Prairie State

Prairie State

Impressions of Illinois, 1673-1967,
By Travelers and Other Observers

———

Compiled and Edited by

PAUL M. ANGLE

With the assistance of Mary Lynn McCree

The University of Chicago Press

Chicago and London

Library of Congress Catalog Card Number 68–22231

The University of Chicago Press, Chicago 60637
The University of Chicago Press, Ltd., London W.C.1

Printed in the United States of America

An Illinois Sesquicentennial Book

This year, 1968, the State of Illinois is observing its 150th anniversary. Three years ago Governor Otto Kerner appointed a commission, authorized by the General Assembly, to decide upon the most effective and suitable means of commemorating this milestone in the state's history. The commission decided that a series of historical publications was called for, and a committee of prominent historians selected the subjects to be covered. High on the list was an anthology of writings by travelers and other observers describing Illinois from the beginning of its recorded history to the present. This volume, *Prairie State*, compiled and edited by the Sesquicentennial Commission's Director of Historical Publications, stems from that decision.

For their support of the sesquicentennial historical program I wish to thank Governor Otto Kerner, the Illinois General Assembly, and the members of the Illinois Sesquicentennial Commission:

Hon. Hudson R. Sours, Hon. Thomas A. McGloon, and Hon. Paul J. Randolph, Vice Chairmen; Gene H. Graves, Secretary; William K. Alderfer; James W. Cook; Hon. Lawrence DiPrima; Patrick H. Hoy; Goffrey Hughes; Hon. Henry J. Hyde; Hon. J. David Jones; Hon. Richard R. Larson; Hon. Edward Lehman; Daniel MacMaster; Virginia L. Marmaduke; Hon. Edward McBroom; Hon. Robert W. McCarthy; Hon. Tom Merritt; Hon. Richard H. Newhouse; Hon. James Philip; Hon. Paul Powell; Walter Schwimmer; John H. Sengstacke; Glenn H. Seymour; Hon. Harold D. Stedelin; Milton D. Thompson; Clyde C. Walton.

RALPH G. NEWMAN, *Chairman*

Editor's Preface

The literate, articulate explorer and traveler in North America have been with us from the age of discovery. Christopher Columbus and Americus Vespuccius wrote accounts of their voyages; Cabeza de Vaca recorded, as a participant, the ill-fated expedition of Pánfilo de Narváez to Florida in 1527; Samuel de Champlain published four books describing his adventures in Canada; and Captain John Smith wrote memorable accounts of the English colonists in Virginia. And these were only the forerunners of many thousands who, from their day to ours, have traversed the continent or part of it and recorded their experiences and impressions.

The literature of exploration and travel takes several forms: official reports; diaries, sometimes published as they were written, sometimes touched up for literary effect; letters to friends, families, or newspapers; books, especially by foreigners, produced in the hope that they would defray the cost of an American trip and perhaps show a profit; and, in recent times, articles obviously commissioned by magazine editors. Whatever the nature of travelers' accounts, the reader should expect to find in them a variable quota of prejudice and misinformation. One visitor may characterize a tavern keeper as little less than a villain; another, coming on the heels of the first, may describe the same man as affable and attentive. Statistics—on population, crop yields, trade, and manufacturing, for example—must be taken with caution unless official sources are cited.

Despite their failings, travelers' accounts are an invaluable source of history. Often they concern subjects not to be found in more formal narratives: dress, speech, amusements, manners, and customs now forgotten. The face of many an embryonic city would have been lost were it not for a Charles Fenno Hoffman or a Patrick Shirreff. The forests and prairies, now so sadly altered, come to view again in the descriptive passages of hundreds of men and women who saw them before despoliation had begun. Not all was idyllic, of course, and it may be some small comfort to a deeply concerned present generation to learn from travel narratives that violence and lawlessness have marred American life from early times.

This book relates solely to Illinois—the area that has been known successively as the Illinois Country, Illinois Territory, and the State of Illinois. (The boundaries are not identical.) In the nineteenth century Illinois became the peculiar state it is today, comprising one huge city and metropolitan area containing more than half the total population, with the remainder distributed among much smaller cities, small towns, and farms. This division poses a problem for the anthologist, and indeed for the formal historian. How much attention should be devoted to Chicago and the Chicago region, and how much to what the Illinoisan calls "downstate"? The problem is complicated by the fact that all too many visitors, particularly in the twentieth century, came only to Chicago, leaving a plethora of descriptions of the big city and a paucity concerning the rest of the state. Having lived in a downstate city for twenty of my forty-two years as an Illinoisan, I have been especially concerned with striking a fair balance between the state at large and the metropolis.

I have also tried to strike a balance between different parts of the state, between the larger cities and the small towns, and between towns both large and small and the farming areas. Readers, I have no doubt, will disagree on the measure of my success.

Throughout, my emphasis has been on the descriptive rather than the narrative. I could have included firsthand accounts of a Lincoln-Douglas debate, the first nomination of Lincoln, the funeral of Stephen A. Douglas, and other notable events in the history of Illinois, but I believe such accounts belong to a different kind of book.

I have tried to present as much fresh material as possible, but not to the exclusion of all well-known writers. In my opinion, a reader should expect to find Charles Dickens, Harriet Martineau, Anthony Trollope, and other familiars in an Illinois travel anthology, even though what they wrote about the state may have been reprinted a dozen times.

The line drawings and the maps illustrating each section have been specially drawn, respectively, by Virgil Burnett and Barbara Long.

A word about editorial practices. The capitalization, punctuation, abbreviation, and spelling (except for obvious errors) of the originals have been retained. Footnotes are those of the authors unless identified by "Ed."

PAUL M. ANGLE

Contents

I

Explorers and Missionaries *1673–1698*   1

II

A Few Scattered Villages *1765–1796*   35

III

IV

V

War and Recovery *1861–1876*   329

VI

The End of the Century *1876–1899*   397

VII

A New Era *1905–1927*   443

VIII

Mid-Century *1934–1967*   487

Index   603

List of Maps

I

Explorers
and
Missionaries

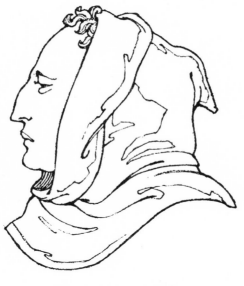

1673-1698

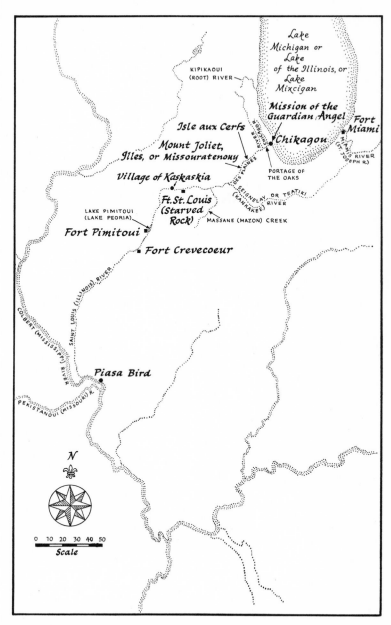

Illinois 1673–1698

Jacques Marquette, French-born Jesuit missionary, and Louis Jolliet, a native of Canada who, though a young man, had already won a reputation as an explorer and map-maker, were the first white men to see what would soon be called the Illinois Country. This distinction slights the five voyageurs who accompanied the expedition, but their names seem to have been lost beyond hope of recovery.

Jacques Cartier, French navigator, discovered the Saint Lawrence River in 1534. On his second voyage, in the following year, he sailed up the river as far as the site of Quebec and took possession of the entire valley in the name of France. But it remained for Samuel de Champlain to establish firmly and exploit Cartier's discoveries. Between 1603 and 1615, Champlain made, in all, eleven trips to eastern Canada. He has gone down in history as the founder of Quebec and the first governor of New France.

In 1634 Champlain sent Jean Nicolet far to the west to find, if he could, the long-sought passage to the western sea and the Far East. Nicolet made his way as far as Green Bay on the western side of Lake Michigan, realized that he had only discovered another nation of Indians (known ingloriously as "The Nation of Stinkers"), and returned to Quebec.

In the next thirty years, parties from New France pushed hesitantly into the region that Nicolet had brought to notice. The fur traders Grosseilliers and Radisson visited Green Bay at least twice; they also skirted the south shore of Lake Superior. Missionaries strove to establish missions there on Chequamegon Bay, at Sault Sainte Marie, and on Green Bay. Not until 1670, however, did New France fully commit herself to the exploitation of the upper lakes. Jean Talon, intendant of the colony, determined to occupy and hold the interior of the continent. The first step toward this goal, he well knew, was exploration.

In the summer of 1670 Talon ordered the Sieur de Saint-Lusson, a French officer who had lived in New France for seven years, to search the shores of Lake Superior for copper and to take formal possession of the territory. The expedition could not start until October, too late for the journey to be completed before the onset of winter. Saint-Lusson, accordingly, stopped at Manitoulin Island in Lake Huron. While his men spent the time in hunting, he sent an emissary familiar with the country, Nicholas Perrot, to summon the tribes to Sault Sainte Marie in the following spring. Early in May, 1671, Perrot, with delegations of Miami, Sacs, Winnebago, and Menominee arrived at the meeting place, where they found Saint-Lusson and his party.

In mid-June, fourteen tribes or their delegates gathered at the Chippewa village and Jesuit mission at the foot of the rapids. On the top of a hill nearby a large wooden cross had been made ready. Around the cross Saint-Lusson assembled his fifteen men, all armed, and four Jesuits in their robes. The Indians surrounded the little group, silent but absorbed in the spectacle. Father Claude Dablon, Superior of the Missions of the Lakes, blessed the cross, which was then planted in the ground. The Frenchmen, uncovered, sang the *Vexilla regis*. Beside the cross the men planted a post on which a metal plate, bearing the royal arms, was mounted. Saint-Lusson's followers raised their voices in the *Exaudiat*, and one of the Jesuits spoke a prayer for the king. Then Saint-Lusson, sword in one hand, clod of earth in the other, sonorously recited the *prise de possession*, by which France claimed sovereignty over "Lakes Huron and Superior, the Island of Manitoulin, and all countries, rivers, lakes, and streams contiguous and adjacent thereunto,—both those which have been discovered and those which may be discovered hereafter, in all their length and breadth."

At the conclusion of the recital the Frenchmen shouted "Vive le roi!" and fired their guns; the Indians, catching the spirit of the occasion if not its meaning, added their shouts to the din.

Saint-Lusson's party included Jolliet, who had already made one trip to the Sault. In this young man—he was then only twenty-six—Talon found the perfect leader for a new expedition. Now the goal was to be the great river which flowed southward to a distant sea. To accompany Jolliet, Talon chose Father Marquette.

Late in 1672 Jolliet proceeded to the Mackinac mission of Saint Ignace, where Marquette was stationed. There the two men spent the winter. In the spring of 1673 they waited impatiently for the ice to break, but May was half gone before they and their voyageurs felt safe in slipping their two birchbark canoes, loaded with Indian corn and smoked meat, into the cold waters of Lake Michigan. They paddled along the shore to Green Bay, then to the mouth of the Fox River. Entering that stream, they proceeded for a hundred miles (forty leagues by the French measure of distance). The Jesuit Claude Allouez, whom they had found at Green Bay, had told them what to expect: a river broadening often into small lakes, where swarms of pelicans would be encountered, marshy banks covered with wild rice, and, in every direction, prairies broken by groves of elm, oak, plum, and apple trees laced with the vines of the wild grape. On the prairies roamed herds of buffalo, frequently numbering four or five hundred.

On June 7 the party reached the Indian village at the headwaters of the Fox River. Here, where three nations— Miami, Mascouten, and Kickapoo—lived together, they stayed three days. The Indians tried to dissuade the Frenchmen from proceeding, but the explorers shouldered their canoes and undertook the portage. Seven or eight miles brought them to the headwaters of the Wisconsin. "Thus," Marquette wrote, "we left the waters flowing to Quebeq . . . to float on those which would thenceforward take us through strange lands."

On June 17 the little party entered the Mississippi. They found a broad stream with a gentle current. Very high hills lined the west bank, and "beautiful lands" could be seen on the east.

Thirty or thirty-five miles south of the present Illinois-Wisconsin line, the character of the country changed. The hills disappeared, trees became sparser. Deer and buffalo could be seen at the water's edge, and in the river the canoes of the explorers sometimes collided with "monstrous fish"—huge and slothful catfish and carp. In the vicinity of Rock Island the prairies became more numerous and larger. Few animals beside the buffalo were to be seen.

The members of the little party advanced cautiously, landing only to make a small fire for cooking, then re-embarking to spend the night in their canoes at a distance from the telltale embers. For eight days they saw no sign of human life. Then, on the west bank of the Mississippi near the mouth of the Des Moines River, they discovered footprints and a well-marked path. Jolliet and Marquette decided to reconnoiter. Leaving the voyageurs, they walked five miles until they came to an Indian village. Two more villages were within sight. They shouted to announce their presence. The savages ran out from their lodges, decided that the intruders were peaceful, and deputed four old men to greet them. As Marquette told the story: "I spoke to them first, and asked them who they were. They replied that they were Illinois; and, as a token of peace, they offered us their pipes to smoke."

Other ceremonies took place in the village. A feast followed: cornmeal boiled in grease, fish, the flesh of a dog killed for the occasion, and finally, fat buffalo meat. That night the two explorers slept on buffalo rugs. In the morning hundreds of the Indians escorted them to the river, marveled at the birchbark canoes—their own were heavy dugouts—and watched them glide away on the current of the ever-widening river.

The Frenchmen floated downstream three hundred miles with surprisingly few adventures. They passed the mouths of other rivers, less great—the Illinois, the Missouri, the Ohio—until they came to the mouth of the Arkansas. There the Indians, who belonged to a strange tribe, gave every sign of hostility until they were quieted by the sight of the calumet in Marquette's hands. Proceeding a few miles farther, the members of the little party

6

were lavishly feasted at another village. Here they found an Indian who had lived among the tribes of the Upper Mississippi and could serve as an interpreter. Thus they learned definitely that the Mississippi debouched in the Gulf of Mexico instead of the Gulf of California, and they were warned that if they continued much farther they would encounter hostile Indians and perhaps fall into the hands of the Spaniards. On July 17, exactly one month after they entered the Mississippi, they turned their canoes upstream.

On their way they learned of the short route to Lake Michigan offered by the Illinois River. They paddled up that stream without incident other than a short stop at the Great Village of the Illinois, located midway between the present cities of La Salle and Ottawa. Here Marquette so impressed the Indians that they urged him to return to them the following year. They also sent an escort of young men to guide the explorers to the Chicago portage and Lake Michigan. With the passage of Marquette and Jolliet up the Illinois River and through the Chicago portage, the history of Illinois begins.

1673

Jacques Marquette

The Piasa Bird and the Missouri

Marquette went no farther north than the mission of Saint Francis Xavier at De Pere, on the Fox River near Green Bay. There he wrote an account of his first voyage, from which the following excerpt is taken. The first two paragraphs concern the Piasa Bird, depicted on a cliff on the east side of the Mississippi a short distance north of the present city of Alton, Illinois. The next two paragraphs describe the confluence of the Missouri and Mississippi. These sights he saw during the descent of the great river.

Marquette remained at De Pere until October, 1674, when he set out to redeem the promise he had made to the Illinois Indians. On the Chicago River the priest became seriously ill. With two companions he spent the winter in a small hut. In the spring the three men made their way to the Great Village, where he preached to a vast gathering. Returning to Saint Ignace, he died at the mouth of the Pere Marquette River on the eastern shore of Lake Michigan.

While Skirting some rocks, which by Their height and Length inspired awe, We saw upon one of them two painted monsters which at first made Us afraid, and upon Which the boldest savages dare not Long rest their eyes. They are as large As a calf; they have Horns on their heads Like those of deer, a horrible look, red eyes, a beard Like a tiger's, a face somewhat like a man's, a body Covered with scales, and so Long A tail that it winds all around the Body, passing above the head and going back between the legs, ending in a Fish's tail. Green, red, and black are the three Colors composing the Picture. Moreover, these 2 monsters are so well painted that we cannot believe that any savage is their author; for good painters in france would find it difficult to paint so well,—and, besides, they are so high up on the rock that it is difficult to reach that place Conveniently to paint them. Here is approximately The shape of these monsters, As we have faithfully Copied It.[1]

While conversing about these monsters, sailing quietly in clear and calm Water, we heard the noise of a rapid, into which we were about to run. I have seen nothing more dreadful. An accumulation of large and entire trees, branches, and floating islands, was issuing from The mouth of The river pekistanouï,[2] with such impetuosity that we could not without great danger risk passing through it. So great was the agitation that the water was very muddy, and could not become clear.

Pekitanouï is a river of Considerable size, coming from the Northwest, from a great Distance; and it discharges into the Missisipi. There are many Villages of savages along this river, and I hope by its means to discover the vermillion or California sea. . . .

We have seen nothing like this river that we enter,[3] as regards its fertility of soil, its prairies and woods; its cattle, elk, deer,

Reprinted from *The Jesuit Relations*, ed. Reuben G. Thwaites (Cleveland, 1900), 59:139–41, 161–63.
[1]   The reference is to a drawing which we have not reproduced. Ed.
[2]   The Missouri. Ed.
[3]   The Illinois. Ed.

wildcats, bustards,[4] swans, ducks, parroquets, and even beaver. There are many small lakes and rivers. That on which we sailed is wide, deep, and still, for 65 leagues. In the spring and during part of The summer there is only one portage of half a league. We found on it a village of Ilinois called Kaskasia, consisting of 74 Cabins. They received us very well, and obliged me to promise that I would return to instruct them. One of the chiefs of this nation, with his young men, escorted us to the Lake of the Ilinois, whence, at last, at The end of September, we reached the bay des puantz,[5] from which we had started at the beginning of June.

Had this voyage resulted in the salvation of even one soul, I would consider all my troubles well rewarded, and I have reason to presume that such is the case. For, when I was returning, we passed through the Ilinois of Peouarea, and during three days I preached the faith in all their Cabins; after which, while we were embarking, a dying child was brought to me at The water's edge, and I baptized it shortly before it died, through an admirable act of providence for the salvation of that Innocent soul.

---

[4]   Game bird related to the crane and the plover, probably the Canada goose. Ed.
[5]   Green Bay. Ed.

1673

Louis Jolliet

The Illinois Country

Jolliet, after leaving Marquette at De Pere, returned to Montreal. At the rapids above the city his canoe capsized and he lost all his notes and maps. However, he related his experiences to Father Claude Dablon, who included them in his relation dated Quebec, August 1, 1674. We present here Jolliet's description of the Illinois River and the region through which it flows.

At first, when we were told of these treeless lands, I imagined that it was a country ravaged by fire, where the soil was so poor that it could produce nothing. But we have certainly observed the contrary; and no better soil can be found, either for corn, for vines, or for any other fruit whatever.

The river which we named for Saint Louis, which rises near the lower end of the lake of the Illinois,[1] seemed to me the most beautiful, and most suitable for settlement. The place at which we entered the lake is a harbor, very convenient for receiving vessels and sheltering them from the wind. The river is wide and deep, abounding in catfish and sturgeon. Game is abundant there; oxen, cows, stags, does, and Turkeys are found there in greater numbers than elsewhere. . . .

There are prairies three, six, ten, and twenty leagues in length, and three in width, surrounded by forests of the same extent; beyond these, the prairies begin again, so that there is as much of one sort of land as of the other. Sometimes we saw the grass very short, and, at other times, five or six feet high; hemp, which grows naturally there, reaches a height of eight feet.

A settler would not there spend ten years in cutting down and burning the trees; on the very day of his arrival, he could put his plow into the ground. And, if he had no oxen from France, he could use those of this country, or even the animals possessed by the Western Savages, on which they ride, as we do on horses.

After sowing grain of all kinds, he might devote himself especially to planting the vine, and grafting fruit-trees; to dressing ox-hides, wherewith to make shoes; and with the wool of these oxen he could make cloth, much finer than most of that which we bring from France. Thus he would easily find in the country his food and clothing, and nothing would be wanting except salt; but, as he could make provision for it, it would not be very difficult to remedy that inconvenience.

Reprinted from *The Jesuit Relations*, ed. Reuben G. Thwaites (Cleveland, 1899), **58**:105–9.
[1]   The Illinois River and Lake Michigan. Ed.

1678-1679

Louis Hennepin

The Kankakee Valley
the Buffalo
and Fort Crevecœur

Five years passed before an intrepid adventurer, Robert Cavelier, Sieur de la Salle, shouldered the burden of French exploration and colonization in the Illinois Country. With the backing of Frontenac, Governor of New France, La Salle planned to establish trading posts in the Illinois and Mississippi valleys, win the allegiance of the Indians, and hold the interior of the continent for Louis XIV. His first step was to build a sailing vessel above Niagara Falls. With it he could transport men and supplies to his Illinois colonies and send back to Canada the furs which would finance his enterprise. Mysteriously, the *Griffon* was lost sometime in 1679. Undismayed, La Salle, his associate Henry de Tonty, the Recollect friar Louis Hennepin, and others followed the Saint Joseph, Kankakee, and Illinois River route to Lake Peoria. There, in January, 1680, La Salle erected Fort Crevecœur. Leaving Tonty in charge of the small garrison, La Salle started overland for Fort Frontenac on Lake Ontario for the purpose of placating his creditors, but before he departed he dispatched Hennepin and two others to explore the upper Mississippi.

In their ascent of the Mississippi, Hennepin and his companions were captured by a band of Sioux and taken on several hunting expeditions in the course of which they traveled over much of Minnesota and discovered Saint Anthony's Falls, where Minneapolis now stands. After several months they were rescued by their fellow countryman, the Sieur Duluth, who took them to Canada. Hennepin soon returned to France, where he wrote a book about his adventures, entitled *A Description of Louisiana.*

Hennepin's *A Description of Louisiana* is generally conceded to be reliable, but his later works (*A New Voyage*, 1696, and *A New Discovery*, 1697) are egregious compounds of fact, fiction, and mendacity.

Here we quote from Hennepin's description of the marshes of the Kankakee River, the buffalo, and Fort Crevecœur.

The river Seignelay[1] which flows to the Islinois (Indians,) rises in a plain in the midst of much boggy land, over which it is not easy to walk. This river is only a league and a half distant from that of the Miamis,[2] and thus we transported all our equipage and our canoes by a road which we marked for the benefit of those who might come after us, after leaving at the portage of the Miami river as well as at the fort[3] which we had built at its mouth, letters to serve as a guide to those who were to come and join us by the bark to the number of twenty-five.

The river Seignelay is navigable for canoes to within a hundred paces of its source, and it increases to such an extent in a short time, that it is almost as broad and deeper than the Marne. It

---

Louis Hennepin, *A Description of Louisiana*, ed. John G. Shea (New York, 1880), pp. 149–50, 192–93.
[1]   The Kankakee. Ed.
[2]   The Saint Joseph River. Ed.
[3]   Fort Miami in present-day Michigan. Ed.

takes its course through vast marshes, where it winds about so, though its current is pretty strong, that after sailing on it for a whole day, we sometimes found that we had not advanced more than two leagues in a straight line. As far as the eye could reach nothing was to be seen but marshes full of flags and alders. For more than forty leagues of the way, we could not have found a camping ground, except for some hummocks of frozen earth on which we slept and lit our fire. Our provisions ran out and we could find no game after passing these marshes, as we hoped to do, because there are only great open plains, where nothing grows except tall grass, which is dry at this season, and which the Miamis had burned while hunting buffalo, and with all the address we employed to kill some deer, our hunters took nothing; for more than sixty leagues journey, they killed only a lean stag, a small deer, some swans, and two wild geese for the subsistance of thirty-two men. If our canoe men had found a chance, they would infallibly have all abandoned us, to strike inland and join the Indians whom we discerned by the flames of the prairies to which they had set fire in order to kill the buffalo more easily.

These animals are ordinarily in great numbers there, as it is easy to judge by the bones, the horns and skulls that we saw on all sides. The Miamis hunt them at the end of autumn in the following manner:

When they see a herd, they gather in great numbers, and set fire to the grass every where around these animals, except some passage which they leave on purpose, and where they take post with their bows and arrows. The buffalo, seeking to escape the fire, are thus compelled to pass near these Indians, who sometimes kill as many as a hundred and twenty in a day, all which they distribute according to the wants of the families; and these Indians all triumphant over the massacre of so many animals, come to notify their women, who at once proceed to bring in the meat. Some of them at times take on their backs three hundred pounds weight, and also throw their children on top of their load which does not seem to burthen them more than a soldier's sword at his side.

These cattle have very fine wool instead of hair, and the females have it longer than the males. Their horns are almost all black, much thicker than those of cattle in Europe, but not quite so long. Their head is of monstrous size; the neck is very short, but very thick, and sometimes six hands broad. They have a hump or slight elevation between the two shoulders. Their legs are very thick and short, covered with a very long wool. On the head and between the horns they have long black hair which falls over their eyes and gives them a fearful look. The meat of these animals is very succulent. They are very fat in autumn, because all the summer they are up to their necks in the grass. These vast countries are so full of prairies, that it seems this is the element and the country of the buffalo. There are at near intervals some woods where these animals retire to ruminate, and to get out of the heat of the sun.

These wild cattle or bulls change country according to the season and the diversity of climate. When they approach the northern lands and begin to feel the beginning of winter, they pass to the southern lands. They follow one another on the way sometimes for a league. They all lie down in the same place, and their resting-ground is often full of wild purslain,[4] which we have sometimes eaten. The paths by which they have passed are beaten like our great roads in Europe, and no grass grows there. They cross rivers and streams. The wild cows go to the islands to prevent the wolves from eating their calves; and even when the calves can run, the wolves would not venture to approach them, as the cows would exterminate them. The Indians have this forecast not to drive these animals entirely from their countries, to pursue only those who are wounded by arrows, and the others that escape, they suffer to go at liberty without pursuing them further, in order not to alarm them too much. And although these Indians of these vast continents are naturally given to destroy the animals, they have never been able to exterminate these wild cattle, for however much they hunt them these beasts

---

[4]   A salad green. Ed.

multiply so that they return in still greater numbers the following year.

The Indian women spin on the distaff the wool of these cattle, out of which they make bags to carry the meat, boucanned[5] and sometimes dried in the sun, which these women keep frequently for three or four months of the year, and although they have no salt, they dry it so well that the meat undergoes no corruption, four months after they have thus dressed this meat, one would say on eating it that the animals had just been killed, and we drank the broth with them instead of water which is the ordinary drink of all the nations of America, who have no intercourse with Europeans.

The ordinary skins of these wild cattle weigh from one hundred to a hundred and twenty pounds. The Indians cut off the back and the neck part which is the thickest part of the skin, and they take only the thinnest part of the belly, which they dress very neatly, with the brains of all kinds of animals, by means of which they render it as supple as our chamois skins dressed with oil. They paint it with different colors, trim it with white and red porcupine quills, and make robes of it to parade in their feasts. In winter they use them to cover themselves especially at night. Their robes which are full of curly wool have a very pleasing appearance.

When the Indians have killed any cows, the little calves follow the hunters, and go and lick their hands or fingers, these Indians sometimes take them to their children and after they have played with them, they knock them on the head to eat them. They preserve the hoofs of all these little animals, dry them and fasten them to rods, and in their dances they shake and rattle them, according to the various postures and motions of the singers and dancers. This machine somewhat resembles a tambour.

These little animals might easily be domesticated and used to plough the land.

---

[5]   Boucan: a framework for smoking meat. Ed.

These wild cattle subsist in all seasons of the year. When they are surprised by winter and cannot reach in time the southern land and the warm country, and the ground is all covered with snow, they have the tact to turn up and throw aside the snow, to crop the grass hidden beneath. They are heard lowing, but not as commonly as in Europe.

These wild cattle are much larger in body than ours in Europe especially in the forepart. This great bulk however does not prevent their moving very fast, so that there are very few Indians who can run them down. These bulls often kill those who have wounded them. In the season you see herds of two and even of four hundred.

Many other kinds of animals are found in these vast plains of Louisiana, stags, deer, beaver and otter are common there, geese, swans, turtles, poules d'inde, parrots, partridges, and many other birds swarm there, the fishery is very abundant, and the fertility of the soil is extraordinary. There are boundless prairies interspersed with forests of tall trees, where there are all sorts of building timber, and among the rest excellent oak full like that in France and very different from that in Canada. The trees are of prodigious girth and height, and you could find the finest pieces in the world for ship building which can be carried on upon the spot, and wood could be brought as ballast in the ships to build all the vessels of France, which would be a great saving to the State and would give the trees in our nearly exhausted forests time to grow again.

Several kinds of fruit trees are also to be seen in the forests and wild grape vines which produce clusters about a foot and a half long which ripen perfectly, and of which very good wine can be made. There are also to be seen fields covered with very good hemp, which grows there naturally to a height of six or seven feet. To conclude, by the experiments that we have made among the Islinois and the Issati, we are convinced that the soil is capable of producing all kinds of fruits, herbs and grain, and in greater abundance than the best lands in Europe. The air there is very temperate and healthy, the country is watered by countless lakes, rivers and streams, most of which are navigable. One is scarcely troubled at all by musquitoes or other noxious creatures, and by cultivating the ground, people could subsist there from the second year, independent of provisions from Europe.

This vast continent will be able in a short time to supply all our West India islands with bread, wine and meat, and our French buccaneers and fillibusters will be able to kill wild cattle in greater abundance in Louisiana than in all the rest of the islands, which they occupy. . . .

These reasons and some others of that kind which I made them, persuaded[6] them, and brought all to work with a good grace in building a fort which was called Crevecœur situated four days' journey from the great village of the Islinois descending towards the river Colbert.[7]

A great thaw having set in on the 15th of January, and rendered the river free below the village, the Sieur de la Salle begged me to accompany him, and we proceeded with one of our canoes to the place which we were going to select to work at this little fort. It was a little mound about two hundred paces distant from the bank of the river, which in the season of the rains, extends to the foot of it; two broad deep ravines protected two other sides and a part of the fourth, which we completely entrenched by a ditch which united the two ravines. Their exterior slope which served as a counterscarp, was fortified; we made chevaux de frise and cut this eminence down steep on all sides, and the earth was supported as much as was necessary with strong pieces of timber, with thick planks, and for fear of any surprise, we planted a stockade around, the timbers of which were twenty-five feet long and a foot thick. The summit of the mound was left in its natural figure, which formed an irregular square, and we contented ourselves with putting on the edge a good parapet of earth capable of covering all our force, whose

6   Hennepin persuaded the men that they needed a fort for their own protection. Ed.

7   The Mississippi. Ed.

barracks were placed in two of the angles of this fort, in order that they might be always ready in case of attack. Fathers Gabriel, Zenoble and I lodged in a cabin covered with boards, which we adjusted with the help of our workmen and in which we retired after work, all our people for evening and morning prayer, and where, being unable any longer to say mass, the wine which we had made from the large grapes of the country having just failed us, we contented ourselves with singing Vespers on holidays and Sundays, and preaching after morning prayers.

1695(?)

De Gannes Memoir

The Chicago Portage, Mount Joliet, the Illinois Valley

When La Salle returned to Fort Crevecœur in the fall of 1680 he found only ruins. His men had mutinied and disappeared into the wilderness. A year later, with Tonty, he erected Fort Saint Louis on the rocky eminence now known as Starved Rock. In 1682 La Salle explored the Mississippi to its mouth and took possession, in the name of France, of the whole vast valley. Within five years the great explorer was killed by one of his own men.

Tonty took La Salle's place in exploiting the Illinois Country. One of his early moves was to replace Fort Saint Louis with a new fort, soon to be called Pimitoui, at Peoria. Some time between 1690 and 1700 a French officer, who wrote under the name De Gannes but who was probably the Sieur Deliette, a nephew of Tonty, was stationed there. The "De Gannes Memoir," as it is called, is a valuable account of the Illinois Country and its Indians.

The Illinois country is undeniably the most beautiful that is known anywhere between the mouth of the St. Lawrence River and that of the Mississippi, which are a thousand leagues apart. You begin to see its fertility at Chicago which is 140 leagues from Michillimackinac, at the end of Lake Michigan. The Chicago is a little stream only two leagues long bordered by prairies of equal dimension in width. This is a route usually taken to go to this country. At this river a portage is made, of a quarter of a league in low water and of an arpent[1] in high water. One finds a stream-let for half a league which comes from two little lakes that extend a league and a half, at the end of which, on the rising ground at this point, is made a short portage simply of one's baggage. When the water is favorable one reëmbarks at once, but when it is low it is necessary to go a league. This is called the Portage of the Oaks; and it costs considerable effort to get the boat into this streamlet, which empties into the river which the French call the Illinois. However, this is not the Illinois,[2] as we only come to that stream twenty leagues farther on. The passage is very difficult on account of the low waters which virtually render this river impracticable, because one ordinarily reaches this region only in summer or autumn. There are ten places where for half a league it is necessary to take out half of the baggage, and very often to remove it entirely, until the deep water is reached. It is necessary also sometimes to carry the canoe. There is a place even, called Mount Joliet,[3] where there are four leagues of rapids, and where this must nearly always be done.

This place is called Illes, because a *voyageur* who bore that name was detained here a long time. The Illinois and Miami call

Theodore C. Pease and Raymond C. Werner, eds., *The French Foundations, 1680–1693*, Collections of the Illinois State Historical Library, 23 (Springfield, 1934): pp. 302–6, 326–28, 361–63.

[1]   Approximately 190 ft. Ed.
[2]   Actually the Des Plaines River. Ed.
[3]   A natural mound near the present city of Joliet was a place of interest to travelers for many years. The mound, which consisted of valuable building materials, was gradually destroyed. Ed.

it Missouratenouy, which signifies an earthen vessel. Indeed it has a certain resemblance to one; it is about three arpents in length and half an arpent in width. It is embanked as if it had been purposely shaped, and is about thirty feet high, situated an eighth of a league from the river in a very beautiful valley. The woods on the other side are distant about three arpents; there is only one tree on it. Several Illinois and Miami have tried to persuade me that at the time of the deluge, of which it appears they have learned, it was a vessel which had been made to save all mankind from shipwreck; and that, on the subsiding of the waters, being on a bad bottom, it had upset, and in course of time it had changed to earth.

Here you ordinarily begin to see the buffalo. As for turkeys, there are quantities of them. There is a game bird that is abundant, which is a good deal like the French pheasant, and which is very good. Formerly you found it as far back as Chicago, but since a party of Miami went to settle there, these birds have gone farther off. Four leagues from here is the fork of the real river of the Illinois, which has its source two leagues above the village of the Miami of the St. Joseph River, whence it flows always northward for 120 leagues up to the fork. Afterwards it bends to the southwest and flows on to empty into the Mississippi. Here you begin to see the beauty of this country, both for the soil, which yields bountifully, and for the abundance of animals. You see places on the one side that are unwooded prairies requiring only to be turned up by the plow, and on the other side valleys spreading half a league before reaching the hills, which have no trees but walnuts and oaks; and behind these, prairies like those I have just spoken of. Sometimes you travel a league, seeing all this from your boat. Afterwards you find virgin forest on both sides, consisting of tender walnuts, ash, whitewood, Norway maple, cottonwood, a few maples, and grass, taller in places than a man. More than an arpent in the woods you find marshes which in autumn and spring are full of bustards, swans, ducks, cranes, and teals. Ten steps farther on are the hills covered with wood extending about an eighth of a league, from the edge of which are seen prairies of extraordinary extent. Three leagues from the fork is the river Mazon,[4] which signifies the tow, in which neighborhood are found parrakeets that live in bands of fifty to sixty. They make a very strange noise. They are a little bigger than turtledoves. . . .

In September I received a letter from Monsieur de Tonti, dated from Michillimackinac, informing me that he had learned that Monsieur de la Forest[5] was returning from France and that the court had granted them the country of the Illinois with the same prerogatives as the late Monsieur de la Salle. He said he was coming up with a large number of *engagés*, and that I should therefore sound the Illinois regarding the abandonment of their village, for which they had shown a desire because their firewood was so remote and because it was so difficult to get water upon the rock if they were attacked by the enemy. I assembled the chiefs, and having learned that they had not changed their minds, I bade them choose such place as suited them best. They chose the end of Lake Pimitoui, which means Fat Lake, so called on account of the abundance of game there. This is where the Illinois are at present and where I was for seven years. Monsieur de Tonti arrived in the winter [1691-1692] and started the building of a large fort[6] to which the savages might retire in case of an alarm. The following spring Monsieur de la Forest arrived also with a considerable number of *engagés* and of soldiers, who completed the building of it. It is four years ago this spring that I left the place. I left there something over 260 cabins, which have from one to four fires. I put them at two on the average, and thus calculate about 800 warriors between the ages of twenty and forty. You can see no finer looking people. They are neither tall nor short usually; there are some you could encompass with two hands. They have legs that seem drawn with an artist's pen. They carry their load of wood gracefully, with a proud gait as finely as

4   Mazon Creek in Grundy County, Illinois.
5   François Daupin de la Forest, a lieutenant of La Salle and associate of Tonty in trading ventures in the Illinois Country. Ed.
6   Fort Pimitoui. Ed.

24

the best dancer. They have faces as beautiful as white milk, in so far as this is possible for Indians of that country. They have the most regular and the whitest teeth imaginable. They are full of life, yet at the same time lazy. They are tattooed behind from the shoulders to the heels, and as soon as they have reached the age of twenty-five, on the front of the stomach, the sides, and the upper arms. There is here a certain Villeneuve, who has half his back tattooed in the same manner. They are proud and vain and all call themselves sons or relatives of chiefs; but in spite of this they are given to begging, are cowardly, licentious, entirely given up to their senses. They always take advantage of the weakness of those they deal with; they dress their best when they appear in public; they are as jealous as Italians, thievish, gourmands, vindictive, hypocritical, and perfidious. They would prostitute their daughters or sisters a thousand times for a pair of stockings or other trifle. I have got men to agree a hundred times that their fathers, their brothers, and their children were worse than dogs, because they hoped that I would give them a little red paint or a five-*sol* knife. . . .

Although this nation is much given to debauchery, especially the men, the reverend Jesuit fathers, who speak their language perfectly, manage (if one may say so) to impose some check on this by instructing a number of girls in Christianity, who often profit by their teaching, and mock at the superstitions of their nation. This often greatly incenses the old men and daily exposes these fathers to ill-treatment, and even to being killed. I must say to their glory that they must be saints indeed to take as much trouble as they do for these people. Every day as soon as the sun rises they go into the cabins to find out if anyone is sick; they give them medicines, and if necessary bleed them, and sometimes they even make broth for them, after which they have it cried through the village that they are about to say mass. Then they teach the catechism or they preach sermons; in the afternoon, after having applied themselves to the language, they return to the village to hear the catechism, which always takes two hours. The pieces of wood, husks of Indian corn, and even the stones which are sometimes thrown at them do not dismay them; they continue their discourse, contenting themselves with saying that it is the master of life who orders them to do what they are doing, and that those who do not wish to hear his word may stay away while those who wish to listen to it may do so. In the evening they come again to call to prayer, which is followed by a prayer service for the French. No weather prevents them from going through with the same exercises. Sometimes they are sent for at night to come to the edge of the village, which is more than an eighth of a league long, to assist the dying. I have even had some differences with some of these reverend fathers as to this matter, on account of the dangers to which they exposed us in thus exposing themselves, fearing as I did that some medicine men, jealous at finding themselves cut off from what they might have gained by caring for the sick, might directly or indirectly do them some mischief. But their great zeal always carried them away, no matter what stipulations they made with me.

1698

Jean François Buisson de St. Cosmé

Mission of the Guardian
Angel and Pimitoui

In 1696 Father François Pinet established the Jesuit Mission of
the Guardian Angel on the site of the future city of Chicago.
The following year Frontenac, governor of Canada, closed the
mission, but it was opened again in 1698. In that year the Bishop
of Canada sent Father Jean François Buisson de St. Cosmé and
two other priests from the Seminary at Quebec to establish missions in the Southwest. St. Cosmé's account of their trip, dated
January 2, 1699, was written from the Arkansas country to the
Bishop.

We remained five days at Kipikaoui,[1] leaving on the 17th and after being windbound on the 18th and 19th we camped on the 20th at a place five leagues from Chikagou. We should have arrived there early on the 21st but the wind which suddenly arose on the lake compelled us to land half a league from Chikagou. We had considerable difficulty in landing and in saving our canoes; we all had to jump into the water. One must be very careful along the lakes, and especially Lake Mixcigan, whose shores are very low, to take to the land as soon as possible when the waves rise on the lake, for the rollers become so high in so short a time that one runs the risk of breaking his canoe and of losing all it contains. Many travellers have already been wrecked there. We, Monsieur de Montigny, Davion, and myself, went by land to the house of the Reverend Jesuit Fathers while our people remained behind.[2] We found there Reverend Father Pinet and Reverend Father Binneteau, who had recently arrived from the Illinois country and was slightly ill.

I cannot describe to you, my lord, with what cordiality and manifestations of friendship these Reverend Fathers received and embraced us while we had the consolation of residing with them. Their house is built on the bank of a small river, with the lake on one side and a fine and vast prairie on the other. The village of the savages contains over a hundred and fifty cabins, and a league up the river is still another village almost as large. They are all Miamis. Reverend Father Pinet usually resides there except in winter, when the savages are all engaged in hunting, and then he goes to the Illinois. We saw no savages there; they had already started for their hunt. If one may judge of the future from the short time that Reverend Father Pinet has passed in this mission, we may believe that if God will bless the labors and the zeal of that holy missionary there will be a great number of good and fervent

Louise Phelps Kellogg, ed., *Early Narratives of the Northwest, 1634–1699* (New York, 1917), pp. 346–51.

[1]   The Root River, which empties into Lake Michigan at Racine, Wisconsin. Ed.
[2]   The Mission of the Guardian Angel. Ed.

Christians. It is true that but slight results are obtained with reference to the older persons, who are hardened in profligacy, but all the children are baptized, and the jugglers even, who are the most opposed to Christianity, allow their children to be baptized. They are also very glad to let them be instructed. Several girls of a certain age and also many young boys have already been and are being instructed, so that we may hope that when the old stock dies off, they will be a new and entirely Christian people.

On the 24th of October the wind fell and we sent for our canoes with all our effects, and finding that the water was extraordinarily low, we made a cache in the ground with some of them and took only what was absolutely necessary for our journey, intending to send for the remainder in the spring. We left Brother Alexandre in charge thereof, as he agreed to remain there with Father Pinet's man. We started from Chikagou on the 29th, and slept about two leagues from it on the little river[3] that afterward loses itself in the prairies. On the following day we began the portage, which is about three leagues in length when the waters are low, and is only one-fourth of a league in the spring, for then one can embark on a small lake that discharges into a branch of the river of the Illinois, and when the waters are low a portage has to be made to that branch. On that day we got over half our portage, and would have gone still further, when we perceived that a little boy given us by Monsieur de Muis, and who had set out alone although he was told to wait, was lost. We had not noticed it because all our people were busy. We were obliged to stop to look for him; everybody went and several gun-shots were fired, but he could not be found. It was a rather unfortunate accident; we were pressed for time, owing to the lateness of the season, and the waters being very low, we saw quite well, that as we were obliged to carry our baggage and our canoe, it would take a long time to reach the Illinois. This compelled us to separate. Messieurs de Montigny, de Tonty, and Davion continued the portage on the following day, while I with

3   The south fork of the Chicago River. Ed.

four other men went back to look for the little boy. While retracing my steps I met Fathers Pinet and Binneteau, who were on the way to the Illinois with two Frenchmen and a savage. We looked for the boy during the whole of that day also, without finding him. As it was the day before the feast of All Saints, I was compelled to go to Chikagou for the night with our people. After they had heard mass and performed their devotions early in the morning, they spent the whole of that day also looking for the little boy without getting sight of him. It was very difficult to find him in the long grass, for this country consists of nothing but prairies with a few groves of trees. We were afraid to set fire to the long grass lest we might burn the boy. Monsieur de Montigny had told me to remain only one day, because the cold weather pressed us, and this compelled me to proceed, after giving orders to Brother Alexandre to seek him and to take some Frenchmen who were at Chikagou.[4]

I started in the afternoon of the 2nd of November. I crossed the portage and passed the night at the river or branch[5] of the River of the Illinois. We descended the river as far as an island. During the night we were surprised to see a slight fall of snow, and on the following day the river was frozen over in several places. We had therefore to break the ice and haul the canoe, because there was no open water. This compelled us to leave our canoe and go by land to seek Monsieur de Montigny, whom we met on the following day, the 5th of the month, at the Isle aux Cerfs. They had already gone over two leagues of portage. We still had four leagues to do, as far as Mont Joliet. This took us three days, and we arrived on the 8th of the month.

From the Isle à la Cache to the said Mont Jolliet,[6] a distance

---

4   According to a letter of Thau Mer de la Source in Shea, *Early Voyages* (Albany, 1861), p. 85, the boy came into the mission thirteen days after he was lost. He was completely exhausted. Ed.

5   The Des Plaines River. Ed.

6   One finds both Joliet and Jolliet in travelers' accounts. The explorer spelled his name "Jolliet," but the official spelling of the Illinois city is "Joliet." Ed.

of seven leagues, everything has to be portaged, as there is no water in the river except in the spring. The banks of this river are very agreeable; they consist of prairies bounded by small hills and very fine thickets; there are numbers of deer in them and along the river are great quantities of game of all kinds, so that after crossing the portage one of our men, while taking a walk, procured enough to provide us with an abundant supper as well as breakfast on the following day. Mont Jolliet is a very fine mound of earth in the prairie to the right, descending a little. It is about thirty feet high. The savages say that at the time of the great deluge one of their ancestors escaped, and that this small mountain is his canoe which he upset there.

On leaving Mont Jolliet we proceeded about two leagues by water. We remained two whole days at our short portage, about a quarter of a league in length. As one of our men named Charbonneau had killed several turkeys and bustards in the morning, together with a deer, we were very glad to give our people a good meal and to let them rest for a day. On the tenth we made the short portage and found half a league of water, after which two men carried the canoe for about a league, the others walking behind, each carrying his load; and we then embarked for a league and a half. We slept at a short portage, five or six arpents in length. On the eleventh, after making the short portage, we came to the river Teatiki,[7] which is the true river of the Illinois, that which we descended being only a distant branch. We put all our baggage in the canoe, which two men paddled, while Monsieur de Tonty and ourselves, with the remainder of our men, proceeded by land, walking all the time through fine prairies. We came to the village of the Peangichias,[8] Miamis who formerly dwelt at the falls of the Miçipi and who have for some years been settled at this place. There was no one in the village, for all had gone hunting. That day we slept near Massane,[9] a small river

7   The Kankakee River. Ed.
8   The Piankeshaw. Ed.
9   Mazon Creek in Grundy County, Illinois. Ed.

which falls into the River of the Illinois. On that day we began to see oxen, and on the morrow two of our men killed four; but as these animal are in poor condition at this season we contented ourselves with taking the tongues only. These oxen seem to me to be larger than ours; they have a hump on their backs; their legs are very short; the head is very large and so covered with long hair that it is said a bullet cannot penetrate it. We afterward saw some nearly every day during our journey as far as the Acansças.

After experiencing considerable difficulty during three days in carrying and hauling our baggage in the canoe, owing to the river being rapid, low, and full of rocks, we arrived on the 15th of November at the place called the Old Fort. This is a rock on the bank of the river, about a hundred feet high, whereon Monsieur de la Salle had caused a fort to be built, which has been abandoned,[10] because the savages went to reside about twenty-five leagues further down. We slept a league above it, where we found two cabins of savages; we were consoled on finding a woman who was a thoroughly good Christian. The distance between Chicagou and the fort is considered to be about thirty leagues. There we commenced the navigation, that continues to be always good as far as the fort of Permetaoui,[11] where the savages now are and which we reached on the 19th of November. We found there Reverend Father Binetot and Reverend Father Marais who, owing to their not being laden when they left Chigaou, had arrived six or seven days before us. We also saw Reverend Father Pinet there. All the Reverend Jesuit Fathers gave us the best possible reception. Their sole regret was to see us compelled to leave so soon on account of the frost. We took there a Frenchman who had lived three years with the Acansças and who knows a little of their language.

This mission of the Illinois seems to me the finest that the Reverend Jesuit Fathers have up here, for without counting all

10   Fort St. Louis on Starved Rock. Ed.
11   Pimitoui, at Peoria Lake. Ed.

the children who are baptized, a number of adults have abandoned all their superstitions and live as thoroughly good Christians; they frequently attend the sacraments and are married in church. We had not the consolation of seeing all these good Christians often, for they were all scattered down the bank of the river for the purpose of hunting. We saw only some women savages married to Frenchmen, who edified us by their modesty and their assiduity in going to prayer several times a day in the chapel. We chanted high mass in it, with deacon and subdeacon, on the feast of the Presentation of the most Blessed Virgin, and after commending our voyage to her and having placed ourselves under her protection we left the Illinois on the 22nd of November—we had to break the ice for two or three arpents to get out of Lake Pemsteoui. We had four canoes: that of Monsieur de Tonty, our two, and another belonging to five young voyageurs who were glad to accompany us, partly on account of Monsieur de Tonty, who is universally beloved by all the voyageurs, and partly also to see the country. Reverend Fathers Binneteau and Pinet also came with us a part of the way, as they wished to go and spend the whole winter with their savages.

II

A Few
Scattered
Villages

1765-1796

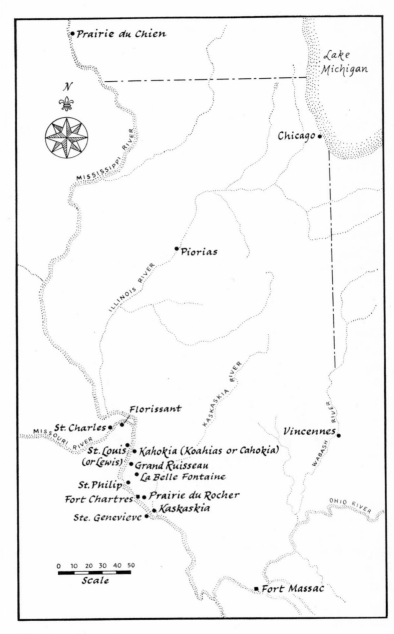

- Prairie du Chien

Lake Michigan

N

MISSISSIPPI RIVER

Chicago •

• Piorias

ILLINOIS RIVER

KASKASKIA RIVER

Florissant

St. Charles •

MISSOURI RIVER

Vincennes •

WABASH RIVER

St. Louis •• Kahokia (Koahias or Cahokia)
(or Lewis) • Grand Ruisseau
• La Belle Fontaine

St. Philip •• Prairie du Rocher
Fort Chartres •• Kaskaskia
Ste. Genevieve •

OHIO RIVER

0 10 20 30 40 50
Scale

• Fort Massac

Illinois 1765–1796

With the closing of the Mission of the Guardian Angel the curtain came down on the history of Chicago until after the Revolutionary War. The Fox Indians, bitter enemies of the French, closed the portage between the Chicago and the Des Plaines rivers. Undoubtedly occasional coureurs de bois slipped through, but they left no records, and, as far as history is concerned, they never existed.

Not so with the southwestern part of the Illinois Country. In 1698 the head of the Seminary of Foreign Missions at Quebec sent three priests to establish a mission among the Illinois tribes that lived along the Mississippi south of the mouth of the Illinois. In the spring of the following year the priests planted the Mission of the Holy Family at a large village of the Tamaroa, or Cahokia, Indians near the site of the present city of East Saint Louis. In 1700 the Kaskaskia subtribe of the Illinois abandoned its villages on the upper Illinois River and moved, under the leadership of the Jesuits, to the right bank of the Mississippi near the southern limit of what is now Saint Louis. In 1703, for reasons now obscure, the Jesuits transferred the mission to Illinois, choosing a site on the right bank of the Kaskaskia River about five miles above its junction with the Mississippi. With this move the French now had establishments about fifty miles apart at both ends of a narrow and enormously fertile alluvial strip, which would come to be known as the American Bottom.

By 1719 the Illinois villages had become too populous to be without protection. Although a census taken in 1723 credited Cahokia with only twelve white residents, 196 were counted in Kaskaskia. For a fortification, a point on the Mississippi ten miles northwest of the latter town was selected. In 1720 a fort of palisades was completed, named Fort de Chartres, and garrisoned. It was rebuilt after seven years, and replaced by a new structure in 1732.

The French settlements, if not populous, were at least picturesque. In all of them agriculture followed the pattern of medieval France: a large common for pasturing stock, with individual farms in strips a few hundred feet wide and a mile or two in length. Farm implements were primitive: plows of wood, and carts with two wheels instead of four. Fertilizing was unknown; the farmers accumulated manure until winter, when they dumped it on the frozen streams to be carried away in the spring thaws.

The houses differed radically from those which American pioneers would erect later. They were made of squared logs placed upright on sills of wood or stone, with the interstices filled with a kind of plaster compounded of mud, stones, and straw. Roofs, steeply pitched, extended over open porches or *galeries* on all four sides of the houses. The more prosperous of the inhabitants brought in much of their furniture—armoires, canopied beds, and sturdy tables and chairs—from New Orleans. The less affluent put up with articles of local manufacture, crudely made because resident craftsmen were few and unskilled.

The settlers followed a variety of occupations. In addition to farmers there were voyageurs: boatmen who took bateaux from Vincennes or Kaskaskia down the rivers to New Orleans and back again or delivered bales of furs to Detroit and Mackinac. Others were coureurs de bois, fur-traders sometimes in the employ of authorized monopolies, more often plying the trade independently and illicitly.

Not until the middle of the eighteenth century did the European wars in which France was involved have any effect on the settlements in the Illinois Country. In 1751, however, the French government, foreseeing a major conflict, ordered Fort de Chartres, which had fallen into disrepair and had been abandoned, replaced by a formidable fortification. Under the direction of a trained engineer, an irregular stone quadrangle, with sides 490 feet long, rose slowly near the site of the old fort. The walls were two feet two inches thick and pierced at regular intervals with loopholes and ports for cannon; a banquette, three feet above the ground, ran along the entire interior. Within the enclosure stood the houses of the commandant and commissary, a storehouse, guard house, and two barracks. The powder magazine, a bakehouse, and a prison were located in the bastions. Although never finished, Chartres was undoubtedly the strongest fortification in North America.

But no hostile shot was ever fired from its walls. Its destiny was settled not on the banks of the Mississippi but in the valley of the Saint Lawrence. As anticipated, the French and Indian War broke out in 1754. The following year the hapless Braddock met defeat in western Pennsylvania, but the British moved relentlessly to conquer Canada. After Montcalm's defeat on the Plains of Abraham in the fall of 1759, only Montreal stood out against the invaders. When that city fell a year later, fighting between the French and English ceased in North America, although hostilities in other parts of the world dragged on for three more years.

By the Treaty of Paris, 1763, France ceded Canada and all her territory east of the Mississippi to Great Britain. But before a British force could be dispatched to the Illinois Country, Pontiac's uprising set fire to the frontier. Not until the fall of 1765 did a detachment of the Forty-second Regiment, the famed Black Watch, succeed in making its way from Fort Pitt to Fort de Chartres. More than a year earlier, De Villiers, then commandant, had transferred the garrison from Vincennes—thus abandoning that post—to Chartres, and had then embarked for New Orleans with most of the troops. Only forty men, in ragged uniforms and poorly armed, could be paraded on October 10, when Saint-Ange, their commander, formally ceded the fort to Captain Stirling.

The British ruled the Illinois Country for thirteen years. Misruled would be a better word. A few of the men who commanded the small garrisons were kindly and honest; others were corrupt and tyrannical. British traders from the East, often in league with corrupt officials, tried to exploit the colony. The British made little effort to understand the French inhabitants and adjust themselves to their ways. When George Rogers Clark and his Virginians took Kaskaskia and the other Illinois villages in the summer of 1778, the Illinois French eagerly shifted their allegiance to the Americans.

For the remainder of the Revolutionary War, Clark succeeded in preventing the British from retaking the Illinois Country. Until 1782, the territory was included in the Virginia County of Illinois. In 1784 Virginia ceded to the United States her claims to land north of the Ohio River. Three years later, Illinois became part of the Northwest Territory, established by the famous Ordinance of 1787. These governmental moves, however, failed to provide an effective government for the inhabitants. The threat of Indian depredations continued. Land titles were involved in a morass of claims and counterclaims. And all too often, serious crimes went unpunished. As the eighteenth century drew to a close, conditions in the Illinois Country were anything but promising.

1765-1768

Philip Pittman

The Illinois Villages

Captain Philip Pittman, an engineer with British troops, arrived in the Illinois Country late in 1765 and spent three years there making surveys and investigations. His account of the settlements at the time of the British occupation is the best available.

The village of Notre Dame de Cascasquias is by far the most considerable settlement in the country of the Illinois, as well from its number of inhabitants, as from its advantageous situation; it stands on the side of a small river, which is about eighty yards across; its source lies north-east, about sixty leagues from the village, and fifteen leagues east of the remarkable rock of Peorya, and it empties itself with a gentle current into the Mississippi, near two leagues below the village.[1] This river is a secure port for large batteaux, which can lie so close to its bank as to load and unload without the least trouble; and at all seasons of the year there is water enough for them to come up. It must be observed here, that it is extremely dangerous for batteaux or boats to remain in the Mississippi, on account of the bank falling in, and the vast number of logs and trees which are sent down, with a violent force, by the rapidity of the current, as also on account of the heavy gales of wind to which this climate is subject. Another great advantage that Cascasquias receives from its river is the facility with which mills for corn and planks may be erected on it: Mons. Paget was the first who introduced water-mills in this country, and he constructed a very fine one on the river Cascasquias, which was both for grinding corn and sawing boards; it lies about one mile from the village. The mill proved fatal to him, being killed as he was working in it, with two negroes, by a party of the Cherokees, in the year 1764. The principal buildings are, the church and jesuits house, which has a small chapel adjoining to it; these, as well as some other houses in the village, are built of stone, and, considering this part of the world, make a very good appearance. The jesuits plantation consisted of two hundred and forty *arpens* of cultivated land, a very good stock of cattle, and a brewery; which was sold by the French commandant, after the country was ceded to the English, for the crown,

Philip Pittman, *The Present State of the European Settlements on the Mississippi; with a Geographical Description of That River* (London, 1770), pp. 42–43, 45–46, 48, 55.

[1]   Pittman refers to the Kaskaskia River. Ed.

in consequence of the suppression of the order. Mons. Beauvais[2] was the purchaser, who is the richest of the English subjects in this country; he keeps eighty slaves; he furnished eighty-six thousand weight of flour to the king's magazine, which was only a part of the harvest he reaped in one year. Sixty-five families reside in this village, besides merchants, other casual people, and slaves. The fort, which was burnt down in October 1766, stood on the summit of a high rock opposite the village, and on the other side of the river; it was an oblongular quadrangle, of which the exterior polygon measured two hundred and ninety by two hundred and fifty-one feet; it was built of very thick squared timber, and dove-tailed at the angles. An officer and twenty soldiers are quartered in the village. The officer governs the inhabitants, under the direction of the commandant at fort Chartres. Here are also two companies of militia. . . .

Fort Chartres when it belonged to France was the seat of government of the Illinois; the head quarters of the English commanding officer is now here, who is, in fact, the arbitrary governor of this country. The fort is an irregular quadrangle, the sides of the exterior polygon are four hundred and ninety feet; it is built of stone and plastered over, and is only designed as a defence against the Indians, the walls being two feet two inches thick, and pierced with loop-holes at regular distances, and with two port-holes for cannon in the faces, and two in the flanks of each bastion; the ditch has never been finished; the entrance to the fort is through a very handsome rustic gate: within the wall is a small banquette, raised three feet, for the men to stand on when they fire through the loop-holes. The buildings within the fort are, the commandant's and commissary's houses, the magazine of stores, corps de garde, and two barracks; these occupy the square. Within the gorges of the bastions are, a powder magazine, a bakehouse, a prison, in the lower floor of which are

[2] Jean Baptiste Bauvais and his son Raphael purchased the property on November 6, 1763. Both were influential members of the Kaskaskia community. Ed.

four dungeons, and in the upper two rooms, and an out-house belonging to the commandant. The commandant's house is thirty-two yards long, and ten broad; it contains a kitchen, a dining-room, a bed-chamber, one small room, five closets for servants, and a cellar. The commissary's house (now occupied by officers) is built in the same line as this, its proportions and distribution of apartments are the same. Opposite these are the store-house and guard-house, they are each thirty yards long and eight broad; the former consists of two large store-rooms (under which is a large vaulted cellar) and a large room, a bed-chamber, and a closet for the store-keeper; the latter, of a soldier's and officer's guard-rooms, a chapel, a bed-chamber and closet for the chaplain, and an artillery store-room. The lines of barracks have never been finished; they at present consist of two rooms each, for officers, and three rooms for soldiers; they are good spacious rooms of twenty-two feet square, and have betwixt them a small passage. There are fine spacious lofts over each building which reach from end to end; these are made use of to lodge regimental stores, working and intrenching tools, &c. It is generally allowed that this is the most commodious and best built fort in North America. The bank of the Mississippi, next the fort, is continually falling in, being worn away by the current, which has been turned from its course by a sand-bank, now encreased to a considerable island covered with willows: many experiments have been tried to stop this growing evil, but to no purpose. When the fort was began in the year 1756, it was a good half mile from the water-side; in the year 1766 it was but eighty paces; eight years ago the river was fordable to the island, the channel is now forty feet deep. In the year 1764 there were about forty families in the village near the fort, and a parish church, served by a Franciscan friar, dedicated to St. Anne. In the following year, when the English took possession of the country, they abandoned their houses, except three or four poor families, and settled at the villages on the west side of the Mississippi, chusing to continue under the French government. . . .

The village of Sainte Famille de Kaoquias is generally reckoned fifteen leagues from Fort Chartres, and six leagues below the mouth of the river Missoury; it stands near the side of the Mississippi, and is masked from the river by an island of two leagues long; the village is opposite the center of this island; it is long and straggling, being three quarters of a mile from one end to the other; it contains forty-five dwelling-houses, and a church near its center. The situation is not well chosen, as in the floods it is generally overflowed two or three feet. This was the first settlement on the river Mississippi. The land was purchased of the savages by a few Canadians, some of whom married women of the Kaoquias nation, and others brought wives from Canada, and then resided there, leaving their children to succeed them. The inhabitants of this place depend more on hunting, and their Indian trade, than on agriculture, as they scarcely raise corn enough for their own consumption: they have a great deal of poultry and good stocks of horned cattle. The mission of St. Sulpice had a very fine plantation here, and an excellent house built on it; they sold this estate, and a very good mill for corn and planks, to a Frenchman[3] who chose to remain under the English government. They also disposed of thirty negroes and a good stock of cattle to different people in the country, and returned to France in the year 1764. What is called the fort is a small house standing in the center of the village; it differs in nothing from the other houses except in being one of the poorest; it was formerly enclosed with high pallisades, but these were torn down and burnt. Indeed a fort at this place could be of but little use....

The first white inhabitants of the Illinois came from Canada; some brought wives and families with them, others married Indian women in those countries; there is still a continual intercourse between them and the Canadians. The men of these countries are very superstitious and ignorant; they are in general

---

[3]   Jean Baptiste Lagrange bought the house and land belonging to the Séminaire des Missions Étrangères when they were sold by Abbé Forget in 1763. Ed.

active and well made; they are as good hunters, can bear as much fatigue, and are as well acquainted with the woods, as the Indians; most of them have some knowledge of the dialects of the neighbouring Indians and much affect their manners. The price of labour in general is very high, as most of the young men rather chuse to hunt and trade amongst the Indians, than apply to agriculture or become handicrafts. At the Illinois a man may be boarded and lodged the year round on condition of his working two months, one month in ploughing the land and sowing the corn, and one month in the harvest. The only trades they have amongst them are carpenters, smiths, masons, taylors, and mill-wrights. The number of white inhabitants in this country, exclusive of the troops, are about two thousand, of all ages and sexes; in this number are included those who live at Fort St. Vincent's, on the Ouabache.[4] Thirty French soldiers were withdrawn from thence in the latter end of the year 1764. The inhabitants at this post live much at their ease, having every thing necessary for their subsistence of their own production. Their commerce is the same as that of the other inhabitants of this country.

[4]   Vincennes on the Wabash River. Ed.

1787

Josiah Harmar

The Illinois Villages

By 1787, conditions in the Illinois Country had become so turbulent that General Josiah Harmar, commander of the army stationed on the Ohio frontier, was ordered to transfer most of his troops from the Falls of the Ohio (Louisville) to Vincennes, Indiana. From there he proceeded with a small detachment to Kaskaskia. His report to the Secretary of War was dated November 24, 1787.

. . . Accordingly, I marched on the 9th of August, from the Post [Vincennes] with a subaltern (Ensign McDowell) and thirty men, through the prairies, and arrived at Kaskaskia on the 16th of the same month. Our march was very fatiguing, as the weather was excessively warm and water very bad and scarce on our route. I was accompanied by two Indians—Pachan, a Miami chief, and his comrade, who hunted and supplied the party with meat (Buffalo and deer), both on the march and on our return. These prairies are very extensive natural meadows, covered with long grass. One in particular which we crossed was eight leagues in breadth. They run, in general, North and South, and, like the ocean, as far as the eye can see, the view is terminated by the horizon. Here and there a copse of woods is interspersed. They are free from bush and underwood, and not the least vestige of their ever having been cultivated. The country is excellent for grazing, and abounds in buffalo, deer, bear, etc. It is a matter of speculation to account for the formation of the prairies. The western side of the Wabash is over flown in the spring for several miles.

On the 17th I was visited by the magistrates and principal inhabitants of Kaskaskia, welcoming us upon our arrival. Baptiste du Coigne, the chief of the Kaskaskia Indians, paid me a visit in the afternoon, and delivered me a speech, expressive of the greatest friendship for the United States, and presented me with one of the calumets, or pipes of peace, which is now sent on. Some of the Pioria Indians likewise visited me. The Kaskaskia is a handsome little village, situated on the river of the same name, which empties into the river Mississippi at two leagues distance from it. It is one hundred and five miles up the Mississippi from the Mouth of the Ohio. The situation is low and unhealthy, and subject to inundation. The inhabitants are French, and much of the same class as those at Post Vincennes. Their number is one hundred and ninety-one, old and young men.

Having but very little time to spare, I left Ensign McDowell

William Henry Smith, ed., *The St. Clair Papers* (Cincinnati, 1882), pp. 30–35.

with the party at Kaskaskia, and on the 18th, set out accompanied by Mr. Tardiveau[1] and the gentlemen of the village, for Cahokia. We gained Prairie du Rocher, a small village five leagues distant from Kaskaskia, where we halted for the night. On the 19th we passed through St. Philip, a trifling village three leagues distant from Prairie du Rocher, and dined at La Belle Fontaine, six leagues further. La Belle Fontaine is a small stockade, inhabited altogether by Americans, who have seated themselves there without authority. It is a beautiful situation, fine fertile land, no taxation, and the inhabitants have abundance to live upon. They were exceedingly alarmed when I informed them of their precarious state respecting a title to their possessions, and have now sent on a petition to Congress by Mr. Tardiveau. On the same day we passed another small stockade, Grand Ruisseau, inhabited by the same sort of Americans as those at La Belle Fontaine, and arrived at Cahokia that evening. Cahokia is a village of nearly the same size as that of Kaskaskia, two hundred and thirty-nine old men and young. I was received with the greatest hospitality by the inhabitants. There was a decent submission and respect in their behavior. Cahokia is distant from Kaskaskia twenty-two French leagues, which is about fifty miles.

On the 21st, in consequence of an invitation from Monsieur Cruzat, the Spanish commandant at St. Louis, we crossed the Mississippi, and were very politely entertained by him. After dinner we returned to Cahokia. St. Louis (nicknamed *Pancour*), is much the handsomest and genteelest village I have seen on the Mississippi. It is about four miles distant from Cahokia, and five leagues above it the river Missouri unites with the Mississippi. The inhabitants are of the same sort as before described, excepting that they are more wealthy. About twenty regular Spanish troops are stationed here. On the 22d, I left Cahokia to return to Kaskaskia. Previous to my departure, at the request of the

---

[1] Barthelemi Tardiveau visited Illinois with Colonel Harmar. He never lived in Illinois. Ed.

inhabitants, I assembled them, and gave them advice to place their militia upon a more respectable footing than it was, to abide by the decision of their courts, etc., and if there were any turbulent or refractory persons, to put them under guard until Congress should be pleased to order a government for them. Exclusive of the intruders already described, there are about thirty more Americans settled on the rich fertile bottoms on the Mississippi, who are likewise petitioning by this conveyance.

On the 23d, I passed by the ruins of Fort Chartres, which is one league above the Prairie du Rocher, and situate on the Mississippi. It was built of stone, and must have been a considerable fortification formerly, but the part next to the river had been carried away by the floods, and is of no consequence at present. I staid about a quarter of an hour, but had not time to view it minutely, as it was all a thicket within. Several iron pieces of cannon are here at present, and also at the different villages. This evening I returned to Kaskaskia.

On the 24th, Monsieur Peruse, the Spanish commandant at St. Genevieve, sent me an invitation to pay him a visit. We crossed the Mississippi accordingly, were politely entertained, and after dinner returned to Kaskaskia. St. Genevieve (nick named Misere) is a village much inferior in every respect to St. Louis. It is about four miles (including the passage of the Mississippi) distant from Kaskaskia. About eight or ten Spanish troops are stationed there. On the 26th, at the request of the inhabitants[2] (which is inclosed), I assembled them, and gave them advice to regulate their militia, and obey their magistrates etc., until Congress pleased to order a government for them. I have to remark that all these people are entirely unacquainted with what Americans call liberty. Trial by jury, etc., they are strangers to. A commandant with a few troops to give them orders is the best form of government for them; it is what they have been accustomed to.

On the 27th I left Kaskaskia, after having received every mark

2   Of Kaskaskia. Ed.

of respect and attention from the inhabitants, in order to set out for the Post. We marched by a lower route. Several of the French, and the Kaskaskia chief, with his tribe (about ten in number), accompanied us, and we arrived safe at Post Vincennes on the afternoon of the 3d of September. I made the distance by the lower route to be about one hundred and seventy miles.

1796

Victor Collot

Illinois at the End
of the Century

Victor Collot first saw America during the Revolutionary War,
when he served on Rochambeau's staff. Returning to France, he
took an active part in the French Revolution, and was rewarded
by being appointed governor of Guadaloupe. By 1796 he was
back in the United States. At the request of the French Minister,
Collot visited the American West. The book in which he recorded
his observations was published in both French and English, but
did not appear until 1826.

After passing Tenessee River, the bed of the Ohio widens considerably, and at the end of eleven miles, leaving several defiles on both sides, with the navigation uninterrupted, we reached Fort Massac. The depth of water in this distance is sixteen, eighteen, and twenty feet. The lands on both sides are low and swampy.

Fort Massac, so called by the Americans, and Fort Massacre by the Canadians,[1] is a post anciently established by the French, and abandoned at the time of the cession of Louisiana; it has lately been repaired, and has been occupied two years past by the Americans.

This fort is erected on a small promontory; it is built with wood, and has four bastions surrounded with palisadoes. . . . The garrison is composed of an hundred men, commanded by a captain; the batteries are mounted with eight pieces of twelve [pounders]. The fault of this position, with respect to the navigation of the Ohio, is, that the channel being on the opposite side, the passage may be effected, especially during the night, without any fear of the batteries.

It is, nevertheless, very important to keep this point, because it communicates by two different roads with the country of the Illinois. One of these, called the lower road, and which is the shortest, is practicable only in very dry seasons, and when the waters are very low; because there are several creeks to pass, which are not fordable in high waters; in this case, the other, called the upper road, must be taken, which is much longer, and which leads along the heights, crossing the creeks or rivers at their sources. This road is passable for carriages, whilst the lower road is practicable only for horse or foot passengers. The distance from hence to Kaskasias by the lower road is reckoned eighty miles, that by the upper road one hundred and fifty.

Victor Collot, *A Journey in North America* (1826; reprinted Florence, Italy: Lange, 1924), 1:191–93, 231–33, 239–40.

[1]   In fact it was named for the Marquis de Massiac, French minister of marine. The original fort was occupied from 1757 to 1764. The Americans built a new fort on the site in 1794 and kept a garrison there until 1814. Ed.

The platform, on which the fort is erected, is about seventy feet above the level of low water, and has consequently nothing to fear from inundations. But the bank being perpendicular, and the fort placed very near the precipice; which is daily giving way, two of the bastions that face the river are in danger of being borne off by the first floods; the ditch and palisadoes having already shared that fate.

Near the fort are seven or eight houses or huts inhabited by Canadians, whose sole occupations are hunting, or dragging boats: they appeared poor and miserable. . . .

The country of the Illinois is situated between the thirty-seventh and forty-fifth degree of northern latitude. The French took possession of this province in 1681, at the same period that William Penn laid the foundation of Pennsylvania.

The settlements on the Spanish side begin from Salt River, and terminate at the Missouri, on the right bank of the Mississipi: those on the American side begin at the river Kaskaskias, and end at Dog's Meadow (Prairie du Chien).

The French settlements which still remain, situated on the Spanish side, are St. Geneviève, St. Lewis, Florissant, and St. Charles. This last is formed on the left side of the Missouri.

On the American side there are still some French at Kaskaskias, the Meadow of the Rock (Prairie du Rocher), St. Philips, Kaokias, Piorias, on the Red River,[2] at Dog's Meadow, near the Ouiscousin, Chicagou, on the lake Michigan, and at Post St. Vincent's, on the Wabash.

These people are, for the most part, traffickers, adventurers, hunters, rowers, and warriors; ignorant, superstitious, and obstinate; accustomed to fatigue and privations, and stopped by no sense of danger in the undertakings they form, and which they usually accomplish.

In domestic life, their characters and dispositions are similar to those of the Indians with whom they live; indolent, careless, and addicted to drunkenness, they cultivate little or no ground,

2   The reference is to the French village at Peoria on the Illinois River. Ed.

speak a French jargon, and have forgotten the division of time and months. If they are asked at what time such an event took place, they answer, "in the time of the great waters, of the strawberries, of the maize, of potatoes:" if they are advised to change any practice which is evidently wrong, or if observations are made to them respecting the amelioration of agriculture, or the augmentation of any branch of commerce, the only answer they give is this: "It is the custom; our fathers did so: I have done well; my children will do the same." They love France, and speak of their country with pride.

The province of the Illinois is perhaps the only spot respecting which travellers have given no exaggerated accounts: it is superior to any description which has been made, for local beauty, fertility, climate, and the means of every kind which nature has lavished upon it for the facility of commerce.

This country is a delightful valley, where winds one of the most majestic rivers on the globe, and which, after receiving the vast Missouri, is still augmented by an infinite number of smaller rivers and creeks, all navigable, and fitted for the construction of mills and machinery of almost every kind. . . .

There are two communications by land from Kaskaskias to Kaokia; one called the lower road, the other the upper. The first is practicable only during the summer, the second the whole year.

From Kaskaskias to the Meadow of the Rock is reckoned fifty miles, and the road lies across natural meadows and a soil extremely loamy, which renders it impracticable in rainy seasons. The vegetation of this soil is so luxuriant, that a man on horseback is covered by the height of the grass; we measured some stalks, which were twenty-one feet high.

The Meadow of the Rock is a small village[3] situated at the foot of the chain of rocks . . . its population is composed of eighty or an hundred inhabitants at most, and the greater part are the produce of a mixture with the Indians.

[3]   Prairie du Rocher. Ed.

At the Meadow of the Rock are two roads; that on the right goes across the heights; the left, which is the continuation of the lower road, traverses the meadows. A mile beyond the Meadow of the Rock, on the left, is a path now covered with grass, the track of which is scarcely to be seen. This path leads to Fort Chartres, situated on the banks of the river, at the distance of a mile: its ruins are the only vestiges that remain of the power by which it was erected. This fort was begun by the French India Company in 1754, and finished in 1762, precisely at the period of the peace by which we lost our territorial possessions on this continent. Its form is square, with four bastions finely proportioned and covered with freestone. A wall surrounds it six feet thick and twenty high, with crannies and embrasures: opposite and parallel to the curtains are four large and magnificent buildings, one of which was destined for officers, one for the garrison, and the two others for military stores. The whole of these buildings are made of freestone, and raised on arches. This establishment was constructed with so much solidity and care, that in spite of time and the neglect in which it is left, the wall and buildings are still in good preservation: the timber has been taken away.

In front of the curtain which faces the river, are seen the remains of a very fine battery of six pieces of twelve that defended the passage of the river, by means of an island which is opposite, and narrows its bed. At a quarter of a mile from the fort, on the left, are the ruins of Chartres, covered with wild herbs.

III

The
Frontier
State

1817-1841

Illinois 1817–1841

Beginning with 1800, the cardinal feature of Illinois history is the growth of settlement. Throughout most of the eighteenth century the population, in large part French, increased slowly. But in the fall of 1779 an influx of new settlers began. Veterans who had served with George Rogers Clark and their families established themselves at Bellefontaine near the present town of Waterloo. (The settlement antedated that at Marietta, Ohio, usually accorded primacy, by nine years.) By 1800, Bellefontaine had 286 inhabitants, and all Illinois counted 2,458.

The newcomers were Americans, mainly from Kentucky and Tennessee. Varied motives drew them to the new region. The soil was reputed to be fertile, game was plentiful, slavery had not become an incubus, and the pioneer who valued solitude could find it. (As early as 1790 Kentucky had 73,677 inhabitants; by 1800 the number had risen to 220,955.)

Between 1800 and 1810, the population of Illinois grew to 12,282; in 1820 the federal census takers counted 55,211. This increase made governmental machinery imperative. As early as 1790 General Arthur St. Clair, governor of the Northwest Territory, created the first Illinois county. With characteristic immodesty, he named it for himself. The second county, Randolph, was established in 1795. In 1800 Congress erected the Indiana Territory, which included the present state of Illinois. On February 3, 1809, Illinois was made a territory in its own right, with what is now Wisconsin included within its boundaries. Ninian Edwards of Kentucky was appointed territorial governor, with his relative and fellow-Kentuckian, Nathaniel Pope, winning the post of territorial secretary.

As settlers came in increasing numbers, agitation for statehood swelled. On April 18, 1818, Congress passed an enabling act, although there is little question that the territory had fewer than the number of inhabitants prescribed by the Ordinance of 1787. On August 26 a convention adopted a constitution, and on December 3, 1818, Illinois came into the Union as the twenty-first state. Its boundaries were the Mississippi on the west, the Ohio on the south, the Wabash and a line northward to Lake Michigan on the east, and on the north, through the imagination and legislative skill of the territorial delegate, Nathaniel Pope, an east-and-west line fifty-one miles north of the tip of Lake Michigan, the boundary stipulated by the Northwest Ordinance. Kaskaskia was designated as the capital.

For the first twenty years of statehood, settlers flowed into Illinois from the south, moving slowly northward. By 1818, Illinois had thirteen counties, all in the southernmost quarter of the state. New towns grew up: Shawneetown, Carmi, and Golconda in southeastern Illinois; Belleville and Edwardsville in the southwestern part of the state. Recognizing the shifting center of population, and deluded into believing that they could make a killing in real estate speculation, the legislators in 1820 moved the state capital to an uninhabited town site, which they named Vandalia, on the Kaskaskia River, eighty-five miles northeast of Kaskaskia.

Northern Illinois did not come into its own until after the Erie Canal had opened an easy route from the East (1825) and the Black Hawk War (1832) had removed the Indian menace. Galena and Chicago, the two most important settlements in the north, amounted to little until southern Illinois was fairly well settled. In 1826 Galena had only four log houses, but in the following year it could boast of 115 houses and stores. When Chicago was incorporated as a village in 1833, it had a population of 350. Four years later, when it obtained a city charter, it had 4,000 residents.

With the rapid growth of population after 1820 (157,445 in 1830; 476,183 in 1840), Illinois moved toward maturity. Farmers put more acres under cultivation and moved, timorously at first, into the prairies. Roads were staked out and sometimes graded, although even such rudimentary surfacing as planks was still years away. Stage lines went into operation, running on uncertain schedules, torturing their passengers, but delivering them to their destinations. Packets on the Mississippi and Illinois offered more comfort, and also, because of the explosive tendencies of their high-pressure boilers—more risk.

All these features of the new state, and many others, are described in the travelers' accounts which follow.

1817

Morris Birkbeck

The Illinois Prairies
and Settlers

For a number of years Morris Birkbeck was the best known man in Illinois. In 1817 this English farmer—a man of wealth even though only a leaseholder—emigrated to the United States with his children. He proposed to establish a colony, with George Flower, another liberal Englishman, where English farmers could own their own land, vote, and not be tithed for the benefit of a church of which they were not members.

Birkbeck and his party made their way overland to south-eastern Illinois, where he expected to locate what would soon be known as the English Settlement. He recorded his experiences and impressions in a book entitled *Notes on a Journey in America, from the Coast of Virginia to the Territory of Illinois*, the first of a long series of books relating to his project. In this excerpt he described the prairies and settlers as he saw them for the first time.

July 26. Left Harmony[1] after breakfast, and crossing the Wabash at the ferry three miles below, we proceeded to the "Big-prairie," where to our astonishment we beheld a fertile plain of grass and arable, and some thousand acres covered with corn, more luxuriant than any we had before seen. The scene reminded us of some open, well-cultivated vale in Europe, surrounded by wooded uplands; and forgetting that we were in fact on the frontiers, beyond which few settlers had penetrated, we were transported in idea, to the fully peopled regions we had left so far behind us.

On our arrival at Mr. Williams' habitation, the illusion vanished. Though the owner of an estate in this prairie, on which at this time are nearly three hundred acres of beautiful corn in one field, he lives in a way apparently as remote from comfort, as the settler of one year, who thinks only of the means of supporting existence.

We had also an opportunity of seeing the youth of the neighbourhood, as the muster of the militia took place this day at his house. The company amounts to about thirty, of whom about twenty attended with their rifles. In performing the exercise, which was confined to handling their arms, they were little adroit; but in the use of them against an invading foe, woe to their antagonists!

The soil of the Big-prairie, which is of no great extent notwithstanding its name, is a rich, cool sand; that is to say, one of the most desirable description. It extends about five miles by four, bounded by an irregular outline of lofty timber, like a lake of verdure most cheering to our eyes just emerging from the dark woods of Indiana.

This prairie is somewhat marshy, and there is much swampy ground between it and the Wabash, which is distant seven miles.

Morris Birkbeck, *Notes on a Journey in America, from the Coast of Virginia to the Territory of Illinois with Proposals for the Establishment of a Colony of English* (Philadelphia, 1817), pp. 133–42.
[1]   The communal settlement of German pietists established in Posey County, Indiana, by George Rapp in 1815. Ed.

The settlers have in consequence suffered from agues and other bilious complaints; but they are now much more healthy than they were on the first settlement. Cultivation seems to alter the character of the soil; where the plough goes, it is no longer a marsh, but dry sandy arable. About thirty miles to the north of this, which was among the earliest prairie settlements of the district, (having been begun four or five years,) there are prairies of higher aspect and uneven surface, to which our attention is directed. We found a few settlers round one of these, who are now watching their crop.

These people are healthy, and the females and children better complexioned than their neighbours of the timbered country. It is evident that they breathe better air. But they are in a low state of civilization, about half Indian in their mode of life. They also seem to have less cordiality towards a "land-hunter," as they, with some expressions of contempt, call the stranger who explores their country in quest of a home.

Their habits of life do not accord with those of a thickly settled neighbourhood. They are hunters by profession, and they would have the full range of the forest for themselves and their cattle. Thus strangers appear among them as invaders of their privileges: as *they* have intruded on the better founded, exclusive privileges of their Indian predecessors.

But there are agreeable exceptions to the coarse part of this general character. I have met with pleasant, intelligent people, who were a perfect contrast to their semi-Indian neighbours; cleanly, industrious and orderly; whilst ignorance, indolence and disorder, with a total disregard of cleanliness in their houses and persons, are too characteristic of the hunter tribe.

Aug. 1. Twenty miles N. of Shawneetown. After viewing several beautiful prairies, so beautiful with their surrounding woods, as to seem like the creation of fancy; gardens of delight in a dreary wilderness; and after losing our horses, and spending two days in recovering them, we took a hunter as our guide, and proceeded across the little Wabash, to explore the country between that river and the Skillet-fork.

Since we left the Fox settlement about fifteen miles north of the Big-prairie, cultivation has been very scanty, many miles intervening between the little "clearings:" this may therefore be truly called a new country.

These lonely settlers are poorly off: their bread corn must be ground thirty miles off, requiring three days to carry to the mill, and bring back the small horse load of three bushels. Articles of family manufacture are very scanty, and what they purchase is of the meanest quality and excessively dear. Yet, they are friendly and willing to share their simple fare with you. It is surprising how comfortable they seem, wanting every thing. To struggle with privations has now become the habit of their lives, most of them having made several successive plunges into the wilderness. And they begin already to talk of selling their "improvements," and getting still further "back," on finding that emigrants of another description are thickening around them.

Our journey across the Little Wabash was a complete departure from all mark of civilization. We saw no bears, as they are now buried in the thickets, and seldom appear by day; but, at every few yards we saw recent marks of their doings, "wallowing" in the long grass, or turning over the decayed logs in quest of beetles or worms: in which work the strength of this animal is equal to that of four men. Wandering without track, where even the sagacity of our hunter guide had nearly failed us, we at length arrived at the cabin of another hunter, where we lodged.

This man and his family are remarkable instances of the effect on the complexion, produced by the perpetual incarceration of a thorough woodland life. Incarceration may seem to be an epithet less applicable to the condition of a roving backwoodsman, than to any other; and especially unsuitable to the habits of this individual and his family; for the cabin in which he entertained us, is the third dwelling he has built within the last twelve months; and a very slender motive would place him in a fourth before the ensuing winter. In his general habits the hunter ranges as freely as the beasts he pursues, labouring under no restraint, his activity is only bounded by his own physical powers: still he is incarcerated, "shut from the common air," buried in the depth of a boundless forest, the breeze of health never reaches these poor wanderers; the bright prospect of distant hills fading away into the semblance of clouds never cheered their sight. They are tall and pale, like vegetables that grow in a vault, pining for light.

The man, his pregnant wife, his eldest son, a tall, half-naked youth, just initiated in the hunter's art; and three daughters growing up into great rude girls, and a squalling tribe of dirty brats of both sexes, are of one pale yellow without the slightest tint of healthful bloom.

In passing through a vast expanse of the backwoods, I have been so much struck with this effect, that I fancy I could determine the colour of the inhabitants, if I was apprised of the depth of their immersion; and, vice versa, I could judge of the extent of the clearing, if I saw the people. The blood, I fancy, is not supplied with its proper dose of oxygen from their gloomy atmosphere, crowded with vegetables growing, almost in the dark, or decomposing, and, in either case abstracting from the air this vital principle.

Our stock of provisions being nearly exhausted, we were anxious to provide ourselves a supper by means of our guns, but could meet with neither deer nor turkey; however, in our utmost need we shot three racoons; an old one to be roasted for our dogs, and the two young ones to be stewed up daintily for ourselves. We soon lighted a fire and cooked the old racoon for the dogs, but famished as they were, they would not touch it, and their squeamishness so far abated our relish for the promised stew, that we did not press our complaining landlady to prepare it: and thus our supper consisted of the residue of our "corn" bread, and *no* racoon. However, we laid our bearskins on the filthy earth, (floor there was none,) which they assured us was "too damp for fleas," and, wrapt in our blankets, slept soundly enough; though the collops[2] of venison, hanging in comely rows in the smoky fireplace, and even the shoulders put by for the dogs, and which were

---

[2]   Small portions or slices. Ed.

suspended over our heads, would have been an acceptable prelude to our night's rest, had we been invited to partake of them; but our hunter and our host were too deeply engaged in conversation to think of supper. In the morning the latter kindly invited us to cook some of the collops, which we did, by toasting them on a stick, and he also divided some shoulders among the dogs: so we all fared sumptuously.

The cabin, which may serve as a specimen of these rudiments of houses, was formed of round logs with apertures of three or four inches between. No chimney, but large intervals between the "clap-boards" for the escape of the smoke. The roof was, however, a more effectual covering than we have generally experienced, as it protected us very tolerably from a drenching night. Two bedsteads of unhewn logs, and cleft boards laid across two chairs, one of them without a bottom, and a low stool, were all the furniture required by this numerous family. A string of buffalo hide stretched across the hovel, was a wardrobe for their rags; and their utensils, consisting of a large iron pot, some baskets, the effective rifle, and two that were superannuated, stood in the corner; and the fiddle, which was only silent when we were asleep, hung by them.

Our racoons, though lost to us, and our hungry dogs, furnished a new set of strings for this favourite instrument. Early in the morning the youth had made good progress in their preparation, as they were cleaned, and stretched on a tree to dry.

1819

Ferdinand Ernst

Edwardsville, Vandalia, and the Sangamon Country

In 1819 Ferdinand Ernst, a cultivated, wealthy German philanthropist from Hanover, visited Illinois for the purpose of acquiring land for twenty-five or thirty families immigrating to the United States. His observations were published at Hildesheim in 1820 under the title, *Bemerkungen auf einer Reise durch das Innere der Vereinigten Staaten von Nord-Amerika im Jahre 1819.* The parts relating to Illinois were translated by E. P. Baker and published by the Illinois State Historical Society. Ernst took up land in the vicinity of Vandalia, but most of his colonists died within a year of their arrival.

Towards evening of the 27th of July I reached Edwardsville, a pretty town about six or seven miles from the bluffs of the Mississippi and 25 miles from St. Louis. This fertile region is covered with fine farms, where one has opportunity of admiring the astonishing productiveness of the soil. I found the maize from 12 to 15 feet high on an average. The gardens which have sufficient age for fruit settings are luxuriant with peach trees and other fruit trees. The peach is a kind of fruit which flourishes admirably here; the seedling producing fruit in four years, and, almost without exception, bears every year afterward so full that its branches have to be propped. Peach brandy and dried peaches are very common here.

On the other hand I have seldom in all America found the plum tree except in (New) Harmony; but there are apples in great quantities, excellent in all old orchards, and I have met with many fine varieties among them. Moreover the gardens produce melons, especially watermelons, in great quantity and of unusual size—the latter are regarded as a more healthful food than the others. That all other kinds of garden fruits will thrive here may be supposed from what has been said. The pumpkin at times reaches the gigantic size of 3 feet in diameter. Brown and red cabbage I have found nowhere in America, and the ground seems to be too rich for potatoes and many other growths. Potatoes, for example, cannot be planted until very late, often not until July; early planted ones almost never thrive. Maize, wheat and oats grow excellently, barley and rye I have not found.

Here, in Edwardsville, I met again my travelling companion, Mr. Hollmann,[1] and it may not be disagreeable to the reader to receive some report of his journey. I shall therefore give here a brief extract from his diary.

"On the 11th of July, (1819) I, in company with ten travelers on horse, crossed the Wabash and entered the State of Illinois. If the traveler from the coast of the Atlantic Ocean to this point

Transactions of the Illinois State Historical Society, 1903, pp. 155–59.

[1]   Frederick Hollmann, with Ernst, owned a store in Vandalia. Hollmann was also an early member of the village board of trustees. Ed.

has grown weary of the endless journey in the forests then he believes himself transferred to another region of the world as soon as he crosses the Wabash and beholds those great prairies alternating with little wooded districts. Yet, this is one of the largest prairies and, on account of the scarcity of wood, not very well adapted to cultivation.

"After a journey of 22 miles through these prairies we reached the tavern; it was full of travelers. Nevertheless each one was served well enough, the horses were well cared for, and only with respect to the lodgings was the comfort not great. Each one had to prepare his own bed upon the floor as well as he could, and even here the American shows a peculiar ease which is the result of his noble freedom. Everything is done without ado and without ceremony. This manner of living, which was to me at first very strange and disagreeable, soon received my entire approval— little by little one feels himself free among free, honest people. The character of the Americans, which at first was so little agreeable to me, is, nevertheless, on the whole, good. This opinion may be due to the fact that my living with them has, little by little, changed my judgment, or that the people themselves here are better than in the eastern states.

"The road leads through prairies where one all day long sees no house, no, not even a tree, so that protected from the burning heat of the sun, one could rest in its shade. In the middle of this prairie, 24 miles wide, an axle of my wagon broke, whereby I got into no small difficulty. My mounted traveling companions could not help me and had to leave me; but two pedestrians, who had made the journey afoot from Baltimore in this manner, proved friends in need. They went back three miles to get a tree trunk which we had seen lying there by the road. With great difficulty we then took the wagon to the next house. These honest Americans repaid me evil with good. They had been in our company for some time, and at the crossing of the river I did not wish to permit them to take a place in my wagon.

"When we arrived at the next tavern the remaining traveling companions had already sent for a wheelwright, and thus through the kind aid of my comrades it was possible for me to continue the journey with them on the next morning. Toward noon the heat became oppressive and the flies so intolerable that we resolved to make a halt. Not until towards 6:00 o'clock did we continue our journey. Traveling at night time in these prairies is very much to be preferred. One can, without the aid of the moon, find the beautiful level road, and the horses are not tormented by either heat or flies.

"The landlord at the next tavern received us with the remark that tavern keeping was only a secondary matter with him, and he requested of his guests that they accommodate themselves to his wishes, and whoever would not consent to this might travel on. The company of travelers regarded the words of the landlord as very strange, but resolved to put up here as the next tavern was quite a distance off, and men and horses were very tired. After supper the landlord with his family began to pray and sing so that the ears of us tired travelers tingled. Many of the travelers would have gladly requested them to desist from this entertainment if the landlord had not taken the above precautions upon our entrance. After prayers the landlord related to me that he had often been disturbed in his religious exercises, and even been shamefully ridiculed by travelers; he therefore had been obliged to make that condition upon the reception of guests. He was a Quaker.

"On the 23d of July I entered Edwardsville. The most remarkable curiosity which met me here was the camp of the Kickapoo Indians who were now sojourning here in order to conclude a treaty with the plenipotentiaries of the United States, whereby they renounced all their rights and claims to the lands on the Sangamon, Onaquispasippi,[2] and in the entire State of Illinois. Their color is reddish-brown; their face irregular, often horribly colored with bright red paint; their hair is cut to a tuft upon the crown of the head and painted various colors. Very few are clothed, in summer a woolen covering, in winter a buffalo skin, is their only covering. They seem to be very fond of adornments,

[2]   Vermilion River. Ed.

as of silver rings about the neck and arms. They likewise carry a shield before the breast."

Vandalia, 1819.

Immediately after I had joined my traveling companion, Mr. Hollmann, in Edwardsville, we visited our countryman, named Barensbach, whose farm was about four miles from the village, to ask him to show us the lands which are to be sold at public auction, at the land office in Edwardsville, on the first of August this year. He granted our request not only with the greatest readiness, but to this excellent man we owe for many other courtesies and much information. His experience and his advice we have found at all times very helpful. So greatly is he respected in this entire region that we have almost never heard his name mentioned by the inhabitants without its being accompanied by great praise. In spite of his disinclination for every public service they have called him to the important office of judge.

The 24 townships which are to be sold lie between this place and Edwardsville on Shoal creek and Sugar creek and Silver creek. There are many good lands among them, and we would certainly have purchased land at this auction if it had been possible to get anything really as good in the vicinity of the town of Vandalia, that is now about to be laid out.

According to the Constitution of the State of Illinois this town is to be the seat of the government of the State, and the lots will be publicly sold on the 6th of September of this year. In the vicinity of this town is a large amount of fine lands; but everyone is full of praise for those which lie about 60 to 80 miles northward upon the river Sangamon. The Indians have concluded their treaty with Congress, and the latter is now in full possession of these so highly prized regions. In consideration of all this we regarded it more advisable to wait, and resolved for the present to settle in the town, Vandalia, and then from here purchase land in time. In order to use the interval to as good advantage as possible, we began to build a little house here from logs, after the manner of the Americans—the logs are laid one upon another, the ends let down into grooves. As soon as the building was far enough advanced so that my companion was able to finish it alone, I started upon a journey to view the wonderful land upon the Sangamon before I returned to Europe. On the 27th of August I, accompanied by a guide set out upon this little journey. We were both mounted, and had filled our portmanteaus as bountifully as possible with food for man and horse, because upon such a journey in those regions, one can not count upon much. A fine, well-traveled road leads thither from Edwardsville. In order to reach this we rode out from Vandalia across Shoal creek, and then northward into the prairie. We left the forests about the sources of Sugar and Silver creeks to the south, and in the vicinity of the groves about the sources of the Macoupin we came upon this road. We now touched upon points of timber on some branches of this river, and then came into that great prairie which extends from the Illinois river through the greater part of the State from west to east and disappears about the source of the Okaw (Kaskaskia) and upon the banks of the Wabash. This great prairie is the dividing line of the waters flowing southward to the Mississippi and northward to the Sangamon; but is, however, of no considerable height (elevation). East of the road are some lakes or swamps from which the two branches of Shoal creek receive their first water. The entire region south of this prairie elevation is especially distinguished by the elevation of the prairie and by the smoothness and fertility of the land; however, no spring or river water is to be found anywhere in it. In general the few springs which may possibly be there occur only in the bordering timber. The banks of the rivers are very high and hilly, upon these alone are found the patches of forest. All rivers here have but little fall and form many stagnant bodies of water, while in dry seasons the rivers dry up almost completely, and thereby are produced those vapors which make the air unhealthy.

As soon as one arrives upon the elevation and northern side of this prairie the grass of the prairie changes and the ground becomes visibly better. The river banks decline in a gentle slope from the prairie to the water, and are likewise covered with woods, which also shows the greater fertility of the soil. We find here in the State of Illinois almost the same variety of woods that are found in Ohio; and I found, in addition to the soft maple, the sugar tree which, in its leaves differs but little from it. The inhabitants regard the latter as far better for the production of sugar.

On Sugar creek, where we passed the second night, we found, right at the point of the timber, a family who had not yet finished their log cabin. Half a mile farther three families had settled near an excellent spring, and here we passed the night. Upon this little stream, which about 15 miles to the north of its source empties into the Sangamon, about 60 farms have already been laid out and indeed all since this spring of 1819. They have only broken up the sod of the prairie with the plow and planted their corn, and now one sees these splendid fields covered almost without exception with corn from ten to 15 feet high. It is no wonder that such a high degree of fruitfulness attracts men to bid defiance to the various dangers and inconveniences that might, up to this time, present themselves to such a settlement. And one can therefore predict that possibly no region in all this broad America will be so quickly populated as this. Nevertheless, one must regard as venturesome daredevils all settlers who this early have located here for they trespassed upon the possessions of the Indians, and ran the risk of being driven out, or killed during the great annual hunt of the Indians,[3] if that treaty at Edwardsville had not fortunately been made. But now how many will migrate hither since everything is quiet and safe here! Let us consider these

[3] Every autumn the Indians within the entire circuit of their possessions hold a grand hunt. They then set fire to the dry grass of the prairie, and the flame with incredible rapidity spreads over all the country. Before it all wild game flees, having been frightened from their safe retreats, and fall victim to the fatal shot of the red hunters. This destructive custom of burning off the prairies is the reason that timber is confined to the banks of streams and a few other places. The heat of the fire not only prevents entirely further extension of the forests but even diminishes their area. Upon these annual hunts the Indians forcibly eject all white settlers from their territory.

present farmers in respect to their property right upon these their plantations. How extremely dangerous is their position in this regard! The land is not even surveyed, and therefore cannot be offered for sale for three or four years. And then, when offered for sale, anyone is at liberty to outbid the present settler for his farm which is already in cultivation. If now all these considerations and actual dangers could not restrain men from migrating to this territory, this then is the most convincing proof of its value and that it is justly styled "the beautiful land on the Sangamon."

1819-1821

John Woods

The English Settlement, the Illinois Pioneer

John Woods was a well-to-do English farmer who settled on the English Prairie in 1819. By that time Birkbeck and Flower had quarreled, and the Settlement was divided into two different camps. Flower had founded the town of Albion; two miles away Birkbeck had established a settlement named Wanborough for his leasehold in England. Woods not only described the English Settlement two years after its founding but also wrote engagingly of the Illinois pioneer.

[*Sept.*] *14th.* [*1819*]. At day-light we got off the sand-bar and passed the mouth of the Wabash, a large river that separates the states of Indiana and Illinois for many miles. Having passed this river, we had Kentucky on the left, and Illinois on the right. When we reached Browns' Island, five miles from the Wabash, and four from Shawneetown; the wind obliged us to anchor on the left side, close to three large flat boats, loaded with flour, bacon, whiskey, tobacco, horses, and pine and cherry planks, for the Orleans' market. They had been 24 days from the falls of Louisville to this place, owing to the state of the water. This day we only came nine miles.

15th. In the morning we moved opposite to Shawneetown, and anchored close to some rocks, amongst keel-boats, arks, &c., some of them for sale. Many disembark here to go by land to Kaskaskia, and St. Louis, on the Mississippi river; and some for the English settlement at the Prairies. It is subject to floods, and that retards its growth. It is the nearest inhabited spot below the mouth of the Wabash, and in the neighbourhood of the United States Saline works, where about 300,000 bushels of salt are made annually. It is the county town of Gallatin, and has a land office for the sale of the government lands, situated in the south east part of the state of the Illinois; extending 80 or 90 miles from the Ohio river towards the north; these united causes draw many to it, and make it a brisk place. There is a bank called the "Bank of Illinois," in good repute, many stores, and several taverns; the principal one, the Steam-boat Hotel, kept by Mr. Hobson from the north of England. There are about 80 houses, mostly of wood, and a wooden jail. The situation of the town is handsome; but being surrounded by low land, that is liable to be inundated, it is rather unhealthy, at least it was so when we were there. We paid off our two men, who soon hired themselves to go with

John Woods, *Two Years' Residence in the Settlement on the English Prairie, in the Illinois Country* . . . *with an Account of Its Animal and Vegetable Productions, Agriculture, &c. &c., a Description of the Principal Towns, Villages, &c. &c. with the Habits and Customs of the Backwoodsmen* (London, 1822), pp. 128–30, 140–42, 160–62, 212–14, 243–46, 292–95.

a keel-boat to Nashville, in Tennessee, 200 miles up the Cumberland. . . .

25th. After breakfast we went on towards the Prairies; after walking two miles we took the wrong road, being deceived by the marks on the trees, viz. three notches, the road to Palmyra being marked the same. We afterwards inquired and got into the right road; passing through the woods we found many dwarf hazels, with vast quantities of nuts on them; and we soon loaded ourselves with them. We called at a cabin, and there found the gentlemen who had been our companions for the last two days, but we left them there. Two of them are since settled in the English Prairie. About half a mile from the cabin we passed a small Prairie, and soon entered the woods again, and then some barrens. A barren is land nearly destitute of timber, but much overrun with scrubby underwood. A great deal of the land we had passed from Bonpas was good, and some of the timber very fine: I thought these barrens a poor sample of the country. After passing these barrens for more than a mile, we got sight of the Prairies. We first entered the long Prairie, and crossed one corner of it; then passed a small strip of timber, and then entered the English Prairie towards the east corner. Here we had a fine view towards the south-west and north-west, and it was extremely pleasant to see so much open land, with a few trees scattered over it. As we advanced, we saw some men making hay for Mr. Flowers, of Albion; the grass was coarse, and very ripe. We saw some large hay-ricks made in the English manner. Mr. Flowers's flock, of more than 200 hundred sheep, were feeding near the road. I went and looked at them; they were poor and coarse, of different sorts, having been collected from the several places, and on the whole an indifferent flock. We saw the houses of Mr. Flowers and Mr. Birkbeck, and we entered the enclosures of the latter, about a mile from his house. There was a good deal of his land fenced in, but a piece of fallow, of upwards of 20 acres, was all I saw of cultivation. It was towards evening when we reached Mr. Birkbeck's house; we met with a friendly reception from him and his family; we supped with them, and slept at a cabin near. . . .

Mr. Birkbeck's settlement, called Wanborough, is situated at the north-west corner of the English Prairie, and contains 25 cabins, a tavern, a store or two, and several lodging houses; and several carpenters, bricklayers, brick-makers, smiths, wheelwrights, and sawyers; also a taylor and butcher.

A horse or ox mill is building, a malt-house planned out, and a new brick building for a tavern, and several new houses began. As water is scarce, there are some more wells digging. Mr. Birkbeck, in July, found a tolerable good spring, by digging only six feet, about 300 yards from his house; but several of the wells lately dug have but little water in them.

Mr. Birkbeck's house is situated south of the village, a frame and log building of good size; it stands pleasantly, and commands a fine view of the prairie.

The building lots, at Wanborough, are some of five, and others of two and a half acres, laid out, like most of the American towns, in streets that cross each other at right angles, running north and south; the cross ones east and west. The lots are in the woods, but a considerable quantity of the wood is now cleared.

Albion, Mr. Flower's settlement, lies two miles east of Wanborough; it is also situated in the woods, a little north of the English Prairie. It has about 20 cabins, a place of worship, a market-house, two taverns, two stores, a surgeon, several carpenters, brick-makers, bricklayers, wheelwrights, smiths, sawyers, and a shoemaker. Several wells have lately been dug in and near it, but water is still scarce.

Mr. Flower's house is to the south-east of Albion, a large log-building, well placed to enjoy the prospect of the prairie.

Many cabins are built round the prairies, but mostly just in the woods. The English that do not reside in the two villages, are scattered round the different prairies, mostly in single cabins.

About four miles to the east of Albion, at Bonpas-bridge, there is a saw-mill lately built, but it is not yet got to work, having had the mill-dam carried away by a flood in February. I believe it is a place very short of water; it is the property of Messrs. Le Serre and Grutt, late of Jersey or Guernsey, I do not know which: it has a tavern and store also. . . .

The price of corn last fall was mostly 50 cents a bushel delivered, and now 50 cents in the place. But near us there is very little to be procured at any price. On the Wabash, where the country has been longer settled, it is lower and plentiful. It is gathered in October and November, when they only take off the ears; but as the ears are covered with a large husk, they carry them as they are to the corn-crib, and then all the neighbours collect together to help to husk it, and put it into the corn-crib. This is a high day with the Americans, and is called a Husking Frolic; plenty of whiskey is generally to be found at one of these frolics. I never was present but at one; I suppose there were near forty people present; I did not stop, but I understood it concluded with a dance. We did not make any frolic in husking our corn, but did it ourselves; but the Americans seldom do any thing without having one. Thus, they have husking, reaping, rolling frolics, &c. &c. Among the females, they have picking, sewing, and quilting frolics. Reaping frolics, are parties to reap the whole growth of wheat, &c. in one day. Rolling frolics, are clearing wood-land, when many trees are cut down, and into lengths, to roll them up together, so as to burn them, and to pile up the brushwood and roots on the trees. I think this one is useful, as one man or his family can do but little in moving a large quantity of heavy timber. Picking cotton, sewing, and quilting frolics, are meetings to pick cotton from the seeds, make clothes, or quilt quilts; in the latter, the American women pride themselves. Whiskey is here too in request, and they generally conclude with a dance.

Raisings, are a number of men getting together to raise a piece of building, that is, to lift the logs on each other; this is practised by the English as well as the Americans; nor is whiskey here omitted. . . .

I will now give a slight and very brief sketch of the American character; but in speaking of our American neighbours, it must be recollected, that the greater part of them are backwoodsmen.

Mr. Collins, of whom I bought some land, behaved in the most honourable manner, for which I shall ever respect him. Mr. Anderson, of whom I purchased my other farm, I never saw; Mr. Birkbeck transacting the business while I was at Shawnee-town. My family have several American neighbours at Birks' Prairie, from whom they have received the most friendly treatment; and those with whom I have had dealings, have been uniformly civil and obliging. As we live at the entrance of Wanborough, we have frequently the first offer of game and other provisions brought for sale, and whether we buy or not, we never receive the slightest incivility from them. In selling, they always take care to ask enough, as they can fall their price with a good grace; in short, they are Jews in this respect, nor are they very punctual in their payments.

Most of them are well acquainted with law, and fond of it on the most trifling occasions: I have known a law-suit brought for a piggin or pail, of the value of 25 cents. (1s. 1½d.) Another failing in their character is drunkenness; and they are extremely quarrelsome when intoxicated. Many of them are sometimes truly industrious, and at other times excessively idle. Numbers of them can turn their hands to many things, having been accustomed to do for themselves in small societies. They are a most determined set of republicans, well versed in politics, and thoroughly independent. A man who has only half a shirt, and without shoes and stockings, is as independent as the first man in the States; and interests himself in the choice of men to serve his country, as much as the highest man in it, and often from as pure motives,— the general good, without any private views of his own. Most of them are from the south, from North and South Carolina, Georgia, and Tennessee; and though now living in a free State, they retain many of the prejudices they imbibed in infancy, and still hold negroes in the utmost contempt; not allowing them to be of the same species of themselves, but look on *negers*, as they call them, and Indians, as an inferior race of beings, and treat them as such.

Those of whom I purchased my farms, and some others, are moved off to the Red River, 700 miles to the south-west, and, as

I have said before, many of our neighbours are true backwoods-men, always fond of moving: there are others, who wish to sell their land, with its improvements, to go to the Sagamond river, 150 miles towards the north-west. This river runs into the Illinois river, and the country near it is highly spoken of, as to soil, timber, and water. They have but few diversions amongst them except hunting and shooting, here both called hunting; they use rifles, and many of them are excellent shots. In this employment or amusement, they spend much of their time, and depend partly on what they kill in making a livelihood. . . .

With regard to the language of this country, I have found no difficulty to understand any of the Americans I have met with, a few words only excepted. I have seen several from England, that came from a distant part from that in which I resided, that I have had far more trouble to understand. Yet the manner of discourse among the true Back-woods-men is rather uncouth to an English ear. I will attempt to give a specimen of it, in a conversation between two of them, who meet each other on the road; one an Esquire, the other a Judge.

Esq. Well, Judge, how do you do? I hope you are well.

Judge. Well, Squire, I am tolerably bad. How do you do?

Esq. Well, I am a heap better than I was; but I have been powerfully sick lately.

Judge. But, Squire, you have a powerful chance of plunder on your creature. What are you going to do with it?

Esq. Well, I am going to town with a tolerable chance of plunder, to get it carded at the mill.

Judge. Well, so you have got your wool to be carded; I could not calculate what truck you had got.

Esq. Well, I fancy you have been to town. How goes times there?

Judge. Times are dull; I calculated to sell my creature there, and then when I got home, to turn in and earn some money to get me another.

Esq. Well, as you could not trade away your creature, you must turn in and work, as well as you can. I also must turn in, and build a cabin or two, to raise a little cash.

Judge. Well, Squire, have you done any hunting lately? I have followed it steadily for some time.

Esq. Well, Judge, I also have hunted steadily; and I calculated to make a heap of money of my truck, but I have got none.

Judge. Well, what truck have you got, to trade away to make money?

Esq. I have got a few beefs, and a tolerable chance of corn.

Judge. Well, I also have got some beefs, and a powerful chance of corn, and some wool, that I must toat to town and trade away.

Esq. Well, Judge, I must go on and toat my truck to mill, and then get right strait home.

Judge. Well, I must also get on, as my woman is powerfully sick and weak, and I am fetching her some whiskey.

Esq. Well, but Judge, where did you get your creature? It is a powerfully fine looking one.

Judge. Well, Squire, mine is a great little horse, I bought him of our general; but I must be going; farewell.

Well begins most sentences. Plunder and truck include almost every thing. A horse is generally called a creature. Beefs are cows. Toat means to carry any thing. Strait and turn in, are words they frequently use. Woman,—they always call their wives their women. Many of them, instead of saying yes, make a sort of noise, like "him, him," or rather like pronouncing "m, m," with the mouth shut.

In this remote part of America, judges, generals of militia, colonels, captains, and esquires, are not generally men of property or education; and it is usual to see them employed in any common kind of labour. Yet I have seen men among them that possess very good abilities; far from ignorant, and much better informed than could be expected from their appearance.

1823

William H. Keating

Fort Dearborn and Chicago

In 1823 Secretary of War John C. Calhoun sent an expedition under Major Stephen H. Long to explore the headwaters of the Mississippi River. William H. Keating, professor of mineralogy and chemistry at the University of Pennsylvania, accompanied the expedition as geologist and historiographer. As will be seen from what he wrote about the adventures of the explorers, Keating took a sour view of Chicago and its prospects.

Fort Dearborn is situated in the State of Illinois, on the south bank, and near to the mouth of Chicago river; the boundary line between this state and that of Indiana strikes the western shore of Lake Michigan ten miles north of its southernmost extremity, and then continues along the shore of the lake until it reaches the forty-second and a half degree of north lattitude, along which it extends to the Mississippi. The post at Chicago was abandoned a few months after the party visited it. Its establishment had been found necessary to intimidate the hostile and still very powerful tribes of Indians that inhabit this part of the country; but the rapid extension of the white population to the west, the establishment along the Mississippi of a chain of military posts which encloses them, and at the same time convinces them of the vigilance of the government, and of the inevitable destruction which they would bring upon themselves by the most trifling act of hostility on their part, have, it is thought, rendered the continuance of a military force at this place unnecessary.[1] An Indian agent remains there, in order to keep up amicable relations with them, and to attend to their wants, which are daily becoming greater, owing to the increasing scarcity of game in the country.

We were much disappointed at the appearance of Chicago and its vicinity. We found in it nothing to justify the great eulogium lavished upon this place by a late traveller, who observes that "it is the most fertile and beautiful that can be imagined." "As a farming country," says he, "it unites the fertile soil of the finest lowland prairies with an elevation which exempts it from the influence of stagnant waters, and a summer climate of delightful

---

William H. Keating, *Narrative of an Expedition to the Source of St. Peter's River . . . 1823 . . . under the Command of Stephen H. Long, U. S. T. E.; Compiled from the Notes of Major Long, Messrs. Say, Keating and Calhoun* (Philadelphia, 1824), 1: 163–67.

[1] The first Fort Dearborn, erected in 1803, was destroyed by the Indians in 1812. A new fort was built on the site in 1816. As Keating stated, the garrison was withdrawn in 1823, but five years later, with Indian hostilities threatening, the fort was manned again. Except for one year (1831) troops remained at Fort Dearborn until 1836. Ed.

serenity." [2] The best comment upon this description of the climate and soil is the fact that, with the most active vigilance on the part of the officers, it was impossible for the garrison, consisting of from seventy to ninety men, to subsist upon the grain raised in the country, although much of their time was devoted to agricultural pursuits. The difficulties which the agriculturist meets with here are numerous; they arise from the shallowness of the soil, from its humidity, and from its exposure to the cold and damp winds which blow from the lake with great force during most part of the year. The grain is frequently destroyed by swarms of insects. There are also a number of destructive birds of which it was impossible for the garrison to avoid the baneful influence, except by keeping, as was practised at Fort Dearborn, a party of soldiers constantly engaged in shooting at the crows and blackbirds that committed depredations upon the corn planted by them. But, even with all these exertions the maize seldom has time to ripen, owing to the shortness and coldness of the season. The provisions for the garrison were, for the most part, conveyed from Mackinaw in a schooner, and sometimes they were brought from St. Louis, a distance of three hundred and eighty-six miles up the Illinois and Des Plaines rivers.

The appearance of the country near Chicago offers but few features upon which the eye of the traveller can dwell with pleasure. There is too much uniformity in the scenery; the extensive water prospect is a waste uncheckered by islands, unenlivened by the spreading canvas, and the fatiguing monotony of which is increased by the equally undiversified prospect of the land scenery, which affords no relief to the sight, as it consists merely of a plain, in which but few patches of thin and scrubby woods are observed scattered here and there.

The village presents no cheering prospect, as, notwithstanding its antiquity, it consists of but few huts, inhabited by a miserable race of men, scarcely equal to the Indians from whom they are descended. Their log or bark-houses are low, filthy and

---

[2]   Henry H. Schoolcraft, *Narrative Journal of Travels* (1821), p. 384. Ed.

disgusting, displaying not the least trace of comfort. Chicago is, perhaps, one of the oldest settlements in the Indian country; its name, derived from the Potawatomi language, signifies either a skunk, or wild onion; and each of these significations has been occasionally given for it. A fort is said to have formerly existed there. Mention is made of the place as having been visited in 1671 by Perrot,[3] who found "Chicagou" to be the residence of a powerful chief of the Miamis. The number of trails centering all at this spot, and their apparent antiquity, indicate that this was probably for a long while the site of a large Indian village. As a place of business, it offers no inducement to the settler; for the whole annual amount of the trade on the lake did not exceed the cargo of five or six schooners, even at the time when the garrison received its supplies from Mackinaw. It is not impossible that at some distant day, when the banks of the Illinois shall have been covered with a dense population, and when the low prairies which extend between that river and Fort Wayne, shall have acquired a population proportionate to the produce which they can yield, that Chicago may become one of the points in the direct line of communication between the northern lakes and the Mississippi; but even the intercourse which will be carried on through this communication, will, we think, at all times be a limited one; the dangers attending the navigation of the lake, and the scarcity of harbours along the shore, must ever prove a serious obstacle to the increase of the commercial importance of Chicago. The extent of the sand banks which are formed on the eastern and southern shore, by the prevailing north and northwesterly winds, will likewise prevent any important works from being undertaken to improve the post of Chicago.

[3]   Nicolas Perrot, French emissary to the Indian tribes of the Mississippi valley. Ed.

1828

James Hall

Shawneetown
and the Salines

James Hall was the first Illinois man of letters. A native of
Philadelphia, veteran of the War of 1812, and practicing lawyer,
he settled at Shawneetown in 1820. There he became editor and
part owner of the *Illinois Gazette*, the second newspaper to be
published in the state. In 1828 he was appointed state treasurer
and moved to Vandalia. In addition to his official duties, which
he performed capably, he edited the *Illinois Intelligencer* and
founded (1830) the *Illinois Monthly Magazine*, the first literary
periodical west of Ohio.

The first of Hall's many books was *Letters from the West*, published in 1828. It consisted principally of letters which had
appeared in the *Port Folio*, a magazine edited and published by two
of his brothers, and in his own *Illinois Gazette*. Hall's account of
Shawneetown and the nearby Salines is especially valuable.

Shawnee Town occupies a beautiful situation on the western bank of the Ohio, nine miles below the mouth of the Wabash, and one hundred and twenty miles above the junction of the Ohio and Mississippi. Its distance from Pittsburgh, by water, is about a thousand miles, and from New Orleans about eleven hundred. The town stands on a level plain, and embraces a view of the river of four or five miles in each direction.

There was formerly a village of Shawnee Indians at this spot, but it was forsaken before the whites attempted a settlement, and no vestige of it now remains but two small mounds. A few cabins were afterwards built by the French traders; but these had also disappeared, and the ground was covered with bushes, when the present town was established. As recently as the year 1808, there was not a house on the ground; in February 1812, an office for the sale of public lands was established at this place; and in March 1814, an act was passed by Congress, providing that two sections of land adjoining Shawnee Town should be laid out into town-lots, streets, avenues, and outlets, and sold in the same manner as other public lands. The town now contains about one hundred houses, of which five or six are of brick, several of frame, and the remainder of log. It has twelve stores, at which a large and active trade is carried on, besides a number of shops of a smaller description; two excellent taverns, an independent bank, and a branch of the state bank; a land office, a post office, two printing offices; and furnishes employment to carpenters, cabinet makers, blacksmiths, tailors, shoe-makers, bakers, and other mechanics, of whom a number are settled here.

The ground, as is usually the case in bottom lands, is higher on the edge of the river, where the town stands, than at some distance back, and the town is often insulated, when not actually overflowed. The waters begin to swell in February or March, and continue rising for several weeks. The greatest rise, from the

James Hall, *Letters from the West; Containing Sketches of Scenery, Manners, and Customs; and Anecdotes Connected with the First Settlements of the Western Sections of the United States* (London, 1828), pp. 220–23, 228–33.

lowest to the highest point, is about fifty feet. The greatest floods of which we have any account, were in 1813 and 1815, when the water covered all the streets, and entered the lower apartments of the dwellings, reaching nearly to the second floors. Since that time the inhabitants have not been expelled by the conquering element, although the water annually covers the plain in the rear of the town, and advances in front to their very doors. The inconvenience and alarm occasioned by the inundations are not so great as might be supposed. The alarm is little, and that little is imaginary, because the irruption is not sudden, nor accompanied with any violent current, or destructive consequence; and the inconvenience is temporary, as the waters subside in a few days, and the soil being sandy, and its surface uneven, no moisture remains. A small deposit of decayed vegetable matter is left, but not enough to corrupt the atmosphere: and even this, before the weather becomes warm, loses its deleterious quality by evaporation, or yields its juices to the vegetable kingdom. When the river first begins to swell, it usually rises as much as three or four feet in twenty-four hours; but as the volume of water increases, its velocity becomes greater, while the widening of the banks affords it room to expand, and the rise becomes daily less perceptible. At length it begins to fill the bayoux, backs up the channels of the tributary streams, and at last spreads over the banks, covering the bottoms for miles. This gradual process affords ample time to the inhabitants to secure their cattle, and to retreat if necessary. The largest body of water naturally flows in the deepest channel, and here of course is the swiftest current, while the shallow waters which cover the alluvial, flow backwards in eddies, or have no perceptible motion. For this reason, dwellings are not *swept away*, and the inhabitants retreat with safety when the dwellings are no longer tenable. . . .

Before the introduction of steam-boats upon this river, its immense commerce was chiefly carried on by means of *barges*—large boats, calculated to descend as well as to ascend the stream, and which required many hands to navigate them. Each barge carried from thirty to forty boatmen, and a number of these boats frequently sailed in company. The arrival of such a squadron at a small town was the certain forerunner of riot. The boatmen, proverbially lawless and dissolute, were often more numerous than the citizens, and indulged, without restraint, in every species of debauchery, outrage, and mischief. Wherever vice exists will be found many to abet and to take advantage of its excesses; and these towns were filled with the wretched ministers of crime. Sometimes, the citizens, roused to indignation, attempted to enforce the laws; but the attempt was regarded as a declaration of war, which arrayed the offenders and their allies in hostility; the inhabitants were obliged to unite in the defence of each other, and the contest usually terminated in the success of that party which had least to lose, and were most prodigal of life and careless of consequences. The rapid emigration to this country was beginning to afford these towns such an increase of population as would have ensured their ascendancy over the despots of the river, when the introduction of steam-boats at once effected a revolution.

The substitution of machinery for manual labour, occasioned a vast diminution in the number of men required for the river navigation. A steam-boat, with the same crew as a barge, will carry ten times the burthen, and perform her voyage in a fifth part of the time required by the latter. The bargemen infested the whole country, by stopping frequently, and often spending their nights on shore; while the steam-boats pass rapidly from one large port to another, making no halt but to receive or discharge merchandise, at intermediate places. The commanders of steam-boats are men of character; property to an immense amount is intrusted to their care; their responsibility is great; and they are careful of their own deportment, and of the conduct of those under their control. The number of boatmen is therefore not only greatly reduced, in proportion to the amount of trade, but a sort of discipline is introduced among them, while the increase of population has enabled the towns to maintain their police.

During the reign of the bargemen, Shawnee Town, and other places on the river, were described as presenting the most barbarous scenes of outrage, and as being the odious receptacles of every species of filth and villany. These accounts were probably exaggerated; but that they were true to a certain degree, is readily conceded. But the disorderly character acquired by these towns in the manner I have related, is unjustly attributed to them now, when the fruitful cause of their worst vices has been removed, and when wholesome regulations ensure protection to the peaceable and industrious. Shawnee Town is now a quiet place, exhibiting much of the activity of business, with but little dissipation, and still less of outbreaking disorder.

The Saline Reserve commences a few miles from Shawnee Town, and embraces a tract of ninety thousand acres. There are a number of wells of salt water, the nearest of which is seven and the farthest fourteen miles from town. The Indians resorted to these Salines, for the purpose of making salt, previous to their discovery by the whites; earthen vessels, of different sizes, used by them in the manufacture, have been found in large numbers by the persons employed in digging wells. Some of these are large, and display no small ingenuity of workmanship; they are generally fractured; but one or two have been found entire. Gigantic bones of quadrupeds have also been disinterred, resembling the huge remains which have been dug from the *Licks* in Kentucky. Previous to the erection of the Illinois Territory into a state, the Saline was leased to individuals by the United States; but at the reception of this state into the Union, this valuable tract was granted to it in perpetuity, with a restriction that it should not be leased at any time for a longer term than ten years. There are now five salt works in operation in the hands of different individuals, at the whole of which an aggregate of immense amount in bushels of salt are manufactured annually, which sells at from thirty-seven and a half to fifty cents a bushel, at the works, or in Shawnee Town. It is sold by weight, the bushel being estimated at sixty pounds; about one hundred and twenty gallons of water yield sixty pounds of salt. The large tract of land reserved is devoted solely to the purpose of making salt, no part of it being leased for tillage; the object of this regulation is to preserve a supply of timber for fuel. Beds of stone-coal have recently been discovered near the furnaces, but they have not yet been brought into use. The constitution of this state, while it prohibited slavery, allowed the salt makers to hire slaves within the Saline boundary, until the expiration of the year 1825. While this privilege, which was suggested by the scarcity of labourers in a new country, continued to exist, the labour of salt making was performed by negroes, hired from the people of Kentucky and Tennessee. A temporary suspension of operations has been caused by the change from the old to the new order of things. What will be the ultimate effect of the new system is bare matter of conjecture; the better opinion seems to be that the change will be beneficial.[1]

---

[1] Production at the Salines continued until 1875. Ed.

1830

James Stuart

Jacksonville
and Springfield

James Stuart, scion of "the noble house of Moray," onetime
student at Edinburgh University, Whig politician and editor,
came to the United States in 1828 and remained until 1831.
During those years he traveled extensively in the East and South
and as far west as Illinois, to which he devoted three chapters of
his book, *Three Years in North America*. We quote his impressions
of Jacksonville and Springfield, not yet the state capital.

Next morning, the 1st May, we passed through a fertile tract of country in the county of Green for ten miles to Carrolton, its chief town. Wherever we saw land cultivated in this ride, the soil was a dark deep loam, and the wheat plants well coloured, vigorous, and far advanced. We had an excellent breakfast at Bletsoe's hotel at Carrolton, where I chanced to meet Dr. Heaton, the Æsculapius of this district, who recommends all that part of the Sangamon country, which is not in the neighbourhood of the river Illinois, as most eminently healthy. The alluvial land on the side of the river is, of course, frequently visited with the bilious fever of the country.

From Carrolton we had one of the most beautiful rides I ever enjoyed in so fine a country to Jacksonville, the capital of Morgan county. It appeared to me that we passed through the most delightful as well as the richest district I had ever seen. The form and appearance of the prairie and of the surrounding woods were most beautiful. Think of Windsor Park, or Strathfieldsaye, or of parks for all the noblemen and wealthy landholders in Britain to be had here at a dollar and a-quarter an acre, in the neighbourhood of such rivers, and all consisting of land of the richest soil, and of the most beautiful waving shape and smooth surface, all laid out by the hand of Nature, as English parks are,—the wood far more beautifully.

The plough alone is required to make this land produce the most abundant crops;—manure would destroy it. We bivouacked on the prairie on our way to Carrolton, and did not reach Jacksonville until the evening. In the last field which I passed through, before coming into the town, there was growing a crop of wheat of great extent, and the most promising in appearance that it is possible to conceive.

I made inquiry on the road from some passengers as to the hotels at Jacksonville, and was told there were two, neither of them good, but that Bentley's was the best. I found on going into

James Stuart, *Three Years in North America* (Edinburgh and London, 1833), 2:342–47, 358–59.

the house that the tea and supper were nearly finished; and it was not without some difficulty, and rather uninviting looks from a young lady who was acting as waiter, that I procured a fresh supply of coffee and eggs. This was Saturday evening, and the young ladies, after having cleared the table and again covered it with the necessary articles, sat down to their meal with me on a footing of the most perfect equality. I found them very inquisitive: far more so than any of the New Englanders I ever met with; but I afterwards learned that these people had lately come from a remote part of the country, where probably there were no schools. Such silly conduct, in respect to their own interest, as they were guilty of during the forty hours I remained with them, is generally the offspring of ignorance. I found the hotel-keeper a masterpiece of rudeness; and very soon got a candle and retired to my bed-room. I was told that the breakfast-hour was half past seven, but I started from my pillow on the following morning at six, when I heard other people stirring so early, and the breakfast had commenced before I was able to get to the parlour. I asked how this happened: but I found from the answer that it was quite unnecessary to have any further discussion with such a barbarian as Squire Bentley. He did not care for the custom of the British. His forefathers had left England to avoid tyranny, and they did not care for seeing foreigners here.

Jacksonville is situated on a rising ground surrounded by hills, some of which are covered with trees. The town was only begun three years ago, and consists almost entirely of one square, with 600 or 800 inhabitants. A church is building, but not yet finished; but the situation of the place is in all respects so attractive, that already a large academy,[1] for which Congress has made a grant of land, amounting to 46,080 acres, under the superintendence of teachers from New England, has been set agoing in a charming situation, at the foot of one of the wooded hills, about half a mile from the town. Jacksonville is about eighteen miles from the river Illinois; but its distance from Naples, its port on the Illinois, is

---

[1]   Illinois College, founded in 1830. It graduated its first class in 1835. Ed.

twenty-five miles. The population of this county is said to consist of about 8000 individuals; and that of Green county to be not much different. The population of Sangamon county is said to amount to nearly 20,000 persons.

After breakfast I walked out to the high ground on which the academy is built, and from thence to the edge of the hill, near which there is a nice-looking plantation, with a good garden and orchard. Mr. Wilson, to whom the farm belongs, happened to be out of doors, and we immediately joined in conversation. He told me that he was the second settler in this county ten years ago, and continued as much attached to the situation as when he came here; that the soil of all his farm was at least three feet deep, and very rich. He never thought of giving a particle of manure to his land, and always kept in wheat or in maize, generally two years of the one, and two years of the other. His wheat never yields less than forty bushels per acre, and he has had second crops of wheat without sowing any seed, yielding thirty-four bushels per acre. He pointed out to me a field of wheat, at present on his farm, on which he had sown no seed and in which the plants were looking vigorous and well. In explaining to me the advantages of the situation, he particularly noticed the excellence of the roads in the dry prairie ground, without any road-making. Having mentioned to Mr. Wilson that I was at Bentley's house, and what a sad place I found it to be, he said, "I don't frequent the house. Tom Bentley was a farmer, and should have staid where he was. He is as fit to be a lawyer as to keep such a house. T'other house is not much better; but you should have gone to a private house kept (I think he said) by Widow Taylor." I afterwards saw one of the ushers of the academy, from whom I learned that the boarding of the academy was at the rate of a dollar and a-half per week; and that all the necessaries of life were so cheap, that boarding is generally to be had in the town at a dollar and a-quarter per week. On my way back to the village, I went into Mr. Hayne's plantation of eighty acres. He has a charming view of the town and adjoining grounds, from a very pretty cottage he has erected. The only difficulty he has found in the management of the land occurs on the first breaking up. The roots of the prairie grass are so firmly interwoven with the soil, that it requires all the power and steadiness of oxen to tear up the ground; but after the first ploughing with six or eight oxen, horses do the work well, and crops are raised with more ease than in any other country which Mr. Hayne has seen. Eight oxen are most generally employed for the first ploughing.

The church not being finished, I attended public worship in a school-house in the town. Mr. Ellis, who generally officiates was not at home, but Mr. Sturtevant of the Illinois academy officiated for him, and gave us a good discourse.[2] I see, by a notice in the Western Observer of Jacksonville, (for every town or village has its newspaper,) that the annual expense for the teachers of the academy is for English alone twelve dollars, and for the languages, mathematics, philosophy, &c. sixteen dollars. The Reverend Mr. Beecher,[3] a son of the eminent Dr. Beecher of Boston, the head of the orthodox clergy of that city, is now principal of this seminary. . . .

Springfield is a straggling village, somewhat larger than Jacksonville, but the situation is not at all equal to it in point of beauty or interest. The hotel was very nearly as bad as that at Jacksonville. Hornden was the name of the landlord.[4] It was difficult to say whether he, his wife, or his daughter, was the sauciest. They certainly were as rude untutored Americans as I have seen. The lady undertook to wash some linen for me, and there was no difficulty about it, as I got to her house early in the afternoon,—but she delayed and delayed, so that I was obliged to carry them away only half dry next morning after seven o'clock. There is a Presbyterian minister here.

2   The Rev. John M. Ellis was one of the founders of the First Presbyterian Church of Jacksonville and was its second pastor; John M. Sturtevant was one of the founders of Illinois College. Ed.

3   Rev. Edward Beecher, Congregational minister and first president of Illinois College, was the son of Rev. Lyman Beecher and the brother of Harriet Beecher Stowe. Ed.

4   Archer G. Herndon, proprietor of the Indian Queen Tavern. He was the father of William H. Herndon, Lincoln's law partner and biographer. Ed.

In walking about the town in the evening, I met Mr. Straw-bridge, formerly a farmer in Donegal, in Ireland; a gentleman seventy-five years old, who brought a family of five children with him to this country twenty years ago, all of whom have done well. He was first settled in the state of Ohio; but hearing of the prodig-ious fertility of the soil of this part of Illinois, he disposed of 100 acres which he had improved in Ohio, and purchased 640 acres about eight miles to the north-west of Springfield, great part of which he has now improved, and where he also has a mill. His description of his land and of its produce was quite equal in point of quality and quantity to that of Mr. Kerr: and he added, that parts of his land had produced forty bushels of wheat to the second crop without sowing. He has advantages, too, in point of situa-tion, by being nearer to the Galena lead mines, to which he last year sold 8000 wooden posts, at three dollars per hundred. No person can be fonder of this country than Mr. Strawbridge. He had been in Scotland; but there was no land in that country to be compared (he said) to that of his farm; and he viewed this district as quite a paradise or garden. Finding him so much dis-posed to praise, I asked him how he was off for servants. His answer was marked. "You have hit the nail on the head. It is difficult to get servants here, and more difficult to get good ones." This difficulty has, I find, been increased of late, in consequence of the number of labourers required at the Galena lead mines, where great inducements are held out to them; the number not long ago amounted to not less than 10,000 persons. Farming is per-mitted free of rent to those persons, wherever it can be done with-out interfering with the timber needed for mining purposes. The labourers are entitled to the free use of timber for building and fuel.

1832

William Cullen Bryant

The Illinois River; Morgan, Sangamon, and Tazewell Counties

William Cullen Bryant, poet ("Thanatopsis," "To a Water-fowl"), editor (*The New York Evening Post*), and political leader, had a brother, John Howard, who settled at Jacksonville in 1831. The following year William Cullen came west for a visit and to see the Illinois country for himself. His visit coincided with the Black Hawk War. He recorded his impressions in a series of letters to his wife, which were not published until 1884.

June 12. . . . I saw nothing remarkable on the Mississippi until we arrived within a few miles of its junction with the Missouri. I then perceived that the steamboat had emerged from the thick, muddy water, in which it had been moving, into a clear, transparent current. We were near the eastern bank, and this was the current of the Mississippi. On the other side of us we could discern the line which separated it from the turbid waters of the Missouri. We at length arrived at the meeting of these two great streams. The Missouri comes in through several channels between islands covered with lofty trees, and where the two currents encounter each other there is a violent agitation of the waters, which rise into a ridge of short, chopping waves, as if they were contending with each other. The currents flow down side by side unmingled for the distance of twelve miles or more, until at length the Missouri prevails, and gives its own character and appearance to the whole body of water.

At a place called Lower Alton, a few miles above the mouth of the Missouri, we stopped to repair one of the boilers, and I climbed up a steep grassy eminence on the shore, which commanded a very extensive view of the river and surrounding country. Everything lay in deep forest. I could see the woods beyond the Missouri, but the course of that stream was hidden by the gigantic trees with which it is bordered. On every side was solitude, vast, dark, and impenetrable.

When I awoke the next morning we were in the Illinois, a gentle stream about as large as the Connecticut, with waters like the Ohio, somewhat turbid. The Mississippi has generally on one side a steep bank of soft earth ten or twelve feet in height which the current is continually wearing away, and which is constantly dropping in fragments into the water, while on the other side it has a sandy beach. But the Illinois has most commonly a shore which presents no appearance of being eaten by the current, but which slopes as regularly to the water as if it had been smoothed by the spade. As we proceeded up the river, bluffs began to make

William Cullen Bryant, *Prose Writings* (New York, 1884), 2:12–20.

their appearance on the west side. They consisted of steep walls of rock, the tops of which were crowned with a succession of little round eminences covered with coarse grass and thinly scattered trees, having quite a pastoral aspect, though the country does not appear to be inhabited. We stopped to take in wood on the west shore, and I proceeded a few rods through the forest to take my first look at a natural prairie. It was one of the wet or alluvial prairies. The soil was black, and rather moist and soft, and as level as if the surface had been adjusted by some instrument of art. To the north and south along the river it stretches to an extent of which I can not judge, but to the east it was bounded at the distance of about five miles by a chain of rounded eminences, their sides principally covered with grass and their summits with wood, forming the commencement of the uplands on which the dry prairies are situated. The prairie itself was covered with coarse, rank grass four or five feet in height, intermingled with a few flowers. Here and there stood a tall and lonely tree in the midst of a wilderness of verdure.

We arrived at Jacksonville about eleven o'clock. I supped at the tavern at a long table covered with loads of meat, and standing in a room in which was a bed. I was afterward shown into an upper apartment in which were seven huge double beds, some holding two brawny, hard-breathing fellows, and some only one. I had a bed to myself, in which I contrived to pass the time until four o'clock in the morning, when I got up, and, having nothing else to do, took a look at Jacksonville. It is a horribly ugly village, composed of little shops and dwellings, stuck close together around a dirty square, in the middle of which stands the ugliest of possible brick court-houses, with a spire and weather-cock on its top. The surrounding country is a bare, green plain, with gentle undulations of surface, unenlivened by a single tree save what you see at a distance in the edge of the prairie, in the centre of which the village stands. This plain is partly enclosed and cultivated, and partly open and grazed by herds of cattle and horses. The vegetation of the unenclosed parts has a kind of wild aspect, being composed of the original prairie plants, which are of strong and rank growth, and some of which produce gaudy flowers. This is not, however, the flowering season. About a fortnight since they were red with the blossoms of the violet, wood-sorrel, and the phlox (*Divaricata lychnidia*) of our gardens. They will soon be yellow with syngenesious plants.

June 12: I have been to look at my brother's farm. There is a log-cabin on it, built by a squatter, an ingenious fellow, I warrant him, and built without a single board or sawed material of any sort. The floors and doors are made of split oak, and the bedstead, which still remains, is composed of sticks framed into the wall in one corner of the room and bottomed with split oak, the pieces being about the size of staves. The chimney is built of sticks, plastered with mud inside. There are two apartments, the kitchen and the parlor, although most of the houses have but one room. The kitchen is without any floor but the bare ground, and between that and the parlor there is a passage on the ground, roofed over but open on the sides, large enough to drive a wagon through.

June 13th: To-day I am to set out with brother John on horseback on a tour up the Illinois. I carry my "plunder" in a pair of saddle-bags, with an umbrella lashed to the crupper, and for my fare on the road I shall take what Providence pleases to send. I have told you little about the natural productions of the soil and other peculiarities of the country. The forests are of a very large growth, and contain a greater variety of trees than are common to the eastward. The soil of the open country is fat and fertile, and the growth of all the vegetable tribes is rapid and strong to a degree unknown in your country. There is not a stone, a pebble, or bit of gravel in all these prairies. A plough lasts a man his lifetime, a hoe never wears out, and the horses go unshod. Wild plums grow in large thickets, loaded with a profusion of fruit said to be of excellent flavor. The earth in the woods is covered with May-apples not yet ripe, and in the enclosed prairies with large, fine strawberries, now in their perfection. Wild gooseberries with smooth fruit are produced in abundance. The prairie and the forest have each a different set of animals. The prairie-hen, as you walk out, starts up and whirs away from under you, but the spotted prairie-squirrel hurries through the grass, and the prairie-hawk balances himself in the air for a long time over the same spot. While observing him we heard a kind of humming noise in the grass, which one of the company said proceeded from a rattlesnake. We dismounted, and found, in fact, that it was made by a prairie-rattlesnake, which lay coiled around a tuft of herbage, and which we soon despatched. The Indians call this small variety of the rattlesnake the Massasauger. Horses are frequently bitten by it, and come to the doors of their owners with their heads horribly swollen, but they are recovered by the application of hartshorn. A little farther on one of the party raised the cry of wolf, and, looking, we saw a prairie-wolf in the path before us, a prick-eared animal of a reddish-gray color, standing and gazing at us with great composure. As we approached, he trotted off into the grass, with his nose near the ground, not deigning to hasten his pace for our shouts, and shortly afterward we saw two others running in a different direction. The prairie-wolf is not so formidable an animal as the name of wolf would seem to denote; he is quite as great a coward as robber, but he is exceedingly mischievous. He never takes full-grown sheep unless he goes with a strong troop of his friends, but seizes young lambs, carries off sucking-pigs, robs the hen-roost, devours sweet corn in the gardens, and plunders the watermelon patch. A herd of prairie-wolves will enter a field of melons and quarrel about the division of the spoils as fiercely and noisily as so many politicians. It is their way to gnaw a hole immediately into the first melon they lay hold of. If it happens to be ripe, the inside is devoured at once; if not, it is dropped and another is sought out, and a quarrel is picked with the discoverer of a ripe one, and loud and shrill is the barking, and fierce the growling and snapping which is heard on these occasions. It is surprising, I am told, with what dexterity a wolf will make the most of a melon, absorbing every remnant of the pulp, and hollowing it out as clean as it could be scraped with a spoon. This is when the allowance of melons is scarce, but when they are abundant he is as careless and wasteful as a government agent.

I believe this to be the most salubrious, and I am sure it is the most fertile, country I ever saw; at the same time I do not think it beautiful. Some of the views, however, from the highest parts of the prairies are what, I have no doubt, some would call beautiful in the highest degree, the green heights and hollows and plains blend so softly and gently with one another.

Jacksonville, June 19th: I set out, as I wrote you I should do, from this place on Wednesday, the 13th of this month, on a little excursion toward the north. John accompanied me. The first day brought us to Springfield, the capital of Sangamon County, where the land office for this district is kept, and where I was desirous of making some inquiries as to the land in market. Springfield is thirty-five miles east of Jacksonville, situated just on the edge of a large prairie, on ground somewhat more uneven than Jacksonville, but the houses are not so good, a considerable proportion of them being log-cabins, and the whole town having an appearance of dirt and discomfort. The night we spent at a filthy tavern, and the next morning resumed our journey, turning toward the north. The general aspect of Sangamon County is like that of Morgan, except that the prairies are more extensive and more level. We passed over large tracts covered with hazel bushes, among which grew the red lily and the painted cup, a large scarlet flower. We then crossed a region thickly scattered with large trees, principally of black or white oak, at the extremity of which we descended to the bottom-lands of the Sangamon, covered with tall, coarse grass. About seven miles north of Springfield we forded the Sangamon, which rolls its transparent waters through a colonnade of huge button-wood trees and black maples, a variety of the sugar-maple. The immediate edge of the river was muddy, but the bottom was of solid rock, and the water was up to our saddle-skirts. We then mounted to the upland by a ravine, and, proceeding through another tract of scattered oaks, came out again on the open prairie. Having crossed a prairie of seven or eight miles in width, we came to a little patch of strawberries in the grass a little way from the edge of the woodland, where we alighted to gather them. My horse, in attempting to graze, twitched the bridle out of my hand, and, accidentally setting his foot on the rein, became very much frightened. I endeavored to catch him, but could not. He reared and plunged, shook off the saddle-bags which contained my clothing and some other articles, kicked the bags to pieces, and, getting into the wood by which we came, galloped furiously out of sight toward Springfield. I now thought my expedition at an end, and had the comfortable prospect of returning on foot or of adopting the method called "to ride and tie." I picked up the saddle-bags and their contents, and, giving them to John, I took charge of the umbrellas, which had also fallen off, and walked back for two miles under a hot sun, when I was met by a man riding a horse, which I was very glad to discover was the one that had escaped. A foot-passenger, who was coming on from Springfield, had stopped him after he had galloped about four miles, and had taken advantage of the circumstance to treat himself to a ride. I then went back to the strawberries and finished them.

As it was now three o'clock, we went to a neighboring house to get something to eat for ourselves and our horses. An old scarlet-faced Virginian gave our horses some corn, and his tall, prim-looking wife set a table for us with a rasher of bacon, a radish, bread and milk in pewter tumblers. They were Methodists, and appeared to live in a comfortable way, there being two rooms in their house, and in one of them only one bed. A little farther on we forded Salt Creek, a beautiful stream, perfectly clear, and flowing over pebbles and gravel—a rare sight in this country. A small prairie intervenes between this and Sugar Creek, which we also forded, but with better success than two travellers who came after us, who, attempting to cross it in another place, were obliged to swim their horses, and one of them was thrown into the water. At evening we stopped at a log-cabin on the edge of a prairie, the width of which we were told was fifteen miles, and on which there was not a house. The man had nothing for our horses but "a smart chance of pasture," as he called it, in a little spot of ground enclosed from the prairie, and which appeared, when we saw it the next morning, to be closely grazed to the very roots of the herbage. The dwelling was of the most wretched description. It consisted of but one room, about half of which was taken up with beds and cribs, on one of which lay a man sick with a fever, and on another sprawled two or three children, besides several who were asleep on the floor, and all of whom were brown with dirt. In a cavernous fireplace blazed a huge fire, built against an enormous backlog reduced to a glowing coal, and before it the hostess and her daughter were busy cooking a supper for several travellers, who were sitting under a kind of piazza or standing about in the yard. As it was a great deal too hot in the house, and a little too cool and damp in the night air, we endeavored to make the balance even by warming ourselves in the house and cooling ourselves out of doors alternately. About ten o'clock the sweaty hostess gave us our supper, consisting of warm cakes, bacon, coffee, and lettuce, with bacon-grease poured over it. About eleven, preparations were made for repose; the dirty children were picked up from the floor, and a feather bed was pulled out of a corner and spread before the great fire for John and myself, but on our intimating that we did not sleep on feathers, we had a place assigned to us near the door, where we stretched ourselves on our saddle-blankets for the night. The rest of the floor was taken up by the other travellers, with the exception of a small passage left for the sick man to get to the door. The floor of the piazza was also occupied with men wrapped in their blankets. The heat of the fire, the stifling atmosphere, the groans and tossings of the sick man, who got up once in fifteen minutes to take medicine or go to the door, the whimperings of the children, and the offensive odors of the place, prevented us from sleeping, and by four o'clock the next morning we had caught and saddled our horses and were on our journey.

We crossed the fifteen-mile prairie, and nearly three miles beyond came to the Mackinaw, a fine, clear stream (watering Tazewell County), which we forded, and about half a mile beyond came to a house where live a Quaker family of the name of Wilson. Here we got a nice breakfast, which we enjoyed with great relish, and some corn for our horses.

Seven or eight miles farther brought us to Pleasant Grove,[1] a fine tract of country, and ten miles from Wilson's we came to a Mr. Shurtliff's, where we had been advised to stop for the purpose of making some inquiries about the country. Shurtliff lives near the north end of Pleasant Grove, and within four miles of the northern limit of the lands in market. The soil is fertile and well watered, the streams being rather more rapid than in Jacksonville, and the region more than usually healthy. It is within eight miles of Pekin, on the Illinois River, so that it is within convenient distance of a market; there is plenty of stone within a few miles, and saw-mills have been erected on some of the streams. I am strongly inclined to purchase a quarter-section in this place. We were now within two days' ride of Dixon's, where the American army is to be stationed; but, being already much fatigued with our journey, the weather being hot, and our horses, though young and strong, so very lazy and obstinate as to give us constant employment in whipping them to keep them on a gentle trot on the smoothest road, we concluded to proceed no farther. The next morning, therefore, we set out on our return. I should have mentioned that every few miles on our way we fell in with bodies of Illinois militia proceeding to the American camp, or saw where they had encamped for the night. They generally stationed themselves near a stream or a spring on the edge of a wood, and turned their horses to graze on the prairie. Their way was marked by trees barked or girdled, and the road through the uninhabited country was as much beaten and as dusty as the highways on New York Island. Some of the settlers complained that they made war upon the pigs and chickens. They were a hard-looking set of men, unkempt and unshaved, wearing shirts of dark calico, and sometimes calico capotes.[2]

---

[1]   A settlement in Elm Grove Township, Tazewell County, no longer in existence. Ed.

[2]   One of these militia companies had for its captain a raw youth, in whose quaint and pleasant talk Mr. Bryant was much interested. He learned some years afterwards that the name of the youth was Abraham Lincoln.

1833

Colbee C. Benton

Chicago

Colbee C. Benton, a young merchant of Langdon, New Hampshire, embarked on a journey to the West for no reason other than curiosity. He traveled across New York by stage and canal boat, and from Buffalo to Detroit by steamer. In Detroit he bought a horse and proceeded on horseback to Chicago, and later to the Indian villages in northern Illinois. In his diary he wrote his impressions of Chicago in the year it was incorporated as a village.

Monday Aug 19. Today has been very pleasant and I am still in Chicago. Previous to my arriving here I had heard that the Indian Agent at this place was going to send out runners to inform the Indians belonging to the Pottawattami tribe that their annual pension or payment would be paid to them the tenth day of September. I immediately made up my mind to go with one of the runners, provided I should not be obliged to wait too long. This morning, or rather about noon, I called upon the Agent and he was absent. I called after dinner again and found him.[1] I told him what my wishes were. He said I should find it rather a hard journey, but if I wished to go, and was determined to go, he would recommend a young man by the name of Louis Wilmot,[2] a half Indian, he being the most companionable of the three whom he had employed, and he said that he might take which route I should prefer. I did not then determine, for I had almost given up the journey, it being two days before we could start. I thanked the Agent, who is a very pleasant and agreeable man, for his politeness, and we left his house. . . .

I have concluded to wait till Wednesday and take my Indian tramp and have informed the Agent that I should prefer visiting the Indians in the state of Illinois, to which he answered that the young man would be ready on Wednesday. He laughed at me, saying that I should find harder times than I expected, and his pretty wife laughed, no doubt thinking it was a wild goose chase. But I had a great curiosity to see the Indians at home and far away from the whites, and I was unwilling to let so good an opportunity pass without improving it. And I longed to tread on

Colbee C. Benton, *A Visitor to Chicago in Indian Days: "Journal to the Far-Off West,"* ed. Paul M. Angle and James R. Getz (Chicago: The Caxton Club, 1957), pp. 70–77.

[1]   The Indian agent was Thomas J. V. Owen. Owen had been elected one of the five town trustees on August 10. Two days later, at the first meeting of the board, he was chosen president. He is sometimes referred to, in disregard to exact terminology, as Chicago's first mayor. Ed.

[2]   Louis Ouilmette, a son of Antoine Ouilmette, for whom the suburban city of Wilmette is named. Ed.

ground that had never been inhabited by civilized mortals. I wanted to be travelling in the wilderness of the west among the savages where I could be an eye witness to their mode of living. And then again, there is something wild, novel, and romantic about it.

Tuesday Aug 20. Another pleasant day, and I have improved it very much to my satisfaction. I have had a good opportunity to view the town and country about, and I find Chicago a very pleasant place, as I have before thought. It is situated on the southwestern shore of Lake Michigan at the mouth of the Chicago River, and already it has the appearance of considerable business. It is laid out into lots on each side of the river, and between the two branches, which come together about one mile from the lake. On the north side of the river the lots commence on the shore of the lake and extend up to the branch (north), but on the south side the United States Fort and the other buildings connected with it are on the shore of the lake, and the land belonging to the Government extends about one hundred rods up the river. And then the lots commence and run some distance up the south branch.

The first street on the south side of the river is eighty feet wide, bordering on the river, and nearly every lot on this street is occupied already and it is the place of nearly all the business.[3] The lots are one hundred and fifty feet deep and eighty feet front. Another street back of this and another, etc., each and all eighty feet wide. The court house is to be located on this side fronting a little square. On the north side there are lots laid out on the river which will be some more convenient, but will not be so pleasant nor so valuable on account of its not being so natural a place for business. The town is laid out very regular, at least as regular as possible with the situation of the place.

The lots are mostly owned by the United States government and the state of Illinois. Part of the lands, every other section, was

---

[3]   South Water Street, now Wacker Drive. Ed.

given by the United States to the state of Illinois for the purpose of making a canal from the mouth of the Chicago River to the mouth of the Fox River where it enters into the Illinois.[4] The state made sale of a few lots some time since, and the rest remain as they were and cannot be sold until the legislature meet again, which will not take place until sometime in eighteen hundred and thirty four. The lots being owned as they are is of great disadvantage to the place and to the appearance of it. It prevents the erection of good buildings, for no one would be willing to risk a large amount of property on public land which must be brought into market and sold under the hammer.

At present the town presents a singular and very peculiar appearance. The lots, many of them, are improved with temporary buildings, some not more than ten foot square, and they are scattered about like the cattle on the prairie. They are mostly new. I believe there has been one hundred built this year, all without any regard to beauty, and they are set on blocks so that they can move them at the shortest notice. It will depend some on the length of the purse of the occupant whether the building shall be moved at the time the lots come into market.

The north side of the river is partly owned by individuals, but it is not much settled yet; some few buildings near the lake. The settlements are in the forks of the river (which consists of one new tavern house two stories high, one other old-looking tavern, one large store building, and a number of log dwellings), and on the south side is the most, which consists of two large, two-story taverns, three or four large storehouses, and a great number of small dwellings and shops. This street extends to the land occupied for the Fort, and is the principal place of business.

The Fort and public buildings are situated on the shore of the river and lake, and it is much the most pleasant part of the town, rendered more pleasant on account of its being elevated a little higher than the rest of the land about. Fort Dearborn, as it is

[4]   The projected Illinois and Michigan Canal would link the Chicago
        River to the Illinois River rather than to the Fox. Ed.

called, is an old fort and it has that appearance, except that the buildings have lately been whitewashed, which makes it appear a little more respectable. It is surrounded by a post fence which would not be much protection against a few pieces of heavy cannon. It answers, and has answered very well, however, as a good and safe refuge from the revenge and cruelty of the savages. It is occupied at present by two companies of forty-eight men each, but in all probability they will soon be unnecessary residents. If emigration continues at the same rate it has done the past season, the country will very soon be able to defend themselves; when that time comes the soldiers will be removed to some other station and the land will be sold and laid out and made to constitute a part of the town.

The Government have appropriated thirty thousand dollars for the purpose of making a safe and convenient harbour. The work is going on briskly & will probably be finished the next season. At present the vessels are obliged to anchor outside of the bar and unload by means of small boats or lighters, so called, and these have to be rowed more than a mile around the bar. When the river comes onto the beach of the lake it turns almost directly south and follows the beach, making a channel of about fifty yards between the beach and the sand bar, and it cannot be crossed even by small boats until proceeding about half a mile from the turn and then with difficulty sometimes. When the harbour is finished all this expense, time, and trouble will be saved. The work has been commenced on the south side of the river at the turn, and they are extending a wharf directly into the lake, cutting through the sand bar, and when finished the river will have a straight and direct channel into the lake, so that any vessel can come into the river and unload anywhere in town, saving all the distance round the bar with their freight's expense & the danger of anchoring in the lake. It will be a safe harbour and the only one in this part of the lake, and the only one that *can* be except the mouth of the Calemic[5] River. Vessels will be

5   Calumet. Ed.

able to run up the south branch a mile or two, and up the north branch some farther. [6]

The trade of Chicago seems to be with the inhabitants in the vicinity of the Wabash River, at least a considerable share of it. They come with large covered waggons drawn by three or four yoke of oxen, generally loaded with wheat which they exchange for salt. They travel very cheap indeed. Their way is across an extensive prairie nearly the whole distance, which is about one hundred and twenty miles to the Wabash River. They carry their victuals with them, and when night comes they turn their oxen onto the prairie and sleep in their waggons. At Chicago they do the same, and I saw them cooking by their fires, making coffee, kneading bread, and baking it on the coals. A large space is occupied by their teams and there is a number present all the time. They seem to live as comfortable as many of the inhabitants. There are a number of settlements in the vicinity of Chicago which do part of their trading here, but not all.

The country about Chicago, for the distance of twelve miles from the lake, is mostly a low prairie covered with grass and beautiful flowers. Southwest from the town there is not one tree to be seen; the horizon rests upon the prairie. North, on the lake, is sandy hills and barren. Between there and the north branch is a swampy, marshy place, and there is a marshy place on the south branch. The town stands on the highest part of the prairie, and in the wet part of the season the water is so deep that it is necessary to wade from the town for some miles to gain the dry prairie. Notwithstanding the water standing on the prairie and the low, marshy places, and the dead-looking river, it is considered a healthy place. It has almost a continual lake breeze, which will explain in a measure the healthiness of the place. And another reason is the cleansing of the river water by the winds driving the pure lake water into and then running out again.

---

[6]   At this time the Chicago River took a sharp turn to the south at what is now Michigan Avenue, followed the course of the famous street to Madison Street, then turned east and emptied into Lake Michigan. Ed.

The inhabitants are a singular collection of beings. "All nations and kindred and people and tongues." Black and white and red and grey, and they live in all manner of ways. Some men do their own cooking. I saw one little hovel which contained a family, and near it was two stakes and a pole across it where they hung on the pot and done all their cooking, & all of it in the principal street.

I was surprised to observe the masculine appearance of the women. They were in the streets as much as the men, and seemed to prefer a seat outside of their dwelling places rather than to sit down under their own roof. And finally I have seen a good deal to surprise, interest, and amuse me for the few days that I have remained here.

1833

Charles Joseph Latrobe

Chicago

When Charles Joseph Latrobe visited Chicago in the early fall of 1833, he saw scenes far different from those which had greeted Benton only a few weeks earlier. At the time of Latrobe's visit, commissioners of the United States were negotiating the treaty that would remove the last of the Indians from Illinois, and the author recorded that event with all the color it called for.

Latrobe was born in London in 1801. Trained for the Moravian ministry, he abandoned that calling for a career of travel and writing. In 1824 he took his first trip to Switzerland, where he made a reputation as a mountain climber. Four years later he traveled through the Tyrol on foot. In 1832 he succumbed to the English mania for touring the United States. With a companion, Count Albert Pourtales, Latrobe sailed for New York in the company of Washington Irving. Latrobe spent most of 1832 in the East, but the fall of the following year found him at Chicago.

I have been in many odd assemblages of my species, but in few, if any, of an equally singular character as with that in the midst of which we spent a week at Chicago.

This little mushroom town is situated upon the verge of a perfectly level tract of country, for the great part consisting of open prairie lands, at a point where a small river whose sources interlock in the wet season with those of the Illinois, enters Lake Michigan. It however forms no harbour, and vessels must anchor in the open lake, which spreads to the horizon to the north and east, in a sheet of unbroken extent.

The river, after approaching nearly at right angles, to within a few hundred yards of the lake, makes a short turn, and runs to the southward parallel to the beach.[1] Fort Dearborn and the light-house, are placed at the angle thus formed. The former is a small stockaded enclosure with two block-houses, and is garrisoned by two companies of infantry. It had been nearly abandoned till the late Indian war on the frontier made its occupation necessary. The upstart village lies chiefly on the right bank of the river above the fort. When the proposed steam-boat communication between Chicago and the St. Joseph's river, which lies forty miles distant across the lake, is put into execution, the journey to Detroit may be effected in three days, whereas we had been upwards of six on the road.

We found the village on our arrival crowded to excess, and we procured with great difficulty a small apartment; comfortless, and noisy from its close proximity to others, but quite as good as we could have hoped for.

The Pottawattomies were encamped on all sides,—on the wide level prairie beyond the scattered village, beneath the shelter of the low woods which chequered them, on the side of the small river, or to the leeward of the sand hills near the beach of the lake. They consisted of three principal tribes with certain

Charles J. Latrobe, *The Rambler in North America*, 2d ed. (London, 1836), 2:203–16.
[1]   See Benton, "Chicago," footnote 6, above. Ed.

adjuncts from smaller tribes. The main divisions are, the Potta-wattomies of the Prairie and those of the Forest, and these are sub-divided into distinct villages under their several chiefs.

The General Government of the United States, in pursuance of the scheme of removing the whole Indian population westward of the Mississippi, had empowered certain gentlemen to frame a Treaty with these tribes, to settle the terms upon which the cession of their Reservations in these States should be made.[2]

A preliminary council had been held with the chiefs some days before our arrival. The principal Commissioner had opened it, as we learnt, by stating, that, as "the Great Father in Washington had heard that they wished to sell their land, he had sent Com-missioners to treat with them." The Indians promptly answered by their organ, "that their Great Father in Washington must have seen a bad bird which had told him a lie, for that far from wishing to sell their land, they wished to keep it." The Commissioner, nothing daunted, replied: "that nevertheless, as they had come together for a Council, they must take the matter into considera-tion." He then explained to them promptly the wishes and in-tentions of their Great Father, and asked their opinion thereon. Thus pressed, they looked at the sky, saw a few wandering clouds, and straightway adjourned *sine die*, as the weather is not clear enough for so solemn a council.

However, as the Treaty had been opened, provision was sup-plied to them by regular rations; and the same night they had had great rejoicings,—danced the war-dance, and kept the eyes and ears of all open by running howling about the village.

Such was the state of affairs on our arrival. Companies of old warriors might be seen sitting smoking under every bush; arguing, palavering, or "powwowing," with great earnestness; but there seemed no possibility of bringing them to another Council in a hurry.

[2] The commissioners were Gov. George B. Porter of Michigan Territory, Thomas J. V. Owen, Indian agent at Chicago, and William Weatherford. Ed.

Meanwhile the village and its occupants presented a most motley scene.

The fort contained within its palisades by far the most enlightened residents, in the little knot of officers attached to the slender garrison. The quarters here consequently were too confined to afford place of residence for the Government Commissioners, for whom and a crowd of dependents, a temporary set of plank huts were erected on the north side of the river. To the latter gentlemen we, as the only idle lookers on, were indebted for much friendly attention; and in the frank and hospitable treatment we received from the inhabitants of Fort Dearborn, we had a foretaste of that which we subsequently met with everywhere under like circumstances, during our autumnal wanderings over the Frontier. The officers of the United States Army have perhaps less opportunities of becoming refined than those of the Navy. They are often, from the moment of their receiving commissions, after the termination of their Cadetship at West Point, and at an age when good society is of the utmost consequence to the young and ardent, exiled for long years to the posts on the Northern or Western frontier, far removed from cultivated female society, and in daily contact with the refuse of the human race. And this is their misfortune—not their fault;—but wherever we have met with them, and been thrown as strangers upon their good offices, we have found them the same good friends and good company.

But I was going to give you an inventory of the contents of Chicago, when the recollection of the warm-hearted intercourse we had enjoyed with many fine fellows whom probably we shall neither see nor hear of again, drew me aside.

Next in rank to the Officers and Commissioners, may be noticed certain store-keepers and merchants resident here; looking either to the influx of new settlers establishing themselves in the neighbourhood, or those passing yet farther to the westward, for custom and profit; not to forget the chance of extraordinary occasions like the present. Add to these a doctor or two, two or three lawyers, a land-agent, and five or six hotel-keepers. These may be considered as stationary, and proprietors of the half a hundred clap-board houses around you.

Then for the birds of passage, exclusive of the Pottawattomies, of whom more anon—and emigrants and land-speculators as numerous as the sand. You will find horse-dealers, and horse-stealers,—rogues of every description, white, black, brown, and red—half-breeds, quarter-breeds, and men of no breed at all;—dealers in pigs, poultry, and potatoes;—men pursuing Indian claims, some for tracts of land, others, like our friend Snipe,[3] for pigs which the wolves had eaten;—creditors of the tribes, or of particular Indians, who know that they have no chance of getting their money, if they do not get it from the Government agents;—sharpers of every degree; pedlars, grog-sellers; Indian agents and Indian traders of every description, and Contractors to supply the Pottawattomies with food. The little village was in an uproar from morning to night, and from night to morning; for, during the hours of darkness, when the housed portion of the population of Chicago strove to obtain repose in the crowded plank edifices of the village, the Indians howled, sang, wept, yelled, and whooped in their various encampments. With all this, the whites seemed to me to be more pagan than the red men.

You will have understood, that the large body of Indians, collected in the vicinity, consisted not merely of chiefs and warriors, but that in fact the greater part of the whole tribe were present. For where the warrior was invited to feast at the expense of Government, the squaw took care to accompany him;—and where the squaw went, the children or pappooses, the ponies, and the innumerable dogs followed;—and here they all were living merrily at the cost of the Government.

[3]   "Snipe" was a farmer from the St. Joseph country who came to Chicago in the same stage as Latrobe. He had a claim against the Indians for hog-stealing. By his account he had put fifty-five hogs into the woods; a few months later only thirty-five could be found. Snipe blamed the Indians, but Latrobe believed that wolves were the real culprits. Ed.

The features of the Pottawattomies are generally broad and coarse; their heads large, and their limbs fuller than the Osages. Among their warriors you rarely see one with the head shaved, retaining nothing but the scalp-lock. On the contrary, they wear it bushy and long, frequently plaited into long tails, sometimes hanging back in the nape of the neck, and at others over the face in front. Their sculls are remarkably flat behind.

Of their dress, made up as it is of a thousand varieties of apparel, but little general idea can be given. There is nothing among them that can be called a national costume. That has apparently long been done away with, or at least so far cloaked under their European ornaments, blankets, and finery, as to be scarcely distinguishable. Each seemed to clothe him or herself as best suited their individual means or taste. Those who possessed the means, were generally attired in the most fantastic manner, and the most gaudy colours. A blanket and breech-cloth was possessed with a very few exceptions by the poorest among the males. Most added leggings, more or less ornamented, made of blue, scarlet, green, or brown broad-cloth; and surcoats of every colour and every material; together with rich sashes, and gaudy shawl or handkerchief-turbans.

All these diverse articles of clothing, with the embroidered petticoats and shawls of the richer squaws and the complicated head-dress, were covered with innumerable trinkets of all descriptions, thin plates of silver, beads, mirrors, and embroidery. On their faces, the black and vermillion paint was disposed a thousand ways, more or less fanciful and horrible. Comparatively speaking, the women were seldom seen gaily drest, and dandyism seemed to be more particularly the prerogative of the males, many of whom spent hours at the morning toilet. I remember seeing one old fool, who, lacking other means of adornment and distinction, had chalked the whole of his face and bare limbs white.

All, with very few exceptions, seemed sunk into the lowest state of degradation, though some missionary efforts have been made among them also, by the American Societies. The

Pottawattomie language is emphatic; but we had no means of becoming acquainted with its distinctive character, or learning to what class of Indian tongues it belonged.

All was bustle and tumult, especially at the hour set apart for the distribution of the rations.

Many were the scenes which here presented themselves, portraying the habits of both the red men and the demi-civilized beings around them. The interior of the village was one chaos of mud, rubbish, and confusion. Frame and clapboard houses were springing up daily under the active axes and hammers of the speculators, and piles of lumber announced the preparation for yet other edifices of an equally light character. Races occurred frequently on a piece of level sward without the village, on which temporary booths afforded the motley multitude the means of "stimulating"; and betting and gambling were the order of the day. Within the vile two-storied barrack, which, dignified as usual by the title of Hotel, afforded us quarters, all was in a state of most appalling confusion, filth, and racket.[4] The public table was such a scene of confusion, that we avoided it from necessity. The French landlord was a sporting character, and every thing was left to chance, who, in the shape of a fat housekeeper, fumed and toiled round the premises from morning to night.

Within, there was neither peace nor comfort, and we spent much of our time in the open air. A visit to the gentlemen at the fort, a morning's grouse-shooting, or a gallop on the broad surface of the prairie, filled up the intervals in our perturbed attempts at reading or writing in doors, while awaiting the progress of the treaty.

I loved to stroll out towards sun-set across the river, and gaze upon the level horizon, stretching to the north-west over the surface of the Prairie, dotted with innumerable objects far and near. Not far from the river lay many groups of tents constructed of coarse canvas, blankets, and mats, and surmounted by poles,

4   Mark Beaubien's Sauganash Hotel. Ed.

supporting meat, moccasins, and rags. Their vicinity was always enlivened by various painted Indian figures, dressed in the most gaudy attire. The interior of the hovels generally displayed a confined area, perhaps covered with a few half-rotten mats or shavings, upon which men, women, children, and baggage were heaped pell-mell.

Far and wide the grassy Prairie teemed with figures; warriors mounted or on foot, squaws, and horses. Here a race between three or four Indian ponies, each carrying a double rider, whooping and yelling like fiends. There a solitary horseman with a long spear, turbaned like an Arab, scouring along at full speed;— groups of hobbled horses; Indian dogs and children, or a grave conclave of grey chiefs seated on the grass in consultation.

It was amusing to wind silently from group to group—here noting the raised knife, the sudden drunken brawl, quashed by the good-natured and even playful interference of the neighbours; there a party breaking up their encampment, and falling with their little train of loaded ponies, and wolfish dogs, into the deep black narrow trail running to the north. You peep into a wig-wam, and see a domestic feud; the chief sitting in dogged silence on the mat, while the women, of which there were commonly two or three in every dwelling, and who appeared every evening even more elevated with the fumes of whiskey than the males, read him a lecture. From another tent a constant voice of wrangling and weeping would proceed, when suddenly an offended fair one would draw the mat aside, and taking a youth standing without by the hand, lead him apart, and sitting down on the grass, set up the most indescribable whine as she told her grief. Then forward comes an Indian, staggering with his chum from a debauch; he is met by his squaw, with her child dangling in a fold of her blanket behind, and the sobbing and weeping which accompanies her whining appeal to him, as she hangs to his hand, would melt your heart, if you did not see that she was quite as tipsy as himself.

Here sitting apart and solitary, an Indian expends the exuberance of his intoxicated spirits in the most ludicrous singing and gesticulation; and there squat a circle of unruly topers indulging themselves in the most unphilosophic and excessive peals of laughter.

It is a grievous thing that Government is not strong-handed enough to put a stop to the shameful and scandalous sale of whiskey to these poor miserable wretches. But here lie casks of it for sale under the very eye of the Commissioners, met together for purposes, which demand that sobriety should be maintained, were it only that no one should be able to lay at their door an accusation of unfair dealing, and of having taken advantage of the helpless Indian in a bargain, whereby the people of the United States were to be so greatly the gainers. And such was the state of things day by day. However anxious I and others might be to exculpate the United States Government from the charge of cold and selfish policy toward the remnant of the Indian tribes, and from that of resorting to unworthy and diabolical means in attaining possession of their lands,—as long as it can be said with truth, that drunkenness was not guarded against, and that the means were furnished at the very time of the Treaty, and under the very nose of the Commissioners,—how can it be expected but a stigma will attend every transaction of this kind. The sin may lie at the door of the individuals more immediately in contact with them; but for the character of the people as a nation, it should be guarded against, beyond a possibility of transgression. Who will believe that any act, however formally executed by the chiefs, is valid, as long as it is known that whiskey was one of the parties to the Treaty.

"But how sped the Treaty?" you will ask.

Day after day passed. It was in vain that the signal-gun from the fort gave notice of an assemblage of chiefs at the council fire. Reasons were always found for its delay. One day an influential chief was not in the way; another, the sky looked cloudy, and the Indian never performs any important business except the sky be clear. At length, on the 21st of September, the Pottawattomies resolved to meet the Commissioners. We were politely invited to be present.

The Council-fire was lighted under a spacious open shed on the green meadow, on the opposite side of the river from that on which the Fort stood. From the difficulty of getting all together, it was late in the afternoon when they assembled. There might be twenty or thirty chiefs present, seated at the lower end of the enclosure; while the Commissioners, Interpreters, &c. were at the upper. The palaver was opened by the principal Commissioner. He requested to know why he and his colleagues were called to the council? An old warrior arose, and in short sentences, generally of five syllables, delivered with a monotonous intonation, and rapid utterance, gave answer. His gesticulation was appropriate, but rather violent. Rice, the half-breed Interpreter, explained the signification from time to time to the audience; and it was seen that the old chief, who had got his lesson, answered one question by proposing another, the sum and substance of his oration being —"that the assembled chiefs wished to know what was the object of their Great Father at Washington in calling his Red Children together at Chicago!"

This was amusing enough after the full explanation given a week before at the opening session; and, particularly when it was recollected that they had feasted sumptuously during the interval at the expense of their Great Father, was not making very encouraging progress. A young chief rose and spoke vehemently to the same purpose. Hereupon the Commissioner made them a forcible Jacksonian discourse, wherein a good deal which was a-kin to threat, was mingled with exhortations not to play with their Great Father, but to come to an early determination, whether they would or would not sell and exchange their territory: and this done, the council was dissolved. One or two tipsy old chiefs raised an occasional disturbance, else matters were conducted with due gravity.

The relative positions of the Commissioner and the whites before the Council-fire, and that of the Red Children of the Forest and Prairie, were to me strikingly impressive. The glorious light of the setting sun streaming in under the low roof of the Council-House, fell full on the countenances of the former as they faced the West—while the pale light of the East, hardly lighted up the dark and painted lineaments of the poor Indians, whose souls evidently clave to their birth-right in that quarter. Even though convinced of the necessity of their removal, my heart bled for them in their desolation and decline. Ignorant and degraded as they may have been in their original state, their degradation is now ten-fold, after years of intercourse with the whites; and their speedy disappearance from the earth appears as certain as though it were already sealed and accomplished.

Your own reflection will lead you to form the conclusion, and it will be a just one,—that even if he had the will, the power would be wanting, for the Indian to keep his territory; and that the business of arranging the terms of an Indian Treaty, whatever it it might have been two hundred years ago, while the Indian tribes had not, as now, thrown aside the rude but vigorous intellectual character which distinguished many among them, now lies chiefly between the various traders, agents, creditors, and half-breeds of the tribes, on whom custom and necessity have made the degraded chiefs dependant, and the Government Agents. When the former have seen matters so far arranged that their self-interest, and various schemes and claims are likely to be fulfilled and allowed to their hearts' content,—the silent acquiescence of the Indian follows of course: and till this is the case, the Treaty can never be amicably effected. In fine, before we quitted Chicago on the 25th [of September], three or four days later, the Treaty with the Pottawattomies was concluded,—the Commissioners putting their hands, and the assembled chiefs their paws to the same.

By it, an apparently advantageous "swop" was made for both parties;—the main conditions of which, if the information we received was correct, were,—that the Indians should remove from the territory they now occupied, within three years time— being conveyed at Government expense across the Mississippi, and over the State of Missouri, to the western boundary of the latter, where five millions of acres of rich and fine land were to be set apart for them;—and that they were to be supported for one year after their arrival in their new possession. Moreover, the Government bound itself to pay them over and above, a million of dollars; part of this sum being set aside for the payment of the debts of the tribe—part for a permanent school-fund—and part for agricultural purposes, presents, and so forth.

1833

Patrick Shirreff

Peoria, Pekin, Springfield, and the Prairies

Patrick Shirreff, a Scottish farmer from East Lothian, toured the United States to determine whether his younger brother should try his fortunes as an American farmer. The three chapters of Shirreff's book which he devoted to Illinois constitute one of the most perceptive accounts of the state at this time.

Peoria takes its name perhaps from the tribe of Indians called Peorias, and which is now almost extinct. It is situated on a lake, or an expansion of the river, two miles wide, and four or five in length, at some elevation above the water, and commanding a view of the lake and fine wooded banks on the opposite side.

The village exhibits marks of considerable age, but none of prosperity. I found the dinner hour past, and fared indifferently. There being nothing to attract attention at Peoria, I recrossed the ferry, where the horse was still standing, and bent my way to Pekin, which I reached a little before sunset.

Pekin, sometimes called Pekin-on-the-hill, is situated on the Illinois, and is progressing rapidly. The hotel was filled with permanent boarders, who seemed to be engaged in the different mechanical arts. The landlord was crawling about the house in a debilitated state, and evidently a fever patient. The people assembled at table addressed me by the name of stranger, and showed considerable attention; a female, as usual, filling out tea.

For three days past I had been without shoe-ties, both having broken after leaving Chicago, the bark of trees having since then been substituted. I made application for a supply at different stores in Pekin, without success. In one instance I found the storekeeper stretched at full length, with his back on the counter, and his feet touching the roof. At first I did not observe him, as the light from a candle was faint, and I was surprised at hearing human sounds proceeding from such an unseemly thing. He answered my enquiries regarding shoe-ties dryly, without altering his position. On retiring I purposely left the door of the store open, with the view of rousing him from his unelegant posture. My stratagem did not, however, succeed, and I began to think the individual might be a philosopher engaged in study; instead of a demi-savage, which his behavior at first led me to suppose.

Patrick Shirreff, *A Tour through North America; Together with a Comprehensive View of the Canadas and the United States as Adapted for Agricultural Emigration* (Edinburgh, 1835), pp. 238–50.

On retiring to bed, I was deposited in a pretty large apartment, containing seven or eight beds, some of which were occupied by sick people, and others were passing to and fro, at all hours of the night. I rose early in the morning, and bent my course towards Springfield, in Sangamon county, leaving the river Illinois to the westward. I applied for breakfast, at an early hour, at a solitary house, which an overgrown young woman readily supplied, baking bread and stewing a fowl in a very short space of time, for which she charged well. In course of conversation, I learned her husband was from the State of New York, and had lived some-time in Indiana. Her children were evidently unhealthy, and she said sickness was no great misfortune, as it was so easy to get a living in the country. After breakfast I passed several small prairies and the river Mackinaw, when I entered on a large and uninhabited one, sixteen miles across. The day being very warm, I felt a good deal fatigued, and was anxious to obtain dinner and shelter from the sun, but on gaining the only house on the road, I was told the whole family were sick, and it was impossible for me to obtain dinner. I proceeded to a hotel on Salt creek, which I reached with scarcely sufficient light remaining to distinguish the house.

The landlord of the hotel, Mr. Music, was from home, and two daughters and a son did the honours of the house. These people seemed in good circumstances, having a well-stocked farm and abundance of Indian corn. On my arrival, I was asked whether I would have bread of Indian corn or wheat, and all seemed sur-prised to hear I had never tasted the former. Two other travellers on horseback arrived, and bread of both kinds was presented at table.

One of the travellers was on his way to Galena, for the purpose of getting payment of horses he had sold some time before. He was originally from Kentucky, and now resided in the neighbourhood of Jacksonville. His manners were somewhat rough, and with this individual I had much conversation. At first he was most anxious to engage me as a farming-help, admitting that he himself had become too lazy to work hard, and pressed me again and again to name my terms. To him and others who wished my assistance as farming-help, I uniformly expressed thankfulness for their kindness, and assured them that circumstances did not admit me to reside in the country. Before separating, he offered me a letter to his wife, who would give me free board at his house till he returned, and his sons would drive me over the adjoining country. I took down his address and left him, with a promise to visit Mrs. Taylor if time permitted me.

The travellers breakfasted at Salt creek before setting out on their journey, which is good policy in thinly settled districts. The day was excessively warm, and I suffered considerably from thirst. On passing a cottage, before reaching Sangamon river, a girl was drawing water, from whom I asked a drink; she went into the house and brought a tumbler, which she filled with indifferent water, and handed over the rails. When about to depart, a woman of prepossessing appearance came to the door, and asked me to enter the house and shelter myself from the sun. I thanked her, and in return, said I was anxious to reach Springfield in time for dinner. She told me her husband, who was sick, liked above all things to converse with travellers, and hoped for his sake I would enter the house. There was something so earnest in the woman's manner that I would have found difficulty in resisting her entreaties at any time, and on the present occasion my inclination yielded a willing assent.

The husband was stretched on a clean uncurtained bed, and appeared in a most debilitated state. He brightened up by degrees, and showed he possessed a good deal of information. He was particular in his enquiries about Ottawa, on the river Illinois, to which he had some thoughts of removing, as he had resolved to leave his present situation, where he had resided for six years, on account of the scarcity of water. His health and that of all his family had been good until the present time, when he was seized with fever, which he thought the doctor had broken. He regretted that his weakness could not stand cooking meat in the house, but if I could partake of other food, his wife would place it before me. A snow-white cloth was spread on the table, followed by bread, milk, butter, and preserved fruits of excellent quality, and to which I did justice. On departing, I received an invitation to call at the house if ever I passed in the direction. Soon afterwards, crossing the Sangamon river in a boat, although the stream was not more than eighteen inches deep, I reached Springfield about two o'clock.

Dinner was readily promised at the hotel, although past the regular hour, and in the meantime I prepared to wash and shave. On asking for a bedroom, the landlord personally brought water, and on a second application, soap and a mirror. I had now discovered that I also wanted a towel, and at last, conscious of the impropriety of keeping the master of the house running up and down stairs on my account, I moved off to the pump-room and apologized for my past conduct, on the score of being a stranger in the country, and unacquainted with its customs. I had no cause to regret this proceeding, the landlord being remarkably attentive during my stay, pointing out what was worthy of notice, and offering his horse to visit them.[1] . . .

Springfield is an irregular village of wooden houses, containing about 1200 souls. It is three miles from Sangamon river, which is only navigable for small boats at the melting of the snow in spring. There are good stores of all descriptions in the village. . . .

Having reached Chicago with an unsocial party of travellers, and gradually passing from the forests and oak openings of Michigan, it was not until after crossing the river Des Plaines that I became fully sensible of the beauty and sublimity of the prairies. They embrace every texture of soil and outline of surface, and are sufficiently undulating to prevent the stagnation of water. The herbage consists of tall grass, interspersed with flowering plants of every hue, which succeed each other as the season advances. The blossoming period was nearly over at the time of my journey. Sunflowers were particularly numerous, and almost all the plants

---

[1]   This was the same tavern keeper, Archer G. Herndon, whom James Stuart, three years earlier, described as an oaf. See Stuart, "Jacksonville and Springfield," above. Ed.

had yellow blossoms. Every day brought me in contact with species formerly unobserved, while others with which I had become familiar, disappeared. Occasionally, clumps of trees stood on the surface, like islands in the ocean. The bounding forest projected and receded in pleasing forms, and the distant outlines appeared graceful. I had no time for searching out and studying scenery, and perhaps conceptions of beauty and grouping of trees, formed in the artificial school of Britain, are inapplicable to the magnificent scale on which nature hath adorned the country between Chicago and Springfield. The works of man are mere distortions compared with those of nature, and I have no doubt many prairies, containing hundreds of square miles, exceed the finest English parks in beauty as much as they do in extent. Sometimes I found myself in the midst of the area without a tree or object of any kind within the range of vision, the surface, clothed with interesting vegetation around me, appearing like a sea, suggested ideas which I had not then the means of recording, and which cannot be recalled. The wide expanse appeared the gift of God to man for the exercise of his industry; and there being no obstacle to immediate cultivation, nature seemed inviting the husbandman to till the soil, and partake of her bounty. Mr. Malthus's doctrine, that population increases faster than the means of subsistence, appeared more than doubtful, and involving the unhallowed thought of a Being of infinite goodness and power leaving man, a favoured object of creation, without the means of subsistence. If a considerable portion of mankind ever are in want of food, the cause will be found to arise from human agency, and not from nature refusing to do her part. I felt grateful at beholding a field so well fitted to relieve the depressed and starving population of Great Britain and Ireland, while the conduct of their land-owning and tithe-eating legislators, in restricting the circulation of nature's bounty, appeared sinful.

It has already been observed, that fire passes annually over the prairies, which may perhaps account for the absence of clovers and fibrous-rooted grasses, the herbage consisting chiefly of three or four tall growing species, the creeping roots of which escape destruction, and continue to exist without renewal from seed. At this advanced period of the season, the coarse withered grass seemed unpalatable to animals, and the cattle were, generally, browsing on parts which had been burned, with a view of affording a succession of nutritious food. I collected the seeds of many plants without knowing any thing of their usefulness or beauty. On the banks of Meadowcrow creek, a small tributary of the river Illinois, I first met the indigenous hop, apparently identical with that of England, and from the Sangamon brought the leguminous and earth seeds of *Glycine Monica*, a species of hazel exceeding four feet in height, and indigenous to the whole extent of country through which I travelled on the American continent, and which commonly fringed the prairie, and graduated the change from forest to open plain. They were loaded with small nuts, which sometimes satisfied my hunger.

The most numerous of birds were the ruffed grouse, or prairie-hen. They frequent roads, particularly in the morning, perhaps to escape from the effects of dew, and with the aid of a gun, I might have shot many hundreds of them without leaving the pathway. On the skirts of the forest around Springfield, quails, or partridges as they are called in the language of the country, are abundant, and so tame, that they might have been killed with stones. Notwithstanding the numbers of such birds, Illinois cannot boast of gamekeepers, and I only observed one individual shooting grouse. Many cranes, swans, ducks, and wild-geese, were seen hovering above the prairies, and on different occasions I disturbed owls reposing amongst withered grass. The forests abounded with green coloured paroquets, which fluttered about with a disagreeable noise, in flocks of six or seven.

Deer were frequently seen bounding across the plain, and prairie wolves skulking amongst the tall grass. The prairie wolf is a small animal, not much larger than the fox of Britain, and whose habits are not widely different. In forests on the banks of the river Illinois, grey coloured squirrels were extremely numerous, and seemed actively engaged in collecting nuts, with which the ground was strewed. Near Pekin I walked a mile or two with a person returning from shooting squirrels, and who bestowed four or five on a woman who asked them for a sick boy. In Canada, the colour of the squirrel is red; in Michigan, black; and in Illinois, grey. The gopher is a red-coloured quadruped, in size and shape resembling the weasel of Britain. It burrows in the prairies, forming passages, and throwing up earth like the mole. It subsists on vegetables, and is sometimes a source of annoyance to the farmer. I was told it is furnished with pouches for carrying earth from its excavations.

The wild bee was the most numerous of insects, and crowded the few remaining blossoms of the sunflower. They live in the hollows of decaying trees, and a considerable quantity of their honey is collected by the inhabitants. In the Canadas, the maple-tree supplies saccharine matter, and in Illinois, where this species of plant is rare or unknown, the bee forms the chief source of this commodity. Thus, the maple, bee, and cane, contribute the same ingredient to man, and are illustrative of the economy and diversity of nature.

The country from Chicago to Springfield, through which I passed, may be termed prairie, the portion of forest land being quite inconsiderable. In the immediate neighbourhood of these villages, the surface is nearly level, and in the intermediate space, sufficiently undulating for usefulness and beauty. The forest trees on the margins of the prairie are of small size, and chiefly oak; those on bottom, or interval, land, on the banks of rivers, are of immense size. Forests generally clothe the banks of streams, but sometimes prairies descend to the water's edge, on both sides, and no general rule can be laid down for the prevalence or want of timber. After crossing the river Des Plaines, there was no indication of marsh or wetness of soil, and I only observed one lake, of very small extent. Rocks were not seen protruding above the surface, although stones of considerable size were observed on the wayside. The beds of the rivers Des Plaines, Du Page, and Vermillion, at the places where I crossed, were strewed with stones. The freestone rock, seen in crossing the Illinois, and of which a considerable sized island was composed, was observed for several miles below in the channels of tributary streamlets. I examined seams of coal on the banks of the river Sangamon, in the vicinity of Springfield. My view was imperfect, as the seams had never been worked. They appeared about two feet in thickness, of bituminous quality, and fifteen feet above the level of the river. A contract was entered into at the time of my visit, to furnish coal, by removing the incumbent earth, at three cents per bushel.

The soil of this district embraces almost every description, from poor sand to rich clay of strong texture. It is of all colours, and generally of superior quality. The poorest soil was on the banks of the Sangamon, the richest on those of the Illinois. The black sand, of which the prairies are partly composed, seems of a penetrating nature, and adheres to the skin like soot. Before being aware of this circumstance, I marvelled at the filthy appearance of some of the inhabitants, who did not wear stockings, and at evening I sometimes found my feet and ankles coated with black dust, after having been washed half a dozen times, in course of the day, in wading streams. The burning of the herbage prevents the accumulation of vegetable matter on the soil, and the creeping rooted grasses, with which it is occupied, perhaps exhaust rather than enrich it. First crops are seldom too luxuriant, and land is said to improve after the breaking up of the prairie.

Agriculture embraces the growth of wheat and Indian corn and the rearing of live stock; but, from the limited number of inhabitants, the cultivated fields form a mere speck on the surface of the prairie. The wheat stubbles in the neighbourhood of Springfield betokened luxuriant crops, and the height and thickness of Indian corn filled me with amazement. At the date of my visit, 23d September, most of this crop had been severed from the earth, and was standing in conical piles on the field, where it remains during winter, or until such time as it is wanted. There are many kinds of Indian corn, differing widely in habits of growth, and I was unable to determine whether the uncommon luxuriance of that in this district was owing to a particular variety, or congeniality of soil and climate, but I supposed the latter.

The herbage of the prairie, consisting of strong-rooted grasses, is difficult to plough for the first time, and is commonly accomplished with the aid of six oxen. The first ploughing is sometimes performed by contract at $2 per acre. The plough for breaking up the prairie is furnished with a broad share, and cuts a turf seventeen or eighteen inches broad, by two or three in depth. Indian corn is dropped into every third furrow, a bushel being sufficient for ten acres, and covered with the next cut turf. This crop receives no farther cultivation of any kind, is termed sod corn, and said to yield fifty bushels per acre. A wheat crop follows without a second ploughing, the soil being simply harrowed, receiving half-a-bushel of seed, and yielding twenty-five bushels per acre. When Indian corn is grown on land not newly broken up, it is commonly planted on hills four feet square, and four seeds are allowed to each hill. The grasses do not appear amongst sod corn, and annual weeds are not often troublesome, until after four or five years' cultivation.

I witnessed the process of seeding land with wheat, during my visit to Mr. Humphries.[2] Four oxen were dragging a small harrow, driven by his son, who left them standing while he sowed ridge by ridge, and he was the only individual engaged in the operation. The previous crop had been Indian corn, and the land had not been ploughed since its removal. Dung is not applied to the fields, though sometimes to the gardens, in which melons and potatoes are chiefly cultivated. At Springfield, the potato of Britain is not of fine quality, and passes by the name of Irish potato, to distinguish it from the sweet potato, a species of convolvulus. These potatoes seem not to be suited to the same climate. Here, and farther to the south, the sweet potato was of large size, and more palatable than the Irish one, although not equal to this root when grown in a colder region. I observed a few plants of Guinea corn, which its cultivators said answered as a substitute for coffee, but none of them seemed to have given it a trial.

[2]   Owen Humphreys settled near Mechanicsburg, Sangamon County, in 1828. Ed.

Clovers, or any description of herbage plant, did not come under my notice. The prairie grasses, when closely depastured for a series of years, fall off, and are said ultimately to disappear. This circumstance was a source of uneasiness to some settlers, who looked forward to the time when there would be a scarcity of food for cattle, and which seemed to me as irrational as the Canadian farmers' fear of wanting firewood.

I did not see breeding-horses or sheep in any part of my journey, although I have no doubt there are plenty of both in the country. The cattle were not numerous, but of good size, and in tolerable condition. The prairie herbage was so completely withered, that I could not form an opinion of its feeding qualities in spring. What had been burned to afford a fresh supply, was so closely cropt by the cattle, that its reproductive properties could not be estimated. In some situations near Springfield, where stock is pretty numerous, and the prairie has been cropt by them for years, the herbage appeared thin and unnutritious. Pigs were frequently seen running about the forest, and were, like all others seen at large in course of my tour, perfect starvelings. The acorn season had arrived, and I was amused at the pigs scrambling for this fruit. They ran grunting from tree to tree, and the noise of a falling acorn was the prelude to a race and fight.

The inhabitants are thinly scattered over the country, and chiefly settled on the skirts of the forest, the middle of prairies being altogether unoccupied, and I was told untaken-up land, or such as had not been bought from government, existed within a mile of Springfield. Proximity to forest is chosen for the facility of obtaining building, fencing, and fuel timber; and a settler regards the distance of half a mile from forest an intolerable burden. The dwelling-places are log-houses, larger than those of Canada, and somewhat better finished. Frequently a nail or piece of iron is not used in the whole creation, the door is without lock or latch, and the beds in the cock-loft lighted by chinks in the walls. In such places, the owners of hundreds of acres and scores of cattle reside. How powerful is habit and fashion in all things! Labour is scarce and highly remunerated. A good farming help obtains

$120, and an indifferent one $100 a-year, with bed and board. A female help receives in private families a dollar a-week. The hotel-keeper at Springfield pays two female helps each $2 weekly in cash, and told me if it were not for a desire young girls have for fine clothes, he could not get one on any terms. Board, at the hotel, with bed, is $3 for short periods, and for long periods $2½ per week.

In the Springfield market, butter is worth eight cents per pound, and eggs six cents per dozen. Beef, in small quantities, is worth three, and pork two cents per pound, respectively, and much cheaper by the carcass. Wheat sells for thirty-seven and a-half, oats eighteen, and Indian corn ten cents per bushel. Good muscovado sugar costs ten, and coffee twenty cents per pound.

1834

Morris Sleight

Naperville and the Region around It

A letter written by Morris Sleight in 1834 describing the settlement that would come to be called Naperville and the region around it is evidence that at last northern Illinois was attracting its share of settlers. Sleight, a former sea captain, left his home and family in Hyde Park, New York, to explore the opportunities offered by the West. He took his time in coming to a decision, so it was not until 1837 that he made extensive land purchases and brought his family to Illinois. He was elected treasurer of Du Page County in 1839 and served as the village president of Naperville in 1861–62.

Sleight wrote the letter quoted here to his wife Hannah in Hyde Park.

Chicago, Illinois, July 9 1834

My dear H.

I received yours today of the 21 June which is the first I have received. You mention sending a Letter to Detroit. My goods have not yet arrived and I shall be detained here perhaps a week longer. As Mr. Douglass returns by Detroit I have directed him to send it to me by private conveyance if Possible.—My health continues first rate and I grow thiner and Darker every day. . . . You do not say one word about your health. Remember to tell me that in your next.—To give you a minute description of all passing events, as they occur only for the space of one week would make a small vollume. In a letter I can only mention a few. I have a thousand Idias and at the time I am determined to communicate them to you, but when I sit down to write, I forget them.—However I have one that I do remember. Mr. Douglass and myself started a week ago tomorrow for Fox River with the Stage with the Idea of being [gone] about 3 days. We left our Baggage at the Hotel at Chicago and I remember having a very dirty Shirt when I returned today. I am very much Pleased with the Land about Capt. Napers Settlement,[1] 28 miles west of Chicago, and with the whole country after getting 12 miles west of this Place. I am highly Pleased with Michigan but I am Delighted with Illinois. Mr. Stuarts account I think is not exaggerated.[2] The first view of a Michigan Prairie is Delightfull after Passing the oak openings & thick forest, but the first view of an Illinois Prairie is Sublime, I may almost say awfully Grand, as a person needs a compass to keep his course—but the more I travel over them the better I like them. There is a great variety of Flowers now on the Praries, but they tell me in a month from this time they will be much prettyer. I have sent you a few of them by Mr. Douglass, which will be all faded by the time you get them, but they will be interesting to you, as you

Manuscript in the library of the Chicago Historical Society.
[1]   Joseph Naper, of Ashtabula, Ohio, settled in Du Page County in 1832 and platted the Town of Naperville. Ed.
[2]   The reference is to James Stuart's *Three Years in North America*. Ed.

can be sure they were picked from the Prarie of Illinois. There is a number of other kinds on the dry Praires. Some Resembl Sweet William, some Pinks, Sun flowers, and almost every variety that grows in our gardens. In crossing the Prarie about 2 miles west of Chicago this morning we startled a dear little gazelle but the little thing hid itself in the long grass, and we could not find it.— I have also sent you a few Pebbles that I this evening picked up on the Shore of lake Michigan; there is nothing remarkable about them only the Interest one Takes in things far fetch[d]. The Shore of the lake is Charming. A short distance from the Shore the wind has blown the Sand in a great many curious shapes. Some resemble hay cocks, some Hay Stacks and some Sheaves of Wheat, all having small bunches of Bushes on the top that resemble the water willow. On the sands of some of those places the sand is very smooth and hard, very tempting to write with ones finger, on one of those delightful places. I wrote the name of my wife, and all the little ones. This when finished looked more like home than any thing I have Seen. What would I have given to have had you all with me in this delightful Ramble. I think it not Impossible, that you may yet see the spot, as distance is nothing when one is traveling. Ten or ten thousand miles I should think nothing of had I an object to gain by the under-taking. Traveling is so delightfull. Every person I see traveling no matter how far they have come even by land and I have seen a number of families from the Destrict of Maine that all appear Delighted, and well they may be.—I wrote Mr. Russell[3] yesterday by mail from Capt Napers Settlement on the River Dupage. That letter and the accounts Mr. Douglass will give will show you how we have spent our last weeks. Mr. Douglass has made a Purchase on the DuPage River joining Capt. Naper and I have the Refusal of the Place adjoining should I conclude to take it before I leave the country. It is a beautiful Place well timbered and watered. It has one of the Best springs close to a beautiful

---

[3]   James Russell was postmaster of Staatsburgh, Hyde Park, Dutchess County, New York. Ed.

Building Spot and the Dupage River, a Small but pretty Stream, runs near the Door. It has now on it a Double Log house, and 50 or 60 acres of wheat, oats & corn. It looks like an old farm as does the whole county around it. It likewise has on it the Fort and Block houses used in the late Indian war. They are now used for a barn & yard. I suppose on the place there is from 150 to 200 acres inclosed and a Chance to enclose 500 acres more of as good land as ever laid out doors. This *Preemption* I can get for $1000. I suppose the Improvents has cost 6 or 700. None of this land has come in market yet nor will it under 2 or 3 years. It is not yet Surveied, but the *Premption Law* has pass^d, which gives the person that occupied the land up to the 13 day of June last the right to take 160 Acres of Land at $1.25 per acre. This they take where there is timber and a good Building Spot and good Springs, and a plenty of Stock water. This place has all those advantages. The prarie adjoining Such places, they suppose can be got yet for some time after the Land comes in market for $1.25 per acre.—This is the Best country I ever saw for a Poor man or a rich one, an Industrious man or a Lazy one.—I see no kind of business but looks Promising, and I believe the country is perfectly Healthy. I do not Know nor see what can make it otherwise. The Place I mention above has but one disadvantage. It is 28 miles to Chicago, and 40 miles to Ottawa. The Proposed Canal will run from Chicago to Ottawa, the head water of the Illinois, and the place lays about 8 or 9 miles from the rout of the Canal. It has the advantage of Grist Mills & Saw Mills, with half a mile also a Store and tavern, and a thick Settled neighborhood. As people build in the Groves you cannot see many of your neighbors. I will not say houses yet, but Cabbins. In a few years I think I can say *Mansions*. But do not think because I have said so much about the place that I think seriously about purchasing, because I understand that I am to see much handsomer, but as a gentleman observed those beautiful places are all the time a little ways ahead, but I have already overtaken a good many of them.—I to day met Mr. Johnson. We were at the same house some time before we recognized each other, so you may suppose what Beautiful Brunetts you are to see should we ever return. We have spent a very pleasant day together. I have had the pleasure of introducing him to the commanding officer of the Garrison at Chicago, who had come to visit us at the Hotel, and to [visit] several other Gentlemen. He starts tomorrow morning for the east. I believe he intends visiting Montral and Quebeck. I have made acquaintance with all the Principle men of Chicago. I have several invitations to dine out. I have promised to dine with Capt Baxley, the Commdg officer of the Garrison; and he has politely offered me his Horse & Gig whenever I choose to take a ride or he will go hunting or fishing with me when ever I choose. The business men are all verry sociable and want me to settle among them. They say there is business enough for all, however I intend to look before I leap. Mr. Johnson mentions that there is some Cholra on south but nothing alarming. The news in Chicago respecting it was very much exagerated as is always the case. I am glad I have seen Mr. J. or I should not liked to have ventured far South.—Mr. J. says I ought not to miss this opportunity, and he thinks there is no danger. . . . —Tell uncle Russell, that there is farms in Illinois, that can be purchased for $5 p acre that the Best farm in Staatsburgh will not compare with. It is Perfectly astounding to see the number of Persons that are emigrating to this country, and how jealous people are of their rights of *Premtion*. I have seen some Places within 3 miles of the Place I mentioned that the Premption could not be got for less than $3,300; and I do not like it near as well as the one I can purchase for $1000—It is uncertain, at what time I shall leave this place. I see one Speculation here that will cost me but a Small Sum to try an experiment. If it does not Succeed I must eventually make considerable by it and if it does—and as yet I cannot see any reason why it will not—it will be a Fortune. The Idea struck me when I first entered Chicago, and since I have returned it looks still better. There is nothing to loose by it and Much to gain. I shall examine the subject [and] will see that all is Right and if so, I'll *go ahead*—It is not worth while to say much about my views as I am not detrmd on anything yet, and perhaps

I may return for the Present without doing anything. *But*—I will make no promises for hereafter, if my views meet your aproba- tion.—Tell the Children, that I should be pleased to see them all turned out on one of those Beautiful Praries, to see what a frolick they would have in gathering Flowers, and Dear little Rose and I would Catch the Dear Gazells. Those beautiful Flowers make a sweet hiding place for them—

Tell Delsar that I was riding through a little grove on the Prarie searching for water and I Started a fine Buck and his Doe. They started out on the open Prarie on high ground and it was a beautifull Sight to see them streak it over the Ground. Dandy would be no touch to them. It is amusing to hear the different names that is given to the People of the different States and territorys in this Vacinity, and you can almost tell them by their Peculiarities as well as we can the 5 Nationers—or the Yankees Dutch or Irish. The Michiganers are calld Woolfverines, the Illinois Suckers, the Indianians Hooshers, and the Missourians Pukes, and the N. Yorkers Eels, and the People of Detroit Hollow Heads. Although there is many Peculiarities in their manners they all appear to be very friendly to Strangers. Give my respects to all enquiring friends. I should be very glad to see you all, but I am on a voyage of discovery and I cannot say when I shall return. I may at some time come upon you on surprize. Until I return you must get along as well as you can. . . .

M. Sleight

1834

Charles Fenno Hoffman

Galena

"He is chivalric to a fault, enthusiastic, frank without discourtesy, an ardent admirer of the beautiful, a gentleman of the best school—a gentleman by birth, by education, and by instinct." So wrote Edgar Allan Poe of Charles Fenno Hoffman, whose book, *A Winter in the West*, is one of the liveliest, most informative contributions to American travel literature.

Hoffman, born in New York City in 1806, lost his right leg in an accident at the age of eleven. He attended Columbia College but did not graduate, studied law, and was admitted to the New York bar. He found his real vocation, however, in writing and editing. In October, 1833, he decided to tour the Northwest on horseback. To defray his expenses he wrote a series of letters to the *New-York American*, and later published them in book form in New York and London.

Hoffman continued to write verse and fiction until 1849, when his mind failed and he entered the state hospital at Harrisburg, Pennsylvania. He remained there until his death in 1884.

The population of Galena is about 1000, and that of Jo-Davies's county, in which it is situated, is computed at 5000; a very large proportion of which is engaged in mining operations. The town, for its size, is one of the busiest places in the Union. The value of goods imported into this place last season amounted to $150,000; the exports of lead amounted to seven millions of pounds, at $4.50 per hundredweight. There were ninety-six departures and ninety-seven arrivals of steamboats during the last season; three of which were owned by persons engaged directly in the trade. This, for a frontier-town, built indifferently of frame and log-houses, thrown confusedly together on the side of a hill, is certainly doing very well. People now hold their property by a somewhat precarious tenure, which prevents them from making improvements. When government gives them title-deeds to the lands they occupy, both Galena and the adjacent country will assume a very different appearance.

I took quite an extensive ride in the neighbourhood yesterday. There was to be a public meeting of the miners and other residents, held about twelve or fifteen miles from town, upon the subject of petitioning Congress in relation to the sale of lands; and having procured a tolerable saddle-horse, I started with Colonel H.,[1]— whose family-name is already known among the very first in our history, and whose acknowledged talents and influence in this quarter will ensure his making a figure in public life, when the new State of Ouisconsin shall take her place in the confederacy.[2]

Charles Fenno Hoffman, *A Winter in the West* (New York, 1835), 2:40–53.

[1] William S. Hamilton, a son of Alexander Hamilton, soldier, surveyor, and lead miner, was the leading citizen of Galena at this time. Ed.

[2] A period much less remote than many would think it. The country between Rock River and Ouisconsin combines perhaps more advantages for emigration than any described in the whole of this tour. That lying between Fox River and Lake Michigan is represented as being equally good; and, supposing the Indian difficulties to be now for ever terminated in this quarter, this region will fill with northern emigrants the moment it becomes known. A glance at the map will show how favourably it is situated for trade, commanding the markets alike of Buffalo and New-Orleans.

But a few years have elapsed since he left the city of New-York, a mere youth, to try his fortune in the West,—since then he has followed at different times the various occupations of a lawyer, a drover, a miner, and lastly a smelter, besides taking an active part in two Indian wars, where his early West Point education came favourably into play. Colonel H. is, perhaps, second only to General Dodge[3] in knowledge of frontier-affairs, and popularity with the backwoodsmen in this quarter. . . .

I had an opportunity of hearing Mr. H. address a public meeting on the evening of my arrival in Galena, and was much struck with the logical precision and force with which he spoke; and with his fluency, clear enunciation, and thorough command of himself and his audience. His features, when animated in speaking, bore a striking resemblance to those of his great and lamented father, as exhibited in the plaster casts which are familiar to every one.

"Colonel H.," said the gentleman who introduced me, "is at present disguised in a suit of broadcloth; to have him in character, sir, you should see him in his leather shirt and drawers, driving his ox-team with a load of lead into town." Mr. H. laughed in reply, and our horses being ready, we mounted, and soon escaping from the muddy town, found topics enough for conversation while galloping through the oak openings on the hills beyond. The gathering proved to be not so numerous, when we arrived at the place of meeting, as I had hoped; and, though in the grouping of wild-looking figures, with their variety of strange faces and striking costumes, Inman's bold pencil might have found some fine studies, yet I was wholly disappointed in any outlandish exhibitions of character. They were, in fact, as civil and well-behaved a set as would come to the call of a committee in any of the best-inhabited wards in your city. Their civility to me, indeed —being a stranger—could not be exceeded; I never approached the fire, but two or three rose to offer me a seat; and scarely one of the company called for any thing to drink, but, turning round,

3   Henry Dodge, Governor of Wisconsin Territory, 1836–41. Ed.

he would add, "Stranger, won't you join us?" As we spent several hours among them merely talking and moving round, without getting up any formal meeting, I had ample leisure to study the different appearances of the company, as some bent over a card-table, where the pieces of dirty pasteboard were rapidly compelling the small piles of money collected there to change hands; while others lay stretched in the sun upon the wood-pile before the open door, listlessly whittling a piece of stick with their long hunting-knives. One of the most striking figures was a tall young man of about seven or eight-and-twenty, whose delicate features, though somewhat imbrowned with toil and exposure, were only relieved from effeminacy by a dark beard trimmed around his oval face and depending from his chin, much in the style that Sir Walter Raleigh and Shakspeare are painted,—either of whose fine heads, his high, pale, and expressive forehead would not have misbecome. His figure, about six feet in height, was set off by a close-fitting hunting-shirt of black buckskin, lightly embroidered on the collar and arms with straw-coloured silk, which, from long use, had grown so dingy as scarcely to be detected upon the rusty leather it was meant to adorn. Others there were with the common cotton hunting-shirt of the west belted around them. But the majority were dressed in rough blanket-coats of every possible colour; while a vest of the most costly description, with pantaloons of Kentucky jean, would often complete their incongruous apparel.

I could form a tolerable estimate of the intelligence of this collection of people, from observing the language which my new friend used in talking to them upon the subject that brought them together; and, when speaking in earnest, it was invariably such as one educated gentleman would use to another when comparing views upon any new topic of interest. Upon my commenting upon this, after we had bid them farewell, and were riding off together, my companion observed, that there were not only many strong-minded men of ordinary education who had adopted the way of life which I saw prevailing around me, but that, had I time to remain longer in that section of country, he could point out to me a number of regularly educated persons, the graduates of more than one of our eastern colleges, who were seeking their fortunes in this region in the capacity of common miners. While he was yet speaking, we were accosted by a poorly clad and in every respect ordinary-looking person, to whom my companion replied with great politeness; and then resuming the subject after we had passed the forlorn shantee which the individual called his house,—"*Par example*," he exclaimed, "that man—and a shrewd, sensible fellow he is—was bred to the bar in your State; he looks poor enough now, it is true, but I hear that he has lately struck a lead, and a few years will probably find him in independent circumstances. We are now, you observe, among his diggings; and though at this moment he has hands to help him, I believe he began, like most of us, with his single pick. Clear that trench, now, and guide your horse through those pitfalls on the right, and I will take you to a point where you may see how we get up the ore."

Following my conductor along a mile or two farther of pretty rough road, we came at last to a spot where a huge mound of earth, with piles of lead-ore scattered here and there on the adjacent ground, showed that a mine was very successfully worked beneath; and giving our horses to an accommodating fellow that stood by, we threw off our overcoats and prepared to descend into it. The orifice on the top of the mound, over which a windlass was placed, was about three feet square, being lined with split logs crossing each other at the angles down to the original surface of the soil, below which point the adhesiveness of the earth seemed to be all that kept the sides of the pit together. It was so dark, however, at this part of the passage down, that other precautions may have escaped me. Taking the rope from above in my hands, and placing my foot in a wooden hook attached to the end of it, I swung myself from the top, and in a few moments descended some seventy or eighty feet below the surface. The narrow chamber was of course excessively dark to one just coming from the light of day; and landing upon the edge of a tub immediately beneath the aperture through which

I had descended, I lost my foothold and pitched head over heels in the water with which the bottom of the mine was flooded. "Any one hurt?" cried a voice behind me; and looking round as I sprang to my feet, I found myself in a long horizontal passage or narrow gallery, with a grim-looking miner approaching me with a lantern in one hand and a pickaxe in the other. The next moment the form of my companion darkened the opening above, and then, after landing by my side, he introduced me to the miner, who proceeded to show us about these subterranean premises. They consisted of three or four galleries, generally terminating in a common centre, though one or two short ones, just commenced, appeared to run off at right angles to the rest; and the lead-ore, which glitters like frosted silver in its native bed, appeared to lie in thick horizontal strata along their side. The masses were readily separated by the pickaxe from the neighbouring clay, and we remained long enough to see several tubsful hauled up by the conveyance which had admitted us into these dusky regions. The labour and exposure of these miners is very great; but the life, to those who have an interest in the work, is said to be so exciting, that the most indolent man, when he has once fairly burrowed under ground, and got a scent of what is called "*a lead*," will vie in devotion to his toil with the most industrious of those who labour in the light of heaven. His stimulus, indeed, resembles that of the gold-hunter; for the lead, when delivered at Galena, is as good as coin in his pocket; while, if he chances to strike a rich *lead* of mineral, he at once becomes independent,—as, if he does not choose to work it on his own account, there are houses in Galena which will purchase him out for a handsome sum, for the sake of speculation.

It was late in the evening, when, after taking this wide circuit, I once more regained my lodgings at Galena. I found the tavern entirely deserted, and upon inquiring the cause, and learning that there was "a play to be acted in town," I rode off at once to the door of the theatre. It proved to be in an unfinished building on the side of a hill, the basement of which, opening on a lower street, was a stable; and, there being no flooring to the apartment above it, one stepped over the naked beams above the horses' heads, if deviating from the plank which formed a passage-way to a rude staircase leading into the histrionic realms in the uppermost story. The company consisted of four grown persons and a child about ten years old, and the play was the melo-drama of The Woodman's Hut. A thing so easily turned into ridicule would be game not worth hunting down, and I mean, therefore, to disappoint any ill-natured expectations you may have of the picture I could give of Galena theatricals. That the rest of the audience were at least as liberal as myself, you may gather from the fact of their showering half-dollars like peas upon the stage, to express their delight of the little girl's dancing between the acts, which certainly did not surpass that of the Vestris, not to mention Taglioni. In the midst of the performance of the melo-drama, I happened to be standing in the apartment below, when I was not a little startled at the passage of a heavy missile by my ears, which, striking fire from a beam near to where I was standing, concluded its career by giving a hearty thump to a horse who was ruminating in his stall beneath. The mystery was presently cleared up by a little negro dropping at a bound from the entrance to the Thespian hall above, and exclaiming, "Did you see a gun come by here, sir? The count went to stand it in the corner, and it slipped between the planks of the floor." I directed the imp to the realms below, and starting at once for my lodgings, had no further opportunity to study these unrehearsed stage effects.

The want of a regular theatre many will think a merit in so small a town as Galena; but there is another defect in the place, and, indeed, in almost all western towns where you get so far beyond the mountains, that is not so easily got over, and that is, the want of female society. The number of males in proportion to females on the frontiers is at least five to one; and girls of fifteen (I might say twelve), or widows of fifty, are alike snapped up with avidity by the disconsolate bachelors. In the mines a few years since their eyes were so seldom cheered with the sight of the better part of creation, that I was told by an old borderer, "he had travelled twenty miles only to get a look at a petticoat, where it was rumoured that there was actually one in the neighbourhood." Even now they talk seriously in Galena of getting up an importation of ladies, for the especial amelioration and adornment of the place. How so delicate a matter is to be managed in our fastidious age I am unable to divine, unless, indeed, they should invite the blooming ones hither, under the ostensible purpose of getting up *a fair*, and then persuade them to remain and cheer these monastic abodes. I have been more than once feelingly appealed to to make the languishing condition of these hermits of the prairies known in more favoured parts of the country; while, not wishing to betray the slenderness of my influence with the fair parties they would conciliate I have avoided making rash promises of using my feeble offices in their favour. The only method of serving their cause I have yet hit upon is, to have inserted in the newspapers after my arrival home, under the head of "Singular fact," "Remarkable phenomenon," "Unequalled spirit," or "Sudden disappearance," some such paragraph as this:—"It is attested by credible witnesses, among whom are some of the oldest and most respectable inhabitants of Galena, that single ladies, visiting their friends in that place, never see 'a second winter.'"

1835

Chandler R. Gilman

By Stage and Packet, with Views of Ottawa and Alton

In 1835 Chandler R. Gilman, a New York physician with literary aspirations, toured the Great Lakes. After stopping at Chicago he traveled by stage to Ottawa and Peoria, and then to Alton by an Illinois River packet. The letters he wrote on the trip were collected and published in book form in 1836, a year after his first book, *Legends of a Log Cabin*, had appeared.

This morning at five, we took our seats in the post coach at Chicago, and left for Ottawa. It was quite dark, and we could only judge of the face of the country by the motion of the carriage. We passed over a continued plain, intersected every now and then with a soft spot of ground, where the wheels sank deeply into the soil. At the dawn of day we found ourselves on a wide prairie, with scarce a tree in sight. The appearance of the prairies disappointed me very much; the tall brown grass, coarse and scattered, gave to the whole a ragged appearance; the ground was low and marshy, and at short intervals we passed through what they here call slews. I thought, at first, that these slews were rivulets, whose streams were dried up by the long drought; but I believe their true character is long narrow ponds, or rather mud holes. There is little or no water visible; here and there a small dark pool dots the surface of the soft black mud. Clumps of grass, the size of my hat, are also sprinkled around. 'Twas by the help of these clumps that we crossed these mud holes, as the carriage sank so deep we were all obliged to get out to enable the horses to drag it through. . . .

At half-past eight we stopped at a small log hut to breakfast. The public part of the establishment (for it was a sort of inn) consisted of two little rooms; in one was a table, which, when we entered, the combined exertions of a black wench, a tall strapping country girl, and the landlady (the very ugliest woman I ever saw by the by) were covering with materials for a substantial breakfast. In one corner of the other room was a straw bed, on which a poor palid wretch was extended; his shrunk features, wasted form, and the general appearance of debility, plainly indicating a victim to the fever of the country. Opposite the sick man's bed, another corner of the room was occupied by a bar, at which several persons were taking in *poison*—in other climates the seeds of disease, in this of death—in the shape of

Chandler R. Gilman, *Life on the Lakes* (New York, 1836), 2:245–61 with elisions, 267, 270–74.

antifogmatics, fever killers, &c. The other end of the room was crowded with the persons and the luggage of an emigrant family; a mother sat in the corner tending her sick child, a boy of ten, whom the fever was burning up; around her huddled several other children; while a bigger boy, stretched on some blankets, pale and wasted away, was striving to amuse himself as well as he could, and enjoy, if that were possible, his *well day*.

From the contemplation of these miserable emigrants we were summoned to our breakfast. The supplies were abundant in quantity, if not very choice in quality; two luxuries, you will be surprised to hear, we could not obtain—good butter and milk; the butter was of the very worst quality, milk there was none. We had excellent coffee, tolerable pork steaks, good bread, both corn and wheat; the gem of the feast, however, was a large stew, which sent up fragrant incense from the centre of the table. Almost every person (our stage-driver and two wagoners were of the party) was helped to that stew. Various were the opinions given as to its component parts. One held up a scraggy bone, and proclaimed it venison; another displayed what he deemed a bit of the breast, and swore 'twas turkey; a third decided, from its exquisite flavour, that it must be the far-famed prairie hen; finally, however, the Major decided the question by producing a long leg, which could belong to no animal but a rabbit or a squirrel, (a cat, of course, we would not allow ourselves to think of). It was stewed rabbit. This favourite dish having been entirely emptied, and a mark made on the pork steaks and beef, appetite cried, "Hold, enough!" we arose from the table, and took our places in the stage. . . .

Our ride from the Desplaines river, near which we breakfasted, to Ottawa, was rather uninteresting. The prairie became drier after we crossed the river, and the proportion of woodland rather greater, though still, I think, less than will be required by the future settlers. We passed during the day eight or ten farms. The wheat was already housed, of course we could not judge of the crop; but the Indian corn was standing, and nearly every hill blasted by the frost. The season opened this year very late, and an early frost in September cut off all the corn crop. Some of the farmers had small droves of cattle, generally of the best breeds and in capital order. A few hogs were ranging through the prairie grass; they were miserable animals; long shanks, huge heads, narrow flanks; the horses also were poor, but the oxen, Col. D——, who is quite an amateur agriculturalist, could never sate his eye in gazing on them or stint his tongue in their praise.

About nine this evening we arrived at Ottawa, having previously crossed the Fox River. At the tavern we saw a large fire of bitumenous coal; it is found in great abundance in this vicinity, and is, I should think, from a casual examination, of decidedly better quality than that of Pittsburgh; in fact nearly equal to Liverpool. It will be of incalculable advantage to the country, the thinness of the forests will very speedily lead to a scarcity of wood for building purposes; it is therefore all important that as little as possible should be used as fuel. The town of Ottawa was laid off by the canal commissioners in 1830, on both sides of the Illinois at its junction with the Fox River. Here we had hoped to find a steamer.—There was none, however. The shoals and rapids in the Illinois river a few miles (eight or ten) below this place, impede the navigation, except in very high water, and even then the larger steamers do not like to venture up lest a sudden fall should shut them in. We spent a pleasant evening in the bar room, chatting with some travellers and a few of the town folks. . . .

Alton, Ill. Sunday, Oct. 5.

All day yesterday on the Illinois river, having left Peoria about nine o'clock at night. On going on board the steam boat I was surprised to find, that forward she looked exactly like a mud-scow; scarcely any deck, and an open hold exposed to the weather; aft, there was a comfortable cabin with good berths. The captain gave his boat the soubriquet of Cat Fish, from the resemblance her bow bears to the mouth of that fish. She draws very little water, and makes about six miles the hour down stream. The Illinois is a calm placid river, with little or no current, and full of sand bars. The banks are well wooded, though very low; the spring freshets overflow them far and wide. We saw, during the day, two or three flocks of paroquets; they present a most beautiful appearance when on the wing, their green plumage glittering in the sun beams. This morning, at 7, the captain called us on deck that we might take our first view of Alton. We had entered the Mississippi during the night, and were now about twenty miles below the mouth of the Illinois. I will not attempt a description of the Father of rivers, but rather hurry forward to Alton. You will readily imagine that I looked with great eagerness for the first glance of a place of which I had heard much, and where I hoped to find friends. The situation at first disappointed me, the land is exceedingly rough; a ledge of rocks lies to the North, and below, steep, broken hills, rise immediately from the river bank: a creek makes in just in the middle of the town, giving yet more irregularity to the surface. The landing is very good, the boat runs close alongside a rock, which forms a natural wharf; so that a short plank is only wanted to put any thing ashore. To this landing our boat approached. There were two large steamers fast, one from New-Orleans, the other from up the Missouri; a third was just casting off, she was bound to Galena. What an idea does the destination of these three boats and our own give of the extent of navigation! Galena, Peoria, the upper Missouri, St. Louis, and New-Orleans; not to name Pittsburg, Cincinnati, and Louisville, with which places the intercourse is free and constant. We landed at the wharf of which I have spoken. There are two large stone ware-houses just opposite, and three or four are building below. Here we deposited our luggage, and went in search of our friends. On our way to the tavern we passed through the main street near half a mile; it is principally occupied by stores, some large and of stone, others smaller, and by their slight structure evidently used only as temporary make-shifts. . . .

Alton, Oct. 9

In my last I mentioned our arrival at Alton on Sunday morning. After a pleasant hour spent with our friends, we attended church in the new Presbyterian Meeting-house, built and presented to that denomination by Captain G———.[1] It is a small, neat, stone building. Standing on high ground, at a short distance and in full view of the river, it forms a very pleasing feature in the landscape, and gives it a character which cannot fail to gladden the eye of the Christian beholder. . . .

The whole of Monday was spent by us in rambling round the town. The number of buildings in progress is very great, and many are large and substantial. We went into one store, which is of stone, three stories high, thirty feet front, and one hundred deep; alongside this the foundations of several others of the same size are laid. There is a great appearance of business here; the streets thronged with wagons from the country, bringing produce and taking away goods. I met with several individuals from up the country, who were laying in their fall stock of goods; one of these was from far up the Missouri.

We called on Mr. G———[2] at the Bank, a neat stone building. It is a branch of the newly incorporated Bank of Illinois, and has just gone into operation; its friends are very sanguine of its success. Just north of the town is the State Penitentiary, a large stone building surrounded by a substantial wall; all made, as I understand, by the few convicts there confined.[3]

The main street, which runs parallel with the river, is intersected by several cross streets; these are yet very irregular from the broken surface of the ground, but men and carts are now busily employed levelling and grading them. All has an appearance of stability, as though the men of to-day expected to be here to-morrow, which contrasts favourably with some other places. Gen. Mitchell has just left Alton, having completed the survey of a route for a rail road from this place to Springfield.

It proved on examination more favourable than had been expected, and the Company will soon open the books for subscription. This will be a very important link in the chain of inter-

[1] Benjamin Godfrey, banker and philanthropist. Ed.
[2] Winthrop S. Gilman, Godfrey's partner. Ed.
[3] This, the first state penitentiary, opened in 1833, and was used until 1857. Ed.

communication between the Mississippi and the Atlantic border; from Springfield a road is already surveyed to the Wabash, and thence to Lake Erie; a charter has also been granted for a rail road from Alton to the Wabash, at the termination of the Wabash canal; and a third from Alton to Shawnee town. Great efforts are being made to have the National road cross the river here on its way to Jefferson City. That a connexion will be soon formed by means of one of these rail roads with the Western termination of that noblest of our works of internal improvement, the New-York and Erie rail road, cannot be doubted. This chain of works, once completed, what miracles in the way of travelling may we not expect. On a continuous line of rail road from the Hudson to the Mississippi, the trip from New-York to Alton will be but a pleasure jaunt of a few days; and the rich products of the Mississippi valley be as easily, as rapidly, and almost as cheaply conveyed to New-York as now to New-Orleans.[4]

On Tuesday we rode out to Upper Alton, three miles from the river, and thence through the wide prairie which lies back of it. There is a college at Upper Alton, under the charge, I believe, of the Baptist church; it is in a very flourishing condition. A large building is being constructed for a female seminary in the neighbourhood.[5] The Prairie land is dry, with a deep rich soil, the very sight of which would gladden the heart of an agriculturist. We passed several large fields of corn, that looked rich and fully ripe. The Major had planned a jaunt to Carlinville, but inexorable necessity compelled us to hurry homeward. After two more happy days at Alton, we embarked this morning on board the Tiskilwa, a steam boat which plies regularly between that place and St. Louis; and, bidding farewell to our dear friends, are again under way.

---

[4]   The projects mentioned here were parts of the ill-fated internal improvements system of Illinois. See Part IV, below. Ed.

[5]   The college at Upper Alton was Shurtleff College, founded at Rock Spring in 1827 and moved to Upper Alton in 1831. It is no longer in existence. The female seminary was Monticello College, which opened in 1838. Ed.

1835

Alfred Brunson

A Prairie Fire and a
Claim Association

Alfred Brunson, a Methodist circuit rider, traveled on horseback
from Meadville, Pennsylvania, to Prairie du Chien, Wisconsin, in
1835. On his return trip he passed through Galena and Peoria
on his way to Springfield, where he attended the Illinois confer-
ence of his church in October. In his journal he noted features
of the northern Illinois scene which many travelers failed to
record.

Oct. 15 [1835]. . . . We went from this to Beauro or Robinsons River, & through Princeton, & to *Dad Joe Smiths* that night 35 miles further, making 55 that day. The last 12 miles we travelled after sundown, & by fire light over Prairie, it being on fire. This was the grandest scene I ever saw, the wind blew a gale all day, the grass was dry, & the fire being in the Prairie, at a distance, where we entered it some men were kindling fire to burn it *away* from their fences & then let it run—no odds who it burnt up. As the dark came on, the fire shone more brilliant. A cloud of smoke arose on which the fire below shone, & the reflection could be seen for miles—in some instances 40. We passed 3 different fires in this 12 miles, having to turn out & get round them when they reached the road. The wind blew acrosst our road, & the *long* ways of the fire was with the wind, in which direction it went nearly as fast as the wind. But when a streak was run, in the direction of the wind, then the fire worked side ways. By this means we had in view at one time from one to 5 miles of fire in a streak, burning from 2 to 6 feet high. In *high* grass it sometimes burns 30 feet high, if driven by fierce winds. By the light of this fire we could read fine print for $\frac{1}{2}$ a mile or more. And the light reflected from the cloud of smoke, enlightened our road for miles after the blaze of the fire was out of sight.

Till I saw this, I could never so well understand one part of the scripture. The cloud which overspread the camp of Israel & kept off the rays of the sun by day, was *a pillar of fire by night*. It was literally so with the smoke which rose from these fires. By day the cloud was often so dense & so great, as to hide the sun from the view of the traveller, but by night this same cloud would reflect the light which shone on it from below, so as to enlightin the country for miles around it. The reason why the cloud over the camp of Israel gave light, was, because the glory of God, which rested in the tabernacle, shone upon it.

Alfred Brunson, "A Methodist Circuit Rider's Horseback Tour from Pennsylvania to Wisconsin, 1835," *Wisconsin Historical Collections*, **10** (1900): 275–78.

Before we reached our lodgings, Bro. Weigleys[1] horse gave out & attempted to lie down, apparently with the cholic, tho' probably from fatiague. We had to walk him about 4 miles,—Weigley on foot by his side. When we reached the place the people were in bed. She got up, however, & gave us some supper.

Oct. 16. We were obliged to take it more moderate on account of the sick horse. We passed more burning Prairies, & large quantities of lost or primitive Rock scatered over the Prairies. And where they were burnt they could be more easily discerned.

We left the most beaton road, to take a new one, said to be much nearer than the old one. We crossed Rock River at Bushes ferry, 5 miles below Dixon's, but we paid dear for our saving. It was with difficulty we got any thing to eat our selves, but could get nothing but Prairie hay & pumpkins for our horses. It began to rain on us, & at length blew a gale. Dark came on before we reached a house. At lingth we reached a Hixite quakers, where we fared very well our selves, but our horses had no stable or shed to break off the storm & nothing but Prairie hay to eat.

Oct 17th. We started with the break of day, & travelled 6 miles before we could get any grain for our horses, or breakfast for our selves. We passed through one of the most beautiful groves, this morning, we had seen in all the Prairie country. It was 6 miles thro' it, & composed of young thrifty timber, on the waters of Elkhorn creek.

Here we learned a little of the way of settling this new country. The lands had been surveyed into townships, but not into sections, & of course not yet in Market. About 40 families had settled themselves about this grove. They had, in the absence of all other law, met & made a law for themselves. They have surveyed the township & assertained that section 16, the school section, was within the grove, & they staked it off & appointed commissioners to take care of it, preserve the timber &c. so as to make it valuable as possible when the township should be regularly

---

[1]   Wellington Weigley, then a young Methodist minister, later a member of the Galena bar. Ed.

settled according to law. They had also meted & bounded every man *wood land*, allowing each family 40 acres of timber, & as much Prairie as he pleased to take up. Timber being the great disideratum of the country, they would not allow any one man to monopolise. Forty acres was thought to be sufficient timber land, to make & sustain the fence, buildings & fires of a farm.

As this land was not in market at the time, & the pre-emtion law having run out, we asked what security they had, that speculators would not buy their lands & improvements, or make them pay what their own improvements were worth? The reply was, that there was an understanding in the country, equivolent to a law of the land, that the settlers should sustain each other against the speculator, & no settler should bid on anothers land.

If a speculator should bid on a settlers farm, he was knocked down & dragged out of the office, & if the striker was prosecuted & fined, the settlers paid the expense by common consent among themselves. But before a fine could be assessed, the case must come before a jury, which of course must be selected from among the settlers. And it was understood that no jury would find a verdict of *guilty* against a settler, in such a case, because it was considered a case of *self defence*. And if these means could not protect the settler, the last resort would be to "burn powder in their faces." These things being under stood no speculator dare bid on a settlers land, & as no settler would bid on his neighbor, each man gets his land at congress price, $1.25 pr. acre.

We this day reached *Apple River*, at Bro. Jewels. Here was a fort in the late Indian War, (1832) made & defended by the inhabitants. About 200 Indians under Black Hawk attacked this fort, defended by about 40 men & boys, besides a few women. A Mrs. Armstrong[2] assumed the command. She had some women making catridges, others loading guns for the men to fire, while she drove round the fort like a fury, cursing & swearing like a pirate. She had all the children drove into one room & one

---

2   Elizabeth Armstrong. The town of Elizabeth, Jo Daviess County, is named for her. Ed.

woman, with a club in hand, appointed to guard them, with strict orders [to] keep them from crying, lest the Indians should think they were frightened, & should thereby be encouraged.

The Indians heard her hallooing at the men, & knowing her voice, said afterwards that she was *very mad*. The Indians were defeated with considerable loss, while but one man was killed & one wounded in the fort. And both these men were shot when gratifying their curiosity by looking over the pickets. The bravery of this woman is allowed, by some, to have saved the fort. But it is a great drawback upon her credit, being so profane.

1835

Richard H. Beach

Farmers and Craftsmen
in Central Illinois

Some of the most interesting and illuminating accounts of Illinois were written without thought of publication. Such is the following letter of Richard H. Beach, written in 1836 but describing conditions in Illinois as he saw them a year earlier. Beach, born in New York City in 1808, married Eliza Baldwin in 1832. The young couple came west to Morgan County, where Beach taught school. The next year they moved to Springfield, where they lived for the remainder of their lives. Beach, with his partner E. R. Wiley, founded a clothing store, which continued in business for many years.

Springfield, Illinois, April 4th, 1836.

Dear Sister:

The following pages were written something like twelve months since, with a view of sending them on by Mr. Baldwin for your perusal, as well as the rest of my friends, but as Mr. B. did not take Illinois on his return, you and the rest of our family were disappointed in not receiving the long expected "Manuscript" and as it was too voluminous to be sent by mail it has lain unfinished until now. An opportunity offers of sending it by private conveyance, and I willingly embrace it. It is well perhaps that you did not receive it sooner, as my impressions were written down at the moment and I find on looking over my lines that in some instances many of my views were incorrect. Even now I do not wish to convey the idea that the view I have taken of things is such that a person wishing to make the western world his home may implicitly rely on them. What is here written is to be read this way, "to the best of his knowledge."

The information I can give may be of use to yourself and others who are thinking of the "Far West" as a home. Read and judge, then form your own conclusions. The subject has three points which are particularly prominent and for the sake of order I shall notice under these points, whatever I deem worthy connected with them, viz: Agriculture, Commerce and Manufactures. Everything comes under these three, although in estimating the relative value of each, the order in which they stand would have to be altered. I mean their value as to making money fast or slow. I would place the order thus, First Commerce, Second Manufactures, and Third Agriculture. I am aware that the farmer is the bone and sinew of my country, but the merchant possesses the most power, because he turns the most money, altho perhaps in the end he does not possess as much as the farmer. But of this I shall say nothing further, my business is with facts.

Richard H. Beach, "A Letter from Illinois Written in 1836," *Journal of the Illinois State Historical Society*, 3, no. 3: pp. 91–98.

The agriculture is of a different character to that of the east; the farmer raises his corn with half the labour we used to do; his pork costs him but little during the summer and his cattle and horses also, with the exception of salting them, say once a week. Pasture during the summer costs nothing, the cattle, hogs and horses range at large undisturbed on the Prairies. Fields for pasture alone are not common, unless it be indeed for oxen or working cattle, that they may be found at any time. This is the state of the case at present; when the country is all settled and the land generally enclosed, every farmer will have to provide his own pasture. The cows, after calving in the spring are not separated from their calves, as with us, and fed by hand. This would prevent their coming up regularly to be milked. The calf is shut up during the day, and at night when its mother comes home it is allowed to have a taste and but a taste, for after a few draws or two on the teats of its mother it is driven off very unceremoniously and shut up in the pen for the night, to eat straw, hay or cornstalks for the balance of his supper.

The principal crop is corn, and to the Illinois farmer this is everything. It feeds and clothes him and pays his store account sometimes without any money, or but little, passing through his hands, as the merchant receives his corn and pork and produce in general, in exchange for goods. The farmers' business commences generally from the middle of March or first of April. I judge not sooner, often. Oats are raised in great abundance; that is when they come to perfection. They are not a sure crop. It is often the case that a few days before they are ready to cut, a storm of rain or wind lays them level with the earth, and not saved at all. I have seen whole fields thus prostrated and going to waste. They are not altogether lost however, if the succeeding winter is open and no use made of the land, hogs, horses and cattle make good use of the privilege they have of seeking for the grain and straw. My oat field of about four acres gave my cattle, from twenty-five to thirty head, employment for a considerable length of time. My hogs were by far the most diligent. The cause of this failure of oats is the richness of the soil. They grow tall and have not sufficient strength to withstand the wind. The general price of oats is 25 cts. There have been great wheat crops in this country, but not since I came into it. Last year the wheat through the country generally was lost. It froze out, as there was but one fall of snow during the winter of '35, and that did not lay but two or three days. This season it is the same as far as my knowledge extends. The winter has been very open. Some farmers begin to turn their attention strongly to winter wheat. Good crops have been raised, but last year, in many instances the ground on which it stood was ploughed up and planted in corn. Flour sold one year ago, or eighteen months, for $3.00 per barrel, now it is $8.00 and $9.00. As I have said, corn is the principal dependence of the farmer. When he cannot buy flour at a reasonable price, he can use "corn dodgers" or hoe cake, in other words, corn bread. Corn in a good season sells for 20 to 25 cents. The usual plan of the farmer is to feed his corn to fatten his hogs, which is better than selling it for 25 cents. Pork sold last season at $3.00 per hundred. It was from two and a half to three the year before. Beef is not very abundant, from some cause or other; it usually sells for 2½ to 3 cents a pound, tallow eight to ten and twelve cents and quite scarce at that. Lard is often made a substitute for tallow and burnt in an open lamp, which answers every purpose, although not so handy. It sells from 4 to 6 cents a pound. The corn in this country is never hoed. The plough is used altogether, and one man will plough and tend from 25 to 30 acres, which when gathered will yield from 40 to 60, or 80 bushels an acre. It has come up to 100 by good management. About the first of June or thereabouts, they begin to "lay it by" as the term is. From that time on to the first of October and so on till January, nothing is done to it. It is then gathered, either by shucking, husking or cutting it up for winter fodder. Shucking is by far the most common way. The corn is pulled off with all the shucks on and carried to the crib, generally a square pen made of rails, and thrown in, to be fed out when wanted, to the hogs, cattle, etc. etc. When husked on the stalk there is more care taken of the corn, but the husks and stalks are left to bleach in the storm and sun until the ground will bear the cattle, when they are turned in and no care taken of them for six weeks or two months. Wheat is often sown in the corn between the rows, which in my opinion is a very slovenly way, but it is very common. Perhaps one cause of the failure of the wheat crop is this careless way of putting it in. I leave this for the more experienced to determine. It has struck me as very odd that farmers here do not cut any hay, or but little, some of them, I mean. Their dependence is upon corn stalks, and yet the cattle appear to do well. Manure is no object. It is not saved at all, and I have heard of men who, when their stable became filled, instead of cleaning it remove it to another place. Chickens are raised in great abundance and sell for a dollar a dozen; eggs from $6\frac{1}{4}$ cents up to an Illinois shilling 16 $\frac{2}{3}$ cts. Butter is 8, 10 and 16 cents, according to its abundance. Through the summer it will command 8 cents and in the winter double this sum.

This land is destined to become the greatest grazing country in the world. Its advantages for that branch of business are very great indeed, and at the present time many are turning their attention to it entirely, to the exclusion of everything else.

It will be perceived from the tenor of my remarks that all the necessaries of life are abundant and cheap. The only articles to be purchased are tea, coffee, sugar, clothing, and even this last may be made in the family and often is. The principal wealth of the farmer at present lies in the rise in value of his land, but this will not be the case always. Past experience has shown that as the country becomes settled, produce rises in value, markets are made where none was found before. By means of railroads and canals the surplus will be transported to less favored portions of our land and find a ready market. Some years ago pork could be bought in abundance at $1.25 per hundred, butter at a "Picaoon" ($6\frac{1}{4}$) a pound and a half bushel of eggs for 25 cents, other things in like proportion. It was because there was no market. I have heard a story since I came here of one man who took a half bushel to Springfield and not being able to get even

25 cents a ½ bushel, took them out into the Prairie and broke them all. This may be true or not, I can not vouch for it. Upon the whole I think this is the greatest farming country in the world. Farms are made the quickest here, of any place that I ever read or heard tell of. No trees to cut down or stones to pick off. The only thing to be done in making a farm is to fence, plough and plant, and the first year's crop will go a great way towards paying the price of the land and fencing.

As yet there is but little manufacturing done in the county, the supplies necessary are brought from the east. But still the mechanic has a fair field open for his enterprise. All kinds of trade do well, such as are adapted to a new country. Especially carpenters, blacksmiths, shoemakers, tanners, cabinet-makers, turners, wheel-wrights, masons, tinners, etc. The finer kinds of trades are not much carried on at present, but still there is room for them and enterprising young men in particular, whether mechanics or not. The trades I have mentioned are much wanted. Buildings can not be put up for want of workmen. Carpenters command good wages; many are in the business who are but quacks in the art. What wages are I can not say, but from the scarcity of hands I suppose they are high.

A french bedstead sells for from $8. to $10.; a cherry table, turned legs with halves, for $7. Cabinet work is high as well as mechanical work in general, owing to the scarcity of hands and high price of lumber, many who would build are obliged to defer it till a more favorable opportunity. The price for brick, every expense, included, in the walls, is $10. per thousand. Whether this is high or low I am not sufficient judge to say. Brick alone sells for $4. and $5. per thousand at the kiln. There is a great scarcity of houses in this place, so that persons who wish to be any way comfortable are obliged to build for themselves. Still after a residence of two years I think this country just the place for a poor family, and for a poor young man of any enterprise at all, the best place I know of. A shoemaker might, I should think, do well here in the mending and making line. I mean to carry on his business pretty extensively, I know

RICHARD H. BEACH

of no reason why the making of boots and shoes could not be carried on to great advantage. Let an enterprising man come here from shoe-making New Jersey or Connecticut and establish himself as a manufacturer not of customers work entirely, but with the idea of carrying on his business as he has been used to, and I have no doubt he will do better than he could at home. It is true he will have to pay a higher price for his leather and materials, but he also will get a higher price for his manufactures. If he should import his leather direct from the East the only additional expense in the price of a pair of shoes to him would be the cost of transportation; then add to this the cost of house rent, fuel and living, and the result would be a larger profit on his labour and capital than he can get at the East. A word or two here about the expense of living. In Springfield perhaps this is nearly the same with New York. This depends in some measure according as you are situated. House rent is nearly the same. Firewood about one-half; groceries higher, clothing higher. Flour at present $9. and $10. per barrel, but this is uncommon. Beef and pork very cheap. My family of six persons has lived on beef twice a day for a week at a cost of *seventy-five cents*! Beat this in New York if you can. But the cheapest way of living is to have a small garden spot and raise your own vegetables, potatoes, cabbage, etc., and rear and fat your own hogs.

I think take all things into consideration, living is much cheaper here than with you and I wonder that many who are now struggling in New York with high living do not seek this western world and better their condition, as assuredly they would. I often think of our Cousin Daniel Hulse. I think he might do well here, and a hundred others I might mention.

I am glad to hear Charley is getting to be such a smart boy. Tell him to go on and get a good education; it is a fortune in itself. Remember me to Mr. Beahs folks. I should have written to them but have not time.

Your affectionate
Brother
Rich'd H. Beach.

1836

Harriet Martineau

The Prairies and Joliet

Harriet Martineau, daughter of an English textile manufacturer, was thirty-two years old when she came to the United States in 1834. Although she had started life as a seamstress, she had published her first article at the age of nineteen, and continued with articles and books on economic and social problems. In Boston she was lionized, but her public advocacy of Abolition caused her to be ostracized in some circles. Undaunted, she remained in the country for two years, visiting the Northwest and Chicago in 1836.

Miss Martineau's impressions of Chicago are well known. Less familiar is her description of the prairies, which she traversed on a trip to Joliet.

From Chicago, we made an excursion into the prairies. Our young lawyer-friend threw behind him the five hundred dollars per day which he was making, and went with us.[1] I thought him wise; for there is that to be had in the wilderness which money cannot buy. We drove out of the town at ten o'clock in the morning, too late by two hours; but it was impossible to overcome the introductions to strangers, and the bustle of our preparations, any sooner. Our party consisted of seven, besides the driver. Our vehicle was a wagon with four horses.

We had first to cross the prairie, nine miles wide, on the lake edge of which Chicago stands. This prairie is not usually wet so early in the year; but at this time the water stood almost up to the nave of the wheels: and we crossed it at a walking pace. I saw here, for the first time in the United States, the American primrose. It grew in profusion over the whole prairie, as far as I could see; not so large and fine as in English greenhouses, but graceful and pretty. I now found the truth of what I had read about the difficulty of distinguishing distances on a prairie. The feeling is quite bewildering. A man walking near looks like a Goliath a mile off. I mistook a covered wagon without horses, at a distance of fifty yards, for a white house near the horizon: and so on. We were not sorry to reach the belt of trees, which bounded the swamp we had passed. At a house here, where we stopped to water the horses, and eat dough nuts, we saw a crowd of emigrants; which showed that we had not yet reached the bounds of civilisation. A little further on we came to the river Aux Plaines, spelled on a sign board "Oplain."[2] The ferry here is a monopoly, and the public suffers accordingly. There is only one small flat boat for the service of the concourse of people now pouring into the prairies. Though we happened to arrive nearly first of the crowd of today, we were detained on the bank above an hour; and then our horses went over at two crossings, and

Harriet Martineau, *Society in America* (London, 1837), 1:355–64.
[1]   Joseph N. Balestier, author of the first history of Chicago. In 1841 he returned east to practice law in New York City. Ed.
[2]   Now called the Des Plaines. Ed.

the wagon and ourselves at the third. It was a pretty scene, if we had not been in a hurry; the country wagons and teams in the wood by the side of the quiet clear river; and the oxen swimming over, yoked, with only their patient faces visible above the surface. After crossing, we proceeded briskly till we reached a single house, where, or nowhere, we were to dine. The kind hostess bestirred herself to provide us a good dinner of tea, bread, ham, potatoes, and strawberries, of which a whole pailful, ripe and sweet, had been gathered by the children in the grass round the house, within one hour. While dinner was preparing, we amused ourselves with looking over an excellent small collection of books, belonging to Miss Cynthia, the daughter of the hostess.

I never saw insulation, (not desolation,) to compare with the situation of a settler on a wide prairie. A single house in the middle of Salisbury Plain would be desolate. A single house on a prairie has clumps of trees near it, rich fields about it; and flowers, strawberries, and running water at hand. But when I saw a settler's child tripping out of home-bounds, I had a feeling that it would never get back again. It looked like putting out into Lake Michigan in a canoe. The soil round the dwellings is very rich. It makes no dust, it is so entirely vegetable. It requires merely to be once turned over to produce largely; and, at present, it appears to be inexhaustible. As we proceeded, the scenery became more and more like what all travellers compare it to,— a boundless English park. The grass was wilder, the occasional footpath not so trim, and the single trees less majestic; but no park ever displayed anything equal to the grouping of the trees within the windings of the blue, brimming river Aux Plaines.

We had met with so many delays that we felt doubts about reaching the place where we had intended to spend the night. At sunset, we found ourselves still nine miles from Joliet;[3] but we were told that the road was good, except a small "slew" or two; and there was half a moon shining behind a thin veil of clouds;

[3]   When platted in 1834 the town was named Juliet. In 1845 the state legislature changed the name to Joliet. Ed.

so we pushed on. We seemed latterly to be travelling on a terrace overlooking a wide champaign, where a dark, waving line might indicate the winding of the river, between its clumpy banks. Our driver descended, and went forward, two or three times, to make sure of our road; and at length, we rattled down a steep descent, and found ourselves among houses. This was not our resting-place, however. The Joliet hotel lay on the other side of the river. We were directed to a foot-bridge by which we were to pass; and a ford below for the wagon. We strained our eyes in vain for the foot-bridge; and our gentlemen peeped and pryed about for some time. All was still but the rippling river, and everybody asleep in the houses that were scattered about. We ladies were presently summoned to put on our water-proof shoes, and alight. A man showed himself who had risen from his bed to help us in our need. The foot-bridge consisted, for some way, of two planks, with a hand-rail on one side: but, when we were about a third of the way over, one half of the planks, and the hand-rail, had dis-appeared. We actually had to cross the rushing, deep river on a line of single planks, by dim moonlight, at past eleven o'clock at night. The great anxiety was about Charley; but between his father and the guide, he managed very well. This guide would accept nothing but thanks. He "did not calculate to take any pay." Then we waited some time for the wagon to come up from the ford. I suspected it had passed the spot where we stood, and had proceeded to the village, where we saw a twinkling light, now disappearing, and now re-appearing. It was so, and the driver came back to look for us, and tell us that the light we saw was a signal from the hotel-keeper, whom we found, standing on his door-step, and sheltering his candle with his hand. We sat down and drank milk in the bar, while he went to consult with his wife what was to be done with us, as every bed in the house was occupied. We, meanwhile, agreed that the time was now come for us to enjoy an adventure which we had often anticipated; sleeping in a barn. We had all declared ourselves anxious to sleep in a barn, if we could meet with one that was air-tight, and well-supplied with hay. Such a barn was actually on these premises.

We were prevented, however, from all practising the freak by the prompt hospitality of our hostess. Before we knew what she was about, she had risen and dressed herself, put clean sheets on her own bed, and made up two others on the floor of the same room; so that the ladies and Charley were luxuriously accommodated. Two sleepy personages crawled down stairs to offer their beds to our gentlemen. Mr. L.[4] and our Chicago friend, however, persisted in sleeping in the barn. Next morning, we all gave a very gratifying report of our lodgings. When we made our acknowledgments to our hostess, she said she thought that people who could go to bed quietly every night ought to be ready to give up to tired travellers. Whenever she travels, I hope she will be treated as she treated us. She let us have breakfast as early as half-past five, the next morning, and gave Charley a bun at parting, lest he should be too hungry before we could dine.

The great object of our expedition, Mount Joliet, was two miles distant from this place. We had to visit it, and perform the journey back to Chicago, forty miles, before night. The mount is only sixty feet high; yet it commands a view which I shall not attempt to describe, either in its vastness, or its soft beauty. The very spirit of tranquillity resides in this paradisy scene. The next painter who would worthily illustrate Milton's Morning Hymn, should come and paint what he sees from Mount Joliet, on a dewy summer's morning, when a few light clouds are gently sailing in the sky, and their shadows traversing the prairie. I thought I had never seen green levels till now; and only among mountains had I before known the beauty of wandering showers. Mount Joliet has the appearance of being an artificial mound, its sides are so uniformly steep, and its form so regular. Its declivity was bristling with flowers; among which were conspicuous the scarlet lily, the white convolvulus, and a tall, red flower of the scabia form. We disturbed a night-hawk, sitting on her eggs, on the ground. She wheeled round and round over our heads, and, I hope, returned to her eggs before they were cold.

4   Ellis Gray Loring, Boston lawyer and abolitionist. Ed.

Not far from the mount was a log-house, where the rest of the party went in to dry their feet, after having stood long in the wet grass. I remained outside, watching the light showers, shifting in the partial sunlight from clump to level, and from reach to reach of the brimming and winding river. The nine miles of prairie, which we had traversed in dim moonlight last night, were now exquisitely beautiful, as the sun shone fitfully upon them.

We saw a prairie wolf, very like a yellow dog, trotting across our path, this afternoon. Our hostess of the preceding day, expecting us, had an excellent dinner ready for us. We were detained a shorter time at the ferry, and reached the belt of trees at the edge of Nine-mile Prairie, before sunset. Here, in common prudence, we ought to have stopped till the next day, even if no other accommodation could be afforded us than a roof over our heads. We deserved an ague for crossing the swamp after dark, in an open wagon, at a foot pace. Nobody was aware of this in time, and we set forward; the feet of our wearied horses plashing in water at every step of the nine miles. There was no road; and we had to trust to the instinct of driver and horses to keep us in the right direction. I rather think the driver attempted to amuse himself by exciting our fears. He hinted more than once at the difficulty of finding the way; at the improbability that we should reach Chicago before midnight; and at the danger of our wandering about the marsh all night, and finding ourselves at the opposite edge of the prairie in the morning. Charley was bruised and tired. All the rest were hungry and cold. It was very dreary. The driver bade us look to our right hand. A black bear was trotting alongside of us, at a little distance. After keeping up his trot for some time, he turned off from our track. The sight of him made up for all,—even if ague should follow, which I verily believed it would. But we escaped all illness. It is remarkable that I never saw ague but once. The single case that I met with was in autumn, at the Falls of Niagara.

I had promised Dr. F. a long story about English politics, when a convenient opportunity should occur. I thought the present an admirable one; for nobody seemed to have anything to say, and it was highly desirable that something should be said. I made my story long enough to beguile four miles; by which time, some were too tried, and others too much disheartened, for more conversation. Something white was soon after visible. Our driver gave out that it was a house, half a mile from Chicago. But no: it was an emigrant encampment, on a morsel of raised, dry ground; and again we were uncertain whether we were in the right road. Presently, however, the Chicago beacon was visible, shining a welcome to us through the dim, misty air. The horses seemed to see it, for they quickened their pace; and before half-past ten, we were on the bridge.

The family, at my temporary home, were gone up to their chambers; but the wood-fire was soon replenished, tea made, and the conversation growing lively. My companions were received as readily at their several resting-places. When we next met, we found ourselves all disposed to place warm hospitality very high on the list of virtues.

1838

Abner D. Jones

Tremont

Abner D. Jones, a young New Englander, visited Illinois in the summer of 1838 to form his own opinion of the prospects of the state. He traveled from Saint Louis through Alton and Peoria to the little town of Tremont in Tazewell County, where he remained for several weeks. Tremont was young, and typical of many northern Illinois towns founded and peopled by New Englanders. At Tremont, Jones witnessed an observance of the cherished national holiday, the Fourth of July.

I reached Tremont, Wednesday morning before breakfast—having taken the stage for that purpose at Peoria—the 10th of June, and became immediately domiciliated in the "Tazewell Hotel," kept by Capt. H. B. Sampson, a native of Duxbury, Mass., and for years a shipmaster from that port. I found several acquaintances here, by whom I was soon made acquainted with nearly the whole population of this social corporation.

Tremont is the shire town for Tazewell county,[1] and is situated in a delightful prairie, bounded on the east and south by a large belt of forest, on the Mackinaw creek, and on the north and west, by another on Dillon's creek, and called "Pleasant Grove."[2] The "timber"—as all forests are here called—is distant from the village, from one and a half to three miles, and is plainly visible on every hand from the point at which I am now writing. Tremont is on the east side of the Illinois river, and distant in a direct line about seven or eight miles. Pekin, nine miles distant, is the landing place for all merchandise coming up the river and destined for this place. Tremont is beautifully laid off in squares, with streets of an hundred feet in width, running at right angles with each other—parallel to the sectional lines by which the whole state is divided into townships and sections. In the centre of the town ten acres are thrown into a public square, with a broad street passing through its centre each way, cutting it into four equal sections. These are intended to be enclosed with a neat, white paling, which will no doubt be accomplished whenever the times improve. With a real public spirit which has marked nearly all the actions of this intelligent colony, they have planted ornamental trees along the lines of these squares, which already beautify, and will one day be a great ornament to the place. On all sides of this area, but chiefly on the western and

Abner D. Jones, *Illinois and the West, with a Township Map, Containing the Latest Surveys and Improvements* (Boston, 1838), pp. 71–77.

[1] The county seat was Tremont from 1836 to 1850, when it was moved to Pekin. Ed.

[2] See Bryant, "The Illinois River; Morgan, Sangamon, and Tazewell Counties," footnote 1, above. Ed.

northern sides, the dwellings, stores, offices, and workshops are scattered, giving the town an extended aspect entirely unlike anything at the east. The buildings are frame, and generally painted white, which gives an exceedingly neat and pleasant aspect, as contrasted with the deep and brilliant green of the prairie which embosoms it.

The character of the place is New England, there being three quarters of the population from that section of our country. There are besides a very intelligent class of citizens from New York, Kentucky, and other places in the Union, whose sectional feelings are all merged in the general interest. Indeed I have rarely ever witnessed less of this powerful influence than appears in this village. For a high moral tone of feeling, temperance, good order, industry, public spirit and real intelligence, I believe Tremont not to be surpassed in the whole west, and rarely equalled in our country towns at the east. A brisk business is here driven with the neighboring farmers, who have "located" themselves all along the line of the prairie in the edge of the "timber." One of the most pleasing features of this place is the respect paid by its inhabitants to Sabbath institutions. There is yet no church in the place—measures are on foot by the Unitarian parish for the erection of one the ensuing winter—but there is a very convenient schoolhouse which the various denominations occupy alternately on the Sabbath; and there is never a Sabbath without some religious service. The Episcopalians are fitting up a room which they will occupy exclusively, and when the church alluded to shall be erected, the place will be abundantly provided with places for public worship. There is a kind and generous feeling cherished by each sect to all the others, which would do much toward destroying any intolerant feelings, were not the influence of the clergy—to their shame be it written—used to draw closer and tighter the narrow lines of sectarianism.

I have seen no place of its size in the west where there is so little intemperance as in Tremont. There is a respectable temperance society here, and it has been my pleasure to be present at two of their meetings—which are held monthly through the year—

where I was edified and instructed with remarks of gentlemen appointed to address us on those occasions. A "celebration of Independence" was got up here for the present anniversary of the "Declaration," by the young men of the village—and on temperance ground. No ardent spirits or wine were on the table during dinner, although every individual was permitted to furnish it, after the cloth was removed, at extra expense. It was a very cheering sight to witness the predominance of *tumblers* over *wine glasses* on the table, more than half the company toasting in pure *cold water*. Nor did I perceive any lack of inspiration or want of edge in the toasts manifested in the water-drinkers. Indeed the most uproarious man at the table was a water-drinker—it was the generous ebullition of a happy spirit. Nor did I witness a single instance of undue excitement by wine in one of the company. All was orderly, though somewhat noisy, and everything passed off without an angry word or an unkind feeling. The dinner was preceded by the usual services. The oration was a very respectable performance, and the music did great credit to the young men of Tremont. An ode, written for the occasion by a resident lady— a very clever performance—was sung to the tune of the "Bonny Boat," with great spirit and taste. After the regular toasts, many voluntary ones were given. Two, alluding to the delegation from Tazewell county, in general assembly, called up two candidates who were present, thus resolving the civic assemblage to a political caucus—into which, however, it must be said, that no *party* politics were permitted to enter. It was the first opportunity I had been afforded of listening to a "stump oration," and I was not sorry for the change. There was something in the frank *naïveté* of the first speaker, a plain Kentucky farmer, which pleased me, and a straightforwardness in his homely "speech," which showed the honest and skilful politician. He was succeeded by a physician, who, although he did well, did no better than his unread predecessor. It strikes a New Englander oddly enough to hear a man talk as familiarly of his political plans and purposes, of what he has done, and *can* do, and will do, "if he be elected," and of his entire devotion to the interests of those he addresses, as if he were in his own castle. Our spouters were repeatedly interrupted with shouts of applause, and calls from individuals among the throng for an expression of opinion on some political question. It is considered the privilege of any of his constituents, while in this attitude, to demand of the electioneering candidate, his opinion on any question which may agitate the community; and he feels bound to give it. It is the custom in many parts of the west to appoint a place and time when the opposing candidates for office may be heard by all the inhabitants of that section, on the questions of policy pertaining to their duties. It is not uncommon, on such occasions, to assemble the whole county or precinct: to roast a whole ox, and to provide every luxury the season can afford.

1840

Eliza R. Steele

By Packet from Peoria to Alton, and the Towns along the Way

Mrs. Eliza R. Steele was one of those indefatigable women who toured the West for the purpose of writing a book. She traveled from New York by way of the Great Lakes to Chicago, thence to Peoria and, by way of the Illinois River, to Alton and Saint Louis. Her account of river travel is lively and informative. A contemporary reviewer in Hunt's *Merchants' Magazine* commented: "We have passed over a portion of the route occupied by the writer, and can, therefore, as far as our observation extends, bear testimony to the general accuracy of her descriptions."

July 9th [*1840*]—While wandering along the shore this morning, we descried the smoke of our expected steamboat, and hastened back to the hotel to pack our trunks. It was the Home, from Peru to St. Louis, and we were to take passage in her for Alton, on the Mississippi. We bade adieu to sweet Peoria with regret. The remembrance of it will long "perfume our minds," as old Izaak Walton says. Its situation, its excellent society, and religious privileges, and its good schools, must certainly make it a desirable place of residence, or of trade. It is two hundred miles from St. Louis, and one hundred and seventy from Chicago. When in the saloon of the Home we were presented with a book in which to write our names, place of residence, whither bound, and *our politics*. While leaving this, our eyes fell upon a piece of pink satin, framed, which hung against the wall, upon which was printed the rules of the boat. Among other things it forbid "any gentleman to go to table without his coat, or any other garb to disturb the company. No gentleman must pencil-work or otherwise injure the furniture"; (I suppose whittling was meant. Upon our lake boat we saw the boxes of merchandize and barrels on deck, fast disappearing under the whittling knife. A piece a foot long and two inches wide would be torn from the box and cut to pieces by a restless passenger.) Beside these, we were told "no gentleman was to lie down in a berth with his boots on, and none enter the ladies' saloon without permission from them." We found in this boat, three indications of being near the south, liquors upon the table, gambling in the gentlemen's cabin, and a black chambermaid *slave* to the captain. . . .

Twelve miles below Peoria we stopped at the town of Pekin, built upon a bank elevated fifteen feet above the water during high tide; but now, all these places are much higher. The captain told us he should be here some time taking in merchandize, and we employed the interval in seeing the lions of the town. . . .

Eliza R. Steele, *A Summer Journey to the West* (New York, 1841), pp. 155–56, 158–71.

Pekin is a small place and only contains eight or nine hundred inhabitants, and five or six streets. The shops seemed well filled with goods, and presented a goodly show of tin, ironware, dry-goods, crockery, provisions, etc. I purchased a green gauze veil here and several small articles, all of which I found much more expensive than in our Atlantic shops, freight being high on the Mississippi. In paying for them I found a new currency here, my shillings and sixpences being transformed into *bits* and *pics* or picayunes. The Pekin Express lay upon the counter which we amused ourselves looking over while waiting for change. The person who kept the shop turned out to be the oldest inhabitant of the place, that important personage who, in a storm, always determines if there has been ever a greater one or no. He might very well be the oldest, as the town is but ten years in existence. "Pekin," he said, "would have been ere this far ahead of any town upon the river, were it not that there were two parties among the commissioners who were to lay it out; these pulling different ways the town was nearly lost between them. The rich country behind, and the river in front, had befriended them, and they soon expected to have their branch of the railroad finished to Mackinaw river, whose water power and timber bluffs were very valuable." We remarked as we walked, a large hotel nearly finished; a presbyterian, methodist, and several other meeting-houses; office of the "Tazewell Telegraph"; academy, and some dwellings. We lay here four hours with a hot sun reflecting from the sandy bank, impatiently watching the barrels of flour which seemed as they would never cease rolling from the large store-house upon the bank, down to our vessel. These barrels are from the steam flour mills, which turn out two hundred barrels a day. Beside these, we took in a hundred sacks of corn, and some other merchandize. The captain seemed well pleased with his morning's work, saying he had a *streak of luck* that day. Three miles below this he had another "streak." At the mouth of Mackinaw river scows were waiting him, loaded with bundles of laths and staves, and long dark boards, which I took for mahogany, but which proved to be black-walnut. The Mackinaw is a clear stream, having rich bottom land, bounded by bluffs covered with white oak and cedar. The prairies through which it flows, are rolling and tolerable land with several mill seats.

The Illinois looked beautiful this afternoon. Its glassy waters scarcely moved, and it seemed so content with its sweet resting place, and at the silent admiration of those stately trees, which were sending their cool flickering shadows over her and gazing down at loveliness, that it would fain linger upon its course, as some young languid beauty, conscious of a graceful position which is winning admiring glances from every beholder. . . .

We passed several towns to day, as Liverpool, Havanna, Beardstown—the former a small settlement, but which its inhabitants intend to make larger, as they have already a railroad in contemplation across the Mississippi. Beardstown is a place of some importance. It is a county town, and its commerce greater than any upon the river. Mechanics of all descriptions are to be found here, as bakers, shoe makers, tailors, blacksmiths, cabinet makers, silversmiths, carpenters, joiners, coopers, painters &c, &c. There are also here steam flour mills, saw mills, breweries, distilleries, &c. A canal is projected here, to connect the Illinois with the Wabash, (which divides the state of Illinois from Indiana,) by means of the Sangamon and Vermilion forks.[1] While passing these towns one is surprised at their rapid growth, for when Schoolcraft[2] rowed his canoe up this river twenty years since, it was a wilderness only inhabited by Indians. Opposite Havanna, the Spoon river enters the Illinois. Its Indian name is Amequeon, which means *ladle*, and is much prettier than its present name. It is one hundred and forty miles in length, navigable most of the way, and capable of being cleared further. The soil is dry undulating prairie, with considerable timber—and some of it upon the forks of the Spoon is the richest in the state—its forks and tributaries affording good mill seats. It is in the military bounty land, which commences just above it, and terminates

---

[1]   The canal was never built. Ed.
[2]   Henry R. Schoolcraft, explorer and ethnologist. Ed.

at the junction of the Illinois with the Mississippi, making a triangle of five million three hundred and sixty thousand acres, about ninety miles along the Illinois, and the base of the triangle, ninety miles across to the Mississippi, near Quincy. This is appropriated by Congress to the soldiers of the regular army in the war between the United States and Great Britain. Two thirds of this land is prairie, and the rest timbered, crossed by a variety of rivers and creeks. The soil is generally a black vegetable mould from fifteen to thirty inches deep. Much of the best of this land has been bought up by a company who have opened an office at Quincy, where they sell it from three to ten dollars a acre, while other parts are sold at the price government established for its lands all over the States, one dollar and twenty-five cents an acre. Government has given to the State of Illinois every other section. Sangamon river comes gliding down over its pebbly floor, a pure transparent stream, between Liverpool and Havanna. It runs through Sangamon county, of whose fertility, beautiful scenery, crowded population, rich prairies, numerous streams, and valuable timber groves, we have heard such flourishing accounts. . . . In this famed county is Springfield, the capital of the State. The Sangamon river is one hundred and eighty miles long, and navigable nearly to the capital, seventy-five miles, by small steamboats.[3] With a small expense it can be cleared. We do not see the Illinois in all its grandeur, as the water is low. It falls, our captain says, one and a half inches a day, and has fallen eight feet since June. It will arise in the autumn, and when its present channel is full overflows the bottom land to the bluffs. This makes the river shore, unless very elevated, rather unhealthy, and consequently uninhabited. Soon after passing the Sangamon, we stopped to take in wood, and we embraced the opportunity to take a sunset stroll in the forest. A small cottage embowered among woodpiles, inhabited by a woodman and his family, were

[3]   Only two steamboats ever ascended the Sangamon: the *Talisman*, in 1832, which managed to make Springfield but barely made the return trip; and the *Utility*, in 1836, which was stranded at New Salem and later broken up. Ed.

the only signs of human life we saw. These sylvan solitudes how-ever, are not without their denizens, for the birds were skipping from bough to bough, the turtle were romantically reclining upon the logs beside the water, the wild fowls, and the paroquets were chattering in concert with the mocking bird. There the squirrel also

"Sits partly on a bough his brown nuts cracking,
And from the shell the sweet white kernal taking."

Here however in these pretty nooks he sits undisturbed, for no boys "with crooks and bags" can molest his quiet haunts. We enjoyed the deep forest walk very much having been now so long cramped in a steamboat, and wandered along among the stately beech and graceful linden, the black walnut and locust, swung upon the festoons of the enormous vines which hung down from the trees, and breathed with much satisfaction the perfume from the dewy herbage, grape vine buds, and yellow jassamin which climbed the boughs around us. The steamboat bell recalled us to the shore in time to see a steamboat pass, being the second we had met this morning. . . .

July 10.—Off Meredosia. This is a thriving town, built upon one of those elevated terraces which occur frequently along the river as if on purpose to raise the settlements above the damp alluvion, and to give them a pretty effect. It is in a good situation to rise, as it is a sort of business port to Jacksonville, to which a railroad of twenty-three miles is in operation; and Morgan county, upon which it is situated, is a thickly peopled district, having good timbered lands, mill streams, quarries of lime and free stone; and is watered by many streams. Jacksonville is a large town where there are several churches, a court house, mills and shops. The Quincy and Danville railroad passes through Meredosia, to the Wabash river, two hundred and twenty miles.[4] Through this river, communication is held with the lakes. Their

---

[4]   This railroad existed on paper only, and would not be built for many years. Ed.

exports are between two and three hundred thousand dollars, and imports five hundred thousand dollars. Here we took in several passengers. Six miles below Meredosia is Naples, a small collection of shops and dwellings, situated upon a high bank. Upon one house, larger than the rest, I read the name "Napoleon Coffee House." I looked around for Vesuvious, but saw it not, nor any other Neopolitan traces. The names upon this river are very ludicrous, and striking monuments of the want of taste in those who bestowed them. One would imagine, from reading my last letter, I had been travelling in seven league boots, or in a balloon, as I have touched at Peru, Pekin, Havanna, Liverpool, Naples, Brussels,[5] Rome, (part in the night,) &c. While the Indian names are so pretty, why are they neglected for such worn out European designations. Peoria, and Illinois, and Ottowa are very pretty; Hennepin is very well, as given in honor of one of the early discoverers of this county from France, and it might be thought a debt of gratitude, but every pioneer has not so good a name, and if this custom is followed, it saddles us with such names as already abound, viz: Jo Daviess County, Pike, Cook, Higgonbottom, Hancock, Buggsville, Toddtown, Dodgeville.[6] Moreover, the Indians were the first explorers, and if any, they are entitled to this honor. To obviate this it has been proposed to take something local, but unless persons of taste are consulted, we shall hear of more Bigbonelicks, Bloodyruns, Mud Lakes or Crab Orchards. I wish Congress would take the matter in hand, and form a committee of nomenclature to name every new settlement.

We are constantly passing steamboats. In 1836, at Beardstown, there were four hundred and fifty arrivals and departures, and at Naples their account was the first year, 1828, nine; from March to June, 1832, one hundred and eight, and now, of course all these figures must be doubled. . . .

---

[5]   Brussels, in Scott County on the Illinois River, had a brief existence. Ed.
[6]   If Higgonbottom, Buggsville, Toddtown and Dodgeville ever existed, they have long since disappeared. Ed.

This morning we passed one of those machines employed by government, during low water for the purpose of clearing away the sandbars. It is a large wooden ark, worked by steam. A great shovel takes up the mud, brings it up, and throws it into the scow at the other side which is emptied upon the shores. The State has appropriated $100,000 to improvements upon this river. There are several sandbars, and below Ottowa ledges of sandstone which, if removed, would render the navigation unimpeded at all seasons of the year quite to Ottowa, two hundred and ten miles above the mouth of the river. We stopped so often to take in freight and passengers, that we began to be fearful we should not reach the mouth of the river and behold its junction with the stately Mississippi before dark—however, "we came a good jog" this morning, to use our old Kentucky lady's phrase, and now after tea we are sitting upon the guards watching for it. We are continually passing streams which run into this river—Crooked creek, comes down about one hundred miles through a very fertile region of country with a soil of argillaceous mould from one to four feet deep. Its banks are lined with oak, maple, hickory, black walnut and much other valuable timber. Bituminous coal, and free stone quarries are also found there. Apple creek, at whose mouth is a small settlement; Macoupin creek, its name taken from the Indian Maquapin, a water plant, whose smooth leaf floats upon the bayous and lakes in this region; its esculent root, after being baked under heated stones is a favorite food with the native tribes. There is a settlement upon this last named stream commenced in eighteen hundred and sixteen, which then was the most northern white settlement of Illinois. The population of the State four years after, in eighteen hundred and twenty, was fifty-five thousand two hundred and eleven, and now, eighteen hundred and forty, it is four hundred and twenty three thousand nine hundred and thirty four, a great increase in twenty years. We have now upon each hand, the two last counties which border the Illinois. Green, on the east, contains excellent land, well settled by eastern families, many from Vermont. It is one of the richest portions of land in the State, traversed by fine water courses and bounded by two large rivers,—containing beautiful prairies, and excellent timber. In the cliffs which border the Mississippi on this county, bituminous coal is found among the sandstone and limestone strata, and crystal springs flow from their sides. Calhoun county on our right is the southern point of the triangle containing the military bounty lands. The point where the Mississippi and Illinois meet is low prairie subjected to inundation and consequently unhealthy; coal has been found here, and the large trees are famous for their honey. . . . The afternoon is beautiful; we are peeping up the forest glades, as the channel runs near the shore, or inhaling the rich perfume which the summer breeze shakes out from the trees. Suddenly the forest is passed and we gaze over the low prairie which lies between the two rivers, bounded by a line of round green hills which range across the country. "The bluffs of the Mississippi!" exclaimed my companion, "and we soon shall see its famous waters." We hastened up to the hurricane deck, and placed ourselves in a good situation for beholding the scenery; a little excited at the thought of looking upon the grand and celebrated stream. The Illinois flowed as straight and still as a canal, about four hundred yards wide, we glided over its waters and soon found ourselves in a broad majestic stream which came rolling down between a range of bluffs; here, a mile broad, upon whose bosom some lonely islands stretched across from the mouth of the Illinois. The view was delightful upon each side; the fair plains of Missouri at our right, and upon the Illinois side, bold beautiful cliffs, or green cone-like hills, covered with a soft carpet of verdure, sinking down upon the east side into lovely green dells. This style of hill is called by the French, Mamelle. In one of these pretty nooks, nestled at the foot of a bluff, is the town of Grafton, from whose balconies the inhabitants obtain a fine view up the Mississippi. This town is only a few years old, but expects soon to rival Alton, as most of the travelling from the interior to the Missouri towns opposite, is through it. It has already laid out upon paper a railroad to Springfield, the capital. The rapid tide of the "father of waters," presented a great contrast to the languid Illinois. The color is brown, but of a different tint from the Illinois, being a dark coffee brown, but clear and sparkling. We looked a last farewell to the fair Illinois, upon whose banks, or on whose water we had travelled for four days and four nights, a distance of nearly four hundred and fifty miles, if we include the Des Plaines. The loveliness of the scenery all this distance merits the encomiums made upon it by the early French writers. This was a favorite river with the French, and La Salle, Charlevoix, and Marquette, describe the beauty of its shores in glowing terms.

1841

Ebenezer Welch

Monmouth and
Warren County

We know nothing about the author of the following letter except that his name was Ebenezer Welch and that he came from Maine. Although his spelling and punctuation were somewhat erratic, he was obviously an intelligent and perceptive man.

Monmouth [*Illinois*], *Friday, September 19, 1841*

Dear Brother Milton

Believing as I do that you would receive with a hearty welcome a letter from an absent, wandering brother, I deem it a duty, as well as a privilege, to devote the present opportunity in conversation with you, and in so doing I shall not attempt to give you fine sounding words, or nice sentances, but merely let you know about matters and things in general. I have many things to write & you must take them as they come. I rec'd a letter from you some time since & should have answered it ere this but as Otis wrote home I thought it propper to defer mine.

Time & again I visited the P. O. with the earnest hope and expectation of getting a letter from you but all in vain. At last I gave it up & concluded that you had forgotten me & I was determined to go no more, when to my joy one Sabbath morn Otis came with the welcome messenger. I read it, reread it and put it away. It contained many things of interest to me and much news, all of which I thank you for. I have also rec'd a letter from Searey dated Hallowell August 18, & a number of papers from home which I am ever glad to receive. Mother's paper came safe to hand and she has my sincere thanks for it. Last Monday had a Journal & [*illegible*] from you.—You must excuse me for not sending papers as I seldom see any except those I have from Maine.—The Season has been very hot & dry; there has scarcely been any rain since I have been here, but as the soil is very deep a drouth does not do the damage that it does in Maine. The crops are generally good exceptting potatoes & grass. Gardens have also been damaged considerably. On account of the dryness in the East the price of wheat has advanced considerably. It is now worth 50 cents in cash here and at Chicago it is worth $1. per bushel. Farmers have just finished haying, & are now engaged in sowing wheat. Many of them sow in among the corn. The corn is now ripe & from 10 to 12 feet high. Mellons

Manuscript letter in the library of the Chicago Historical Society.

196

of all kinds have been so plenty for 6 weeks past that they were free for all. They continue yet. One of my neighbors has 10 acres of watermellons in his corn, another 5. Here they grow as large as Yanke pumkins with out touching a hoe to them. What do you think of that? Often as I have visited these loved places, & stuffed my chops with their red cores, have I thought of those who would gladly partake of these luxuries if it were not for leaving *home*. Poor Souls how I pity you, contented to drag out a miserable life in a land where grasshoppers can hardly live, where toads can be seen crying for a little sorrell, and even the poor *weevils* had to *emigrate* in order to get a little *wheat*, & I don't blame them for it. Ah no it shows wisdom in them & should teach man an important lesson.

Here in the west things grow allmost spontaneously. At any rate they far exceed my expectations. I think a man can raise 10 bu. of corn with less labor than he can one in Maine. I have seen 30 acres of corn which was brushed in with a bush which has not been hoed & is now ripe & will average from 20 to 30 bu per acre!!

A few days since I visited a field of corn containing 60 acres, and as I strolled through it, I could but laugh heartily, for it seemd as though I was in a world of corn. I could see nothing else except the sun which heated the black soil so hot that I could hardly bear my hand on it. At a distance I saw something move, I hastened to the spot. It was the old farmer getting a load of mellons. Here he had 5 acres of them, many of which were nearly as large as a water pail. I looked at them. I wished you [were] here, and at it I went eating until I could hardly turn round. The old man told me to come with my waggon and fill it—but I found a plenty at home.—But enough of this for I fancy I can almost see Rodney with his knife open ready to cut one & the rest egar to set a slice.

The summer was so hot that I suffered much with the heat and often I thought of the old Pond where I had so often bathed, for I have not been in aswimming but once this season & then I went out to the Mississippi a distance of 18 miles, this was our nearest bath.

For several days past we have had cold unpleasant weather. We have had a frost twice. I worked for Emery until the 8 of August when I was taken sick. I had all the appearances of a violent fever, called a Doctor who bled me gave me an emetic, pills, powders etc. I was confined to my bed 5 days during this time. I was constantly under the operation of medicine in order to drive off the fever. The weather was hot & the flies thick enough I assure you. The 2d week I was able to sit up a part of the time, & the 3d week I could walk about although I was very weak & had lost much flesh. From that time to this I have been able to work for my board. I am now in good health, but out of employment. There are but few who pay money for work but will give provision or stock, which I do not want. Besides hands that work out have to pay from 5 cts to *one dollar* per dozen for washing. This must be cash!!

I shall now tell you something of the people. They are generally very easy to get acquainted with, sociable and open hearted. They dress very plain and in short their manners are far different from the people of New England, but very much as they were in *"the days when I was a boy."* It is no uncommon thing to see two women riding one horse, or a man & a woman! Only think how your "down east" girls would feel in going to meting on a horse with a man.—Riding on horse back is much practiced by the Ladies here.

The most of their houses consist of only one room, many of them made of logs. In this they do all their work. All lodge & all stay contentedly. "To be content their natural desire." Their greatest desire seems to be to live easy. In their work they are slovenish, & care but little about improvements.

Many of them live almost entirely on "whole hog bacon," corn meal doggers, & mush, & milch. In fact you see but few tables set in "down east" style. They think that Yankees are very extravagant in their living, building, dress etc.—Many of the customs of the people I dislike very much—As most of the wood land belongs to Eastern men, they go on to it, cut & slash where ever they wish until the timber is all destroyed, &

then go to another. At length the owner comes to sell his land, but finds only a few stumps left. Of course no one knows any thing about it!!! There are but few who buy wood, and they even hook (or steal) timber to build meeting houses of!! When a man wishes to be married he has only to buy a license & it is a custom for all the men & boys to turn out the first night after marriage, surround the house, & then with tin pans, cow bells, tin pails & every thing else, they make such a noise that can often be heard several miles, until the married man will give them money enough to have a *drunk* on. This they take, go to the grocery, & spend the night in a "spree."

This is merely civil amusement.—Rum drinking (or rather whiskey) is quite fashionable here, & it is not uncommon to see boys 8 or 9 years old *drunk*. But you can judge something of the society when I tell you that we employ 7 Lawyers in this place, & have a court nearly every day.—I shall now give you some of the words they use here—a wedge is called a *glut*, a stream is called a *slew*, a hill, a *bluff*, wheat bread, *prote*, etc. The word *reckon* is used instead of "guess" and quite as much. The word *heap* is a kind of degree of comparison and is applied to every thing.—They tell about a "heap of rain," a "heap of mud," "a heap of wind," and "a heap of business," "a heap of hot weather" & a heap of every thing else. If you enquire the distance to any place, your answer would probably be, "It's a right smart chance of distance." This is another degree of comparison, & every thing is "right smart" with them. But I will give you a western sentence & you may translate it. "On Friday week, (a week from Friday) I took the *glut*, passed over *yon slew*, by the side of *yon bluff*, & found a *right smart chance* for splitting a *heap* of rails. I felt *powerful* weak so I returned home."

The Mormons are increasing very fast in this State. They are building a City 60 miles from here, & they are flocking from all quarters to it. I counted at one time 17 large covered waggons in one string that passed through this town, bound for Nauvoo, loaded with people, & in one week there were about 200 people passed through it, but this is but a small part of what come.

Many of them are not able to build houses so they live in their carts, but I think winter will give them a shaking.—They are erecting a temple of stone 110 feet square. They have also made 12 oxen of wood to be gilded over & placed in it. &c &c &c.

I have had an opportunity of seeing their bible & it really seems like a mess of nonsense to me. It is an account of a part of the lost tribe of Israel written & signed by Mormon & his Son, on plates of gold, which were sealed up to be kept until some future generation. At length the world became corrupt so the Lord sent an Angel with the plates, who gave them to Jo Smith, & gave him power to translate them, & then they were sealed up again!!! It seems to me that the Author of this tried to imitate the style of the bible, but he done it awkwardly. Although they say it was written several thousand years before Christ, yet, they have many passages in the new testament in it word for word, and even Christ's sermon on the mount is in it, revised a little. Strange that men can believe such folly! Good night—E.S.W.

IV

The
Maturing State

1842-1858

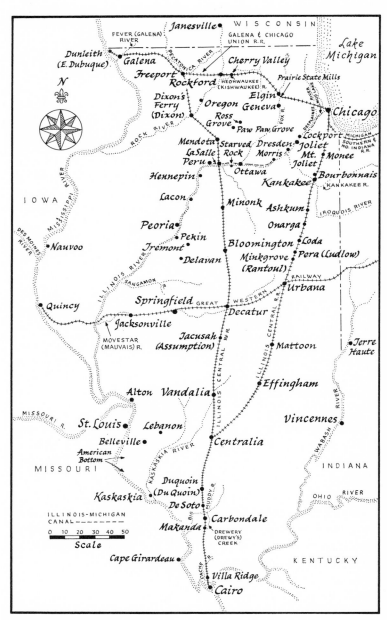

Illinois 1842–1858

When a party like that of Charles Dickens, venturing into the prairies in the vicinity of Belleville, could carry a supply of sherry and champagne, and lemons and sugar for punch, one can assume that the pioneer period had come to an end. Hard statistics support this conclusion. In twenty years, from 1840 to 1860, the population of Illinois jumped from 476,183 to 1,711,951, with the biggest increase taking place in the northern part of the state. Chicago began its spectacular growth in the same years. The 4,853 residents counted by the census takers in 1840 had become 112,172 by 1860. Much of the increase was accounted for by immigration. Irish poured into Illinois to work on the canal and railroads; Germans, leaving their country after the unsuccessful revolution of 1848, found Chicago and Illinois congenial; colonies of French-Canadians settled in the Kankakee country, and Swedes at Bishop Hill in Henry County.

In 1836–37 Illinois had embarked on a grandiose system of internal improvements. The first project was the Illinois and Michigan Canal, connecting Lake Michigan and the Illinois River. Work began in 1836 on borrowed money, which the state expected to repay through tolls and the sale of canal lands granted to it by the federal government. But the canal would be only a beginning. The principal rivers would be improved for navigation. Three great railroads were planned: the Illinois Central from the terminus of the Illinois and Michigan Canal to Cairo, the Northern Cross from Quincy through Springfield to the Indiana line, and the Southern Cross from Alton to Mount Carmel on the Wabash River. Various local projects—new roads and the improvement of existing ones—rounded out the system.

Before much could be done, the severe depression of 1837 brought the entire country to a standstill. In Illinois, as elsewhere, money dried up, and credit could not be had. Of the railroads, only a section of the Northern Cross—from Meredosia on the Illinois River to Springfield—was completed. Work on the Illinois and Michigan Canal continued longest, but even that was abandoned in 1842.

By the middle of the decade the country was on the way to recovery. In Illinois a strong governor, Thomas Ford, worked out new financing for the Illinois and Michigan Canal; work was resumed, and the first boat passed through in the spring of 1848. Almost simultaneously, trains started to run over the first few miles of the Galena and Chicago Union, Chicago's first railroad. Within two years Congress would make a land grant of 2,595,000 acres to support construction of the Illinois Central Railroad to connect Galena and Cairo, with a "branch line" to Chicago. Seven hundred miles of track were finished by 1856. In 1860 Illinois had 2,790 miles of railroad in operation, ranking second only to Ohio.

The twenty years between 1840 and 1860 saw the beginnings of great Illinois industries. Cyrus H. McCormick, a Virginian, established his reaper plant at Chicago in 1847, and within three years was selling his machines throughout the country. About the same time John Deere transferred his plow-making plant from the tiny town of Grand Detour to Moline, and in ten years was turning out 10,000 plows annually.

To adapt the governmental machinery to a growing, changing state, the people of Illinois adopted a new constitution in 1848. During the '50s a system of public schools went into operation. New colleges appeared: Knox in 1837, and in 1857, the original University of Chicago, Illinois State Normal, and Blackburn. The theater blossomed in Chicago, and traveling lecturers and entertainers carried some measure of culture to the smaller cities.

1842

Charles Dickens

The Looking-Glass Prairie, Belleville, and Lebanon

The fame of Charles Dickens as a novelist was well established when he visited the United States in 1842. Welcomed warmly at first, he offended many of his hosts by his comments, in public, on literary piracy, of which American publishers were guilty, and on Abolition, which he favored. Dickens took his revenge in his *American Notes*, published after his tour. In Illinois he visited Cairo, which he satirized in *Martin Chuzzlewit*, and made a trip from Saint Louis through Belleville and Lebanon to the Looking Glass Prairie.

I may premise that the word Prairie is variously pronounced *paraaer*, *parearer*, and *paroarer*. The latter mode of pronunciation is perhaps the most in favour.

We were fourteen in all, and all young men: indeed it is a singular though very natural feature in the society of these distant settlements, that it is mainly composed of adventurous persons in the prime of life, and has very few grey heads among it. There were no ladies: the trip being a fatiguing one: and we were to start at five o'clock in the morning, punctually.

I was called at four, that I might be certain of keeping nobody waiting; and having got some bread and milk for breakfast, threw up the window and looked down into the street, expecting to see the whole party busily astir, and great preparations going on below. But as everything was very quiet, and the street presented that hopeless aspect with which five o'clock in the morning is familiar elsewhere, I deemed it as well to go to bed again, and went accordingly.

I awoke again at seven o'clock, and by that time the party had assembled, and were gathered round, one light carriage, with a very stout axletree; one something on wheels like an amateur carrier's cart; one double phaeton of great antiquity and unearthly construction; one gig with a great hole in its back and a broken head; and one rider on horseback who was to go on before. I got into the first coach with three companions; the rest bestowed themselves in the other vehicles; two large baskets were made fast to the lightest; two large stone jars in wicker cases, technically known as demi-johns, were consigned to the "least rowdy" of the party for safe keeping; and the procession moved off to the ferry-boat, in which it was to cross the river bodily, men, horses, carriages, and all, as the manner in these parts is.

We got over the river in due course, and mustered again before a little wooden box on wheels, hove down all aslant in a morass, with "MERCHANT TAILOR" painted in very large letters over the

Charles Dickens, *American Notes for General Circulation* (London, 1842), 2:123–30, 134–40.

door. Having settled the order of proceeding, and the road to be taken, we started off once more and began to make our way through an ill-favoured Black Hollow, called, less expressively, the American Bottom.

The previous day had been—not to say hot, for the term is weak and lukewarm in its power of conveying an idea of the temperature. The town had been on fire; in a blaze. But at night it had come on to rain in torrents, and all night long it had rained without cessation. We had a pair of very strong horses, but travelled at the rate of little more than a couple of miles an hour, through one unbroken slough of black mud and water. It had no variety but in depth. Now it was only half over the wheels, now it hid the axletree, and now the coach sank down in it almost to the windows. The air resounded in all directions with the loud chirping of the frogs, who, with the pigs (a coarse, ugly breed, as unwholesome-looking as though they were the spontaneous growth of the country), had the whole scene to themselves. Here and there we passed a log hut; but the wretched cabins were wide apart and thinly scattered, for though the soil is very rich in this place few people can exist in such a deadly atmosphere. On either side of the track, if it deserve the name, was the thick "bush"; and everywhere was stagnant, slimy, rotten, filthy water.

As it is the custom in these parts to give a horse a gallon or so of cold water whenever he is in a foam with heat, we halted for that purpose, at a log inn in the wood, far removed from any other residence. It consisted of one room, bare-roofed and bare-walled of course, with a loft above. The ministering priest was a swarthy young savage, in a shirt of cotton print like bed-furniture, and a pair of ragged trousers. There were a couple of young boys, too, nearly naked, lying idly by the well; and they, and he, and *the* traveller at the inn, turned out to look at us.

The traveller was an old man with a grey gristly beard two inches long, a shaggy moustache of the same hue, and enormous eyebrows; which almost obscured his lazy, semi-drunken glance, as he stood regarding us with folded arms: poising himself alternately upon his toes and heels. On being addressed by one of the party, he drew nearer, and said, rubbing his chin (which scraped under his horny hand like fresh gravel beneath a nailed shoe), that he was from Delaware, and had lately bought a farm "down there" pointing into one of the marshes where the stunted trees were thickest. He was "going," he added, to St. Louis, to fetch his family, whom he had left behind; but he seemed in no great hurry to bring on these encumbrances, for when we moved away, he loitered back into the cabin, and was plainly bent on stopping there so long as his money lasted. He was a great politician of course, and explained his opinions at some length to one of our company; but I only remember that he concluded with two sentiments, one of which was, Somebody for ever! and the other, Blast everybody else! which is by no means a bad abstract of the general creed in these matters.

When the horses were swollen out to about twice their natural dimensions (there seems to be an idea here, that this kind of inflation improves their going), we went forward again, through mud and mire, and damp, and festering heat, and brake and bush, attended always by the music of the frogs and pigs, until nearly noon, when we halted at a place called Belleville.

Belleville was a small collection of wooden houses, huddled together in the very heart of the bush and swamp. Many of them had singularly bright doors of red and yellow; for the place had been lately visited by a travelling painter, "who got along," as I was told, "by eating his way." The criminal court was sitting, and was at that moment trying some criminals for horse-stealing: with whom it would most likely go hard: for live stock of all kinds being necessarily very much exposed in the woods, is held by the community in rather higher value than human life; and for this reason, juries generally make a point of finding all men indicted for cattle-stealing, guilty, whether or no.

The horses belonging to the bar, the judge, and witnesses, were tied to temporary racks set up roughly in the road; by which is to be understood, a forest path, nearly knee-deep in mud and slime.

There was an hotel in this place which, like all hotels in America, had its large dining-room for the public table. It was an odd, shambling, low-roofed out-house, half-cowshed and half-kitchen, with a coarse brown canvas table-cloth, and tin sconces stuck against the walls, to hold candles at supper-time. The horseman had gone forward to have coffee and some eatables prepared, and they were by this time nearly ready. He had ordered "wheat-bread and chicken fixings," in preference to "corn-bread and common doings." The latter kind of refection includes only pork and bacon. The former comprehends broiled ham, sausages, veal cutlets, steaks, and such other viands of that nature as may be supposed, by a tolerably wide poetical construction, to "fix" a chicken comfortably in the digestive organs of any lady or gentleman. . . .

From Belleville, we went on, through the same desolate kind of waste, and constantly attended, without the interval of a moment, by the same music; until, at three o'clock in the afternoon, we halted once more at a village called Lebanon to inflate the horses again, and give them some corn besides: of which they stood much in need. Pending this ceremony, I walked into the village, where I met a full-sized dwelling-house coming down-hill at a round trot, drawn by a score or more of oxen.

The public-house was so very clean and good a one, that the managers of the jaunt resolved to return to it and put up there for the night, if possible. This course decided on, and the horses being well refreshed, we again pushed forward, and came upon the Prairie at sunset.

It would be difficult to say why, or how—though it was possibly from having heard and read so much about it—but the effect on me was disappointment. Looking towards the setting sun, there lay, stretched out before my view, a vast expanse of level ground; unbroken, save by one thin line of trees, which scarcely amounted to a scratch upon the great blank; until it met the glowing sky, wherein it seemed to dip: mingling with its rich colours, and mellowing in its distant blue. There it lay, a tranquil sea or lake without water, if such a simile be admissible, with the day going down upon it: a few birds wheeling here and there: and solitude and silence reigning paramount around. But the grass was not yet high; there were bare black patches on the ground; and the few wild flowers that the eye could see, were poor and scanty. Great as the picture was, its very flatness and extent, which left nothing to the imagination, tamed it down and cramped its interest. I felt little of that sense of freedom and exhilaration which a Scottish heath inspires, or even our English downs awaken. It was lonely and wild, but oppressive in its barren monotony. I felt that in traversing the Prairies I could never abandon myself to the scene, forgetful of all else; as I should do instinctively, were the heather underneath my feet, or an iron-bound coast beyond; but should often glance towards the distant and frequently-receding line of the horizon, and wish it gained and passed. It is not a scene to be forgotten, but it is scarcely one, I think (at all events, as I saw it), to remember with much pleasure, or to covet the looking-on again, in after life.

We encamped near a solitary log-house, for the sake of its water, and dined upon the plain. The baskets contained roast fowls, buffalo's tongue (an exquisite dainty, by the way), ham, bread, cheese, and butter; biscuits, champagne, sherry; lemons and sugar for punch; and abundance of rough ice. The meal was delicious, and the entertainers were the soul of kindness and good humour. I have often recalled that cheerful party to my pleasant recollection since, and shall not easily forget, in junketings nearer home with friends of older date, my boon companions on the Prairie.

Returning to Lebanon that night, we lay at the little inn at which we had halted in the afternoon. In point of cleanliness and comfort it would have suffered by no comparison with any village alehouse, of a homely kind, in England.

Rising at five o'clock next morning, I took a walk about the village: none of the houses were strolling about to-day, but it was early for them yet, perhaps: and then amused myself by lounging in a kind of farm-yard behind the tavern, of which the leading features were, a strange jumble of rough sheds for stables; a rude colonnade, built as a cool place of summer resort; a deep well; a great earthen mound for keeping vegetables in, in winter time; and a pigeon-house, whose little apertures looked, as they do in all pigeon-houses, very much too small for the admission of the plump and swelling-breasted birds who were strutting about it, though they tried to get in never so hard. That interest exhausted, I took a survey of the inn's two parlours, which were decorated with coloured prints of Washington, and President Madison, and of a white-faced young lady (much speckled by the flies), who held up her gold neck-chain for the admiration of the spectator, and informed all admiring comers that she was "Just Seventeen": although I should have thought her older. In the best room were two oil portraits of the kit-cat size,[1] representing the landlord and his infant son; both looking as bold as lions, and staring out of the canvas with an intensity that would have been cheap at any price. They were painted, I think, by the artist who had touched up the Belleville doors with red and gold; for I seemed to recognise his style immediately.

After breakfast, we started to return by a different way from that which we had taken yesterday, and coming up at ten o'clock with an encampment of German emigrants carrying their goods in carts, who had made a rousing fire which they were just quitting, stopped there to refresh. And very pleasant the fire was; for, hot though it had been yesterday, it was quite cold to-day, and the wind blew keenly. Looming in the distance, as we rode along, was another of the ancient Indian burial-places, called The Monks' Mound; in memory of a body of fanatics of the order of La Trappe, who founded a desolate convent there, many years ago, when there were no settlers within a thousand miles, and were all swept off by the pernicious climate: in which lamentable fatality, few rational people will suppose, perhaps, that society experienced any very severe deprivation.[2]

[1]   A portrait less than half-length. Ed.
[2]   Monks' Mound is 100 feet high, 1080 feet long, and 710 feet at its
greatest width. The Trappist colony was established in 1809 and
abandoned four years later. Ed.

The track of to-day had the same features as the track of yesterday. There was the swamp, the bush, the perpetual chorus of frogs, the rank unseemly growth, the unwholesome steaming earth. Here and there, and frequently too, we encountered a solitary broken-down waggon, full of some new settler's goods. It was a pitiful sight to see one of these vehicles deep in the mire; the axletree broken; a wheel lying idly by its side; the man gone miles away, to look for assistance; the woman seated among their wandering household goods with a baby at her breast, a picture of forlorn, dejected patience; the team of oxen crouching down mournfully in the mud, and breathing forth such clouds of vapour from their mouths and nostrils, that all the damp mist and fog around seemed to have come direct from them.

In due time we mustered once again before the merchant tailor's, and having done so, crossed over to the city in the ferry-boat: passing, on the way, a spot called Bloody Island, the duelling-ground of St. Louis, and so designated in honour of the last fatal combat fought there, which was with pistols, breast to breast. Both combatants fell dead upon the ground; and possibly some rational people may think of them, as of the gloomy madmen on the Monks' Mound, that they were no great loss to the community.

1843

Sarah Margaret Fuller

The Fox River Valley
and the
Rock River Country

Sarah Margaret Fuller, the precocious daughter of a Massachusetts lawyer, received an education that gave her a sound knowledge of literature and languages. She published her first book, a translation of Eckermann's *Conversations with Goethe*, in 1839, when she was twenty-nine. From 1840 to 1842 she edited the *Dial*. Among her friends she counted Emerson, Hawthorne, William Henry Channing, and James Freeman Clarke.

On a tour of the Great Lakes in 1843, Miss Fuller visited Chicago, Dixon, and the Rock River country, an experience that she recorded with verve.

Margaret Fuller's later career was notable, and ended tragically. In 1844 she became the literary critic of Horace Greeley's *New York Tribune*, holding this position for two years. In Italy in 1847 she married the Marquis Ossoli, an Italian revolutionary. Returning to the United States in 1850, she, her husband, and their child were lost when their ship was wrecked off the Long Island coast.

Notwithstanding all the attractions I thus found out by degrees on the flat shores of the lake, I was delighted when I found myself really on my way into the country for an excursion of two or three weeks. We set forth in a strong wagon, almost as large, and with the look of those used elsewhere for transporting caravans of wild beasteses, loaded with every thing we might want, in case nobody would give it to us—for buying and selling were no longer to be counted on—with a pair of strong horses, able and willing to force their way through mud holes and amid stumps, and a guide, equally admirable as marshal and companion, who knew by heart the country and its history, both natural and artificial, and whose clear hunter's eye needed neither road nor goal to guide it to all the spots where beauty best loves to dwell.

Add to this the finest weather, and such country as I had never seen, even in my dreams, although these dreams had been haunted by wishes for just such an one, and you may judge whether years of dullness might not, by these bright days, be redeemed, and a sweetness be shed over all thoughts of the West.

The first day brought us through woods rich in the moccasin flower and lupine, and plains whose soft expanse was continually touched with expression by the slow moving clouds which

> "Sweep over with their shadows, and beneath
> The surface rolls and fluctuates to the eye;
> Dark hollows seem to glide along and chase
> The sunny ridges,"

to the banks of the Fox river, a sweet and graceful stream. We reached Geneva just in time to escape being drenched by a violent thunder shower, whose rise and disappearance threw expression into all the features of the scene.

Geneva reminds me of a New England village, as indeed there, and in the neighborhood, are many New Englanders of an excellent stamp, generous, intelligent, discreet, and seeking to

Sarah Margaret Fuller, *Summer on the Lakes in 1843* (Boston, 1844), pp. 35–51.

win from life its true values. Such are much wanted, and seem like points of light among the swarms of settlers, whose aims are sordid, whose habits thoughtless and slovenly.

With great pleasure we heard, with his attentive and affectionate congregation, the Unitarian clergyman, Mr. Conant,[1] and afterward visited him in his house, where almost everything bore traces of his own handywork or that of his father. He is just such a teacher as is wanted in this region, familiar enough with the habits of those he addresses to come home to their experience and their wants; earnest and enlightened enough to draw the important inferences from the life of every day.

A day or two we remained here, and passed some happy hours in the woods that fringe the stream, where the gentlemen found a rich booty of fish.

Next day, travelling along the river's banks, was an uninterrupted pleasure. We closed our drive in the afternoon at the house of an English gentleman, who has gratified, as few men do, the common wish to pass the evening of an active day amid the quiet influences of country life. He showed us a book-case filled with books about this country; these he had collected for years, and become so familiar with the localities that, on coming here at last, he sought and found, at once, the very spot he wanted, and where he is as content as he hoped to be, thus realizing Wordsworth's description of the wise man, who "sees what he foresaw."

A wood surrounds the house, through which paths are cut in every direction. It is, for this new country, a large and handsome dwelling; but round it are its barns and farm yard, with cattle and poultry. These however, in the framework of wood, have a very picturesque and pleasing effect. There is that mixture of culture and rudeness in the aspect of things as gives a feeling of freedom, not of confusion.

I wish it were possible to give some idea of this scene as viewed by the earliest freshness of dewy dawn. This habitation of man

---

[1]   Augustus H. Conant, minister at Geneva and Unitarian missionary from 1841 to 1857. Ed.

seemed like a nest in the grass, so thoroughly were the buildings and all the objects of human care harmonized with what was natural. The tall trees bent and whispered all around, as if to hail with sheltering love the men who had come to dwell among them.

The young ladies were musicians, and spoke French fluently, having been educated in a convent. Here in the prairie, they had learned to take care of the milk-room, and kill the rattlesnakes that assailed their poultry yard. Beneath the shade of heavy curtains you looked out from the high and large windows to see Norwegian peasants at work in their national dress. In the wood grew, not only the flowers I had before seen, and wealth of tall, wild roses, but the splendid blue spiderwort, that ornament of our gardens. Beautiful children strayed there, who were soon to leave these civilized regions for some really wild and western place, a post in the buffalo country. Their no less beautiful mother was of Welsh descent, and the eldest child bore the name of Gwynthleon. Perhaps there she will meet with some young descendants of Madoc, to be her friends; at any rate, her looks may retain that sweet, wild beauty, that is soon made to vanish from eyes which look too much on shops and streets, and the vulgarities of city "parties."

Next day we crossed the river. We ladies crossed on a little foot-bridge, from which we could look down the stream, and see the wagon pass over at the ford. A black thunder cloud was coming up. The sky and waters heavy with expectation. The motion of the wagon, with its white cover, and the laboring horses, gave just the due interest to the picture, because it seemed as if they would not have time to cross before the storm came on. However, they did get across, and we were a mile or two on our way before the violent shower obliged us to take refuge in a solitary house upon the prairie. In this country it is as pleasant to stop as to go on, to lose your way as to find it, for the variety in the population gives you a chance for fresh entertainment in every hut, and the luxuriant beauty makes every path attractive. In this house we found a family "quite above the common," but, I grieve to say, not above false pride, for the father, ashamed of being caught barefoot, told us a story of a man, one of the richest men, he said, in one of the eastern cities, who went barefoot, from choice and taste.

Near the door grew a Provence rose, then in blossom. Other families we saw had brought with them and planted the locust. It was pleasant to see their old home loves, brought into connection with their new splendors. Wherever there were traces of this tenderness of feeling, only too rare among Americans, other things bore signs also of prosperity and intelligence, as if the ordering mind of man had some idea of home beyond a mere shelter, beneath which to eat and sleep.

No heaven need wear a lovelier aspect than earth did this afternoon, after the clearing up of the shower. We traversed the blooming plain, unmarked by any road, only the friendly track of wheels which tracked, not broke the grass. Our stations were not from town to town, but from grove to grove. These groves first floated like blue islands in the distance. As we drew nearer, they seemed fair parks, and the little log houses on the edge, with their curling smokes, harmonized beautifully with them.

One of these groves, Ross's grove,[2] we reached just at sunset. It was of the noblest trees I saw during this journey, for the trees generally were not large or lofty, but only of fair proportions. Here they were large enough to form with their clear stems pillars for grand cathedral aisles. There was space enough for crimson light to stream through upon the floor of water which the shower had left. As we slowly plashed through, I thought I was never in a better place for vespers.

That night we rested, or rather tarried at a grove some miles beyond, and there partook of the miseries so often jocosely portrayed, of bedchambers for twelve, a milk dish for universal handbasin, and expectations that you would use and lend your "handkercher" for a towel. But this was the only night, thanks to the hospitality of private families, that we passed thus, and it was well that we had this bit of experience, else might we have

---

[2]   Now Shabbona Grove, De Kalb County. Ed.

pronounced all Trollopian records of the kind to be inventions of pure malice.[3]

With us was a young lady who showed herself to have been bathed in the Britannic fluid, wittily described by a late French writer, by the impossibility she experienced of accommodating herself to the indecorums of the scene. We ladies were to sleep in the bar-room, from which its drinking visitors could be ejected only at a late hour. The outer door had no fastening to prevent their return. However, our host kindly requested we would call him, if they did, as he had "conquered them for us," and would do so again. We had also rather hard couches; (mine was the supper table,) but we yankees, born to rove, were altogether too much fatigued to stand upon trifles, and slept as sweetly as we would in the "bigly bower" of any baroness. But I think England sat up all night, wrapped in her blanket shawl, and with a neat lace cap upon her head; so that she would have looked perfectly the lady, if any one had come in; shuddering and listening. I know that she was very ill next day, in requital. She watched, as her parent country watches the seas, that nobody may do wrong in any case, and deserved to have met some interruption, she was so well prepared. However, there was none, other than from the nearness of some twenty sets of powerful lungs, which would not leave the night to a deadly stillness. In this house we had, if not good beds, yet good tea, good bread, and wild strawberries, and were entertained with most free communications of opinion and history from our hosts. Neither shall any of us have a right to say again that we cannot find any who may be willing to hear all we may have to say. "A's fish that comes to the net," should be painted on the sign at Papaw grove.

In the afternoon of this day we reached the Rock river, in whose neighborhood we proposed to make some stay, and crossed at Dixon's ferry.

This beautiful stream flows full and wide over a bed of rocks,

[3]   The reference is to Frances Trollope's derogatory book, *Domestic Manners of the Americans* (1832). Ed.

traversing a distance of near two hundred miles, to reach the Mississippi. Great part of the country along its banks is the finest region of Illinois, and the scene of some of the latest romance of Indian warfare. To these beautiful regions Black Hawk returned with his band "to pass the summer," when he drew upon himself the warfare in which he was finally vanquished. No wonder he could not resist the longing, unwise though its indulgence might be, to return in summer to this home of beauty.

Of Illinois, in general, it has often been remarked that it bears the character of country which has been inhabited by a nation skilled like the English in all the ornamental arts of life, especially in landscape gardening. That the villas and castles seem to have been burnt, the enclosures taken down, but the velvet lawns, the flower gardens, the stately parks, scattered at graceful intervals by the decorous hand of art, the frequent deer, and the peaceful herd of cattle that make picture of the plain, all suggest more of the masterly mind of man, than the prodigal, but careless, motherly love of nature. Especially is this true of the Rock river country. The river flows sometimes through these parks and lawns, then betwixt high bluffs, whose grassy ridges are covered with fine trees, or broken with crumbling stone, that easily assumes the forms of buttress, arch and clustered columns. Along the face of such crumbling rocks, swallows' nests are clustered, thick as cities, and eagles and deer do not disdain their summits. One morning, out in the boat along the base of these rocks, it was amusing, and affecting too, to see these swallows put their heads out to look at us. There was something very hospitable about it, as if man had never shown himself a tyrant near them. What a morning that was! Every sight is worth twice as much by the early morning light. We borrow something of the spirit of the hour to look upon them.

The first place where we stopped was one of singular beauty, a beauty of soft, luxuriant wildness. It was on the bend of the river, a place chosen by an Irish gentleman,[4] whose absenteeship

---

[4]   Alexander Charters of New York City, whose estate, "Hazelwood," was a show place for many years. Ed.

seems of the wisest kind, since for a sum which would have been but a drop of water to the thirsty fever of his native land, he commands a residence which has all that is desirable, in its independence, its beautiful retirement, and means of benefit to others.

His park, his deer-chase, he found already prepared; he had only to make an avenue through it. This brought us by a drive, which in the heat of noon seemed long, though afterwards, in the cool of morning and evening, delightful, to the house. This is, for that part of the world, a large and commodious dwelling. Near it stands the log-cabin where its master lived while it was building, a very ornamental accessory.

In front of the house was a lawn, adorned by the most graceful trees. A few of these had been taken out to give a full view of the river, gliding through banks such as I have described. On this bend the bank is high and bold, so from the house or the lawn the view was very rich and commanding. But if you descended a ravine at the side to the water's edge, you found there a long walk on the narrow shore, with a wall above of the richest hanging wood, in which they said the deer lay hid. I never saw one, but often fancied that I heard them rustling, at daybreak, by these bright clear waters, stretching out in such smiling promise, where no sound broke the deep and blissful seclusion, unless now and then this rustling, or the plash of some fish a little gayer than the others; it seemed not necessary to have any better heaven, or fuller expression of love and freedom than in the mood of nature here.

Then, leaving the bank, you would walk far and far through long grassy paths, full of the most brilliant, also the most delicate flowers. The brilliant are more common on the prairie, but both kinds loved this place.

Amid the grass of the lawn, with a profusion of wild strawberries, we greeted also a familiar love, the Scottish harebell, the gentlest, and most touching form of the flower-world.

The master of the house was absent, but with a kindness beyond thanks had offered us a resting place there. Here we were taken care of by a deputy, who would, for his youth, have been assigned the place of a page in former times, but in the young west, it seems he was old enough for a steward. Whatever be called his function, he did the honors of the place so much in harmony with it, as to leave the guests free to imagine themselves in Elysium. And the three days passed here were days of unalloyed, spotless happiness.

There was a peculiar charm in coming here, where the choice of location, and the unobtrusive good taste of all the arrangements, showed such intelligent appreciation of the spirit of the scene, after seeing so many dwellings of the new settlers, which showed plainly that they had no thought beyond satisfying the grossest material wants. Sometimes they looked attractive, the little brown houses, the natural architecture of the country, in the edge of the timber. But almost always when you came near, the slovenliness of the dwelling and the rude way in which objects around it were treated, when so little care would have presented a charming whole, were very repulsive. Seeing the traces of the Indians, who chose the most beautiful sites for their dwellings, and whose habits do not break in on that aspect of nature under which they were born, we feel as if they were the rightful lords of a beauty they forbore to deform. But most of these settlers do not see it at all; it breathes, it speaks in vain to those who are rushing into its sphere. Their progress is Gothic, not Roman, and their mode of cultivation will, in the course of twenty, perhaps ten, years, obliterate the natural expression of the country.

This is inevitable, fatal; we must not complain, but look forward to a good result. Still, in travelling through this country, I could not but be struck with the force of a symbol. Wherever the hog comes, the rattlesnake disappears; the omnivorous traveller, safe in its stupidity, willingly and easily makes a meal of the most dangerous of reptiles, and one whom the Indian looks on with a mystic awe. Even so the white settler pursues the Indian, and is victor in the chase. But I shall say more upon the subject by-and-by.

While we were here we had one grand thunder storm, which added new glory to the scene.

One beautiful feature was the return of the pigeons every afternoon to their home. Every afternoon they came sweeping across the lawn, positively in clouds, and with a swiftness and softness of winged motion, more beautiful than anything of the kind I ever knew. Had I been a musician, such as Mendelsohn, I felt that I could have improvised a music quite peculiar, from the sound they made, which should have indicated all the beauty over which their wings bore them. I will here insert a few lines left at this house, on parting, which feebly indicate some of the features.

Familiar to the childish mind were tales
    Of·rock-girt isles amid a desert sea,
Where unexpected stretch the flowery vales
    To soothe the shipwrecked sailor's misery.
Fainting, he lay upon a sandy shore,
And fancied that all hope of life was o'er;
But let him patient climb the frowning wall,
Within, the orange glows beneath the palm tree tall,
And all that Eden boasted waits his call.

Almost these tales seem realized to-day,
When the long dullness of the sultry way,
Where "independent" settlers' careless cheer
Made us indeed feel we were "strangers" here,
Is cheered by sudden sight of this fair spot,
On which "improvement" yet has made no blot,
But Nature all-astonished stands, to find
Her plan protected by the human mind.

Blest be the kindly genius of the scene;
    The river, bending in unbroken grace,
The stately thickets, with their pathways green,
    Fair lonely trees, each in its fittest place.
Those thickets haunted by the deer and fawn;
Those cloudlike flights of birds across the lawn;
The gentlest breezes here delight to blow,
And sun and shower and star are emulous to deck the show.

Wondering, as Crusoe, we survey the land;
Happier than Crusoe we, a friendly band;
Blest be the hand that reared this friendly home,
The heart and mind of him to whom we owe
Hours of pure peace such as few mortals know;
May he find such, should he be led to roam;
Be tended by such ministering sprites—
Enjoy such gaily childish days, such hopeful nights!
And yet, amid the goods to mortals given,
To give those goods again is most like heaven.

Hazelwood, Rock River, June 30th, 1843.

The only really rustic feature was of the many coops of poultry near the house, which I understood it to be one of the chief pleasures of the master to feed.

Leaving this place, we proceeded a day's journey along the beautiful stream, to a little town named Oregon. We called at a cabin, from whose door looked out one of those faces which, once seen, are never forgotten; young, yet touched with many traces of feeling, not only possible, but endured; spirited, too, like the gleam of a finely tempered blade. It was a face that suggested a history, and many histories, but whose scene would have been in courts and camps. At this moment their circles are dull for want of that life which is waning unexcited in this solitary recess.

The master of the house proposed to show us a "short cut," by which we might, to especial advantage, pursue our journey. This proved to be almost perpendicular down a hill, studded with young trees and stumps. From these he proposed, with a hospitality of service worthy an Oriental, to free our wheels whenever they should get entangled, also, to be himself the drag, to prevent our too rapid descent. Such generosity deserved trust; however, we women could not be persuaded to render it. We got out and admired, from afar, the process. Left by our guide—and prop! we found ourselves in a wide field, where, by playful quips and turns, an endless "creek," seemed to divert itself with our attempts to cross it. Failing in this, the next best was to whirl down a steep bank, which feat our charioteer performed with an air not unlike that of Rhesus, had he but been as suitably furnished with chariot and steeds!

At last, after wasting some two or three hours on the "short cut," we got out by following an Indian trail,—Black Hawk's! How fair the scene through which it led! How could they let themselves be conquered, with such a country to fight for!

Afterwards, in the wide prairie, we saw a lively picture of nonchalance (to speak in the fashion of dear Ireland). There, in the wide sunny field, with neither tree nor umbrella above his head, sat a pedler, with his pack, waiting apparently for customers. He was not disappointed. We bought, what hold in regard to the human world, as unmarked, as mysterious, and as important an existence, as the infusoria to the natural, to wit, pins. This incident would have delighted those modern sages, who, in imitation of the sitting philosophers of ancient Ind, prefer silence to speech, waiting to going, and scornfully smile in answer to the motions of earnest life,

> "Of itself will nothing come,
> That ye must still be seeking?"

However, it seemed to me to-day, as formerly on these sublime occasions, obvious that nothing would come, unless something would go; now, if we had been as sublimely still as the pedler, his pins would have tarried in the pack, and his pockets sustained an aching void of pence!

Passing through one of the fine, park-like woods, almost clear from underbrush and carpeted with thick grasses and flowers, we met, (for it was Sunday,) a little congregation just returning from their service, which had been performed in a rude house in its midst. It had a sweet and peaceful air, as if such words and thoughts were very dear to them. The parents had with them all their little children; but we saw no old people; that charm was wanting, which exists in such scenes in older settlements, of seeing the silver bent in reverence beside the flaxen head.

At Oregon, the beauty of the scene was of even a more sumptuous character than at our former "stopping place." Here swelled the river in its boldest course, interspersed by halcyon isles on which nature had lavished all her prodigality in tree, vine, and flower, banked by noble bluffs, three hundred feet high, their sharp ridges as exquisitely definite as the edge of a shell; their summits adorned with those same beautiful trees, and with buttresses of rich rock, crested with old hemlocks, which wore a touching and antique grace amid the softer and more luxuriant vegetation. Lofty natural mounds rose amidst the rest, with the same lovely and sweeping outline, showing everywhere the plastic power of water,—water, mother of beauty, which, by its sweet and eager flow, had left such lineaments as human genius never dreamt of.

1844

Josiah Quincy

Nauvoo and the Mormons

Expelled from Missouri in 1839, the Mormons, or Latter-Day Saints, purchased a townsite on the Mississippi in Hancock County, Illinois, and named it Nauvoo. There they prospered for several years. Although figures are unreliable, it is probable that in 1844, at the time of the following description, Nauvoo had 10,000 inhabitants. A temple, commenced in 1841, neared completion. Joseph Smith, the Prophet, dominated the community.

Smith's visitors in 1844 were Charles Francis Adams, the son of John Quincy Adams and at the time a member of the Massachusetts House of Representatives, and Josiah Quincy, son of Josiah Quincy, then president of Harvard.

Six weeks after the visit of Adams and Quincy, Joseph Smith and his brother Hyrum, then lodged in the jail at nearby Carthage, were murdered by a mob of non-Mormons.

It was on the 25th of April, 1844, that Mr. Adams and myself left Boston for the journey to the West which we had had for some time in contemplation. I omit all account of our adventures— and a very full account of them is before me—until the 14th of May, when we are ascending the clear, sparkling waters of the Upper Mississippi in the little steamboat "Amaranth." With one exception we find our fellow-passengers uninteresting. The exception is Dr. Goforth. A chivalric, yet simple personage is this same doctor, who has served under General Jackson at the battle of New Orleans and is now going to Nauvoo, to promote the election of the just nominated Henry Clay. It is to this gentleman we owe our sight of the City of the Saints, which, strangely enough, we had not intended to visit. Though far from being a Mormon himself, Dr. Goforth told us much that was good and interesting about this strange people. He urged us to see for ourselves the result of the singular political system which had been fastened upon Christianity, and to make the acquaintance of his friend, General Smith, the religious and civil autocrat of the community. "We agreed to stop at Nauvoo," says my journal, "provided some conveyance should be found at the landing which would take us up to General Smith's tavern, and prepared our baggage for this contingency. Owing to various delays, we did not reach the landing till nearly midnight, when our friend, who had jumped on shore the moment the boat stopped, returned with the intelligence that no carriage was to be had, and so we bade him adieu, to go on our way. But, as we still lingered upon the hurricane deck, he shouted that there was a house on the landing, where we could get a good bed. This changed our destiny, and just at the last moment we hurried on shore. Here we found that the 'good bed' our friend had promised us was in an old mill, which had been converted into an Irish shanty. However, we made the best of it, and, having dispossessed a cat and a small army of cockroaches of their quarters in the

Josiah Quincy, *Figures of the Past from the Leaves of Old Journals*, 5th ed. (Boston, 1883), pp. 378–82, 384, 386–90.

coverlet, we lay down in our dressing-gowns and were soon asleep."

We left our lowly bed in the gray light of the morning, to find the rain descending in torrents and the roads knee-deep in mud. Intelligence of our arrival had in some mysterious manner reached General Smith, and the prophet's own chariot, a comfortable carryall, drawn by two horses, soon made its appearance. It is probable that we owed the alacrity with which we were served to an odd blunder which had combined our names and personalities and set forth that no less a man than ex-President John Quincy Adams had arrived to visit Mr. Joseph Smith. Happily, however, Dr. Goforth, who had got upon the road before us, divided our persons and reduced them to their proper proportions, so that no trace of disappointment was visible in the group of rough-looking Mormons who awaited our descent at the door of the tavern. It was a three-story frame house, set back from the street and surrounded by a white fence, that we had reached after about two miles of the muddiest driving. Preeminent among the stragglers by the door stood a man of commanding appearance, clad in the costume of a journeyman carpenter when about his work. He was a hearty, athletic fellow, with blue eyes standing prominently out upon his light complexion, a long nose, and a retreating forehead. He wore striped pantaloons, a linen jacket, which had not lately seen the washtub, and a beard of some three days' growth. This was the founder of the religion which had been preached in every quarter of the earth. As Dr. Goforth introduced us to the prophet, he mentioned the parentage of my companion. "God bless *you*, to begin with!" said Joseph Smith, raising his hands in the air and letting them descend upon the shoulders of Mr. Adams. The benediction, though evidently sincere, had an odd savor of what may be called official familiarity, such as a crowned head might adopt on receiving the heir presumptive of a friendly court. The greeting to me was cordial—with that sort of cordiality with which the president of a college might welcome a deserving janitor—and a blessing formed no part of it. "And now come, both of you, into the house!'" said our host, as, suiting the action to the word, he ushered us across the threshold of his tavern. . . .

On the right hand, as we entered the house, was a small and very comfortless-looking bar-room; all the more comfortless, perchance, from its being a dry bar-room, as no spirituous liquors were permitted at Nauvoo. In apparent search for more private quarters, the prophet opened the door of a room on the left. He instantly shut it again, but not before I perceived that the obstacle to our entrance was its prior occupancy by a woman, in bed. He then ran up-stairs, calling upon us to follow him, and, throwing open a door in the second story, disclosed three Mormons in three beds. This was not satisfactory; neither was the next chamber, which was found, on inspection, to contain two sleeping disciples. The third attempt was somewhat more fortunate, for we had found a room which held but a single bed and a single sleeper. Into this apartment we were invited to enter. Our host immediately proceeded to the bed, and drew the clothes well over the head of its occupant. He then called a man to make a fire, and begged us to sit down. Smith then began to talk about himself and his people, as, of course, we encouraged him to do. . . .

At this point breakfast was announced, and a substantial meal was served in a long back kitchen. We sat down with about thirty persons, some of them being in their shirt-sleeves, as if just come from work. There was no going out, as the rain still fell in torrents; and so, when we had finished breakfast, the prophet (who had exchanged his working dress for a broadcloth suit while we lingered at the table) proposed to return to the chamber we had quitted, where he would give us his views of theology. The bed had been made during our absence and the fire plentifully replenished. Our party was now increased by the presence of the patriarch, Hiram Smith; Dr. Richards, of Philadelphia, who seemed to be a very modest and respectable Mormon; Dr. Goforth; and a Methodist minister, whose name I have not preserved. No sooner were we seated than there entered some half-dozen leaders of the sect, among whom, I think, were Rigdon and Young;[1] but of their presence I cannot be positive. These men constituted a sort of silent chorus during the expositions of their chief. They fixed a searching, yet furtive gaze upon Mr. Adams and myself, as if eager to discover how we were impressed by what we heard. . . .

"And now come with me," said the prophet, "and I will show you the curiosities." So saying, he led the way to a lower room, where sat a venerable and respectable-looking lady. "This is my mother, gentlemen. The curiosities we shall see belong to her. They were purchased with her own money, at cost of six thousand dollars"; and then, with deep feeling, were added the words, "And that woman was turned out upon the prairie in dead of night by a mob." There were some pine presses fixed against the wall of the room. These receptacles Smith opened, and disclosed four human bodies, shrunken and black with age. "These are mummies," said the exhibitor. "I want you to look at that little runt of a fellow over there. He was a great man in his day. Why, that was Pharaoh Necho, King of Egypt!" Some parchments inscribed with hieroglyphics were then offered us. They were preserved under glass and handled with great respect. "That is the handwriting of Abraham, the Father of the Faithful," said the prophet. "This is the autograph of Moses, and these lines were written by his brother Aaron. Here we have the earliest account of the Creation, from which Moses composed the First Book of Genesis." The parchment last referred to showed a rude drawing of a man and woman, and a serpent walking upon a pair of legs. I ventured to doubt the propriety of providing the reptile in question with this unusual means of locomotion. "Why, that's as plain as a pikestaff," was the rejoinder. "Before the Fall snakes always went about on legs, just like chickens. They were deprived of them, in punishment for their agency in the ruin of man." We

---

[1] Sidney Rigdon and Brigham Young. Rigdon had been a Mormon leader since his conversion in 1830. After the death of the Smiths he broke with Young, returned to the East, and attempted to organize his own branch of the church. Ed.

were further assured that the prophet was the only mortal who could translate these mysterious writings, and that his power was given by direct inspiration. . . .

The clouds had parted when we emerged from the chamber of curiosities, and there was time to see the Temple before dinner. General Smith ordered a capacious carriage, and we drove to that beautiful eminence, bounded on three sides by the Mississippi, which was covered by the holy city of Nauvoo. The curve in the river enclosed a position lovely enough to furnish a site for the Utopian communities of Plato or Sir Thomas More; and here was an orderly city, magnificently laid out, and teeming with activity and enterprise. And all the diligent workers, who had reared these handsome stores and comfortable dwellings, bowed in subjection to the man to whose unexampled absurdities we had listened that morning. . . . Near the entrance to the Temple we passed a workman who was laboring upon a huge sun, which he had chiselled from the solid rock. The countenance was of the negro type, and it was surrounded by the conventional rays.

"General Smith," said the man, looking up from his task, "is this like the face you saw in vision?"

"Very near it," answered the prophet, "except" (this was added with an air of careful connoisseurship that was quite overpowering)—"except that the nose is just a thought too broad."

The Mormon Temple was not fully completed. It was a wonderful structure, altogether indescribable by me. Being, presumably, like something Smith had seen in vision, it certainly cannot be compared to any ecclesiastical building which may be discerned by the natural eyesight. It was built of limestone, and was partially supported by huge monolithic pillars, each costing, said the prophet, three thousand dollars. Then in the basement was the baptistry, which centered in a mighty tank, surrounded by twelve wooden oxen of colossal size. These animals, we were assured, were temporary. They were to be replaced by stone oxen as fast as they could be made. The Temple, odd and striking as it was, produced no effect that was commensurate with its cost. Perhaps it would have required a genius to have designed anything worthy of that noble site. The city of Nauvoo, with its wide streets sloping gracefully to the farms enclosed on the prairie seemed to be a better temple to Him who prospers the work of industrious hands than the grotesque structure on the hill, with all its queer carvings of moons and suns. This, however, was by no means the opinion of the man whose fiat had reared the building. In a tone half-way between jest and earnest, and which might have been taken for either at the option of the hearer, the prophet put this inquiry: "Is not here one greater than Solomon, who built a Temple with the treasures of his father David and with the assistance of Huram, King of Tyre? Joseph Smith has built his Temple with no one to aid him in the work."[2]

---

[2]   In 1848, two years after the departure of the Mormons from Nauvoo, the temple, still unfinished, was destroyed by fire. Ed.

1846

William Cullen Bryant

Chicago
and by Stage to Peru

William Cullen Bryant, whom we encountered in Illinois in
1832, made several visits to the state, primarily to see his brother,
who had moved from Jacksonville to Princeton. In 1846 Bryant
traveled by way of the lakes to Chicago, and then by stage to
Peru and Princeton. He related his experiences in letters to his
paper, the *New York Evening Post*, which were later collected and
published in book form.

When we awoke the next morning our steamer was at Chicago. Any one who had seen this place, as I had done five years ago, when it contained less than five thousand people, would find some difficulty in recognizing it now when its population is more than fifteen thousand. It has its long rows of warehouses and shops, its bustling streets; its huge steamers, and crowds of lake-craft, lying at the wharves; its villas embowered with trees; and its suburbs, consisting of the cottages of German and Irish laborers, stretching northward along the lake, and westward into the prairies, and widening every day. The slovenly and raw appearance of a new settlement begins in many parts to disappear. The Germans have already a garden in a little grove for their holidays, as in their towns in the old country, and the Roman Catholics have just finished a college for the education of those who are to proselyte the West.

The day was extremely hot, and at sunset we took a little drive along the belt of firm sand which forms the border of the lake. Light-green waves came to the shore in long lines, with a crest of foam, like a miniature surf, rolling in from that inland ocean, and as they dashed against the legs of the horses, and the wheels of our carriage, the air that played over them was exceedingly refreshing.

When we set out the following day in the stage-coach for Peru, I was surprised to see how the settlement of Chicago had extended westward into the open country. "Three years ago," said a traveller in the coach, "it was thought that this prairie could neither be inhabited nor cultivated. It is so level and so little elevated, that for weeks its surface would remain covered with water; but we have found that as it is intersected with roads, the water either runs off in the ditches of the highways, or is absorbed into the sand which lies below this surface of dark vegetable mould, and it is now, as you perceive, beginning to be covered with habitations."

William Cullen Bryant, *Letters of a Traveller, or, Notes of Things Seen in Europe and America* (New York and London, 1850), pp. 259–63.

If you ever go by the stage-coach from Chicago to Peru, on the Illinois river, do not believe the glozing tongue of the agent who tells you that you will make the journey in sixteen hours. Double the number, and you will be nearer the truth. A violent rain fell in the course of the morning; the coach was heavily loaded, nine passengers within, and three without, besides the driver; the day was hot, and the horses dragged us slowly through the black mud, which seemed to possess the consistency and tenacity of sticking-plaster. We had a dinner of grouse, which here in certain seasons, are sold for three cents apiece, at a little tavern on the road; we had passed the long green mound which bears the name of Mount Joliet, and now, a little before sunset, having travelled somewhat less than fifty miles, we were about to cross the channel of the Illinois canal for the second or third time.

There had once been a bridge at the crossing-place, but the water had risen in the canal, and the timbers and planks had floated away, leaving only the stones which formed its foundation. In attempting to ford the channel the blundering driver came too near the bridge; the coach-wheels on one side rose upon the stones, and on the other sank deep into the mud, and we were overturned in an instant. The outside passengers were pitched head-foremost into the canal, and four of those within were lying under water. We extricated ourselves as well as we could, the men waded out, the women were carried, and when we got on shore it was found that, although drenched with water and plastered with mud, nobody was either drowned or hurt.

A farm wagon passing at the moment, forded the canal without the least difficulty, and taking the female passengers, conveyed them to the next farm-house, about a mile distant. We got out the baggage, which was completely soaked with water, set up the carriage on its wheels, in doing which we had to stand waist high in the mud and water, and reached the hospitable farm-house about half-past nine o'clock. Its owner was an emigrant from Kinderhook, on the Hudson, who claimed to be a Dutchman and a Christian, and I have no reason to doubt that he was either. His kind family made us free of their house, and we passed the night in drying ourselves, and getting our baggage ready to proceed the next day.

We travelled in a vehicle built after the fashion of the English post-coach, set high upon springs, which is the most absurd kind of carriage for the roads of this country that could be devised. Those stage-wagons which ply on Long Island, in one of which you sometimes see about a score of Quakers and Quakeresses, present a much better model. Besides being tumbled into the canal, we narrowly escaped being overturned in a dozen other places, where the mud was deep or the roads uneven.

In my journey the next day, I was struck with the difference which five years had made in the aspect of the country. Frame or brick houses in many places had taken the places of log-cabins; the road for long distances now passed between fences the broad prairie, inclosed, was turned into immense fields of maize, oats, and wheat, and was spotted here and there with young orchards, or little groves, and clumps of bright-green locust-trees, and where the prairie remained open, it was now depastured by large herds of cattle, its herbage shortened, and its flowers less numerous. The wheat harvest this year is said to have failed in northern Illinois. The rust has attacked the fields which promised the fairest, and they are left unreaped, to feed the quails and the prairie-hens.

Another tedious day's journey, over a specially bad road, brought us to Peru a little before midnight, and we passed the rest of the night at an inn just below the bank, on the margin of the river, in listening to the mosquitoes. A Massachusetts acquaintance the next morning furnished us with a comfortable conveyance to this pleasant neighborhood.

1847

J. H. Buckingham

Chicago to Springfield and the Towns along the Way

J. H. Buckingham, son of the founder and publisher of the *Boston Courier*, attended the River and Harbor Convention at Chicago in July, 1847, in the dual role of delegate and reporter for his father's paper. Excited by the West, Buckingham decided to tour Illinois after the convention ended. He traveled by stage and steamer through Peru, Peoria, Springfield, Jacksonville, and Alton to Saint Louis. Then he ascended the Mississippi to Galena and returned to Chicago by way of Dixon. His travel letters were published in the *Courier* in July and August, 1847.

Chicago, July 6, 1847

. . . Chicago is destined, some day hence, and no very far-off day
neither, to be one of the largest cities in the Union; and the
wisdom of its projectors, in laying out its wide streets, is every
where apparent. The streets are all lined with trees, and the
Acacia and Maple and Elm are abundant; the Acacia, in particular, grows very thrifty and beautiful. The soil, even in its worst
places, after you go a few yards from the shore of the lake, is
nothing but the richest garden earth to the depth of many feet,
and its capacity for yielding produce is unfathomable.

The latitude of Chicago is about the same as that of Boston
and the climate, as regards heat and cold, is about the same.
The prevalent breezes are from the North, and blowing over the
pure fresh water of Lake Michigan, are very healthy and invigo-
rating.

To-day I stood in what is called the Old Fort, a spot occupied
by barracks, with a square in the centre, the whole occupying
not more space than the Common on Fort Hill, in Boston; and
in that spot, in 1832, Gen. Scott collected for safety, and to
protect them from the Indians, every inhabitant that lived within
a circuit of thirty miles. In the space of that thirty miles, are now
living nearly fifty thousand people! Twelve years ago, one hundred and fifty inhabitants was a large estimate for the census of
Chicago, and to-day the residents are estimated at twenty
thousand!

A large proportion of the people of this city are of eastern
origin, mostly from New-England, and one would hardly be
aware in the intercourse with the town's people that he was not
in a New-England village. But the persons who come into town
from the country, and from other States, are strongly marked
with the characteristics of the West. The procession of yesterday
exhibited these hardy countenances and sturdy frames to great

J. H. Buckingham, *Illinois as Lincoln Knew It: A Boston Reporter's Record of a
Trip in 1847*, ed. Harry E. Pratt (Springfield, Ill., 1938), pp. 116–22, 128–41,
143–46.

advantage, and if nothing else results from the Convention but a knowledge, by personal inspection, of the traits of character existing in each and all of the different classes of the East and the West, the North and the South, who are here assembled, enough will have been accomplished to pay for all the cost and labor of individuals, and of this community.

The weather is intensely hot, and the roads are dusty. Chicago has no stone, and consequently the streets are not paved. Every street, however, to the end of its settlement—for some of them run out for miles into the prairie, beyond where there are houses,—is accommodated with a wide wooden sidewalk, which is pleasant to walk on. The crossings, too, are generally accommodated with a plank foot path, which is very fortunate, as some times one might run the risk of getting lost by sinking into the rich and fruitful looking earth. The dust is not sand, and the mud is not clay, but it looks more like the soil of a hot-house garden bed, than like any thing else. . . .

The more I see of Chicago, the more I am impressed with the value of its increasing trade with Boston,—for Boston is the Atlantic sea-port of this great country. Everywhere one meets with something new to astonish and delight him, and the only wonder soon gets to be, that we have not sooner made efforts to secure it all to ourselves. To-day I have had a ride on the prairie, and although new to me, I was coolly told that I had seen nothing at all. The flowers growing wildly beautiful, the roads running through miles and miles of unfenced grounds rich with soft black loam, the young trees growing thriftily and luxuriantly, the tall grass,—all, I am told, are nothing. Well, we shall see in a few days, for I am off, to-morrow, for the interior of the state, where I am to find "something" worth looking at.

I could write columns about Chicago, and give statistics upon statistics, to show that it is the greatest place of its age, and is destined to be still greater; but *cui bono*? You would not believe half I should tell you, and instead of writing notes from a plain diary, I should be set down as a romancer. This is a great place for the pork trade, in which article it is destined to rival Cincinnati, and its beef is said to be the finest in the world. Our steamer is now taking on board, as freight, two hundred casks—hogsheads of hams, which are to go through the lakes and the Erie Canal to Troy, and perhaps to Boston. Hundred of barrels of beef and pork are also going on board, all bound East. Even at this season of the year the store-houses are filled with produce, and I this morning went into one where there were stored twenty-eight thousand barrels of wheat.

On one side of the river is the Lake House, which was built in the "times of expansion," as they are called, of 1836 or 1837, for a public house. It is well kept, well furnished, and very comfortable. In its vicinity and for some distance around, are scattered numbers of elegant private dwellings, surrounded by gardens, and the streets are all wide and regularly laid out. One street on this side skirts the river shore, and has on it a few warehouses, and a large number of retail shops, mostly occupied by foreigners,—Dutch and Irish. On the other side of the river is now the principal business, and Lake-street is filled with retail stores of as much beauty of arrangement, and with as valuable stocks of goods, as can be found in any city in America. In fact, Chicago is now, with its present population, as much of a business place as I know of, after our own city. Hundreds upon hundreds of wagons are in its streets, drawn by the finest horses in the world, and laden with every sort of commodity. In the fall of the year they have their wheat brought into the city from the country in immense wagons, called prairie schooners, which hold two hundred bushels at a time, and these may be seen stringing out through the roads for miles and miles.

This is a great place for the lumber trade, although no lumber grows in this neighborhood. The boards, &c., are brought from the Sault St. Marie and Lake Superior, in different kinds of vessels, and stored in the lumber yards, to be transported by wagons into the country. A canal is about being built which will soon afford great facilities for internal transportation.[1] . . .

---

[1]   The Illinois and Michigan Canal, completed in 1848. Ed.

Springfield, Illinois [*July 9, 1847*]

. . . We left Chicago at nine o'clock in the morning, and took our way across the prairies. At first the road was uneven, dusty and uninteresting, exhibiting some cultivated farms, and but little wooded country. Soon we came upon the line of the canal, which we followed, at a short distance, through its whole extent. I have not time, nor inclination, to give a description of the few places we stopped at on the first day, nor to tell of the gross deception, and swindling actions, and gross impertinences of the stage-drivers, of which I could, if so disposed, fill a column or two, and then not tell half. The public houses were worse than the worst taverns ever seen in New-England,—dirty, and ill-found in every respect. An old lady furnished, at short notice, a dinner of boiled eggs, fresh fried pork, and tolerable coffee, which was much more palatable in the participation than in the appearance.

The prairie, where not cultivated, and in many places where it is, remains without fences, for wood is scarce for many miles after we leave Chicago, and the few houses to be met with are sadly lacking in many of the necessary boards and timbers. Corn and wheat grow luxuriantly, and large droves of cattle are to be found grazing at different places. Hogs are numerous, and I can easily conceive that Chicago may, by and by, become a great pork market. When at Chicago, I learned that the beef of this country was very superior, and I had opportunities of testing its good quality. The cattle are large, and grow fat on the prairie grass, at little or no expense, except of the time which it takes to raise them to the proper age to be driven to market. At a small place, called by some name which I have now forgotten, we stopped to examine a boiling spring, the water of which is as bad to the taste, and as much filled with sulphur, as the most enthusiastic lover of watering-places could desire. At several places in the neighborhood the water bubbles up through white sand, and the pool into which it comes looks more like a boiling cauldron than any thing else; but the water is neither warm nor cold. The driver gave it freely to his horses, and the people of the house in the neighborhood use it altogether for all purposes. The driver said it operated upon his horses as a sort of gentle cathartic, and made them healthy.

We came to no village until we arrived at Lockport, a place that is not laid down on any map that I have seen, where there are a number of stores and two or three taverns. Here is to be a large basin on the canal, and we had a fine opportunity to observe the construction of the great work, on which so many hundreds of thousands of dollars have been, and so many more are to be, expended. The canal as far as this place is nearly level and is, for a greater part of the way, already finished; it is faced on the inside with a yellowish stone, which is found at different points, and which appears to be a combination of lime and sand-stone; it is easy to work, and lies in the quarries in layers of unequal thickness, but none of it more than a foot or a foot and a half thick. The canal is not, however, built up of stone throughout its whole extent, although it is for the most of the route. At Lockport the canal must be about two hundred or two hundred and fifty feet in width at the bottom, and the locks and abutments are laid in smooth, handsome masonry, that would do no discredit to any part of our country; there are seven locks in this place, in a distance of a few miles.

We then passed over to a town called Joliet, which was named after an old Frenchman who originally settled here and owned a great part of the land. By some mistake it was originally called Juliet,[2] but the name was changed by act of the legislature a year or two ago, to conform to the proper title of the old original settler. Here are several blocks of stone stores, evidently built with a view to a large trade, which is to come at some future day. The village is laid out on a plain, and on the side of a hill, with a handsome stone bridge crossing the canal; and here, too, is a large, broad basin. The projectors of this canal, and the original directors and engineers, appear to have had in view the immense business which it will take and which it will create, or they must

[2] See Martineau, "The Prairies and Joliet," footnote 3, above. Ed.

have been very extravagant in their notions. It is probable that they knew what they were doing, what the future was to accomplish; but they were then, in a manner, before the age; they spent too much money, and by their financiering, their want of prudence, involved themselves and others in difficulties from which better counsels are now relieving the state. Now it is certain that the canal will be finished, the bonds will be paid, and nothing that I can imagine, not even another revulsion in the financial condition of the country, can prevent the stock from being a paying investment, except some mismanagement take place before the work is finished. The produce raised in the interior of the state is incalculable, and the producers must consume other articles in their turn, both of which, the exports and the imports, will, until a railroad is built side by side with it, pass through the canal to Chicago.

From Joliet to Dresden[3] we had an interesting ride, and at the latter place we took supper, our Yankee landlady serving us up codfish as a luxury, and hashed potatoes. At a small place called Morris, at half past eleven o'clock, we again stopped to change horses, and remained an hour in the most uncomfortable place you can conceive of; the tavern-keeper and all his people were in bed, but we succeeded, after some difficulty, in getting into the house, and had the luxury of two tallow candles, and a little water, which was warm, and not very palatable. On the opposite side of the road was another still smaller tavern, from which proceeded the sound of a violin. We walked over, and found about twenty persons assembled in a room on the lower floor, trying to learn to dance cotillions; the room was lighted by a solitary dip-candle; the teacher, who was also the musician, was in his shirt sleeves, and wore a shocking bad straw hat; the ladies were two little girls, two old women, and two or three fat,

---

[3] Dresden, in Buckingham's time, consisted of an inn and two or three dwellings. After a few years it disappeared. Today the Dresden atomic generating plant of the Commonwealth Edison Company stands near the site and perpetuates the name. Ed.

coarse-looking girls, about twenty; one of the male dancers wore a straw hat, two or three were without coats, and the one who was evidently the dandy of the place—for village it could hardly be called—wore a nankin-colored frock coat, and had his blue pantaloons strapped down so tight that he could scarcely move about. We amused ourselves for some time in witnessing the troubles and disasters which befell the instructor in his attempts to make the company go through correctly with the difficult figures of right and left, cross over, and promenade.

The rest of our ride during the night was as uncomfortable as any enemy, if we had one, could desire. We made progress at the rate of less than three miles an hour; the weather was intensely hot, and not a breath of air was stirring; the horses and carriage raised any quantity of dust, which, of course, rose only high enough to fill the carriage; and we were nine inside passengers, a new one having been taken in to replace the lady we had left at Dresden—[*illegible*]. We arrived at Ottawa about six o'clock in the morning, having seen nothing of the country for many miles, but bearing about as indisputable evidence that the road had led through the same soft and fertile soil that we had had during the whole day before. Ottawa is a considerable village, and has a large court-house, pleasantly situated in a square surrounded with thriving acacia, or locust trees, and a number of stores, besides some half dozen bar-rooms, independent of four taverns.

I have spoken of the want of wood on the prairies. The acacia is easily cultivated, and grows very rapidly wherever it is planted; some people are beginning to appreciate its advantage, and when we come to any considerable settlement, we find that they have commenced setting out trees on the borders of the lots; in some places, large groves have been planted, which will, in a few years, be very valuable. Of bridges, we saw few during yesterday, being obliged to ford most of the streams; as we entered Lockport we forded the river Des Plaines, which is an eighth of a mile wide, although there is a ricketty bridge over it. The whole road from Chicago lies through a tract of country which is a sort of valley—

if you can call that a valley where there are no hills on either side—which was once evidently the bed of a river. The prairie is in many places undulating, or rolling, and the waters of Lake Michigan once undoubtedly flowed uninterruptedly through to the Illinois river; the stones and rock formations show this, and the course of the former current is distinctly marked on the whole line. We forded a number of inconsiderable streams, which I am informed are sometimes—at the season of the year when the lakes and rivers are at the highest—almost impassable, and the greater part of the wood-land is on the borders of these streams.

After breakfast we took up our line of march, for it could hardly be called anything else, at the rate of two or three miles an hour, on the borders of the Illinois river, and passing by the village of La Salle, arrived at the terminus of the Canal at Peru, about twelve o'clock. Peru is next to Lisbon, in St. Lawrence county, New-York, the most uninviting place I ever saw. It is destined to become a great and growing village, the head and centre of a great trade. It is at the head of the navigation of the river, and already there are a number of stores, grog-shops, a barber's shop, and two taverns. In the early days in the history of the Canal, it was built up with log huts and mud cabins, to accommodate the Irish mud-diggers, and they remain in all their primitive ugliness, and with increased nastiness, the larger part of the village— certainly the most peopled, if we count the dirty children and the independent hogs. I ought to state, however, that a little distance from the bank of the river, on the high bluffs, are some good farms, and several nice dwellings; as I had little time to go into the interior from the main village, my remarks must be considered as applying to the terminus of the canal. Mr. Webster once owned a farm in this vicinity, where Mr. Fletcher Webster was a resident for some year or more, but I believe it has been sold to some one else.[4]

[4]   Fletcher Webster, son of Daniel Webster, moved to Peru in 1837 and
       practiced law there for three years. Ed.

Springfield, Illinois [*July 11, 1847*]

After waiting three hours at Peru, in the hope of finding a better conveyance, we embarked on board a small steamboat called the *Dial*, to come down the Illinois river. We were loaded with freight and crowded with passengers. The engine was out-doors, on the lower deck, and altogether the prospect of comfort was very small. The captain, however, did his best for the accommodation of every body, and the steward served up a very good dinner. A company of about fifty raw volunteer recruits for the Mexican army[5] were desirous of coming on board, but the captain refused to take them, and thereby deserves our gratitude; for they were excessively noisy and very drunk. We stopped at several small places on the river, to take in more freight, particularly at Hennepin and at Lacon. At this latter place, our friends J. & N. Fisher of Boston, own considerable property, and carry on a large business in packing pork, &c. It is rather a pretty place, and will, like all other places of the kind, share the fate of all in this Western country, and be a place of great trade. We remained at Lacon for nearly three hours, and took on board two hundred barrels of flour and provisions, two hundred bags of wheat, and some wool. We started again after dark, and arrived at Peoria about two o'clock in the morning. . . .

Peoria is a beautifully situated town on the right bank of the river, and is already the seat of a great business. It commands one of the most grand and interesting views in the world, and is built or laid out something in the New-England style. It has a large extent of back country to supply, and has increased within a few years almost beyond what it would be considered reasonable for me to state. In the little time I remained here, I had little opportunity to see its beauties or to learn of its trade and capacities; but as daylight came gradually on, I saw how it was situated, and soon took a walk around the more settled and business portion of the town. But everybody was asleep. The stores were shut, the night lamps were out or burnt dim, and the early morning

---

5   Recruits for the U.S. Army engaged in the Mexican War. Ed.

dawn only exposed the silent beauties of a landscape without showing vitality. It was a picture of still-life, which any painter might copy, and which, if copied, would be purchased and appreciated by the man of taste, as the richest of his collection.

At four o'clock we took a stage coach for the interior, six inside, in a carriage built to carry but four, and drawn by horses that evidently knew their driver to be bent on making work easy and pay profitable. We crossed the river in a ferry-boat, and then all got out and walked up a long hill, turning every now and then to admire the beautiful scenery, which included the town of Peoria, the river and other objects of interest in the distance.

Our party was again changed. We had two members of Congress from the state of Illinois, one Whig and one Locofoco,[6] and persons of other professions. Query,—Is a member of Congress a professional man or not? We started in a grumbling humor, but our Whig congressman was determined to be good natured, and to keep all the rest so if he could; he told stories, and badgered his opponent, who it appeared was an old personal friend, until we all laughed, in spite of the dismal circumstances in which we were placed. The character of the Western people is in every respect different from ours. Our Locofoco friend is a regular canvasser; he says that he has a way in his district of bowing to everybody, of kissing every man's child, and making love to every man's wife and daughter; he regretted that he did not ask "Long John," as everybody calls Mr. Wentworth, how he should behave in Wentworth's district, because the force of habit is so great with him, he feared he might exceed the bounds of propriety—it may be that the fashion with Long John is more abrupt, and in that case he might be going contrary to established usage. For some miles we were in Wentworth's district, and a tolerably poor district it appeared to be.

We breakfasted at Tremont, a very pretty village on a prairie, but the propriety of the name did not make itself manifest, as

[6]   The Whig Congressman was Abraham Lincoln, and the Locofoco was Robert Smith of Alton, Illinois. Ed.

there were no three hills any where in the neighborhood;—all was level country. Tremont was about twelve years ago an uninhabited prairie, and a gentleman of our party stated that a friend of his, one winter, since 1835, entrusted his wife to his care to go to a town some miles further south. That friend had purchased largely of lands in the present town of Tremont, and had a lithographic map prepared, exhibiting the squares, and the buildings, and the trees which might thereafter be erected and set out. The wife saw the map and wished very much to go through her husband's town; but when she arrived there she was of course disappointed, as no houses, no square, no trees, no any thing, was to be seen, but a level and uninteresting prairie.

Now there are houses; trees have been planted, and as every thing that is planted in this soil grows very rapidly, the squares and the streets are sufficiently marked; there is a meeting-house, and a tavern, lots of good farms, and a number of stores, and several mechanic shops, and a saw-mill worked by horse-power.

After breakfast we were fairly launched on one of the great prairies of the state, and I must acknowledge that I did not see a prairie in the neighborhood of Chicago—that is, comparatively speaking. For miles and miles we saw nothing but a vast expanse of what I can compare to nothing else but the ocean itself. The tall grass, interspersed occasionally with fields of corn, looked like the deep sea; it seemed as if we were out of sight of land, for no house, no barn, no tree was visible, and the horizon presented the rolling of the waves in the far-off distance. There were all sorts of flowers in the neighborhood of the road, which, by the way, did not appear to be a road, and all the colors of the rainbow were exhibited on all sides,—before, behind, east, west, north and south,—as if the sun were shining upon the gay and dancing waters. We saw the white-weed of our New-England, the wild indigo, the yellow mustard, the mullen, the clover, red and white, the purple nettle, the various colored phlox, numerous yellow, pink and crimson flowers, and almost everything else that is beautiful, that we have ever heard of. Occasionally we passed a cultivated spot, where some person had purchased land from the government, and had made a farm,—cattle, too, are numerous, in herds, and horses in large droves, and swine uncountable. In the distance, we saw at intervals, groves of trees, which looked like islands in the ocean, and we learned that they were planted for the purpose of raising timber. Every thing will grow in this state, and the soil is everlasting, never wearing out, and never needing manure.

Again we came to a settlement, or village, called Delavan, where there was a post-office and a tavern. We changed horses and ordered dinner. Two doctors had offices directly opposite each other, and each kept a sort of apothecary shop; but such shops I never saw before. I went into one of them, and found in one corner a bed, the sheets of which appeared as if they had never been washed. On one side of the room was a case of shelves, on which were paraded half a dozen books, probably comprising the whole library of the worthy practitioner, and twice that number of bottles, labeled—*mirabile dictu!*—with understandable names, and two or three gallipots.[7] In one corner was a pair of saddle-bags, and in another corner a saddle; but the doctor was off at a distance to visit a patient. I think I should be patient for some time before I should send for such a son of Esculapius—and yet he may be a patient, pains-taking, learned, and very charitable member of his profession. Appearances are often very deceitful, as has been remarked many hundred times before.

We dined. And such a dinner! The table was set in a bedroom, which was neither plastered nor boarded up, the open air, if there had been any, coming through in all directions. If we had had a rain storm to encounter, we should hardly have been protected from it, and for mid-winter there was nothing to keep out the snow. But the landlord was civil, his wife and daughter barefooted and dirty, and he could only keep off the flies by waving continually over the table a bough which he had cut from one of his locust trees. The table-cloth was stained with the grease

7   Small medicine bottles. Ed.

249

of many former meals, if with nothing worse, and his meat, which he called beef, was swimming in fat. The only things palatable were some fried eggs and some hashed potatoes, with some tolerable bread. However, we satisfied our craving appetites, and started in good spirits, with the hope of doing better next time.

How we speed on our journey for the rest of the day, it is unnecessary to relate. It is sufficient to say that we came, in the course of the afternoon, to a more wooded tract of land, forded several streams, and saw more beautiful flowers, several groves of acacias, and in the distance, what appeared to be hills of trees or islands of forests. Towards Springfield the cultivated farms were more numerous, and we passed through miles and miles of tall corn, the bright and beautiful green of which was almost dazzling in the sunlight; some acres of wheat, tall as an ordinary man; and many fields of oats, with some of barley—all of which appeared ready for the sickle.

We were now in the district represented by our Whig Congressman, and he knew, or appeared to know, every body we met, the name of the tenant of every farm-house, and the owner of every plat of ground. Such a shaking of hands—such a how-d'ye-do—such a greeting of different kinds, as we saw, was never seen before; it seemed as if he knew every thing, and he had a kind word, a smile and a bow for every body on the road, even to the horses, and the cattle, and the swine. His labor appeared to be so great, that we recommended to our Locofoco friend to sit on the other side of the coach and assist in the ceremonies; but he thought that that would be an interference with the vested rights of his friend and opponent, and so he declined, although he was evidently much disposed to play the amiable to several rather pretty girls that we fell in with at one of our stopping places. It seems that as there is honor among thieves, so there is etiquette among Western Congressmen.

On the road, during the afternoon, we met three large wagons loaded with wool, and drawn by three yokes of oxen each, on their way to Chicago, the wool being destined for the Boston market. Think of that. Look at the map. See what an extent of country that wool is to pass over, what will be the distance it is to be carried by water through the lakes, round over the northern part of Michigan, through the lake St. Clair, lake Erie, and thence by the Erie canal to Albany, and then by water down the Hudson and over Long Island Sound, or over our Western Railroad, and judge for yourself if the Ogdensburg Railroad would not, if it were now open, save something in time, if not in money, to the owner of that wool.

I have spoken somewhere of the cheapness of butter and cheese and eggs and poultry, in Northern New-York. On our road to Springfield, we saw a first rate roasting piece of beef—the first cut of the rib—weighing sixteen pounds, which was sold to a tavern-keeper for *four cents a pound*, and that was said to be a good price in this neighborhood. Think of that, ye housekeepers in Boston! Of vegetables we are now in the enjoyment of all the luxuries of the season, such as green peas, cucumbers, string and other beans, and new potatoes. Cherries and strawberries are among the things that were.

We arrived at Springfield early in the evening, after the most fatiguing day's ride that, in all my traveling, I ever experienced. We were all tired and dirty, covered with dust and perspiration, and not in much better humor than we were when we started in the morning. The strangers in Buffalo complained of the impositions, the lies, and the impudence of certain steamboat captains, but I will put an Illinois stage agent or driver against any thing that ever I saw before, in Europe or America, and bet odds upon him for impudence and imposition.

[*Springfield,*] *Illinois* [*July 12, 1847*]
. . . To-day I visited the State House, to listen to the debates of the [Constitutional] Convention.[8] The President is not worth

---

[8]   The Constitutional Convention sat from June 7, 1847, until August 31. The officers were Newton Cloud, of Morgan County, president; Henry W. Moore, of Gallatin County, secretary or clerk; and John Crain, of Washington County, chairman of the committee of the whole. The constitution framed by the convention was ratified by the voters in March, 1848. Ed.

much as a presiding officer, for he understands, or at any rate practises, little of the etiquette necessary for parliamentary government; he seldom rises, never announces the names of the speakers, allows two of them to speak at once, and puts the questions in such a tone of voice that he can scarcely be understood. The chief clerk, who has a tolerably clear intonation, stated the question when I was there this morning, and if it had not been for his assistance, I do not see how the members could have understood what they were voting for. A motion was made and carried, for the Convention to go into committee of the whole, and I expected something better from the new chairman, but he seemed to know but little, if any thing more than the President, and was not any better than that officer in his manner of conducting business. The members of the Convention are to appearance a much more intellectual body of men than the members of our House of Representatives; they have generally marked features, and much character. As for discipline and etiquette, I cannot say much for them. Every member who spoke, rose and put one foot in his chair, and one hand in his breeches pocket, and more than half of the whole sat with their feet on the desks before them, tilting up in their chairs. They looked like sensible men, but they want training, from the President down.

The State-House is at present an unfinished building, of stone, and intended to be well-arranged; but the architect has set it too low on the ground, so that it will never be any ornament to the place. It has a cupola built of wood, and stands in the centre of a large public square. By and by it will have a portico, with several large columns, but the columns are to be laid in blocks like the pillars before St. Paul's Church in Boston and will never present an appearance corresponding to the design of the architect. The interior, even, is not finished, and we ascend to the Representatives' hall, where the Convention assembles, by a flight of temporary stairs. The halls of the two houses will be very pretty when they are finished, but I doubt whether they will not want much remodeling before they will give satisfaction, either to members or to the sovereign people, who wish to listen to the debates of their servants.[9]

Near the State-House is a much handsomer building, which was erected some years ago by the State Bank of Illinois: it has columns, and a porch in front, and looks quite classical. The business of the place is done in stores, which are arranged round and in the neighborhood of the square, and it is even now very considerable. A railroad is to be built from Springfield to Alton, which will enable the farmers in the interior of the state to send their produce to a market; at present the only means of transportation is by wagons, and this summer it has cost seventy-five cents to a dollar a barrel to send flour to Alton on the Mississippi, on its way to New-Orleans. Wheat cannot be sent, at present, at any price, as the cost of freight would absorb all its value,— the only way it can be sent to market, is in its manufactured state. . . .

In the neighborhood of Springfield, and in the city itself, for I believe it is a city, there are many beautiful residences, and one can hardly believe that fifteen years ago, the place contained but two houses, one of which was a common drover's tavern,—that there was, as lately as 1835, but one mail a week brought here from the South, and but one a fortnight from the North,—yet such is the fact.

[9] After the Civil War, Sangamon County took over the State House that Buckingham describes and used it as a court house until 1965. In 1901, to provide more room, it was raised and a new story added. Now the building has been rebuilt in its original form as a historical monument.   Ed.

1850

Arthur Cunynghame

Travel on the Illinois
and Michigan Canal

Arthur Cunynghame, a British army officer stationed in Canada, obtained a few weeks' leave of absence for the purpose of making a tour of the United States. While in this country he traveled down the Illinois and Michigan Canal to La Salle, made side excursions to Princeton and Cambridge, and embarked on a river packet at Rock Island for passage down the Mississippi.

Cunynghame's account of his trip by canal boat is rare and interesting. This mode of travel lasted only a short time until the railroads offered faster and more comfortable transportation.

On Saturday evening, the 12th October, [1850], about five, P.M., I embarked on board the canal boat, the "Queen of the Prairies," bound for La Salle, a town situated south-west of Chicago, about 100 miles distant, and at the head of the navigable portion of the Illinois river. The cabin of this canal boat was about 50 feet in length, 9 feet wide, and 7 feet high. We numbered about ninety passengers within this confined space, in which we were to sleep, eat, and live; the nominal duration of our passage was twenty hours, but it eventually proved to be twenty-five; our baggage was secured on the roof of the boat, and covered with canvass, to screen it from the effects of the weather. A sort of divan surrounded the cabin, the portion appropriated to the ladies being screened off during the night with a curtain.

For the first few miles we, in company with three more canal boats, were towed by a small steamer, but having passed the locks, not very distant from Chicago, three horses were attached, which towed us smoothly along at the rate of five miles an hour.

Soon after we had started, tea with its accompaniments made its appearance, the never-failing beef-steak being as tough as usual. As soon as this was disposed of, all the male passengers were ordered on deck, while the parlour should be transformed into a bed-room; in less than half-an-hour we received permission to return, in which short time no less than fifty sleeping places in this small space had been rigged up, and twenty more spread upon the floor; the remainder of the passengers, about twenty in number, for the most part children, being detailed off to share their tenements with their pa's and ma's. These sleeping-places consisted of shelves placed three deep, the entire length of the cabin, on either side, with a height of two feet between each. In consequence of my being a stranger, I was politely offered the first choice; the selection was difficult indeed, where all appeared equally uncomfortable, but I am happy to have the opportunity of acknowledging this attention. Into these berths we were

Arthur Cunynghame, *A Glimpse at the Great Western Republic* (London, 1851), pp. 35–39.

ordered to get; and after some difficulty, especially amongst those to whom this mode of travelling was new, we obeyed; the remainder of the passengers, selecting their locations in succession, according to the number on their tickets.

I soon became insensible to the uncomfortable position which I occupied, although, only six inches above my face a tremendous man threatened every moment to burst through the sacking which supported him; and had the cords given way, I felt I must have been squeezed as flat as a pancake.

With so many passengers in so confined a space, no wonder that on the following morning I should awake with a severe headache, the effect of the heated nauseous vapours which surrounded us. Not a window was permitted to be opened; I made various endeavours to break through this rule during the night, but every window within my reach was fastened down. This, however, may be considered but a wise precaution; for the malaria from the surrounding marshy land, and especially from Mud Lake, distant about fifteen miles from Chicago, which we passed within a very short distance, is very dangerous.

At early dawn I contrived to slide off my shelf, and effected my ablutions in a bucket on deck, before any of my fellow-passengers had taken themselves down. I found that we had already passed the town of Lockport. Soon after breakfast we came to the junction of the two rivers, the Kaukaki and the La Plaine,[1] which at this point form the Illinois river.

The river La Plaine rises about twenty miles to the northwest of the city of Chicago, shortly before it reaches the town of Lockport: the soil through which it runs becomes rocky, and at an average distance of half a mile from the banks of the stream, which is here an inconsiderable one, on either side, are high bluffs, presenting an unmistakable assurance that at some former period this entire space was the bed or channel of a mighty stream. These high bluffs continue, with scarcely any intermission, all the way to La Salle, increasing, however, in their

---

[1]   The Kankakee and the Des Plaines. Ed.

256

imposing appearance, and slightly in their relative distances from each other. . . .

At about nine, A.M., we reached the small town to which I had previously alluded, called Morris, as being a particularly good spot for "hunting prairie chickens"; and from the general appearance of this settlement, I can readily believe that it abounded in game. Morris is surrounded by fine prairies, with quite enough grain to feed the game. There are few residents who give themselves the trouble to carry a gun; it is easy of access by means of the canal, but too distant from the large cities to make it profitable for the resort of sportsmen who live by the produce of their guns only. Towards the afternoon we arrived at Ottawa; this town is situated in a most beautiful portion of the valley, which is formed by the high bluffs, which are here separated from each other about two miles. The pasturage looked green and pleasant, the town neat and thriving. We remained but a few moments to land some passengers, but this was sufficient for me to recognise the unmistakeable figures of two of my own countrymen, whom I afterwards ascertained were those who were making a brief stay at Ottawa for the purpose of killing prairie grouse, &c. From Ottawa to La Salle is a distance of about twenty miles; rocky islands occasionally present themselves, now surrounded by fertile prairie and corn-fields, which were, no doubt, formerly encircled by the stream. These islands in the plain much resembled some which I had seen in China, within the Yang-tse-kiang river, which, in former days, stood out in the sea, but which by the receding of water had left them islands in the plain, occasionally even one hundred miles distant from the salt water.

At six, P.M., we reached La Salle; here is the termination of the Illinois Canal, and the navigable portion of the Illinois River. We found excellent accommodation at an hotel, scarcely completed, called the Hardy House.

The landlord of this hotel had cleared more than 50,000 dollars in a contract upon the canal, but entering upon all sorts of subsequent speculations, became bankrupt, and in a few weeks all his goods were to be placed in the possession of others. This circumstance, however, is, in the Western States, of too common a nature even to raise a comment.

The Illinois Canal is a fine work, and will eventually do wonders towards the settlement and wealth of this state. The cost of this really great work was more than three millions of dollars; the money being borrowed upon the faith of the state. At first, half of this money was voted towards this undertaking—contracts were given to those who found favour with the government, and the most nefarious peculation of public money is *said* to have resulted; the million and half of dollars being spent, and the work being only half completed, the state, already deeply involved, borrowed another million and a half, principally from British capitalists, and eventually, about three years since, this work was completed, thus connecting the Mississippi with the St. Lawrence, and perfecting the inland navigation from the Atlantic Ocean to the Gulf of Mexico. Since its completion, I was given to understand that it has paid six per cent. upon the second capital, which was borrowed, besides producing a very large amount towards liquidating the principal, and redeeming the state debt. It has every appearance of great prosperity, but I am inclined to think that this account is somewhat exaggerated. It however does not depend entirely upon its tolls, but also upon the sale of a large amount of waste lands in its neighbourhood, which was in the first instance granted by the state to assist in its formation; the moneys accruing from the sale of which have been very considerable, and which are, of course, now immeasurably increased in value, since this large portion of the country has been opened out by means of the canal itself.

This work, however, has had two most opposite effects upon the prosperity of the state of Illinois. By opening out the country it has given it a better chance of developing its agricultural resources. But on the other hand, the state, by entailing upon itself so large a debt, had no resource but to repudiate its debt or increase its taxation. It chose the latter and more honest course, and taxed its citizens proportionally. While therefore the work itself benefited the state, the taxes frightened away emigration towards the less prodigal, but neighbouring state of Iowa, which in consequence has been on the increase, in a ratio far exceeding that of the older state of Illinois. It is contended by some, that had Illinois followed the example of Pennsylvania and Mississippi, and repudiated its obligations for a time, she could have paid interest and compounded interest, and have been more prosperous than at present. I have no doubt that "honesty is the best policy," and that ere long she will reap her reward.

1851

J. P. Thompson

River Travel, Peoria, Jacksonville, and Prairie Farming

Daniel S. Curtiss, author of one of the best guide books of the period, incorporated extensive extracts from letters written by the Reverend J. P. Thompson of New York, who offered firsthand accounts of river travel and the Illinois prairies, and vivid sketches of the fast-growing cities of the state.

The following selections are from Thompson's letters.

A western steamboat is at first sight a novelty to one familiar only with eastern models. The boats on the western waters are very slightly built—mere shells of pine, shallow, long, narrow, flat-bottomed, open and flaring on all sides, just as represented in Banvard's panorama.[1] There is no cabin either below the deck or upon it.

The engines are placed immediately on the lower deck, two huge furnaces flaming upon you as you enter the boat, and giving you rather uncomfortable hints of a choice between fire and water in making your exit from the world.

Huge flaming brands and coals are dropping continually upon the thinnest possible sheeting of sheet-iron, in many places worn through to the plank; heated pipes on which you cannot bear your hand are in immediate contact with boards as dry as tinder, and perhaps already charred; goods, you know not how inflammable, are strown promiscuously around the boilers, while huge piles of dry pine wood, waiting to be consumed, are crowded in the vicinity of the fires. But not every traveler has the habit that I confess to of prying into every thing about him, and therefore few probably enjoy the peculiar sensation of sailing on the rim of a volcano. However, there is nothing like getting used to it, and I learned to sleep quite soundly.

The cabin is up stairs, and extends nearly the whole length of the deck, over which it is perched upon sundry posts that seem too frail for a summer's breeze; this is divided into a long, narrow saloon, from stem to stern, and a row of state-rooms on either hand. An apartment for ladies is curtained off at one extremity, while the main saloon is used for meals, conversation, promenading, card-playing, and whatsoever one may list. The kitchen, pantry, bar, etc., are all contiguous to the saloon; with every convenience for "life above stairs," so that passengers may

Daniel S. Curtiss, *Western Portraiture and Emigrant's Guide: A Description of Wisconsin, Illinois, & Iowa* (New York, 1852), pp. 316–18, 321–26.
[1]   In the 1840's John Banvard painted a three-mile-long panorama of the Mississippi River, which he exhibited throughout the United States and in London. Ed.

spend days in and around this saloon without knowing any thing of the deck life below. Some of the state-rooms that open both into the saloon and upon the guard are very airy and pleasant. If, however, there is any deficiency in regard to neatness and comfort, it is in this department of the boat. We took passage in the *Prairie State*, one of the best boats on the river. The furniture was neat, and the table excellent—always excepting the preponderance of grease in western cookery. But the ideas of civilization exhibited in the state-rooms reminded me of Dr. Bushnell's[2] discourse on Barbarism as the first danger of the West, a sermon that contained some of the truest of his paradoxes. In a cozy chat with the captain, I found him a clever, polite, and attentive gentleman.

The scenery of the Illinois river is rather low and monotonous, but sufficiently picturesque to arrest the eye of a stranger. It savored of the romantic to sail at times through the woods—the water spreading indefinitely among the trees—and in the middle of the stream to bring up at the second story of a house that seemed to say, "For freight or passage apply within."

Peoria is the most beautiful town on the river. Situated on rising ground, a broad plateau extending back from the bluff, it has escaped the almost universal inundation. Indeed, the river here expands into a broad, deep lake, that embosoms the rising flood. This lake is a most beautiful feature in the natural scenery of the town, and is as useful as it is beautiful, supplying the inhabitants with ample stores of fish, and in winter with an abundance of the purest ice. It is often frozen to such a thickness that heavy teams and droves of cattle can pass securely over it. A substantial drawbridge connects the town with the opposite shore. The town is neatly laid out in rectangular blocks, the streets being wide and well graded. A public square has been reserved near the present center. The place wears quite a New England aspect; its schools

[2]   Horace Bushnell, pastor of the North Congregational Church of Hartford, Conn., 1833–59, prolific author and controversial theologian. Ed.

and churches are prosperous, and its society is good. Back of the town extends one of the finest rolling prairies in the State; this region already furnishes to Peoria its supplies and much of its business, which is destined to increase as plankroads and like improvements shall bring the producer nearer to the market. I am struck with the sagacity shown in selecting the sites of many of these Western towns, of which LaSalle and Peoria are examples. May "the children of light" be equally sagacious in choosing their points of action and influence for Christ!

Traveling on these western waters throws one into all sorts of society, and affords a fine opportunity for the study of human nature. I found a number of emigrants, Irish and German, on the deck, occupying sundry extempore bunks, and living on their own bread and cheese.

These emigrants have a hard life of it. Poor fare and exposure to the elements, on the open deck of the boat, often engender disease among them, and break up families before they reach their destined home. There should be an active missionary agency on all the rivers of the West. The deck-hands need such an influence, for they have no Sabbath, and are fearfully addicted to profaneness and intemperance. Their manner of life begets a recklessness of death and of all solemn and sacred things. "A man overboard," no unusual event on boats nowhere guarded by a rail, or a death by cholera, now becoming frequent, make these men callous rather than thoughtful, and render life and death alike cheap in their estimate.

The freedom of the western character, and the independence of the western mind, united with the native love of argumentation in the Anglo-American race, render it easy to engage men in discussion, to while away the listless hours of steamboat traveling. . . .

At first sight of Jacksonville, you wonder how the spot ever came to be chosen for the location of a town. It looks like a village made to order at the East, with neat houses—some wood, some brick—some cottage-shaped, and others more ambitious, with gardens filled with flowers and shrubbery, with wide and cleanly streets adorned with shade trees, with a pleasant public square inclosed with a plain white fence, and graced (except that the rickety building has no grace about it) with the courthouse and public offices, with schools and academies, with churches, and a college, all clustering about the village center, while well-tilled farms stretch along the borders on every side—it looks, I say, like a model New England village made to order, with such improvements as old villages that have grown up gradually do not admit of, and transported hither by some magic machinery and set down in the midst of the prairie, for picturesque effect, or as a wholesale speculation in city lots.

Now that the village is there, you see that it is pretty, and seemly, and convenient; that there was need of it, and that it is likely to prosper, in a moderate way, as a place of business; and when you have heard the forementioned tradition, you understand how there happens to be a village in this precise meridian at all; but when you inquire farther for the propriety of the location, you see no river, no hills, no forests, no streams, nothing in short that should have led to the selection of this particular section of the vast prairie as the site of a town, rather than any other within twenty miles of it. A more careful study, however, of the features of the country shows that it was a lucky accident that hit upon this location; for while there is nothing in or about Jacksonville that can aspire to the name of a hill, the adjacent country is rolling and exhibits sundry mounds, not Indian, but natural, that swell in some instances to the height of forty or fifty feet! While there are no forests, there are sundry beautiful groves, that vary the scenery and also furnish a partial supply of lumber; and, in the absence of a mill-stream, the low, sluggish, muddy, ever devious Movestar, winds itself all about the town. This name, by the way, is a corruption of the French *Mauvaise Terre* (bad country), which for some unknown reason was given to the creek by French explorers at its mouth, where it empties into the Illinois.

But never was there a more decided misnomer. Bad land, forsooth! Let the New England farmer who has spent half his life in gathering the stones and grubbing the stumps out of a five acre lot, and the other half in trying to make lean, jaundiced corn grow in the two inches of soil, come out and look upon these cornfields of hundreds of acres, where the rich black loam is turned up by the plow to the depth of two feet, where is never seen a stick or a stone, where the hoe is never used, but weeds are plowed up by driving the team between the rows, and where, as the season advances, one may ride on horseback through acres of corn without once seeing over the tops of the gigantic stalks, and where in harvest time the wondrous cutting-machine, drawn by horses, like the old scythe-armed chariot of Roman warfare, as it forces its mighty swath through the toppling grain, mocks at the puny efforts of the sickle, and the hot and weary day's work of a man.

To one who has not looked upon these immense fields, waving for the harvest, it is impossible to convey any adequate idea of the richness of the *cereal* products of this region. Here may be realized the statement of the vast wealth of Job in lands, and corn, and stock. In the immediate vicinity of Jacksonville is one farm containing *seven thousand* acres, under cultivation, with thousands of sheep and oxen, and ten thousands of *ephahs* [3] of corn. The proprietor finds it no easy matter to ride over his vast domain, and to superintend the management of its every part.

A prairie farm is always conducted on a magnificent scale. The fences, if there are any, do not cut it up in little acre patches, but divide it into stately squares ranging from forty-acre lots to half a "section." This I found to the sorrow of my aching feet upon going one day to see some buffaloes kept for improving stock. I was told that I would find them "just down at the lower end of the field," in reaching which I had to walk full half a mile or more. The sight of such a farm on a rolling prairie, partly in grass, partly in corn, partly in grain and garden vegetables, as the sun chases over it the cloudy shadows, and the light breeze

---

[3]   A Hebrew dry measure. Ed.

waves the distant grove, to a lover of the beautiful is perfectly enchanting.

But it is not in cereals alone that these prairies are productive. Fruits come to great perfection in this soil and climate. Peaches are very abundant, and the choicest varieties of apples may be introduced by grafting. It is so easy, however, to raise the one great staple, corn, that orchards have been comparatively neglected; indeed they have hardly had time to come to perfection. I had no thought of detracting from the merits of "this country"—to use the current western phrase—when I spoke dubiously of my prospects for the strawberry season, in taking leave of the Erie Railroad. But on the very morning of my arrival I was regaled with finely flavored strawberries swimming in luscious cream; and I found this delicious fruit to be everywhere a common article of the table. It is a gross idea of some Eastern people that the inhabitants of the West live entirely upon pork and corn, in some parts of the West the living is coarse enough; but in such villages as I am describing, the family table is spread with all the comforts and delicacies of the East—excepting of course seafood, which can be had only in pickle or in jars hermetically sealed.

And then the living is *cheap*, even in the choicer articles of food. Think of fine, fat, spring chickens for $1 to $1.50 per *dozen*; of quails (partridges) and pigeons in abundance; of eggs at three or four cents a *dozen*; of beef at six or eight cents a pound; of a turkey weighing nineteen pounds for *fifty cents*; and of flour at $3 or $4 a barrel. A man can live like a prince in Jacksonville for what would barely suffice to pay his house-rent in New York.

And yet how many mechanics and clerks are eking out a scanty subsistence in New York upon a precarious income of from $500 to $1,500, when for the first named sum they might live comfortably in such a western village, and possibly lay up money besides. Many, especially mechanics, could find ready employment in such places at good wages. If, however, *too* many should crowd at once into the same place, competition would ensue, and with it would come many of the evils of city life.

Indeed I almost hesitate to let out the secret of this western paradise, and I surely dread to have its Arcadian repose disturbed by the puffing of the locomotive with an express train from New York.

The great railroads will essentially modify the main features of western life; will equalize prices by finding a market for produce, and by bringing in more abundantly goods from abroad; will introduce more of the city element into business, and will make adventurers and speculators still more abundant. In due time these prairies will be attached to the suburbs of New York; the great West will be but a day's ride into the country; and its inhabitants will be sending to New York for their flour and garden sauce.

The churches contribute to all objects of Christian benevolence. There are also in the village several societies—some formed exclusively of ladies—for aiding the cause of missions and the cause of education. From this source relief is afforded to indigent students in the college, and female teachers are educated for the common schools of the State; the daughters of ministers and of farmers, accustomed to hard fare and hard work, and familiar with western society, are thus qualified for the office of instruction, and these in general prove to be more efficient and adaptive teachers than those sent from the East. The money expended upon Jacksonville is already yielding a good return. Here the Portuguese exiles have found a home, with a congenial climate, warm Christian sympathy, and steady employment and support.[4] They are mostly doing well; and with a little Yankee thrift and tidiness might do far better.

The Charitable Institutions of the State are located at this point. Asylums for the *Deaf and Dumb*, and *Insane*, and the *Blind*, occupy relatively three sides of a quadrangle around the village, each about a mile from its center. The first of these has about one hundred inmates, and is under excellent regulation.

---

[4]   A colony of Portuguese Protestants from the island of Madeira settled in Jacksonville, by invitation, in 1849. Ed.

The institution is sustained wholly by State-tax. Its inmates appeared cheerful and bright, as the deaf and dumb always do. In general they are quick learners, and enjoy the acquisition of knowledge. While I stood by and witnessed their devotions at morning prayer in the chapel, I was so struck with the expressiveness of signs or symbols for religious uses, that I almost became upon the spot a convert to Dr. Bushnell's theory of language. It was affecting to hear the unintelligent, mechanical utterance of sounds by some who had once used the organs of speech, but who, with the loss of hearing, had ceased also to speak. The Asylum of the Insane is not yet in operation. The noble building, like that for the deaf and dumb, occupies a little rise of ground, and is visible at a great distance. From the cupola of either you have an extensive prospect of the prairie sea, diversified with island groves. The institution for the Blind is in successful operation, but the building designed for it not yet completed.

The Methodists have erected at Jacksonville a large Female Seminary, a product of their centenary fund. There is also another Female Academy in the place, of a high order, and of long standing, under the auspices of Congregationalists and Presbyterians.[5] In addition to this, there is a sort of Free Academy, and a good supply of schools of every grade. But to me the chief object of interest, both historically and prospectively, was *Illinois College*.[6] For years I had been familiar with the toils and struggles of the men engaged in founding and rearing that institution, and it was with no common emotion that I looked upon the work of their hands. The site selected for the college is the most beautiful in all the region, and perhaps is not equalled in the State. Upon a rise of ground, skirted with a luxuriant grove, far away from the miasma rivers, the bustle of commerce, and the wrangle of

[5]   Illinois Female College, founded in 1846, became MacMurray College
       in 1930. It is now coeducational. The Jacksonville Female Academy
       (Congregational-Presbytarian), opened in 1833, was absorbed by
       Illinois College in 1903. Ed.
[6]   See Stuart, "Jacksonville and Springfield," footnote 1, above. Ed.

politics, is this seat of learning and religion, which was itself modeled in the main after Yale College.

I was more disturbed than disappointed at finding the college buildings so unsightly and so illy adapted to the present wants of the institution. The main building, which is the primitive chapel pieced out, is so low in the stories and so cramped in all its dimensions, that one has to stoop in order to enter it or to get up the steep and narrow stairway; the recitation rooms are poorly finished, and the whole structure looks old and crazy. It was built with poor brick and in dear times. The *people of Jacksonville* should replace it by one more worthy of their present prosperity; they should not suffer such an eye-sore to mar the most lovely spot in their town. Let them send a committee to Beloit to see the building that the citizens of that infant place have erected for *their* College, and then go to work at once with a subscription paper for their own.

The College is now well manned both in the number and the quality of its instructors. There is need, however, of a Professor of Rhetoric, to impart a polish and finish to the strong, rough materials of the western mind.

To pass from the intellectual to the physical, I saw at Jacksonville a striking connection between these two, in the *hedge* recently introduced by Mr. Turner, formerly Professor in the College. It would puzzle the 'cutest Yankee to guess out the connection between hedges and common schools; but here they must rise or fall together. Years ago, Professor T. attempted to introduce into Illinois the New England system of Common Schools. But he soon found that the farmers, who had located their farms along the borders of the prairies, near the timber, in order to build their fences with ease, were too widely scattered to be formed into school districts after the New England fashion. Before this could be done, some method must be devised of *fencing the prairies*, so that settlements could be made in the centers. Mr. T. experimented with various shrubs for hedging, but without success, until he made trial of the *Osage orange*; this grows rapidly, endures the winter, and is covered with thorns. It has become universally popular, and already stretches across the prairies for hundreds of miles. Now it is practicable to plant a village in the very heart of a prairie, with farms stretching outward to its borders; and in these compact settlements schools and churches can be sustained.[7] So much for the union of natural and moral husbandry. *Apropos* of shrubbery, I may mention that every shade tree in Jacksonville, of which there are hundreds, was set out within the memory of inhabitants not yet gray.

I have now said enough of Jacksonville for one letter, and yet the half is not yet told. But I must hasten on to the Mississippi.

In conclusion I will give only one additional evidence of progress in this region. Fifteen years ago, about the time of the *Alton riot*,[8] the College commencements were held under the restraint of a mob, upon the watch lest any allusion should be made to Liberty. Now, a graduate of Illinois College, an intelligent lawyer residing in Jacksonville, has just been elected to Congress as a known free-soiler.[9]

[7]   Jonathan Baldwin Turner was also a leader in the movement for federal land grants to support colleges of agriculture and mechanical arts, a movement that culminated in the Morrill Act of 1862. Ed.
[8]   In 1837 Elijah P. Lovejoy, Alton abolitionist editor, was killed by a pro-slavery mob. Ed.
[9]   Richard Yates, later Civil War governor of Illinois. Ed.

1852

Elizabeth F. L. Ellet

By Rail and Stage
to Galena

Elizabeth Fries Lummis was born in 1818 at Sodus Point, New York, the daughter of a prominent physician who was also a wealthy landowner. She was educated at the Female Seminary at Aurora, New York. In girlhood she developed a passion for writing, and published her first book when she was sixteen. In 1835 she married William H. Ellet, professor of chemistry at Columbia College, and soon moved with him to Charleston, where he taught at South Carolina College until 1849, when they returned to New York.

Meanwhile, Mrs. Ellet had turned out a succession of books on American history and foreign history and literature. In 1852 she made a tour of the West, traveling extensively in northern and central Illinois. Her account of a trip by rail and stage from Chicago to Galena exhibits the qualities—sharp observation and inclusion of vivid detail—that made her a popular writer.

The evening passed in a charming circle of visitors, and after an early breakfast on the 23d, we bade farewell to our kind friends and drove to the cars of the "Galena and Chicago Union Railroad," which started at half past seven. Happy may the traveller conclude himself when the completion of the road may enable him to have the prospect, even with slow travel, of reaching Galena the same evening. A new route will then be opened to the tourist from the Eastern States, which will bring throngs of summer travellers. It will then be fashionable to visit the Falls of St. Anthony, and to rave about the beauty of the Upper Mississippi, from which those are now cut off who do not care to go down the Ohio and ascend the Great River, and whose love of scenery is not strong enough to induce them to brave eighty or ninety miles of staging over a perilous and fatiguing road. Never was a railroad more needed, nor one which promised a surer or more continual product for the capital invested in its construction; so essential a link will it be in the great chain stretching from the Mississippi to the Hudson.

The first prairies on which you enter are perfectly level—a treeless, shrubless expanse, with groves like islands in the distance, and a line of woods on the verge; the space between much cut up by cultivated fields and farm-houses with flourishing gardens. Fine oak openings are seen at intervals every where. The grass, even on the prairies which had not been grazed over or mown, was little more than a foot high, and profusely sprinkled with pale yellow and flame-colored, or blue and pink flowers. Now and then the prairie squirrel or gopher leaps across the path. The shortness of the grass, owing in some measure to the late drought, much disappointed us in the first views of these "gardens of the desert," especially after ascending to a somewhat higher level, when we came into the region of the rolling prairies. Cultivation, too, has sadly marred the effect of these; one can scarcely conceive how much the sight of a distant corn patch, or

Elizabeth F. L. Ellet, *Summer Rambles in the West* (New York, 1853), pp. 36–46.

field of wheat, or even a fence, or inclosure round a dwelling, takes away from the aspect of romantic wildness usually associated with the idea of a prairie of the West. Its vernal aspect, when the gold and crimson flowers contrast with the tender green, must be such as to inspire what Margaret Fuller[1] called a "fairy land exultation," and there is moreover something in the feeling she describes, that she might continue a walk with any seven-leagued mode of conveyance, hundreds of miles without an obstacle. There is, too, a peculiar beauty in the sunset and moonlight, of the same kind with their loveliness at sea, and the clustering island groves are sheltering nooks for delicate romance; nevertheless, the idea expanded by the poetic dream is not filled by the reality. Who does not associate with the thought of a prairie the swaying of the wind, so that its fleet course may be traced by the bending of the reedy grass, or the tossing of the golden flowers, or the slow moving clouds, which

> "Sweep over with their shadows, and beneath
> The surface rolls and fluctuates to the eye:
> Dark hollows seem to glide along, and chase
> The sunny ridges—"?

Yet on the upland prairies this is rarely or never seen. The motion of tall grass would give to these plains much of the sublimity and magnificence of ocean, which now they resemble only in the grandeur of their vast extent, and the undulating outline defined against the far-off sky like the billowy swelling of the sea. The burning of the grass, which is done every year, presents a splendid spectacle, though less stupendous than the perilous and poetical conflagrations described by glowing pens. Several blackened patches showed where the dry grass had been recently burned.

At Prairie State Mills, about forty miles from Chicago, we came upon the Fox River, a low but graceful stream flowing through a pretty valley on the left, in which herds of cattle were grazing. This river follows us to Elgin, a flourishing business

[1]   See Fuller, "The Fox River Valley . . .," above. Ed.

273

place, and disappears after many picturesque windings. Then comes the Heohwaukee[2] and other smaller streams, and after passing a village or two, the train stopped at Cherry Valley, where the railway then terminated. Our progress had been slow, but we endeavoured to console ourselves by observing the scenery. Miss C. counted eighty different species of plants in flower, which she duly noted in her journal, besides a number of sedges and grasses.

At Cherry Valley private vehicles and coaches were in readiness to convey travellers to their destination; those bound to Galena were consigned to the latter, and were soon jolting over roads, respecting which they were assured every few miles that they were "just passing over the worst." It will be a joyful era in civilization when those heavy, lumbering, leathery horrors are banished from the traveller's knowledge! Since our pilgrimage over the mountains of Virginia and the dusty highways of Tennessee, I had not seen one, and the aspect of four drawn up in file, to be filled by the victims ejected from the cars, was appalling enough, without the addition of a surly, dirty-looking Jehu on the driver's seat of each, whose grim visage and profane tongue checked on the instant the half-formed wish to occupy a seat on the outside. Into one of these purgatories we perforce climbed, and two of us, sighing, took our places on the back seat. It was soon crowded with rather a rough population; but who can blame petulance, under circumstances disagreeable enough to neutralize all the genial effects of Western atmosphere and custom! One woman with a child, who entered last, found a place on the front seat, and complained of her lot; whereat a tall, raw-boned amazon in a white sun-bonnet, who took up the largest third of the middle seat, with a grin meant to be gracious, desired me to change and go to the front. My declining to accommodate the new comer on the plea that I feared being made sick, drew down her indignation and that of the woman's husband and a pert little girl of about thirteen, who echoed whatever the others said,

[2]   The Kishwaukee River. Ed.

enforcing their axioms occasionally by a poke of her needle-like elbow into the sides of whoever she chanced to be near—the while changing her seat every three minutes. "I'm thankful *I* am not disobleeging!—You can have *my* seat any time." (She took care never to suit the action to the word.) "*I* am not fearful of sea-sickness."—"It's cur'ous how timid some folks is!" &c., keeping up a perpetual stream of talk, and mingling the most searching inquiries into the domestic affairs of her neighbors with a voluble autobiography and the private annals of sundry families of her acquaintance, in a manner that would have been ludicrous, had not the sharp and incessant din of her tongue been like daggers in our ears. She speered several questions at me, which were answered with repulsive monosyllables, and then she launched into remarks she meant to be applied, concerning the pride of "some folk, who thought themselves better than some other folk." It was a sensible mitigation of the nuisance, however, to learn that she was going no farther than Freeport.

Rockford, seven miles from Cherry Valley, is beautifully situated on Rock River, a noble stream which flows through the most picturesque part of Illinois. Miss Fuller speaks of it as flowing "sometimes through parks and lawns, then between high bluffs whose grassy ridges are covered with fine trees, or broken with crumbling stone that easily assumes the form of buttress, arch, and clustered columns. Along the face of such crumbling rocks swallows' nests are thick as cities, and eagles and deer do not disdain their summits."[3] Bryant[4] observes that the shores of this river unite the beauties of the Hudson and the Connecticut. Its course is through upland prairie, yet its banks are often bold, and sometimes perpendicular precipices or steep bluffs, rock-turreted, or covered with woods on the low lands. The prairies extend back off the bluffs, from the face of which clear springs gush out, and send their tribute to the river.

A stoppage was made here of an hour for dinner, fifty minutes

3   See Fuller, above. Ed.
4   William Cullen Bryant. Ed.

of which were consumed in the preparation of the meal, leaving the passengers ten in which to eat it and secure their places in the crowded stages. Now came our fit again, and truly it seemed as if all things, including the roads and weather, had conspired to make this journey memorable in the record of the petty miseries of human life. The extreme heat was rendered more oppressive by a slight dampness in the air, and the road exhibited the phenomena of dangerous mud-holes combined with a stifling atmosphere of dust. Into these plunged ever and anon the cumbrous, shackling vehicle, and came out with a violent jerk, to the utter discomfort of the tumbling and grumbling passengers, above whose muttered plaints rose a shrill trio from the woman, whose name the amazon proclaimed to be Mrs. Johnson—her husband, and the hopeful girl, with loud exclamations from the strapping regulator of the movements and sessions of the coachful, who treated our hapless mother tongue with great cruelty. It was an omen of relief, at least from the overpowering heat, when the driver was seen to alight and encase himself in an India-rubber overcoat; and in about an hour the long desired shower came upon us. We had groaned at the dust, but alas, found the rain harder to endure; for it stayed with us, and without cooling the air, added both to the discomforts and dangers of the way. At Freeport a miserable supper was offered, with the like delay in preparing and hurry in dispatching; and then a night's travel was commenced, the like of which one may hope never to encounter again.

Our tormentor in the white sun-bonnet had disappeared— but her influence lingered; she had given whispered instructions, overheard by those interested, to the woman with the infant to go without her tea for the purpose of securing the back seat, and her husband took his place beside her, manfully resolved to do battle for the moiety of comfort it promised. M. quietly yielded to his intrusion on her rights, and edged herself into a corner on the front seat; the only place left was a segment of the back one, which must be filled, for there were nine inside, but which Mr. Johnson was sternly determined should *not* be occupied. The interference of the driver had to be invoked, and as the only alternative was for one of us to get out of the stage, the surly passenger was compelled to give up the point, and suffer the intrusion on the premises he claimed of one of the ladies he had dislodged. I mention this incident as a rare exception to the prevailing custom thoughout the United States; at the West especially I have often seen men reliquish their seats to female passengers, but never before saw one turned out of her seat by a man. No selfish preparations, however, could procure an hour of balmy repose. The rain, which was still falling soft and warm, had reduced the prairie roads to their worst summer condition, and a long line of black mud, checkered by holes at one side or another, and now and then a tumble-down bridge, could be seen by the light of the lamps. But let no one imagine that the mere view can give the least idea of a prairie "slough," or mud-hole! You may see one deceitfully covered with green turf, and suspect no danger till your horses' feet, or one of your wheels, shall be sunk so far as to render recovery impossible without the aid of stakes and ropes brought to the rescue. The story of the pedestrian's cap moving just above the black ooze, while the rider and horse were below, appears no fable. Then the mud—it is of a peculiar quality, coal-black, and tenacious as tar. After our coach had plunged and slipped along an hour or two, lurching almost to an overturn first on one side, then on another, the voice of the driver calling for a light—for he "could not see an inch, and never drove over this road before"—did not tend to reassure those disposed to think of accidents, particularly as the information was added, that a night seldom passed without some stage being overset. The pockets of cigar-smokers were searched for matches, but vain was the attempt to light the lamp, till the last match had been used. Presently the driver in front roared out to "take care of the bridge" which his wheels had just demolished; a caution withheld till ours were in the act of going over it, bringing the stage down with a swing from which it seemed impossible to recover it. Next our driver called in great alarm for help: one of the horses had slipped, and lay sprawling in the mud. A succession of such agreeable incidents during the whole night, kept before our minds the probability of having limbs broken, or of spending the rest of the hours of darkness on the lone, waste prairie, miles from any human habitation, with the wet grass for a couch. These not very exhilarating circumstances were rendered intolerable by the most shocking profanity on the part of the drivers. Ours kept up a soliloquy of oaths, and when an accident or a stoppage brought him into the fellowship of his companions, the concert of blasphemies was absolutely terrifying. Such conduct should never have been permitted by the directors of the road.

The summer of 1853 will probably put an end to similar experiences by finishing the railroad. We took the whole night to accomplish twenty-eight miles, and were glad to escape without any serious accident, though a score of times had we been forced to descend from the coach and wallow through the mud with our thin-soled gaiters coated thickly to the instep, the rain penetrating the destructible part of bonnets, and saturating crape shawls. On arriving at the customary breakfast-house, none of the woe-begone passengers seemed disposed to stop; and as there were no signs of preparation, none of the inmates being up, the driver consented to go on fourteen miles to the next halting place. The prairies passed over at this stage were the finest and wildest we had yet seen; boundless in extent save by the bending horizon, and rolling in majestic undulations. Not a tree or shrub could be seen for miles. Within fourteen miles of Galena that aspect of the country began to change; instead of sweeping prairies a ridge of elevated land presented itself, the summit of which commanded an extensive view of a beautiful and varied landscape, patches of woods, sloping fields, meadows, orchards, etc., all giving evidence of a rich soil and high cultivation. The broken country became bolder, and abrupt conical hills began to rise in front, to be scaled by stony and irregular roads matched nowhere except within seven miles of the Mammoth Cave, in Kentucky. More elevated ranges appeared in the distance. Here and there we came upon "mineral openings," through which descent is made by a windlass to the lead mines for which this region has long been so famous. The workmen were busily occupied around the openings, and wagons loaded with the smelted lead and rough ore were continually passing. Rugged heights of limestone rock, in castellated form, their crevices and summits covered with tangled vines, bushes and trees, rose before us, and after scaling and descending several steep hills, we entered Galena about noon.

1854

Frithjof Meidell

Society in Springfield

A young Norwegian immigrant, writing to his family in the old country, offered humorous comments on American women as he observed them in Springfield. The author, Frithjof Meidell, son of an army officer and educated in Norway and Scotland, tried many jobs in the United States: carpenter's apprentice in Saint Louis, clerk in Iowa, railroad hand and laborer in a lumber yard. The year 1854 found him clerking in a grocery store in the Illinois capital.

Yesterday was Sunday. I went to church in the morning. I had decided to use the afternoon for letter writing and already had pen in hand when the sun came out so beautifully and invitingly that I could not stay inside any longer. So I went for a walk out on the prairie to enjoy the grass. I believe I told you once before that Springfield is situated on a large prairie which borders on woodland. It was beautiful out there. It had rained the night before, and the grass looked so fresh and green that I almost felt like tasting it. But there were no flowers except white clover. The Americans say that nothing can be compared to their flower-covered prairies in June, but I have not seen the flowers yet. It is strange that virtually no flowers here have any scent, even jasmine and lilac give off only a very faint scent. But there is a tree here which they call "locust." Its leaves look like those of the laburnum, and the flowers are white and toward evening give off a wonderful odor. The roses are almost without fragrance, and I have not even seen reseda.

I walked far, far out into the vast grassy plain without meeting a single human being—people were probably in church. The only creatures I met were a botanizing cow or pig. People here are too lazy to care for walking. When they cannot make money on a thing, it does not interest them.

Just now I was interrupted as a man came in and bought a codfish, and as these have a rather homely smell you may well understand that it dissipated the rest of my prairie fantasy. You asked me how the ladies look here. As everywhere, they are very much like angels. But they dress in bad taste, since all they are interested in is to have very expensive-looking clothes. Besides they are unforgivably lazy, truly pampered creatures. All day they sit quietly in a rocking chair and rock themselves, and then they sew a little once in a while by way of change.

Theodore C. Blegen, ed., *Land of Their Choice: The Immigrants Write Home* (Minneapolis, 1955), pp. 304–7. Reprinted by permission of the University of Minnesota Press.

In my opinion they are the rudest persons I have ever met among civilized people, but of course they may very well look like "angels" in spite of that. If you do them a little favor they very seldom thank you for it but treat you as if you had only done your duty and there was no need for them to think of theirs. At present the latest fashion among the ladies is to be ill. One has a pain in her back, another a pain in her side, and a third one has it in her head, but I believe that the most fashionable seat of illness is the chest.

God knows if this ailing condition is not something they have hit upon to ease their bad conscience concerning the unspeakable amount of paint they use to freshen up, with a make-up of rosy red, the color of their skin which may otherwise look a little bit too much like a buttercup yellow. Probably as a result of this extensive use, the paint is very expensive here, especially if it is to be the genuine article. Those who want to be in the competition but cannot afford to get the genuine, unadultered "milk and blood" color, therefore have to content themselves with a substitute, which unfortunately will not stick to the cheek. So when they get warm the whole "daub" runs off, which makes them look as if they were crying bloody tears over their own and the world's vanity. Still further down in society the women cannot even afford to buy the adulterated paint, so here they have to try the most desperate means, for red they must be. What do you think they do? I have not happened to see it, but it is generally said that they pinch their own cheeks, and if they can get away in private where no one sees or hears them—something that is not so very easy in America—rumor has it that they do not hestitate to box themselves on the ears, and by so doing produce the most natural blooming complexion you can imagine. These boxes on the ears are the most well deserved I have yet heard about. But despite these attempts to aid nature, there can be no doubt that the American ladies really do look like angels, and perhaps the similarity is increased by the daub, since for so many years of grace we have seen nothing but painted angels.

You ought to see our Norwegian peasant girls and servant girls here. You would not be able to recognize them or ever think that these lovely creatures had been transplanted from the rocky ground of Norway to this tropical soil. Big-heeled, round-shouldered, plump, good-natured cooks who at home waddled about in all their primitiveness in front of the kitchen fire between brooms and garbage cans here trip about with a peculiar, affected twisting of parasols and fans and with their pretty heads completely covered by veils. Aase, Birthe, and Siri at an incredible speed become changed to Aline, Betsy, and Sarah, and these ladies like to have a little "Miss" in front of their names. Their English is just as incomprehensible as the language of the native Indians.

1857

Gustaf Unonius

Chicago

Gustaf Unonius was born of Swedish parents in Helsingfors, Finland, in 1810. Since Finland was about to come under the domination of Russia, the family moved to Sweden, where Gustaf was educated at Uppsala University. After completing his course he studied law and became a government clerk at Uppsala, a position he held until 1841 when, newly married, he emigrated to the United States with his wife. The couple settled in Wisconsin Territory, where Unonius lived the life of a frontier settler before he decided to enter the Episcopal ministry. After seventeen years in the United States he returned to Sweden, where he lived for the rest of his life. His memoirs, published at Uppsala in 1861 and 1862, were not translated and published in the United States for almost a century.

In the following excerpt Unonius contrasted Chicago in 1857 with the city he had first seen a dozen years earlier.

I remained two weeks in Chicago, the Garden City, as it was called, but at that time anything but a garden. Though most of the houses had a pavilion-like appearance there was nothing beyond that appearance to give them the character of inviting garden pavilions. The surroundings also harmonized with the general character of the city—with few exceptions resembling a trash can more than anything else; the entire area on which that "wonder of the western world" was to grow up might best be likened to a vast mud puddle. The principal site of the city is low and swampy, almost at the same level as Lake Michigan, and most of the buildings were at that time erected close to the lakeshore or on the miry, alluvial soil which time and again was flooded by the river flowing right through the city. Certain other parts consisted of waste expanses of sand without a blade of grass, and from them a floury dust was carried in blinding clouds over the clayey streets, sifting into the houses, making them as dusty inside as the outdoors was muddy and unpleasant. During the rainy season, and sometimes far into the summer, the streets were almost impassable for driving as well as for walking. To be sure they were supplied with board sidewalks, but crossing from one side of the street to the other entailed decided difficulties. I recall how during my first year in Chicago I saw, again and again, elegantly dressed women standing on streetcorners waiting for some dray on which they might ride across the street. But even for vehicles, the streets were sometimes impassable. Horses and wagons sometimes sank down in the clayey mud and had to be pulled out with great labor and difficulty.

This will give the reader an idea of what Chicago was like at that time, when it was estimated that its population was something like 20,000. Twelve years have passed, and what a change in its appearance as well as in its population, which is now 120,000!

Gustaf Unonius, *A Pioneer in Northwest America, 1841–1858: The Memoirs of Gustaf Unonius*, Trans. Jonas Oscar Backlund, Ed. Nils William Olsson (Minneapolis, 1950, 1960), **2**: 174–88. Reprinted by permission of the Swedish Pioneer Historical Society.

GUSTAF UNONIUS

The formerly low, swampy streets have been raised several feet and paved with planks or stone. The river has been dredged and widened; its shores have been supported with piles, evened off, raised well above the water level, and are now occupied by loading piers or used as foundations for gigantic warehouses or factories. The older buildings, most of which had been erected in such a hurry that they would soon have tumbled down anyway, have either been burnt to ashes in the fires that frequently broke out (and which greatly assisted in the improvement of the city) or have been torn down to make way for new buildings of brick, stone, iron, and even marble, on far better foundations. It is now a city in which private and public buildings have been erected that compare favorably both in size and style with the most splendid structures in the capitals of Europe. In a single summer, in 1855, 2,700 new houses were built, many of which would be a source of pride to any city. The following year an even greater number were erected, which, inclusive of churches, railroad stations, and other public buildings, were said to have entailed expenditures of more than four million dollars. Some of the older wooden buildings which had been built in what is now the better part of the city have been moved on sled-like runners to outlying districts where new streets are constantly being laid out; eventually they will be moved even farther away to make room for modern and more beautiful buildings.

Some of the houses thus moved from one place to another are not so small as one might imagine. I have seen even three-story buildings travel down the street. The contrivance by which this is done is really quite simple. A capstan is used, seldom drawn by more than one horse, around which a chain is wrapped and fastened to the rollers placed underneath the building after the foundation has been removed. The capstan is moved from place to place according to the length of the chain, and while the chain is rolled up on it the house is pulled forward; a few men are kept busy moving the planks and rollers under the runners, and the house is pulled evenly and steadily to its new site. When they are to make a turn the capstan is moved to the side, the chains are fastened to the corner of the building, which is carefully turned and faced in a new direction. This kind of work has become almost a new trade in the growing cities, and housemovers are seldom idle or in want of a good income.

Until one has become accustomed to this kind of transportation, it seems rather strange. Often the entire width of the street is blocked by a house that is out for a walk and extends from one side of the street to the other, but neither drivers nor pedestrians complain because they are compelled to make a small detour. Anyway, it does not take long before the street is clear again. Moving the house does not necessarily mean that those living in it must move out. I have seen houses on the move while the families living in them continued with their daily tasks, keeping fire in the stove, eating their meals as usual, and at night quietly going to bed to wake up the next morning on some other street. Once a house passed my window while a tavern business housed in it went on as usual. Even churches have been transported in this fashion, but as far as I know, never with services going on.

The ease with which this house moving is carried on is great, but I doubt that it can be done so imperceptibly as it is described by Oscar Comettant,[1] who relates that in New York vacant houses have been stolen during the night and afterward advertised for in the public press. That is probably one of the numerous fictions with which that author seeks in his easy, entertaining style rather to characterize America than to make his readers believe that his stories are literally true.

When the streets are filled in and raised several feet, the sidewalks as well as the first floors of the houses are much lower than the street level, whence, instead of having steps up to the door, they have to build steps leading down to the entry. Of course this causes much inconvenience where the houses are not so constructed that they can be sold and carted away to make room for other buildings erected with due regard to the change in the

---

[1]   Jean Pierre Oscar Comettant, a French pianist, composer, and music critic who, in 1857, published *Trois ans aux Etats-Unis*. Ed.

grade. The first floors could not be converted into basement floors without heavy expense to the owners, since they are largely made up of well-equipped offices and stores, and what was formerly a second story is too high above the street to be made into a first floor. To have the houses lowered below the street in that fashion is of course far from pleasant, but an American finds a solution for every problem. The streets absolutely had to be raised and graded; hence many decided also to raise their houses and bring them to a level with the new streets. This of course, was accompanied by greater difficulties than house-moving, but still it was done, even with large stone buildings.

The first experiment of this kind was successfully made with a four-story brick house, seventy feet long and forty wide, its weight calculated to be seven hundred fifty tons. They dug underneath the house, and under all the walls they placed heavy timbers resting on two hundred fifty strong iron jacks placed at equal distances from each other. For that work they employed fifty men who at a signal turned the jacks equally at every point until the house was raised not less than six feet two inches above its original foundation. In the meantime they kept constructing new supporting pillars, so that when the timbers and jacks were removed the entire new foundation was completed. Thus the house regained its original appearance, except that it now had an excellent basement which on its former low level it did not have. The entire cost of the raising project was $2,700. While it was going on, business was carried on as usual in the house, and one could not notice that the building was being raised. The trading in the store on the first floor was not interrupted; in fact, it was even brisker than usual because a process which later was to become a rather common occurrence at that time was still new and attracted a great many curious onlookers.

Thus Chicago has undergone a complete transformation. Located on an almost completely level prairie upon which it extends itself farther year by year, lying as it does on the shore of a boundless inland sea, having extensive parks, magnificent buildings and attractive villas surrounded by beautiful flower parterres, orchards, and terraces, it now really deserves the name it has adopted, the Garden City. It is now displaying, perhaps in a greater degree than any other city in the Union, one of the most indisputable proofs of the industrial advance and the virile power which, while it is evidenced in the smaller communities, has lifted, and will continue to lift, the great, robust nation to a position as one of the most powerful dominions in the world. Did we not know it to be an indisputable fact, one might well believe that the description of Chicago, its discouraging beginning, the changes that have taken place in the course of a few years, its incredible growth—ten thousand added to its population in a single year—and the position it occupied today in the business life of America, had been culled from an Arabian Nights tale.

There are persons still living in the city from the time when the first log cabin was erected by the side of the red man's wigwam. When I moved to the city its oldest native-born inhabitant was a rosy-cheeked girl of seventeen. But the oldest inhabitant, reckoned from the time the first white families settled here, is John H. Kinzie, Esq., still in the best years of his manhood, one of the principal and highly honored citizens of Chicago. When the government in 1804 built a small fort at the mouth of the Chicago River, with a garrison of fifty men as a frontier guard against the Indians, Mr. Kinzie's father settled opposite the fort, on the other side of the river, and there built the first dwellinghouse. He also established a trading post among the wild tribes that were roaming the land which they had recently ceded to the United States but which, with the exception of these Indians, was almost completely uninhabited. The son, who at that time was only a few months old, is now occupying a sturdy house on the spot where the original cottage was. As a young man he secured appointment to an office in the service of the government, but after a few years he returned to his hometown, which was then hardly any more advanced than when he left it. There he settled with his talented young wife who has, since then, published a well-written and entertaining story of the early settlements and of the bloody scenes which they were later to witness during the war with England.[2] The Indians, who gained possession of the fort, cruelly and treacherously murdered the greater part of the garrison and the women and children of the settlers, and carried several of them into capitivity, among them a young girl belonging to Mr. Kinzie's own family.[3] Again and again, in that cultured and respectable family, who from our first arrival in Chicago showed us much friendship and kindness, I have listened to their description of the childhood of that remarkable city which they had seen grow up. Kinzie was at first the owner of most of the ground on which Chicago is now built. Had he been able to foresee its future importance, and had he realized that in a few years every foot of the sandhills where he had played as a child would be sold at a price for which he could have purchased an entire section, he would probably not have practically given away tracts that, had he retained them, would have made him one of the richest men in America. He told me, for instance, that he had once traded off for the colt of an Indian pony a few muddy acres which would now be worth over $100,000, not counting the buildings erected on them, though he himself, as well as others, thought at the time that he had made a good trade.

In 1816 the fort which had been destroyed by the Indians was rebuilt and remained standing till only a couple of years ago, as a venerable relic of the childhood of the city. In buildings within that memorable stockade, now without defenses or defenders, a temporary refuge was provided by public benevolence for many Swedish immigrants who, on their way to distant regions in the West, have arrived in Chicago sick and homeless. The modern improvement craze finally committed the sacrilege of razing the monument from a past time and in its place a railroad terminal

---

2   Juliette A. Kinzie, *Wau-bun: The "Early Day" in the North West*
     (New York, 1856). Ed.
3   The massacre did not take place in the fort, as one might infer from
     Unonius' statement, but on the lake shore soon after the garrison and
     settlers had started toward Fort Wayne. Ed.

was erected from which mighty locomotives now roll out of the city on their iron rails, linking Chicago with the Gulf of Mexico and the Atlantic Ocean.[4]

In 1829 the place had five dwellinghouses in addition to the fort and a few outlying log houses. In 1831 the population was increased by a few dozen families. The merchant fleet of the city consisted of four small vessels which unloaded in Chicago everything that was required for the northeastern part of Illinois and the northwestern part of Indiana. As yet the place had no postoffice, but an Indian was sent every other week to bring letters and papers from a small village in Michigan. In 1833 a few more families settled in Chicago and from that year we may date its existence as something more than a pioneer settlement. However, it was not incorporated as a city until four years later when it had acquired a population of 4,170.

The growth of the city during the last sixteen years seems almost miraculous—even for America. In 1848 a canal was completed, a hundred miles long, by which Chicago secured direct communication with the Mississippi River, and consequently also with the Mississippi valley, all the way down to New Orleans, and all the way up to the land around the source of the giant river with its three thousand miles of navigable water. Through this canal the state of Illinois, which in fertility is surpassed by no other state in the Union, became commercially the most important state in the West, and the city of Chicago became the center of trade in products of America and other countries. The canal became the first powerful force leading to the present greatness and is still the artery through which rejuvenating strength flows into the constantly growing city.

However, the web of railroads which Chicago has spun around itself during the last ten years is the thing that more than anything else has contributed to its wealth and progress. In 1851 the

---

[4]   An inaccurate location. No railroad terminal has ever occupied the site of Fort Dearborn. The Illinois Central-Michigan Central station, formerly at the foot of Randolph Street, was not far away. Ed.

first locomotive was to be seen rolling along on a track that extended only a few miles outside the city. Now Chicago is the terminus of more than a dozen trunk lines from which almost twice as many branch lines extend in every direction. Thereby the city has communication with the rich copper districts and other mining regions around Lake Superior, with Canada, with all the Atlantic states, with the rich grain-producing lands beyond the Mississippi, and with the cotton states around the Gulf of Mexico. While a few years ago it took eight to ten days to travel from New York to Chicago, the traveler may now make his choice among three different railroads and cover that distance in thirty to thirty-six hours. More than one hundred twenty trains, some of them consisting of up to forty fully loaded freight cars, arrive and depart each day from the railroad stations in various parts of the city. Some of these stations are still uncomfortable and primitive, showing how people in the West try to get along as best they can with what they have. On the other hand, many compare very well in size, architecture, furnishings, and beauty with the best in other countries. It should be mentioned that all these railroads, altogether measuring five thousand miles in length, which radiate from Chicago as a central point in that immense iron web, the threads of which now cross each other everywhere in the extensive Mississippi valley, are private undertakings. Neither the state nor the city has spent a single dollar on these projects or voted any public funds to realize them. They are ventures entirely undertaken and brought to completion with wonderful energy and foresight by private companies which, operating under a charter issued by the state, independently attend to all the affairs associated therewith; the public has not ventured a penny on these railroads. In that respect Chicago differs from many other American communities which have grown up overnight and engage in extensive undertakings in which unscrupulous demagogues discover some way of fattening their purses at the expense of the general public only to bring eventual loss and dishonor to the community whose confidence they have succeeded in gaining.

But not only canals and numerous railroads have made Chicago one of the most important business centers of the Union, without a doubt the most important in the interior of the country. Its favorable location contributes fully as much if not more. Located at the extreme south end of Lake Michigan, the point of departure for all of the great watercourses, it is, one might say, the source of the extensive navigation maintained on those immense lakes and through the great navigable rivers connected with them. Thus it has direct communication by water with Canada and the Atlantic and even with transatlantic ports. Chicago is connected by the canal with the almost inexhaustible coalfields in southern Illinois and has easy access through the St. Mary's Canal to the mining regions around Lake Superior. These conditions will be important in promoting the future growth and prosperity of the city. It has already become the center for great iron-manufacturing mills which are now employing thousands of workmen and which will in the future certainly be still more developed. . . .

At present grain may be regarded as the city's principal business commodity and export goods. It is possible to form some conception of the scope of the business carried on in that line when we learn that in 1855 a single firm shipped 500,000 bushels to Buffalo. This is natural, for the city is the most easily available and most important trading center for the 130 million bushels of corn and 120 million bushels of wheat which in addition to other grains are produced annually by the fertile state of Illinois alone. This is according to a report of 1855, following which time, since more land has been put under cultivation, the yield must have increased by millions of bushels. . . .

The reader will kindly pardon me if I take him into a grain elevator. I wish to introduce him to Chicago, and since there are no such notable buildings as are generally found in other cities— no museums, art galleries, or other art collections (though if we were to enter the private, comfortable, and tastefully furnished home of a successful businessman we would be likely to find many art treasures testifying to the fact that while his head is filled with stock speculations and plans for grain exports, he is not so ignor-ant of or indifferent to the fine arts as we generally imagine); no antique buildings or moss-covered ancient monuments—since there are no extraordinary sights of that kind to describe, I shall have to present what there is to see, and however prosaic it may seem I beg to invite the reader into a grain elevator, because I have no Madonna or Aphrodite of the Sea or any great library to present.

Atterbom[5] once told me of a visit he had made to a big estate, whose owner, displaying the usual self-satisfaction of a successful agriculturist, and sure that others must be as interested as the owner himself in all the improvements and buildings, led him around to see his new clearings, showed him his cleverly con-structed threshing machine, his great, solidly constructed, prac-tically appointed barn, and other noteworthy things on his farm. Finally he led the professor of aesthetics to what he considered the principal adornment and the greatest evidence of the excep-tional management of the estate—a gigantic manure pile, greater than the "stacks at Wosnosensk." Atterbom, who at the beginning had allowed himself to be led about almost auto-matically among objects which up to that time had been entirely foreign to his experience, was struck with astonishment at the sight of this last exhibit and exclaimed with amazement, "I could never have imagined that it would be possible to find any-thing really poetic about a manure pile."

And so it is. There is nothing really prosaic in life if we look at it from the right point of view. Or rather, energetic activity, hope-ful striving, a powerful spirit in whatever form it may appear, are able to breathe a spirit into the most material objects and make them catch a ray which is refracted into a thousand colors through the prism of ideal art. And that is what the industrial activities in America are able to do. As we look at these structures and undertakings which testify of wonderful strides in material

---

[5] Per Daniel Amadeus Atterbom, Swedish poet and professor at the University of Uppsala. Ed.

advance and prosperity, but which some might be inclined to regard as the apotheosis of the material interests at the expense of more soul-ennobling efforts, we are astounded at the real magnificence revealed in them and we are made to acknowledge that a mighty spirit has stamped these things too with its "Excelsior."

I have seldom realized this as clearly as when I entered for the first time one of those grain elevators in Chicago, and if Atterbom could say that there was something poetic even about a manure pile, I must confess that I found something really sublime in a structure such as this. If I had the poet's ability to describe it, the reader would no doubt realize the same thing; but as it is I am only able to mention briefly and prosaically, a thing that I admired as a gigantic accomplishment in a city which in itself is one of the world's great wonders, leaving the poetic and sublime to be developed by the imagination of the reader.

Here is a solid stone building erected on a pile foundation right at the river's edge, with water on three sides; a building 203 feet long, 101 wide, and 117 feet high. As one enters one is puzzled by a vast number of beams and iron rods which cross each other in every direction, partly to give strength to the structure, partly to form its seven stories. Along one wall run two railroad tracks, spurs from a great nearby main line which, branching out in every direction, connects Chicago with the most fertile grain regions in Illinois and other sections along the Mississippi River. On each of these spurs, six freight cars can be hauled into the elevator for unloading at one time. For that purpose two elevators have been built near the two tracks, and by means of them a train of wheat or corn can be emptied in six minutes—though ten minutes is the regular time in which the load is lifted from the cars and dumped into the grain bins. In the building are 148 such bins, each one 50 feet deep and with a capacity of 5,000 bushels of grain. A carload is generally 350 bushels. After the elevator has gathered up the grain from the car it empties it into a big 500-bushel scoop which is hoisted up to one of the upper stories where it is placed on a scale. After the weight of the 500 bushels has been ascertained, the bottom of the scoop is opened and its contents drop into one of the grain bins. The scoop is immediately lowered to be refilled and once more hoisted. All of this, including the weighing, is done with great speed. Through a simple contrivance 12 to 16 bins may be filled with a single scoop. And so, in ten minutes the grain from a train loaded with about 3,000 bushels is raised by 12 elevators, weighed, and transferred to the bins.

If a vessel is to be loaded it is brought to the side of the elevator, a lid in the bottom of the bin is opened, and the grain runs into the elevator to be hoisted up and weighed, 500 bushels at a time being placed on the scale, whereupon it is run through a spout into the hold of the vessel. All this is done with almost incredible speed. At the time the cars are being unloaded at one side of the elevator, the grain may, if necessary, after it has been hoisted up and weighed, be loaded into the vessel on the other side, to be exported. Thus in less than an hour two ships are loaded with 12,000 bushels apiece.

In this work 25 to 30 men are employed, but the machinery is kept in motion by means of a 30-horsepower steamengine. This engine is separated from the interior of the building by means of heavy fire-walls, and other precautions against fire have also been taken. Great water tanks have been placed in various places in all the seven stories. The elevator can hold 750,000 bushels of grain, but during the shipping season it is seldom filled to capacity. True, one freight train after another arrives every day, loaded with corn and wheat, but the elevators have hardly emptied the cars before they are set in motion again to load the grain from the filled bins. The entire massive building, the steamengine not included, was erected at a cost of about $180,000.

Next to the traffic in grain the lumber business is the most important in Chicago. Illinois, the Prairie State, has no great supply of timber. From the pine woods of Michigan and the northern sections around the lake of that name, masses of boards and other lumber are shipped annually to Chicago, whereupon they are transhipped by railroad to the interior of the country and to the southern states. The businessmen of Chicago dealing in these products are generally also owners of sawmills on the rivers which run through the extensive northern woods and empty into Lake Michigan. Along the shores of the Chicago River there is nothing to be seen for a distance of six miles but lumberyard after lumberyard. The imports of boards and planks to Chicago amounted in 1856 to 457,711,267 cubic feet.

In addition to what has already been mentioned, Chicago has a great number of establishments, all of which testify to the speedy and constant development in all kinds of industries and business undertakings. Great locomotive works, car shops, foundries, and all kinds of machine shops employing thousands of workmen receive orders from almost every state for manufactures that a few years ago could be secured only from the eastern states. Among factories, McCormick's establishment for the manufacture of agricultural machinery deserves mention. Among other things, it annually produces several thousand harvesting machines—Mr. McCormick's invention which is now being used almost everywhere in Europe.

Add to this the fact that Chicago has more than fifty churches, some of them really excellent structures in Gothic style, twenty-five newspaper presses, about a dozen banks, and a countless number of stores and hotels, which in the matter of elegance, comfort, equipment, and stock cannot only be compared with, but also surpass, most establishments of that kind in the European capitals. All of these things will give the reader an idea of how the city has grown from practically nothing during the last twenty years, and he will therefore realize that it is not an exaggeration to predict that within another score of years, when it is likely that the electric spark, crossing the Rocky Mountains, will bring messages from one ocean's shore to the other, and the locomotives which roll across the land from San Francisco and New York will meet in Chicago—that this city will become the central metropolis of the great North American continent, an emporium for the products of Asia, Europe, and America. Not only commercially may we predict for this city a great future of vast importance to the world, but also in other respects. Culture and education have, like Columbus, found land in the West, and the Mississippi valley and its metropolis are a star in the banner of the United States that like the "changeless star of the North" knows no setting.

1855

William Ferguson

Through Illinois on the Illinois Central, with a Look at Cairo

William Ferguson, Scottish scientist born in 1823, preferred to write on nonscientific subjects. His first book, *America by River and Rail*, described his experiences and impressions on a trip to the United States in 1855. He visited Boston, New York, Philadelphia, and the southern states before proceeding to the West. Ferguson devoted six chapters to Illinois. After spending a short time in Chicago, which he did not like, he took the Illinois Central to Urbana. From there he traveled by wagon to Decatur, where he picked up the Illinois Central main line and went on to Cairo. In his account of his American tour, Ferguson strove for accuracy and impartiality, and came close to attaining those goals.

Monday, June 4.—We left Chicago this morning at a quarter past eight, by train on the Chicago branch of the Illinois Central railway, and reached Urbana, one hundred and twenty-eight miles, about four o'clock. The line is only opened to this point at present. By and by, it will be continued, and join the main line from Cairo to Galena. As this is such a new and interesting country, I venture to give pretty detailed notes upon it, and upon the great railway which opens it up. . . .

On leaving the shore of the lake, the railway enters flat prairie land, with some young wood. Some eight or nine miles out, it crosses the line of the Michigan Southern and Northern Indiana railway. Beyond this, it lies for many a mile in open prairie. It is only when approaching the bank of some stream that wood is found. In the pools about, were white water-lilies, like our cultivated ones; and, growing profusely, a blue flower, which also finds a place in our garden borders. The most prominent plant is the resin-weed. It has a palmated leaf, and grows to a considerable height; but is not come to maturity yet. It exudes a resin, and is aromatic to the taste. Horses select it from among hay in winter. It seems to act as a sort of tonic. It has a large, thick root, which affords food to the gophers. These are little burrowing animals, not unlike a gray squirrel in appearance, but possessed of a pouch under their throats. I was informed, that in digging on these prairies the remains of palm-trees are found. At Urbana, wells of sulphuretted hydrogen have been come to. Indigenous plants and grasses retire before those introduced by man; just as the Indians retire before the white man.

One curious feature of these prairies is the occurrence of numerous granite boulders, to which is given the characteristic name of "lost rock." I was told, by one well acquainted with the prairies, that they lie in ridges from north-east to south-west; these belts of them being sometimes half a mile wide. They lie mostly on the surface, but sometimes under it also; and in some

William Ferguson, *America by River and Rail; or, Notes by the Way on the New World and Its People* (London, 1856), pp. 370–88.

places, as near Monee, they are in such quantity as to lower the value of the land for cultivation. They are of a highly crystalline reddish granite.

Until this railway was made, this part of the State was quite inaccessible; and still tracks, miles in extent, are without a house. Stations are put down every ten miles or so; and already little villages are clustering around them, and the lands are being rapidly settled. The early settlements are all on the banks of streams. Reaching the Iroquois river, we find on its banks, a mile and three-quarters from the station, the old French settlement of Bourbonnais. It contained, by the census of 1850, 1719 people; and it presents features of improvement, in new buildings, &c. At the station, a new town, called Kankakee, is springing up. Eighteen months ago, there were at this place one log-hut on an eminence, and one shanty or small house of boards at the station; now, there is a flourishing little town of 1500 to 2000 people. The situation is very favourable for a town, there being a flat meadow bottom along the Iroquois river, and a rising ground beyond, well timbered. It is on the ridge of this rising ground that the town (which is to be the county-town of Kankakee county) is springing up, and a court-house is in the course of erection now.

The eighth station is Ashkum. One of the engineers sent up a sketch of this station—a single barrel, with a solitary crane sitting upon it, labelled, "Ashkum station and its keeper." There is not a house as yet, nor is there any object to be seen along this portion of the line, but the expanse of waving grass, with hazy-looking belts of wood, just visible on the extreme east and west, indicating the course of the Iroquois river and its tributary creeks.

Onarga, another station, has the nucleus of a village,—some dozen houses, two of them stores. Already, though quite new, it is a growing place. Near this, over a wide stretch of prairie, we saw a party of emigrants moving westward, with their covered carts and cattle, in a long line. At this station, I got upon the roof of one of the cars. Nothing was to be seen all around but prairie, with faint lines of wood in the distance, marking the course of streams. Between these and the nearer prairie, there was the appearance of water, a kind of mirage. It would be difficult to fancy anything exceeding the richness of these rolling-lands. At Loda, we saw a farmer breaking up a large tract of prairie, himself meanwhile abiding in two white tents, pitched on a slight eminence; not having had time, as yet, to build even the quickly-erected house of boards. At Pera [1] was perhaps the finest expanse of prairie we saw all day. The whole field of vision was one unbroken meadow of fine undulating grass-land. At Minkgrove, [2] there is a patch of timber, or grove, in the midst of a perfect sea of prairie, just like an island; we saw it for miles after we had passed it, between us and the sky.

The thirteenth station is Urbana—$128\frac{1}{2}$ miles from Chicago. Here we stopped—there remaining 122 miles to be finished before this branch joins the main line at Centralia. There is a patch of wood close to Urbana, of 15,000 acres, and an old and new town; [3] the latter at the railway station, and about two miles from the former. In 1853, the old town contained about 400 inhabitants, and the new town did not exist. It is calculated that the old town now contains 1200 or 1500 inhabitants, and the new town about 800—so rapidly does the building up of towns go on in these new countries.

We observed another interesting instance of the mirage. We were passing over a long reach of level railway, where, without any cutting or embankment, the track was simply laid on the prairie; nevertheless, it assumed the appearance of having disappeared through a deep cutting outlined against the sky, while an engine, following us at some distance, looked as if suspended in the air, some little way above the road.

We reached about four. There is a hotel close to the station, where we got a tolerable tea (our kind cicerone, Mr Johnson, had brought a basket of sandwiches, and we dined on them in the train), and then we got into a waggon with a pair of horses,

1   Now Ludlow. Ed.
2   Now Rantoul. Ed.
3   The new town would become Champaign. Ed.

and drove through the old town of Urbana, and out upon the great prairie. I do not fancy there exists in the old world such a sight as we beheld. From an eminence, as far as the eye could comprehend the scene, it traversed the richest undulating fields of grass, almost unbroken by fence, plough, or house. We walked some distance up to the knees in the luxuriant herbage. It is said that this is the character of the country nearly all the distance from this to the junction with the main line, 122 miles; except that as you get further south there are more streams, and consequently more timber. The agricultural resources of this country are incredible. We made a detour from this edge of the grand prairie, by cultivated fields, till we reached the timber; and skirting it, returned to Urbana.

Tuesday, June 5.—Mine host would have devoted two of us to one bed—the household one, if I mistake not, for there was women's gear about; but at last a bed was "raised" for me in the hall above. It was a good bed, though rather public; for, being at the head of the stair, it had to be passed and repassed by those who slept on that floor. However, I slept very comfortably, till knocked up at half-past five this morning. This is a superior specimen of an Illinois country inn:—a frame-house, with a good deal of accommodation of that rough sort; and good enough food, badly cooked. Withal—what is rarer—a most civil landlord.

We got breakfast, and by half-past six were again seated in the waggon, with a day's provisions, to cross the prairie, sixty miles, to Decatur. There is a shorter route, but we took the one we did to see a herd of fine cattle, belonging to Mr Frank Harris. They were out on an extensive prairie, and we discovered them by means of a glass. We went as straight as we could, through the prairie, some mile or two, to where they were—losing sight of them most of the while, from the rolling of the ground. At last we got near them, and the sight was indeed worth going a long way to see.

There were one hundred and twenty-six of them; one weighed as much as 2600 ℔.; many of the others weighed from 1900 ℔.

to 2100 ℔. They were standing and lying about among the deep grass, in attitudes and groups, such as would have delighted Cooper [4] to paint. A finer lot of fat cattle, I suppose, is not to be seen anywhere. They were tended by a little lad, mounted on a fine high-bred pony. A most intelligent little fellow he was, and right glad to see us, to break the monotony of his occupation. He keeps the cattle penned all night, he told us; brings them out to the prairie about seven in the morning, and, as I understood, tends them there for the most part of the day. He pointed out his favourites with great delight.

As we were walking about among them, one of our party called out, "There's a snake"; and sure enough there lay a rattle-snake, three or four feet long, coiled up, and with elevated head, hissing and shaking his rattling tail. Our herd-boy friend soon made an end of him, planting one heel upon him, he stamped him to death with the other. The rattle, which was carried off in triumph, had eight rings, betokening a serpent of ten years. The boy said, he had killed probably fifty of them. They sometimes bite the cattle, when whisky and tobacco is applied, and this allays the inflammation. It is affirmed, there is no authenticated instance of any one in Illinois having ever died from the bite of these prairie rattle-snakes.

We called for Mr Harris at his house, about two miles from where the cattle were, but did not find him. His farm contains 4200 acres, distributed thus—700 acres Indian-corn; 100 acres oats and wheat; 200 acres meadow; 2500 acres pasturage; and 700 acres wood.

The rest of our route was nearly all the way through the timber which skirts the Sangamon river. About half-way, we stopped in the woods to dine and rest the horses. Drawn up beneath the shade of a spreading live-oak, a napkin was spread out on the front seat of the waggon; and from a miscellaneous collection of sandwiches, cheese, crackers, hard-boiled eggs, and pickled

[4]   Probably George Victor Cooper (1810–78), portrait and landscape painter who did all the illustrations for *California Illustrated* (1853). Ed.

cucumbers (salt was not forgotten), we made an *al fresco* mid-day meal, pretty near the heart of Illinois.

Water is rather scarce on some parts of these prairies. At one cottage, where was a well, the people refused to permit us to take any; but about four in the afternoon, we came to a farm-house, where the people not only permitted us to have water, but helped to draw it. While our horses were drinking, we had some interesting conversation with the farmer and his brother. He owns a farm of 1960 acres. A single field in front of his house contained in one unbroken expanse forty acres of wheat, and seven hundred acres of Indian-corn. He keeps fifteen teams or pairs of horses. We saw eleven of them engaged at one time hoeing the corn. He can make a profit by selling Indian corn at fifteen cents, or sevenpence halfpenny per bushel. He has made, he says, as much money as he wants; and wishes to sell his farm as it stands, with its improvements, at fifteen dollars or three pounds per acre, all round. It is five miles from the Great Western railway of Illinois, and about mid-way between the Chicago branch and the main line of the Illinois Central railway—about sixteen miles from each.

Shortly after leaving this farm, we encountered immense swarms of locusts. They appear periodically in the west. They were on the trees, are about two to three inches long, and were in myriads. The sound they emitted was deafening. They were not eating.

We got into Decatur about half-past eight, by which time it was just dark enough to be out on the prairie; four miles of which we had to cross before entering the town. The whole ride to-day, both in its prairie, and forest, and river features, has been one of very great interest. Such a body of rich land is inconceivable. It must be seen to be appreciated; and even then, its extent and value are beyond what can be duly recognized.

It was too dark to see anything of Decatur when we arrived. As we drove through streets, which were no more than untouched field, we could discover it was a new place. We got an excellent supper, and excellent beds; and enjoyed repose after so long a ride as we had.

Wednesday, June 6.—Breakfasting at the early hour of half-past six, we had more than an hour to wait at the station. We left at nine; but the morning being very wet, we could not to-day, any more than last night, see much of Decatur. It is a large place, and is increasing rapidly. In 1850, its name does not occur in the census report. In 1853, it had about six hundred inhabitants; and the present year, it is estimated to have three thousand. There are several hotels in the town, and one building at the railway-station. A farm was pointed out to us, a little way from the station, which had been offered last autumn, with all its improvements, for $45, or £9 per acre; and the one between it and the town was stated to be likely to fetch $90, or £18 per acre; while land in the town itself would be worth $150, or £30 per acre.

The distance from Decatur to Cairo is 204¾ miles; and the train was due there at 8.35,—a journey of eleven hours and a half; and giving a speed of about eighteen miles an hour, including stoppages once in ten miles, or so. Till we pass Duquoin, which is only 76½ miles from Cairo, the country is chiefly prairie. Here and there it is a little broken, and near the stream it is timbered. Ere we are many hours out of Decatur, the climate becomes perceptibly warmer. The flowers are further out, and different. The prairie-rose is in bloom, also several pink and scarlet flowers, and a showy chrysanthemum, and various others common in our gardens.

Vandalia, 142½ miles from Cairo, is the old capital of the State, and contains about a thousand people. It is a very prettily-situated little town. The country around is finely varied and well-timbered, that is, the trees are large and well-grown. The neighbourhood is fairly settled, and being fast cleared. Fine woods and fields of wheat, together with the general fencing and cultivation, give somewhat the appearance of English scenery. The town itself is not increasing. A little south of the town, the Kaskaskia river is crossed; and there is near it a good deal of broken ground and low-lying bottoms, subject to be overflowed. They were so this morning. The railway is carried through them on trestle-work, which will be ultimately converted into embankments, when experience has taught how much water-way it will be needful to leave.

A little to the north of Duquoin is the first place where it has been attempted to work coal on the line of the road in the south of the State. The train was stopped to allow us to examine the coal-pits. There has been one shaft sunk perpendicularly 74 feet, —in reaching which depth it has passed through a bed of limestone, 4 feet thick, then shales, and lastly, the coal-bed, which is 6 feet 8 inches thick. The limestone is very compact, crystalline, and not fossiliferous, as far as I could judge on a hasty glance. They are now sinking an incline to reach the coal on a slope. They have got down 150 feet, but have not reached the coal yet. As I stood at its mouth looking down, a blast exploded at the bottom, and made me start. A small quantity of coal has as yet been taken out, as the mine is only in course of being opened. It is supposed they have got to about the centre of the basin, for the coal rises on each side from this shaft. It crops out about half a mile to the east, and again on the banks of the Bigmuddy river to the west. It is stated that the coal can be sold at the pit-mouth at $1, or 4s. per ton. The head miner is a Lanarkshire man. There was a large lump of solid coal lying at the pit-mouth, about 4 by 4 by 2, or 32 feet cubic. It was taken out from the bottom of the perpendicular shaft.

We now enter the hilly country of the south, and there is no more prairie. Some sixty miles north from Cairo we crossed Bigmuddy river, which well deserves its characteristic name. It looks small, but it is deep. Coal is found along its banks, and is floated to the Mississippi in barges to supply St Louis, and other towns. In making the railway, the rails were brought by water to this point. Six miles beyond, we reach Carbondale, through a timber country, with clearings here and there. Dead trunks of trees, standing up among the wheat, remind one of Pennsylvania and Ohio. There is fine wheat-land all around. We saw some fields already beginning to change colour. The road is now ascending, at the rate of about thirty-six feet in a mile. Carbondale is a station for some towns near, the country back from the line of railway being well settled. Tobacco is grown in this neighbourhood, and forwarded from Carbondale. As we passed, we saw five hogsheads on the platform, waiting to be taken away.

Passing on, we come to the first stone-cutting, a little to the north of Drewery-creek, apparently in limestone and shale. The country hence becomes very broken and hilly, and the line of the railway very winding, following the lie of the country. In some fourteen miles, the summit is reached. It is about 600 feet above ordinary water-level at Cairo. The railway, for a considerable distance here, lies in a deep gorge, occupied by Drewery-creek, the course of which it follows; indeed, it occupies its channel for miles, a new one having been cut for the stream alongside. It is a very picturesque gorge, bluffs on both sides, 200 feet high, with water-worn faces. It is crossed by ravines leading into the country. All is finely wooded. On the table-lands above, and back into the country, are good farms. The district is pretty well settled. As a proof of the fineness of climate and fertility, we were told that one farmer, whose place is on the rocks above the station at Makanda, makes from his own orchard annually forty hogsheads of peach brandy.[5]

The descent to Cairo is made in forty-four miles. It is through a wild, wooded, beautiful country, till we reach Villa-ridge, ten miles from the terminus. Here we began to see fire-flies in great abundance, and they increased as we got into the low grounds. There were myriads of them. Few at first, they seemed like stars here and there; but they increased in number, till every tree seemed alive with wandering stars. Flitting in brilliant sparkles from leaf to leaf, they made the whole dark wood alive with light. As I called my companion's attention to them, some men at the station informed us, "Them's the lightning bugs!"

Passing this station—the last—we enter Cottonwood-slough, part of the Cache flats, which cover the whole of this delta of the

---

[5] During August of this year, 1855, thirty tons of fruit were forwarded to the north from Jonesborough.

two rivers. A few cypresses grow here, but not many. There are also some cane-brakes. Through this swamp, the railway is carried on a trestle-work, about a mile and a quarter long, and varying in height from eighteen to twenty feet. It creaked as we went slowly over it. By and by, it will be substituted by an embankment. The railway, at a little distance from Cairo, turns abruptly off to the bank of the Ohio, and runs down alongside the river on the levee. When finished, it will encircle the town.

As we neared the town of Cairo, we had the swamp forest, with its multitudes of fire-flies, on the west; and on the east, the broad Ohio placidly reflecting the failing light; beyond, the wood-covered hills of Kentucky; and here and there, on the bosom of the river, the star-like light of some boat.

Presently, we emerged from the thicket, and its place was taken by an open space, flickered here and there by the light from an open window. The train stands still. We are on the high bank of the levee. Down on the one side, the shining waters of the Ohio; down on the other, the shining lights of the few scattered wooden houses which constitute Cairo. It has begun to rain. We descend twenty steps, cross on a gangway of planks some fifty yards of an incipient lake (!), and reach a new hotel—the Taylor-house.

The Taylor-house is large and roomy, but it is new; and many of the rooms are but partially furnished, others not at all. Some of us get rooms supplied with beds on a bedstead; others are not so fortunate, for their beds are spread on the floor. A few months ago, we would have fared worse. Travers, who drove us to-day, has often slept at Cario, stretched, for warmth and shelter, on a board below his engine.

There were lots of people just arrived from New Orleans, all looking wretched in the rain. We are in a different climate altogether from Chicago. I have on the clothes to which the cold winds of the lakes had driven me, and now they are thoroughly wet with perspiration. The air is hot, close, and oppressive. I escape to my room. A solitary chair does duty for itself, wash-stand, and toilet-table. I have placed my lamp upon it, and sit on the bed-side, to read for a little. I open the Olney Hymns, and read—

"Strange and mysterious is my life!"

when a vivid flash of lightning lights up my room, the court, and beyond. Flash succeeds flash, with roll of distant thunder. The rain comes down in torrents, splash, splash, in the already circumambient waters; and thinking I have got into somewhat of a bog, I prepare to put myself to bed in the future "city" of Cairo.

Thursday, June 7.—The breakfast-hour this morning was six; and we were in hopes that we would have had an opportunity to look round Cairo before starting. It rained, however, in torrents; and we were fain to content ourselves with a very cursory inspection. Breakfast over, we carried our traps—in default of help that could be hired—across the space between the hotel and the railway, which, by this time, was a sheet of water. Raining as it was, we walked down the line of rail upon the levee, in hopes we might be able to reach the point, and see the union of the Ohio and Mississippi. We got on pretty well as long as we could step on the sleepers, or better—for even they were covered with mud—balance ourselves upon the rails; but when we came to the end of these, our first step took us up to the ancles in mud. We pushed on through this as far as the levee goes, which is not quite to the point. It turns abruptly north, leaving a low swampy plot between it and a branch of the Mississippi. Beyond this slough there is an island, and the main channel is beyond it.

Cairo is the southern terminus of the railway, situated on the confluence of the Ohio and Mississippi. From this point southward, the river is always navigable, and nearly always free from ice. It is about 180 miles below St Louis, and 509 miles below Cincinnati. To each of these cities, and, consequently, to all places beyond them, the navigation is liable to frequent stoppage, —in summer, from want of depth of water; and in winter, from ice. This point is, therefore, likely to become a great shipping-place for produce going south, and for merchandise, &c., coming from New Orleans; while the saving to passengers going to Cincinnati and St Louis is such, that they are already preferring to land at Cairo and go by railway, although, in the present state of the connecting lines, this route is a long one.

A company was formed in 1841 to build a city at Cairo, but after getting two or three houses erected, it broke up. The place got the name of being "stuck," and people became prejudiced against it. It was said to be a swamp, unhealthy, &c. A new company has recently been formed, called "The Cairo City Property Company," which is possessed of all the land for nearly seven miles north from the point; and through their exertions, and the opening of the railway, attention is again turned to Cairo.[6] It is confidently stated, that the spot is less unhealthy than many other points on the river, where large towns have sprung up. The trustees have cut down the timber on the flats from river to river, for a considerable space; and this permits of the free circulation of air, and has driven away the miasma, which produced chills and fever. Last summer, when there was so much cholera in the other towns on the Ohio and Mississippi, there was not one case of it among the inhabitants of Cairo.

A levee or embankment of most substantial character, one hundred and seventy feet in breadth on the top, surrounds the town, and the tracks of the Illinois Central railway are laid upon it. The greatest range of level in the rivers occurred last year, 1854, when between the lowest and highest water the rise and fall was forty-two feet. The natural level of the ground is about thirty-eight feet above ordinary water. The levee is seven or eight feet higher than the highest water-mark, and the town level is only three and a half feet below highest water. It is thus subject to partial overflows for short periods at a time, in extraordinarily wet seasons. During the heavy rains, too, which occur frequently,

---

[6]   The first attempt to establish Cairo was made in 1818 and failed dismally. The Cairo City and Canal Company was formed in 1837, not 1841, as Ferguson states. Not until 1846, when the company was reorganized as the Cairo City Property Trust, was a permanent settlement planted. Ed.

the town, from being embanked all round, looks somewhat like a lake; but this overabundance of water speedily flows off by natural drainage, through culverts in the levee, at least in ordinary seasons. During high water in the river, this drainage is stopped; and the city, though protected from inundation, is subject to partial overflow. This could be easily remedied by the formation of a large reservoir, at the lowest level, into which the surface-water might flow, and whence it could be forced by steam-power into the river.

It is computed there are from 1000 to 1200 people in Cairo, two-thirds of whom have come here within a year from this time. There are about sixty houses, including the hotel, which is quite full of people. The city is laid out in lots of twenty-five feet front, and one hundred and twenty-five feet in depth. Three of these, on the front level, had been sold at $1500 each, to make a beginning. The price for good lots range as high as $2500. On the back streets they may be had for $350, and upwards.

The high prices for which the trustees are holding out, has helped to delay the rapid development of Cairo; but within a month or two they have adopted a different policy, and several "substantial buildings are now erecting; and in the autumn, others, already contracted for, will fairly start the place."

The levee round the town is the work of the Illinois Central railway. It has been completed sufficiently to protect the town, and for a mile is finished for the accommodation of business. The railway buildings are only partly erected, and but temporary; but both levee and buildings will be finished as fast as the business of the road and the growth of Cairo demand. For this service, the railway receives from the trustees ample land for depôt purposes on both rivers; and when all the arrangements are perfected, the railway will surround the town, leaving it, on the north side, at a point about equi-distant from each river.

1858

Sir James Caird

A Bird's Eye View of Illinois, Prairie Farming, and the State Capital

Sir James Caird was well advanced in a distinguished career when he decided to tour Canada and the United States in 1858–59. Educated at the University of Edinburgh, he became not only a practical farmer but an agricultural expert. Commissioned by the British government, he made a report on Irish farming in 1846. Four years later, for the *Times*, he investigated the distressed state of English agriculture after the adoption of free trade. In 1857 he was elected a Member of Parliament for Dartmouth, Devonshire, and it was while serving his term that he made his American tour. Later in life he served on a number of government commissions and wrote extensively on agricultural subjects.

Before examining particular localities in the State, I was anxious to obtain as it were a bird's-eye view of the country; such a general impression of its surface as would enable me to select points for special inspection. I therefore first traversed the entire State on the line of the Illinois Central Railway, from north-east to south, and from south to north-west, a total distance of about 700 miles. The State of Illinois extends from 37° to 42° 30′ north latitude, being thus nearly the same length as England, but further south, and on the same parallel with Spain and Italy. This first journey occupied three days, the last day of September, and the first and second of October.

Immediately after leaving Chicago we enter on the prairie, which, near Lake Michigan, and for the first twenty miles, is low and wet, better suited for pasture and dairying than the cultivation of corn. The country then begins to rise, and in the next twenty miles the surface becomes dry and undulating; the soil a black mould, varying in depth from twelve to thirty inches, and resting on clay, or a mixture of clay and gravel. From this point to the Kankakee River, the first large stream we cross, the prairie is a series of long and gentle undulations, less abrupt than the chalk downs of England, but otherwise resembling them in general form and sweep. The character of the soil is very uniform, and the face of the wide open country is sparsely dotted with farm-houses. Where the prairie is unbroken, it is covered with long coarse waving grass, from three to four feet high; and in the hollows the grass is so high as to hide completely any cattle that may be grazing there. Before reaching Kankakee we pass through a settlement of 800 French Canadians, which has been growing for the last fifteen years.[1] Each settler has about forty acres, and their farms are laid out along parallel roads at right angles to the railway. They exhibit signs of careful cultivation, and the village and church of the colony are prettily situated near the woods on the river side.

James Caird, *Prairie Farming in America; With Notes by the Way on Canada and the United States* (London, 1859), pp. 35–41, 54–63.
[1]   Bourbonnais. Ed.

The town of Kankakee is finely situated on the river, fifty-six miles south of Chicago. Though there was not a house here five years ago, the population already numbers 3,500, with very good streets and shops, the centre of a rich agricultural district affording a sufficient traffic for a special daily train in and out from Chicago. The land behind it is a fertile, black, sandy loam, lying on limestone, excellent for oats and potatoes, and productive of rich grass.

Crossing the river, which is a broad clear stream, as wide as the Thames at Richmond, running between limestone cliffs clothed with timber, the road traverses a continuous prairie, more or less dotted with houses and farms for the next seventy miles. This is all a good range of country, and though the railroad frequently runs in a perfectly straight line for many miles, the surface while rather flat is very seldom a dead level, as may be at once observed by the varied depth of the cuttings and embankments all along the line. At every eight or ten miles we pass a station round each of which a town is rapidly springing up, very often with a steam flour-mill in its centre capable of manufacturing 150 barrels of flour a day.

At Urbana, 128 miles south of Chicago, there is a flourishing town and station, the population numbering near 4000. I saw a peach plantation in this neighbourhood which was said to be in some seasons extraordinarily productive and remunerative. High prices are paid by the graziers here for the best breeds of cattle to improve their stock, one man whom I met at the station having last year paid 500*l.* for a short-horn bull from England. The soil is very black and rich looking. Generally, even on the flattest prairie, groves of timber are visible somewhere on the horizon, but they become more frequent after we pass southwards of Urbana, and until Mattoon is reached, a few miles from which, and at about 180 miles south of Chicago, the general level of the country falls about eighty feet. This forms the termination of the line of black loamy prairie, the grey wheat-soils of southern Illinois now commencing. The open prairie becomes narrower, and the woods, which are everywhere found along the beds of the rivers and streams, seem to be within little more than a mile apart from each other. The soil is more silicious than the black soil of the upper prairies, and better adapted for winter wheat, of which it seldom fails to produce good crops of fine quality. It is also considered good for grazing cattle; but is not so prolific of Indian corn or oats, nor so suitable for potatoes or sugar-beet, all of which grow very successfully on the black prairie. The face of the country, however, is more picturesque, and the woods more diversified, the white oak growing to a great height. There is also abundance of coal and building stone in this portion of the State, and the winter climate is occasionally so mild that in favourable seasons cattle can live the whole year on the prairies, with the aid of little or no fodder. From this point to Centralia, where the junction is made with the main line of the railroad, and onwards to the south as far as Desoto, which is 301 miles south of Chicago, the same whitish grey prairie soil continues. The country near Duquoin, a station on the line, is all underlaid with coal, in seams from five to nine feet thick, at a depth of seventy to eighty feet. It is easily wrought, but at present there is not much sale for it, as the country is very thinly settled, and there is no scarcity of wood. In the whole country, for nearly the last 150 miles, there was scarcely a settler four years ago, but so rapidly has settlement followed the opening of the railway, that it is estimated that half a million of acres of land have already been brought under cultivation along this part of the road.

From Desoto to the southern boundary of the State the country is all hills and hollows, rocky and wooded, with good farms interspersed. The climate is very mild in winter and hot in summer, and admits of the growth of all kinds of fruits and tobacco. It produces white wheat of the finest quality, and peaches and other fruits are sent in large quantities for the supply of the market at Chicago. This is one of the earliest soils in the Union for the ripening of wheat, the new crop from which may be sent to the northern and eastern markets before their own harvests are ready.

I now retraced my course by the same line to the junction at Centralia, but went northwards from that point by another line, nearly through the centre of the State, meeting with the same characteristics of soil as were noticed on the journey southwards. Near Tacusah[2] there is another considerable settlement of French Canadians from Lower Canada. On again reaching the black prairie, after having been for some time accustomed to the whitish grey soil of the southern prairie, it seemed to me that the land looked richer and the grass greener. But we were now traversing the richest part of Illinois, and for 100 miles north of Tacusah the whole country is very fine, much of it settled and enclosed, and dotted with houses, as far as the eye can see. The cultivation is on a larger and more regular scale, the Indian corn and wheat both showing evidence of more careful management. Hay and corn ricks are more numerous; woodland is to be seen in all directions, and the country is altogether more undulating, rich, and picturesque, than any part of the prairie which I had yet seen. At Bloomington, which is a very rising town, with 7000 people, 10,000 bushels of grain are sent off daily by railroad to Chicago in a good season. The country here is chiefly settled by farmers from the State of New York. About thirty miles farther north, near the station of Minonk, a large colony of about 200 families from Vermont have settled. They sent before them a committee of their most skilful farmers to examine the Western States and choose the most suitable and advantageous position they could find. These men made a very careful inspection of Illinois, and other States farther west, during a four months' tour, and came to the conclusion that no other locality which they had seen presented so great a combination of advantages as this. They bought altogether about 20,000 acres, upon which they have been settled for the last three years.

At La Salle we cross the Illinois river, and have now reached the centre of the coal region of the northern part of the State, a busy populous district, in which the population has increased

---

[2]   Now Assumption, Christian County. Ed.

five fold during the last fifteen years. The value of land has increased in a much greater ratio, land near the station, which then sold at 10s. an acre, being now worth 10l.

At Mendota, about ten miles farther north, the country, which is all open prairie, is well "settled," and the people look unusually lively, healthy, and well fed. White clover may be seen growing very luxuriantly along the railway banks where the natural prairie grass has given way. The same kind of country continues for the next twenty-five miles to Dixon, which is a very handsome town of about 5000 people, finely placed on both sides of the Rock River, a broad navigable stream, flowing at the bottom of shelving wooded banks. For some miles north of Dixon the road runs up the river bank, skirting the woodland, and then emerges on a tract of open undulating prairie, where large farms with corn fields stretch out apparently for miles on either side. This continues for the next thirty or forty miles. In this northern part of the State the air is much cooler than in the south, and the winters are more severe. Cattle require six weeks longer of winter provender. Indian corn is not so productive by one-fourth as it is in the rich midland portion of the State, and winter wheat is so precarious that the spring-sown variety is chiefly cultivated. But this district is admirably suited for oats and potatoes, and for summer grazing. We have now reached Freeport, a flourishing town of 7000 people, on the Pecatonia river, northwards of which, for the next forty or fifty miles to near Galena, the prairie soil is thinner and more rolling, but covered with white clover wherever the natural grass has given way. This terminates the prairie land.

Galena is the great seat of the lead mines in America, and yields annually about thirty million pounds weight. It is a large and thriving town, situated on the banks of Fever river, which is navigable to the Mississippi, some few miles distant. The river smelt noxiously at night, and the principal trading streets lie along its bank. But the residences of the people are prettily scattered up the hillsides on both banks, and the inhabitants themselves, notwithstanding the ominous name of the river, think there are few places in the State to compare with the town of

Galena. From Galena to Dunleith[3] on the Mississippi, and near the north-west boundary of Illinois, the country has no interest of importance to a farmer. It is chiefly woodland, and, where open prairie, it is already "settled" and under cultivation . . . .

From Bloomington I proceeded southwards to Springfield, the capital, and not far from the centre of the State of Illinois. This is a fine town, with good streets and shops, and the neighbourhood is diversified by timber. It is like all other places in this part of the country, surrounded by the wide prairie. The view from the top of the State house very much resembles that of the plain of Lombardy as seen from the Duomo of Milan, except that there is nowhere a boundary of mountains. But there is the same rich far-stretching plain, with trees in lines and groups, the timber becoming denser along the banks of the streams, which have cut out for themselves hollow passages winding about on the panoramic landscape spread before the eye. The inhabitants of the town, like those in the country, are not this season exempt from ague.

I visited the county cattle fair or show which was then being held in a field close by the town. The best short-horn stock were exhibited by Mr. Brown, a celebrated cattle breeder of this State, whose acquaintance I had the good fortune to make in the show yard.[4] He exhibited a short-horn cow, bred by himself, six years old, which had had five calves, a large fat handsome animal, which would have been a prize taker at any English show. He showed also a three-year-old short-horn bull from Lord Ducie's stock, imported last year.[5] The large stock farmers of the West, who are the really monied men, are taking great pains to improve the quality of their cattle by the importation of the best English blood. It is an excellent policy, and they are already abundantly reaping the reward of their enterprise. For, though at this autumnal season, the prairie grass looks coarse and innutritious,

3   Now East Dubuque. Ed.
4   James N. Brown, whose large farm was situated about halfway between Springfield and Jacksonville. Ed.
5   Henry George Francis Moreton, second Earl of Ducie, leading English breeder of short-horned cattle. Ed.

a stranger has only to examine the cattle which are fed upon it to convince himself of its feeding qualities. And, as this grass is everywhere to be had here for nothing, the grazier consults his own interest by incurring some expense in improving the present breeds of cattle, and thus obtaining earlier maturity, better quality, and quicker returns from his extensive grazings. Of the cattle common to the country there were several specimens exhibited, of enormous size. One red and white ox with wide upturned horns, four and a half years old, measured 2700 lb. weight. He handled well, though very strong in the bone and limbs. Another of 2000 lb. gross weight was reckoned on the spot worth only 14*l.* at the current price of beef, viz. about 2*d.* a pound dead weight.

Mr. Brown has been many years in the country engaged in farming. He farms largely, and believes that more money may be made, and has been made, in this State by stock farming than corn growing. Nor is this remarkable, inasmuch as grazing land on the prairies hitherto could be had for nothing, costing neither rent nor taxes, while corn land must be bought, enclosed, and cultivated, and labour has hitherto been expensive. However, till very recently there was no outlet for corn. Railways are rapidly altering the former state of things, and Indian corn is no longer unsaleable at 6*d.* a bushel. He has found short-horn stock the most profitable, which is no doubt chiefly owing to the high prices he is enabled to realise in the sale of well bred stock for improving the breeds of the country. But he has not found them so successful on the natural prairie grass, of which on his own lands he has no longer any. Though the prairie grass may be extirpated in time by close feeding, he has found it the best practice to break it up, and, after a course of tillage, to sow the land out with blue grass and clover. The blue grass is a rich thick succulent grass of a bluish colour, which grows with great success on the limestone soils of Kentucky, and is found to succeed admirably on the prairies when laid down as pasture. It improves every year, and yields feed for six months, besides half feed during the winter, whereas the natural prairie grass is in its best state only for the first four months after spring. Mr. Brown has all his lands now laid down in "tame" grass, as the sown grasses are commonly termed here. He keeps no stock except his thoroughbred short-horns, and lets his surplus grass for grazing at one dollar a month for each animal, during the summer and autumn. He feeds his own stock during winter on the pastures, giving them corn and hay in time of snow. As he can buy Indian corn in his part of the State at an average of 8*d.* a bushel, he has no doubt that this is the kind of farming which best suits Illinois. He had tried sheep, and found them to do well, but having no taste for them he keeps exclusively to cattle.

There were various novel agricultural implements exhibited in the show yard. Ploughs mounted on an axle, with high wheels, the only advantage of which seemed to be that a seat was thus provided for the driver. There were seed planters of ingenious construction, a circular self-cleaning harrow, which always goes round about while being dragged forward,—little hand machines for washing clothes upon, which are said to economise labour 100 per cent,—and a chain-bucket pump, an extremely simple, cheap and efficient article.

I drove a few miles out of town to visit the farm of Mr. M'Connell,[6] who was recommended to me by the Governor of the State as a man of great intelligence, integrity, and experience. I walked and drove over his farm, examined his stock, and received from him very clear and distinct information. He is a practical man who has been all his life engaged in farming, and has fought his way up to a very comfortable independence. He left "the old country" in 1811, farmed in a small way for thirty years in the state of New York, where he first settled, and moved thence to Illinois seventeen years ago. He had always preferred sheep-farming, and brought his small flock of merinos with him. They have been remarkably healthy, increase one-third every year, and his flock now numbers 25,000. His fleeces average four to five

---

[6]   Murray McConnell, lawyer and politician of Jacksonville. His farm was in Morgan County. Ed.

pounds each, and the wool sells for 1s. 8d. to 2s. a pound. He bought his farm at 1l. an acre, and could now sell it at 10l., as it is in a good position near the capital of the State. But he is so firmly persuaded of the rapidly growing wealth of this fine State, that he has no doubt of his farm being worth 20l. an acre a few years hence. He considers the land for 100 miles round Springfield to be the best in the world.

Mr. M'Connell sends his flock to the open prairies in April, places about 1200 under the charge of one shepherd, who tends them and supplies them with salt. They need no other food for six months. He brings them to his enclosed ground in winter, and gives them hay when they need it, and a little corn. His flock has never suffered from any epidemic, but on the contrary have been extremely free from disease. His original flock grew one-fourth in weight and size after being brought from New York State to this better soil. He prefers the merino to the South Down for this climate and soil, and has found from trial that the merinos yield as much mutton and far better wool. He imports pure merino rams from Germany and Spain to improve his flock.

Mr. M'Connell finds that by feeding prairie grass close with sheep, it, in a few years, gives way to blue grass and white clover— which come naturally of themselves and without being sown. But the plan he recommends for laying this land down into good meadow and pasture, is to break up the soil some time between the middle of May and middle of July; a few days earlier or later may be tolerated, but not more, as if prairie land is broken out of season the labour is worse than lost. Sow wheat in end of August, or 1st of September: the following season, after wheat, take a crop of Indian corn, which must be kept clean; after the crop is removed, level the ground well, and in February sow one peck of Timothy to the acre,—if on the snow so much the better, as the dark seeds attract the sun's rays, and gradually melt a passage for themselves to the soil below, and the moment the snow disappears, they, being already imbedded in the damp soil, spring up at once, and take the start of all other vegetation. Late in March add two pounds of clover seed per acre, and a good hay crop will be certain.—I can testify to the success of this management, as I walked over a meadow of many acres on this gentleman's land, on which there was ricked a crop of at least two tons an acre of very excellent mixed clover and grass hay. The aftermath was rich close luxuriant clover, on which a flock of lambs were grazing, just such clover aftermath as we should find in this country on good land after the first crop of hay. I thought it had been the first crop, but learnt to my surprise that the meadow had been sown out twelve years ago, that it had little manure all that time, had borne a crop of hay every year, and been fed close afterwards with sheep, during winter and spring, till the prairie grass grew. I have never seen land in Britain that would bear a close clover aftermath at a period so distant from the time of being seeded, and cannot withhold my belief in the fertile qualities of a soil capable of doing so. Mr. M'Connell has no doubt that the prairie land would benefit by the occasional application of manure, but he never met with any other soil so constantly productive without it. He has known the first wheat crop pay the price of the land, with the cost of fencing it, and all labour, and leave a small balance over.

With regard to sheep-farming, his opinion is that corn and hay should first be provided by a few years' cultivation, before going largely into a flock. The prairie grass will furnish summer keep at little or no cost, but provision must be made for the winter. Good merinos can be bought for 8*s.* to 12*s.* 6*d.* a-head in flocks. There is probably no kind of farming on the prairies from which the returns would be so regular and certain.

Mr. M'Connell had tried a timber country before coming here, and was very energetic in expressing his opinion of the superior advantages to a settler on the prairie.

When in the capital I did myself the honour of visiting the Governor, who lives in a handsome house provided for him by the State, who also grant him the modest revenue of 500*l.* a year.[7]

---

[7]   The governor was William H. Bissell, the first Republican to hold
      that office. He died on March 18, 1860, before the expiration of his
      four-year term. Ed.

He was a distinguished soldier in the Mexican war, and had long been one of the Senators of Congress. He has the highest hopes of the future of Illinois, and he, like other men of character and position to whom I have put the question, expressed the belief that fever and ague in this State are on the decline, though from special causes there had this year been an exceptional prevalence of both.

I visited also the State House, where the two branches of the State Legislature hold their sittings, and in which are the bureaux of the various state officers. The Secretary of State very politely showed me over the building; the State Auditor supplied me with documents showing the valuation and taxation of the State; and the Treasurer, who locks up the money and disburses it exactly like the clerk in a bank, for which he is paid a salary of 400*l.* a year, explained to me the rate of taxation in the State, the desire they all had to pay off their debt, the present increased rate to which they submitted for that object, the probability of a future decrease in expense, and the general frugality of the management. There is a total absence of form and ceremony about these gentlemen, who are high officers of State.[8] The Secretary of State acts also as librarian. He and his clerk conduct the public correspondence and business. While I was there a man, about thirty, with his hat on and his hands in his pockets, came lounging in, and, after listening to our conversation for a while, asked if this was the Secretary, because he wanted to get some information about an old county road of which no record could be found in his county, but which he "reckoned" would be posted up at the capital in the books of the State. The Secretary immediately went off to "fix" him about the road. In the same way the Auditor was at everybody's call, and the Treasurer also. The officers of State are not above doing their own work here.

If there is not much official ceremony, there is a total absence of it in the manners of the bulk of the people. The nasty habit of

---

[8]   Ozias M. Hatch was secretary of state, Jesse K. Dubois was
        state auditor, James Miller treasurer. Ed.

chewing tobacco, and spitting, not only gives them a dirty look, but makes them disagreeable companions. They eat so fast, and are so silent, and run off so soon when they have finished their meals, that really eating in this country is more like the feeding of a parcel of brutes than men. The food is both various and plentiful, but it is generally badly cooked and served.

Violent thunderstorms are not infrequent. Every house on the prairie is fitted with a lightning conductor, but I did not hear that accidents from lightning were very common.

Again taking the railway, I proceeded to Decatur, a station about thirty miles east of Springfield, and drove for a whole day through the prairie country in that neighbourhood. After driving a few miles through the enclosed farms which surround the town, we reached the open unbroken prairie, and turning short off the track on which we had hitherto been driving, we stood across the great plain which stretched out before us. The horses struck without hesitation into the long coarse grass, through which they pushed on with very little inconvenience, although it was in many places higher than their heads. It was not thick, and parted easily before them; then sweeping under the bottom of our waggon it rose in a continuous wave behind us as we passed along. The surface of the ground was firm and smooth. We had fixed our eye on a grove of timber on the horizon as our guide, and drove on for about an hour in a straight line, as we believed, towards it. But stopping now and then to look at the soil and the vegetation, we found that the grove had disappeared. Without knowing it we must have got into a hollow, so we pressed on. But after two hours' steady driving we could see nothing but the long grass and the endless prairie, which seemed to rise slightly all round us. I advised the driver to fix his eye upon a cloud right ahead of us, the day being calm, and to drive straight for it. Proceeding thus, in about half an hour we again caught sight of the grove, still very distant, and the smart young American driver "owned up" that he had lost his way. We had got into a flat prairie about five miles square; one of the horses stepped a little quicker than the other, and we had been diligently driving in a circle for the last two hours. We soon struck upon a track which led us towards the rising ground and among some new settlements.

One man here had entered to an eighty acre lot last spring, had built his house, broken about ten acres and sowed it with wheat, and had his little crop of "sod" corn gathered and stacked out of harm's way, close to his dwelling. The first care of an American settler on the prairie is to provide for the first winter. If he starts in May he ploughs a few acres up, and very commonly plants the Indian corn on it by making a slit with his axe on the tough upturned sod, into which he drops the seed. Rude though this preparation appears, it is generally followed by a crop, sometimes a very good one. Having thus started his "sod" corn, he constructs his house, and spends the rest of the summer in "breaking" the prairie in preparation for a wheat crop, and in cutting and making some prairie hay for the winter provender of his live stock. He also plants a few culinary vegetables and potatoes. In the end of August he sows his wheat, and, when that is completed, he harvests his "sod" corn. This keeps him out of the market the very first winter, as it is often made to suffice for the food both of the family and the live stock. "Hog and Hominy" is not infrequently the only food that the settler has to set before his guest during the first year of his possession. And though homely it is wholesome. When the crop of Indian corn is secured, there is time to begin making fences. The neighbours have a mutual interest in this and assist each other. The fences are made of posts and sawn pine timber; the posts of cedar, seven feet long, cost 3d. each, and both posts and rails are prepared in the forest, so that the settler buys them ready for his purpose, at either the nearest railway station or grove of timber, whichever happens to be most convenient. The holes for the posts are not dug out as with us, but are bored with an auger made for the purpose, and the work of fencing thus goes on with much neatness and regularity, and the fences, being all made in the same manner and with timber of the same dimensions, are very uniform and substantial. At this settlement we found the owner with four of his neighbours all busy in the work of fencing, one boring, one driving in the posts, and the others sorting and nailing on the rails.

The "snake" fence, which is common in all the timbered parts of America, is seldom met with on the prairie, and there only in the neighbourhood of a timber grove. It is a very substantial and excellent fence, but consumes too much timber in any country where that article is somewhat scarce.

In this day's ride, all the older settlers with whom we met, complained of the wheat crop as a failure this season, but the Indian corn was pretty good. One man who had settled here two years ago on good land, for which he then paid 30s. an acre, offered to sell it to us, with his "improvements" as they are called, viz. his house and a little bit of enclosure which he had made, at 62s. 6d. an acre. He was a considerable distance from a railway station.

V

War
and
Recovery

1861-1876

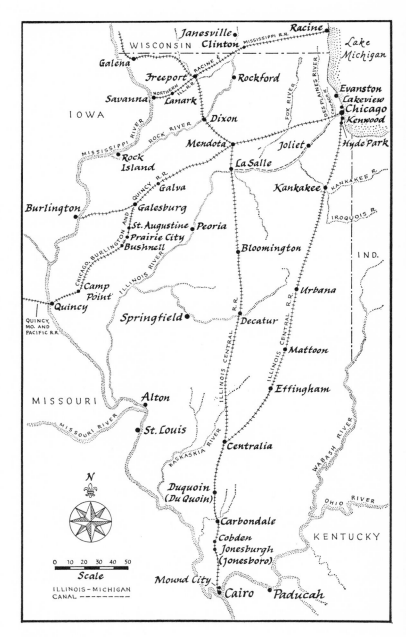

Illinois 1861–1876

No state responded to the challenge of Fort Sumter with more alacrity and enthusiasm than did Illinois. Two days after Major Robert Anderson had surrendered the fort, April 14, 1861, the Secretary of War called on Governor Richard Yates for six regiments of militia for immediate service, and four days later directed the governor to send four regiments to Cairo.

Unfortunately, Illinois had no militia. It did have fifteen or twenty independent military companies, organized more for social than belligerent purposes. In Chicago six of these companies were at full strength. On April 20 these companies were ordered to their arsenals and drill rooms, supplied with such arms as had been rounded up, sworn into the state service, and herded into an Illinois Central train. Twenty-four hours later the men reached Cairo. Quarters were found for them in cattle sheds on the county fair grounds. Thus, in less than two weeks, Illinois troops occupied the strategic junction of the Ohio and Mississippi rivers.

Meanwhile, throughout the state volunteers had been signing muster rolls and gathering at hastily established camps. While the War Department had originally called on Illinois for six regiments, the legislature increased the number to ten, and the additional four were accepted for federal service in June.

After the July and August battles of Bull Run and Wilson's Creek, both Union defeats, Lincoln called for 500,000 additional troops. By early August, Illinois had regiments numbered as high as the 55th. (Out of regard for the six regiments of volunteers raised for the Mexican War, the state started its Civil War regiments with the 7th.) By the end of the war, Illinois had organized 150 regiments of infantry, seventeen regiments of cavalry, two regiments of light artillery, and eight independent batteries. These units represented a military contribution of 260,000 men, a total exceeded only by New York, Pennsylvania, and Ohio. One need hardly mention that the state also contributed the President and, in Ulysses S. Grant, the greatest of Union generals.

Illinois men fought in many of the bloodiest battles of the war: Shiloh, Corinth, Murfreesboro, Vicksburg, Chickamauga, Atlanta, and Nashville, to list only a few. Casualties were heavy, and thousands of men spent long months in Confederate prison camps. To innumerable Illinois homes the war brought anxiety, hardship, and sorrow. No wonder the fact of war hung like a heavy cloud over the state for four years.

Yet the war did not absorb all the energies of the people. In spite of the number of farm laborers drawn into the army the production of corn, wheat, and hogs increased. New coal mines opened. Railroads extended their tracks. New factories were established, not only to turn out munitions and supplies for the armies but also to produce a variety of goods for general consumption. In the cities crowds filled the theaters, concert- and lecture-halls. On the surface, there were few signs of the nation's turmoil.

With peace, Illinois surged forward. Immigration, reduced to a small stream during the war, neared flood stage. By 1870, in a total population of 2,540,000, more than twenty per cent were foreign-born. By far the largest number, 200,000, were Germans. Next came the Irish with 120,000. Substantial groups of Norwegians and Swedes took root. The number of Negroes, 28,762 in 1870, represented a three-fold increase over 1860. During the decade the legislature repealed the infamous Black Laws, which, since territorial days, had deprived the Negro of many fundamental rights. In 1871 the voters of Cook County elected John Jones, a leader in the repeal movement, to the Board of Commissioners, thus making him the first Negro to hold public office in Illinois.

While the total population growth between 1860 and 1870 represented a fifty per cent gain, Chicago almost trebled in size (to 300,000). Smaller cities also grew rapidly. Quincy, counting 24,000, became the second city of the state, outranking Peoria by 1,200. Springfield's population doubled. Only Galena retrogressed, losing more than 1,000 residents in the decade.

Prosperity kept pace with growth. The war over, the railroads speeded up construction, especially in the central and southern parts of the state. By 1869, total mileage had reached 4,031, still second in the country to Ohio. Chicago led the nation as a market for grain, beef, pork, and lumber. Its factories employed more than half of the Illinoisans engaged in manufacturing, and became the center for the production of farm implements, wagons, iron work, brick, and textiles. Smaller cities developed industries of their own. Quincy made stoves in large quantities; Peoria led in distilleries; Elgin turned to the making of watches; La Salle and Ottawa had glass works. And most towns of any size supported a flour mill and saw mill, a wool factory, a carriage and wagon shop, and one or two foundries and machine shops.

By 1870, Illinois had taken a long step toward becoming an industrial state. Progress would be slowed by Chicago's disastrous fire and by the Panic of 1873 and the subsequent depression. But the city recovered from the fire with amazing rapidity. To overcome the effects of the panic took longer.

1861

William H. Russell

From Cairo to
Chicago by Train

William H. Russell came to the United States in 1861 with a reputation. He had reported the Crimean War for *The Times* of London, and his dispatches, collected and published in book form, had made him well known.

In Washington, Russell met Lincoln, Seward, and General Scott; then crossed into the South. There he visited Pensacola, Mobile, and New Orleans. The determination and fighting spirit of the Southerners impressed him, but he was disgusted by what he saw of slavery.

By the time Russell reached Cairo in June, 1861, his letters to *The Times* had made him unpopular in the North. But it was his account of the Battle of Bull Run, fought on July 21, 1861, that infuriated Northern opinion. When McClellan refused to allow Russell to accompany the Army of the Potomac in the Peninsular Campaign, he returned to England, there to resume the journalistic career that brought him further fame and, before the end of his life, a knighthood.

June 23d [*1861*] . . . At four o'clock in the evening I started by the train on the famous Central Illinois line from Cairo to Chicago.

The carriages were tolerably well filled with soldiers, and in addition to them there were a few unfortunate women, undergoing deportation to some less moral neighbourhood. Neither the look, language, nor manners of my fellow passengers inspired me with an exalted notion of the intelligence, comfort and respectability of the people which are so much vaunted by Mr. Seward[1] and American journals, and which, though truly attributed, no doubt, to the people of the New England states, cannot be affirmed with equal justice to belong to all the other components of the Union.

As the Southerners say, their negroes are the happiest people on the earth, so the Northerners boast "We are the most enlightened nation in the world." The soldiers in the train were intelligent enough to think they ought not to be kept without pay, and free enough to say so. The soldiers abused Cairo roundly, and indeed it is wonderful if the people can live on any food but quinine. However, speculators, looking to its natural advantages as the point where the two great rivers join, bespeak for Cairo a magnificent and prosperous future. The present is not promising.

Leaving the shanties, which face the levees, and some poor wooden houses with a short vista of cross streets partially flooded at right angles to them, the rail suddenly plunges into an unmistakeable swamp, where a forest of dead trees wave their ghastly, leafless arms over their buried trunks, like plumes over a hearse— a cheerless, miserable place, sacred to the ague and fever. This occurs close to the cleared space on which the city is to stand,— when it is finished—and the rail, which runs on the top of the embankment or levee, here takes to the trestle, and is borne over the water on the usual timber frame work.

William H. Russell, *My Diary North and South* (London, 1863), 2:77–87.
[1]   William H. Seward, Secretary of State. Ed.

"Mound City," which is the first station, is composed of a mere heap of earth, like a ruined brick-kiln, which rises to some height and is covered with fine white oaks, beneath which are a few log huts and hovels, giving the place its proud name. Tents were pitched on the mound side, from which wild-looking banditti sort of men, with arms, emerged as the train stopped. "I've been pretty well over Europe," said a meditative voice beside me, "and I've seen the despotic armies of the old world but I don't think they equal that set of boys." The question was not worth arguing—the boys were in fact very "weedy," "splinter-shinned chaps," as another critic insisted.

There were some settlers in the woods around Mound City, and a jolly-looking, corpulent man, who introduced himself as one of the officers of the land department of the Central Illinois railroad, described them as awful warnings to the emigrants not to stick in the south part of Illinois. It was suggestive to find that a very genuine John Bull, "located," as they say in the States for many years, had as much aversion to the principles of the abolitionists as if he had been born a Southern planter. Another countryman of his and mine, steward on board the steamer to Cairo, eagerly asked me what I thought of the quarrel, and which side I would back. I declined to say more than I thought the North possessed very great superiority of means if the conflict were to be fought on the same terms. Whereupon my Saxon friend exclaimed, "all the Northern States and all the power of the world can't beat the South; and why?—because the South has got cotton, and cotton is king."

The Central Illinois officer did not suggest the propriety of purchasing lots but he did intimate I would be doing service if I informed the world at large, they could get excellent land, at sums varying from ten to twenty-five dollars an acre. In America a man's income is represented by capitalizing all that he is worth, and whereas in England we say a man has so much a year, the Americans, in representing his value, observe that he is worth so many dollars, by which they mean that all he has in the world would realise the amount.

It sounds very well to an Irish tenant farmer, an English cottier, or a cultivator in the Lothians, to hear that he can get land at the rate of from £2 to £5 per acre, to be his for ever, liable only to state taxes; but when he comes to see a parallelogram marked upon the map as "good soil, of unfathomable richness," and finds in effect that he must cut down trees, eradicate stumps, drain off water, build a house, struggle for high-priced labour, and contend with imperfect roads, the want of many things to which he has been accustomed in the old country, the land may not appear to him such a bargain. In the wooded districts he has, indeed a sufficiency of fuel as long as trees and stumps last, but they are, of course, great impediments to tillage. If he goes to the prairie he finds that fuel is scarce and water by no means wholesome.

When we left this swamp and forest, and came out after a run of many miles on the clear lands which abut upon the prairie, large fields of corn lay around us, which bore a peculiarly blighted and harassed look. These fields were suffering from the ravages of an insect called the "army worm," almost as destructive to corn and crops as the locust-like hordes of North and South, which are vying with each other in laying waste the fields of Virginia. Night was falling as the train rattled out into the wild, flat sea of waving grass, dotted by patch-like Indian corn enclosures; but halts at such places as Jonesburgh and Cobden, enabled us to see that these settlements in Illinois were neither very flourishing nor very civilised.

There is a level modicum of comfort, which may be consistent with the greatest good of the greatest number, but which makes the standard of the highest in point of well-being very low indeed. I own, that to me, it would be more agreeable to see a flourishing community placed on a high level in all that relates to the comfort and social status of all its members than to recognise the old types of European civilisation, which place the castle on the hill, surround its outer walls with the mansion of doctor and lawyer, and drive the people into obscure hovels outside. But then one must confess that there are in the castle some elevating tendencies which cannot be found in the uniform level of citizen equality.

There are traditions of nobility and noble deeds in the family; there are paintings on the walls; the library is stored with valuable knowledge, and from its precincts are derived the lessons not yet unlearned in Europe, that though man may be equal the condition of men must vary as the accidents of life or the effects of individual character, called fortune, may determine.

The towns of Jonesburgh and Cobden have their little teapot-looking churches and meeting houses, their lager-bier saloons, their restaurants, their small libraries, institutes, and reading rooms, and no doubt they have also their political cliques, social distinctions and favouritisms; but it requires, nevertheless, little sagacity to perceive that the highest of the bourgeois who leads the mass at meeting and prayer, has but little to distinguish him from the very lowest member of the same body politic. Cobden, for example, has no less than four drinking saloons, all on the line of rail, and no doubt the highest citizen in the place frequents some one or other of them, and meets there the worst rowdy in the place. Even though they do carry a vote for each adult man, "locations" here would not appear very enviable in the eyes of the most miserable Dorsetshire small farmer ever ferretted out by "S. G. O."

A considerable number of towns, formed by accretions of small stores and drinking places, called magazines, round the original shed wherein live the station master and his assistants, mark the course of the railway. Some are important enough to possess a bank, which is generally represented by a wooden hut, with a large board nailed in front, bearing the names of the president and cashier, and announcing the success and liberality of the management. The stores are also decorated with large signs, recommending the names of the owners to the attention of the public, and over all of them is to be seen the significant announcement, "Cash for produce."

At Carbondale there was no coal at all to be found, but several miles farther to the north, at a place called Dugoine, a field of bituminous deposit crops out, which is sold at the pit's mouth for one dollar twenty-five cents, or about 5s. 2d. a-ton. Darkness and night fell as I was noting such meagre particulars of the new district as could be learned out of the window of a railway carriage; and finally with a delicious sensation of cool night air creeping in through the windows, the first I had experienced for many a long day, we made ourselves up for repose, and were borne steadily, if not rapidly, through the great prairie, having halted for tea at the comfortable refreshment rooms of Centralia.

There were no physical signs to mark the transition from the land of the Secessionist to Union-loving soil. Until the troops were quartered there, Cairo was for Secession, and Southern Illinois is supposed to be deeply tainted with disaffection to Mr. Lincoln. Placards on which were printed the words, "Vote for Lincoln and Hamlin, for Union and Freedom," and the old battle-cry of the last election, still cling to the wooden walls of the groceries often accompanied by bitter words or offensive additions.

One of my friends argues that as slavery is at the base of Secession, it follows that States or portions of States will be disposed to join the Confederates or the Federalists just as the climate may be favourable or adverse to the growth of slave produce. Thus in the mountainous parts of the border States of Kentucky and Tennessee, in the north-western part of Virginia, vulgarly called the pan handle, and in the pine woods of North Carolina, where white men can work at the rosin and naval store manufactories, there is a decided feeling in favour of the Union; in fact, it becomes a matter of isothermal lines. It would be very wrong to judge of the condition of a people from the windows of a railway carriage, but the external aspect of the settlements along the line, far superior to that of slave hamlets, does not equal my expectations. We all know the aspect of a wood in a gentleman's park which is submitting to the axe, and has been partially cleared, how raw and bleak the stumps look, and how dreary is the naked land not yet turned into arable. Take such a patch and fancy four or five houses made of pine planks, sometimes not painted, lighted by windows in which there is, or has been, glass, each guarded by a paling around a piece of vegetable garden, a pig house, and poultry box; let one be a grocery, which means a whisky shop, another the post-office, and a third the store where "cash is given for produce." Multiply these groups if you desire a larger settlement, and place a wooden church with a Brobdignag spire and Lilliputian body out in a waste, to be approached only by a causeway of planks; before each grocery let there be a gathering of tall men in sombre clothing, of whom the majority have small newspapers and all of whom are chewing tobacco; near the stores let there be some light wheeled carts and ragged horses, around which are knots of unmistakably German women; then see the deep tracks which lead off to similar settlements in the forest or prairie, and you have a notion, if your imagination is strong enough, of one of these civilising centres which the Americans assert to be the homes of the most cultivated and intelligent communities in the world.

Next morning, just at dawn, I woke up and got out on the platform of the carriage, which is the favourite resort of smokers and their antithetics, those who love pure fresh air, notwithstanding the printed caution "It is dangerous to stand on the platform"; and under the eye of early morn saw spread around a flat sea-like expanse not yet warmed into colour and life by the sun. The line was no longer guarded from daring Secessionists by soldiers' outposts, and small camps had disappeared. The train sped through the centre of the great verdant circle as a ship through the sea, leaving the rigid iron wake behind it tapering to a point at the horizon, and as the light spread over it the surface of the crisping corn waved in broad undulations beneath the breeze from east to west. This is the prairie indeed. Hereabouts it is covered with the finest crops, some already cut and stacked. Looking around one could see church spires rising in the distance from the white patches of houses, and by degrees the tracks across the fertile waste became apparent, and then carts and horses were seen toiling through the rich soil.

A large species of partridge or grouse appeared very abundant, and rose in flocks from the long grass at the side of the rail or from the rich carpet of flowers on the margin of the corn fields.

They sat on the fence almost unmoved by the rushing engine, and literally swarmed along the line. These are called "prairie chickens" by the people, and afford excellent sport. Another bird about the size of a thrush, with a yellow breast and a harsh cry, I learned was "the sky-lark"; and *apropos* of the unmusical creature, I was very briskly attacked by a young lady patriot for finding fault with the sharp noise it made. "Oh, my! And you not to know that your Shelley loved it above all things! Didn't he write some verses—quite beautiful, too, they are—to the sky-lark." And so "the Britisher was dried up," as I read in a paper afterwards of a similar occurrence.

At the little stations which occur at every few miles—there are some forty of them, at each of which the train stops, in 365 miles between Cairo and Chicago—the Union flag floated in the air; but we had left all the circumstance of this inglorious war behind us, and the train rattled boldly over the bridges across the rare streams, no longer in danger from Secession hatchets. The swamp had given place to the corn field. No black faces were turned up from the mowing and free white labour was at work, and the type of the labourers was German and Irish.

The Yorkshireman expatiated on the fertility of the land, and on the advantages it held out to the emigrant. But I observed all the lots by the side of the rail, and apparently as far as the eye could reach, were occupied. "Some of the very best land lies beyond on each side," said he. "Out over there in the fat places is where we put our Englishmen." By digging deep enough good water is always to be had, and coal can be carried from the rail, where it costs only 7*s*. or 8*s*. a ton. Wood there is little or none in the prairies, and it was rarely indeed a clump of trees could be detected, or anything higher than some scrub brushwood. These little communities which we passed were but the growth of a few years, and as we approached the Northern portion of the line we could see, as it were, the village swelling into the town, and the town spreading out to the dimensions of the city. "I daresay, Major," says one of the passengers, "this gentleman never saw anything like these cities before. I'm told they've nothin' like them in Europe?" "Bless you," rejoined the Major, with a wink, "just leaving out London, Edinbro', Paris, and Manchester, there's nothing on earth to ekal them." My friend, who is a shrewd fellow, by way of explanation of his military title, says, "I was a major once, a major in the Queen's Bays, but they would put troop-sergeant before it them days." Like many Englishmen he complains that the jealousy of native-born Americans effectually bars the way to political position of any naturalised citizen, and all the places are kept by the natives.

The scene now began to change gradually as we approached Chicago, the prairie subsided into swampy land, and thick belts of trees fringed the horizon; on our right glimpses of the sea could be caught through openings in the wood—the inland sea on which stands the Queen of the Lakes. Michigan looks broad and blue as the Mediterranean. Large farmhouses stud the country, and houses which must be the retreat of merchants and citizens of means; and when the train, leaving the land altogether, dashes out on a pier and causeway built along the borders of the lake, we see lines of noble houses, a fine boulevard, a forest of masts, huge isolated piles of masonry, the famed grain elevators by which so many have been hoisted to fortune, churches and public edifices, and the apparatus of a great city; and just at nine o'clock the train gives its last steam shout and comes to a standstill in the spacious station of the Central Illinois Company, and in half-an-hour more I am in comfortable quarters at the Richmond House, where I find letters waiting for me, by which it appears that the necessity for my being in Washington in all haste, no longer exists.[2] The wary General[3] who commands the army is aware that the advance to Richmond, for which so many journals are clamouring, would be attended with serious risk at present, and the politicians must be content to wait a little longer.

---

[2] Russell was anticipating the Battle of Bull Run, still several weeks in the future. Ed.

[3] Winfield Scott, still General in Chief of the U.S. Army. Ed.

1862

Anthony Trollope

Dixon and Chicago in War Time

Anthony Trollope, an Englishman even more famous than "Bull Run" Russell, came next. The third son of Frances Trollope, whose *Domestic Manners of the Americans* had aroused violent resentment in the United States thirty years earlier, arrived in this country in August, 1861. For years he had spent his days as a British postal official, his nights in writing. *The Warden* (1855) and *Barchester Towers* (1857) had made him known wherever English was spoken and read.

Except for the South, Trollope traveled extensively in the United States. He arrived in Cairo in mid-February, 1862, just after the conclusion of the successful Union campaign against Fort Henry and Fort Donelson, and then proceeded north by way of Dixon to Chicago. On the whole he admired the Americans, and the book he wrote about them went far to redress the strictures of his mother, of Dickens, and of Russell.

I have said that corn—meaning maize or Indian-corn—was to be bought at Bloomington, in Illinois, for ten cents (or five pence) a bushel. I found this also to be the case at Dixon, and also that corn of inferior quality might be bought for four pence; but I found also that it was not worth the farmer's while to shell it and sell it at such prices. I was assured that farmers were burning their Indian-corn in some places, finding it more available to them as fuel than it was for the market. The labor of detaching a bushel of corn from the hulls or cobs is considerable, as is also the task of carrying it to market. I have known potatoes in Ireland so cheap that they would not pay for digging and carrying away for purposes of sale. There was then a glut of potatoes in Ireland; and in the same way there was, in the autumn of 1861, a glut of corn in the Western States. The best qualities would fetch a price, though still a low price; but corn that was not of the best quality was all but worthless. It did for fuel, and was burned. The fact was that the produce has re-created itself quicker than mankind had multiplied. The ingenuity of man had not worked quick enough for its disposal. The earth had given forth her increase so abundantly that the lap of created humanity could not stretch itself to hold it. At Dixon, in 1861, corn cost four pence a bushel. In Ireland, in 1848, it was sold for a penny a pound, a pound being accounted sufficient to sustain life for a day; and we all felt that at that price food was brought into the country cheaper than it had ever been brought before.

Dixon is not a town of much apparent prosperity. It is one of those places at which great beginnings have been made, but as to which the deities presiding over new towns have not been propitious. Much of it has been burned down, and more of it has never been built up. It had a straggling, ill-conditioned, uncommercial aspect, very different from the look of Detroit, Milwaukee, or St. Paul. There was, however, a great hotel there, as usual, and a grand bridge over the Rock River, a tributary of the Mississippi, which runs by or through the town. I found that life might be

Anthony Trollope, *North America* (Philadelphia, 1862), 1:172–77.

maintained on very cheap terms at Dixon. To me, as a passing traveler, the charges at the hotel were, I take it, the same as elsewhere. But I learned from an inmate there that he, with his wife and horse, were fed and cared for and attended, for two dollars (or eight shillings and four pence) a day. This included a private sitting-room, coals, light, and all the wants of life—as my informant told me—except tobacco and whisky. Feeding at such a house means a succession of promiscuous hot meals, as often as the digestion of the patient can face them. Now I do not know any locality where a man can keep himself and his wife, with all material comforts and the luxury of a horse and carriage, on cheaper terms than that. Whether or no it might be worth a man's while to live at all at such a place as Dixon, is altogether another question.

We went there because it is surrounded by the prairie, and out into the prairie we had ourselves driven. We found some difficulty in getting away from the corn, though we had selected this spot as one at which the open rolling prairie was specially attainable. As long as I could see a corn-field or a tree I was not satisfied. Nor, indeed, was I satisfied at last. To have been thoroughly on the prairie, and in the prairie, I should have been a day's journey from tilled land. But I doubt whether that could now be done in the State of Illinois. I got into various patches and brought away specimens of corn—ears bearing sixteen rows of grain, with forty grains in each row, each ear bearing a meal for a hungry man.

At last we did find ourselves on the prairie, amid the waving grass, with the land rolling on before us in a succession of gentle sweeps, never rising so as to impede the view, or apparently changing in its general level, but yet without the monotony of flatness. We were on the prairie, but still I felt no satisfaction. It was private property, divided among holders and pastured over by private cattle. Salisbury Plain is as wild, and Dartmoor almost wilder. Deer, they told me, were to be had within reach of Dixon, but for the buffalo one has to go much farther afield than Illinois. The farmer may rejoice in Illinois, but the hunter and the trapper must cross the big rivers and pass away into the Western

Territories before he can find lands wild enough for his purposes. My visit to the corn-fields of Illinois was in its way successful, but I felt, as I turned my face eastward toward Chicago, that I had no right to boast that I had as yet made acquaintance with a prairie.

All minds were turned to the war, at Dixon as elsewhere. In Illinois the men boasted that, as regards the war, they were the leading State of the Union. But the same boast was made in Indiana, and also in Massachusetts, and probably in half the States of the North and West. They, the Illinoisians, call their country the war-nest of the West. The population of the State is 1,700,000, and it had undertaken to furnish sixty volunteer regiments of 1000 men each. And let it be borne in mind that these regiments, when furnished, are really full—absolutely containing the thousand men when they are sent away from the parent States. The number of souls above named will give 420,000 working men, and if, out of these, 60,000 are sent to the war, the State, which is almost purely agricultural, will have given more than one man in eight. When I was in Illinois, over forty regiments had already been sent—forty-six, if I remember rightly—and there existed no doubt whatever as to the remaining number. From the next State, Indiana, with a population of 1,350,000, giving something less than 350,000 working men, thirty-six regiments had been sent. I fear that I am mentioning these numbers *usque ad nauseam*; but I wish to impress upon English readers the magnitude of the effort made by the States in mustering and equipping an army within six or seven months of the first acknowledgment that such an army would be necessary. The Americans have complained bitterly of the want of English sympathy, and I think they have been weak in making that complaint. But I would not wish that they should hereafter have the power of complaining of a want of English justice. There can be no doubt that a genuine feeling of patriotism was aroused throughout the North and West, and that men rushed into the ranks actuated by that feeling, men for whom war and army life, a camp and fifteen dollars a month, would not of themselves have had any attraction. It came to that, that young men were

ashamed not to go into the army. This feeling of course produced
coercion, and the movement was in that way tyrannical. There is
nothing more tyrannical than a strong popular feeling among a
democratic people. During the period of enlistment this tyranny
was very strong. But the existence of such a tyranny proves the
passion and patriotism of the people. It got the better of the love
of money, of the love of children, and of the love of progress.
Wives who with their bairns were absolutely dependent on their
husbands' labors, would wish their husbands to be at the war.
Not to conduce, in some special way, toward the war; to have
neither father there, nor brother nor son; not to have lectured, or
preached, or written for the war; to have made no sacrifice for the
war, to have had no special and individual interest in the war,
was disgraceful. One sees at a glance the tyranny of all this in
such a country as the States. One can understand how quickly
adverse stories would spread themselves as to the opinion of any
man who chose to remain tranquil at such a time. One shudders
at the absolute absence of true liberty which such a passion
throughout a democratic country must engender. But he who
has observed all this must acknowledge that the passion did exist.
Dollars, children, progress, education, and political rivalry all
gave way to the one strong national desire for the thrashing and
crushing of those who had rebelled against the authority of the
stars and stripes.

When we were at Dixon they were getting up the Dement
regiment. The attempt at the time did not seem to be prosperous,
and the few men who had been collected had about them a
forlorn, ill-conditioned look. But then, as I was told, Dixon had
already been decimated and redecimated by former recruiting
colonels. Colonel Dement, from whom the regiment was to be
named, and whose military career was only now about to commence, had come late into the field.[1] I did not afterward ascertain

---

[1]   John Dement, contrary to Trollope's statement, had served in the
Black Hawk War. In 1862 he succeeded in raising only five companies
of the 75th Regiment, Illinois Volunteer Infantry, and did not
take the field himself. Ed.

what had been his success, but I hardly doubt that he did ultimately scrape together his thousand men. "Why don't you go?" I said to a burly Irishman who was driving me. "I'm not a sound man, yer honor," said the Irishman; "I'm deficient in me liver." Taking the Irishmen, however, throughout the Union, they had not been found deficient in any of the necessaries for a career of war. I do not think that any men have done better than the Irish in the American army.

From Dixon we went to Chicago. Chicago is in many respects the most remarkable city among all the remarkable cities of the Union. Its growth has been the fastest and its success the most assured. Twenty-five years ago there was no Chicago, and now it contains 120,000 inhabitants. Cincinnati, on the Ohio, and St. Louis, at the junction of the Missouri and Mississippi, are larger towns; but they have not grown large so quickly nor do they now promise so excessive a development of commerce. Chicago may be called the metropolis of American corn—the favorite city haunt of the American Ceres. The goddess seats herself there amid the dust of her full barns, and proclaims herself a goddess ruling over things political and philosophical as well as agricultural. Not furrows only are in her thoughts, but free trade also and brotherly love. And within her own bosom there is a boast that even yet she will be stronger than Mars. In Chicago there are great streets, and rows of houses fit to be the residences of a new Corn-Exchange nobility. They look out on the wide lake which is now the highway for breadstuffs, and the merchant, as he shaves at his window, sees his rapid ventures as they pass away, one after the other, toward the East.

I went over one great grain store in Chicago possessed by gentlemen of the name of Sturgess and Buckenham.[2] It was a world in itself, and the dustiest of all the worlds. It contained, when I was there, half a million bushels of wheat—or a very great many, as I might say in other language. But it was not as a storehouse that this great building was so remarkable, but as a

---

[2]   The elevator of Sturges, Buckingham & Co. Ed.

channel or a river-course for the flooding freshets of corn. It is so built that both railway vans and vessels come immediately under its claws, as I may call the great trunks of the elevators. Out of the railway vans the corn and wheat is clawed up into the building, and down similar trunks it is at once again poured out into the vessels. I shall be at Buffalo in a page or two, and then I will endeavor to explain more minutely how this is done. At Chicago the corn is bought and does change hands; and much of it, therefore, is stored there for some space of time, shorter or longer as the case may be. When I was at Chicago, the only limit to the rapidity of its transit was set by the amount of boat accommodation. There were not bottoms enough to take the corn away from Chicago, nor, indeed, on the railway was there a sufficiency of rolling stock or locomotive power to bring it into Chicago. As I said before, the country was bursting with its own produce and smothered in its own fruits.

At Chicago the hotel was bigger than other hotels and grander. There were pipes without end for cold water which ran hot, and for hot water which would not run at all. The post-office also was grander and bigger than other post-offices, though the postmaster confessed to me that the matter of the delivery of letters was one which could not be compassed. Just at that moment it was being done as a private speculation; but it did not pay, and would be discontinued. The theater, too, was large, handsome, and convenient; but on the night of my attendance it seemed to lack an audience. A good comic actor it did not lack, and I never laughed more heartily in my life. There was something wrong, too, just at that time—I could not make out what—in the Constitution of Illinois, and the present moment had been selected for voting a new Constitution. To us in England such a necessity would be considered a matter of importance, but it did not seem to be much thought of here. "Some slight alteration probably," I suggested. "No," said my informant, one of the judges of their courts, "it is to be a thorough, radical change of the whole Constitution. They are voting the delegates to-day." I went to see them vote the delegates, but, unfortunately, got into a wrong place—by invitation—and was turned out, not without some slight tumult. I trust that the new Constitution was carried through successfully.[3]

From these little details it may, perhaps, be understood how a town like Chicago goes on and prospers in spite of all the drawbacks which are incident to newness. Men in those regions do not mind failures, and, when they have failed, instantly begin again. They make their plans on a large scale, and they who come after them fill up what has been wanting at first. Those taps of hot and cold water will be made to run by the next owner of the hotel, if not by the present owner. In another ten years the letters, I do not doubt, will all be delivered. Long before that time the theater will probably be full. The new Constitution is no doubt already at work, and, if found deficient, another will succeed to it without any trouble to the State or any talk on the subject through the Union. Chicago was intended as a town of export for corn, and therefore the corn stores have received the first attention. When I was there they were in perfect working order.

From Chicago we went on to Cleveland, a town in the State of Ohio, on Lake Erie, again traveling by the sleeping-cars.

[3] This constitution was rejected at the polls. Ed.

1862

Edward Dicey

Cairo and Lanark

Edward Dicey, the third notable Englishman to visit the United States during the Civil War, was less prominent than Russell and Trollope, but equally capable as an observer and recorder of the American scene. As editorial writer and special correspondent of the London *Daily Telegraph* he spent the first half of 1862 in the United States. After traveling widely in the East he entered Illinois, like his two predecessors, at Cairo. Dicey visited Chicago, as all Englishmen did, but our interest lies in his account of one of the many new towns which the expanding railroads were bringing into existence. Unfortunately Lanark, in Carroll County in northwestern Illinois, never lived up to the hopes of its founders. It survived, but in 1960 had a population of only 1,359.

There are some places in the world which, when you get to, your first thought is—how shall I get away again; and of these Cairo is one. A Yankee legend states, that when the universe was allotted out between heaven, earth, and hell, there was one allotment intended for the third department, and crowded by mistake into the second; and that to this topographical error Cairo owes its terrestrial existence. The inhabitants boast, with a sort of reckless pride, that Cairo is also the original of the "valley of Eden," in which the firm of Chuzzlewit and Co. pitched their location; and a low hut is pointed out, which is said to be the identical one that Dickens had in his mind, when he described the dwelling where Mark Tapley immortalized himself.[1] The description of the Chuzzlewit journey down the Mississippi is utterly inconsistent with this hypothesis; but I felt it would be cruelty to deprive my informant of the one pleasant reminiscence which his city could afford. The Mississippi and the Ohio meet at an acute angle, and on the low narrow neck of land which divides the two, stands Cairo. The whole town is below the level of the river, and would be habitually under water, were it not for the high dykes which bar out the floods. As it is, Cairo is more or less flooded every year, and when I was there the whole town was under water, with the exception of the high jetty which fronts the Ohio. On this jetty, the one great street of the town, the railroad runs, and opposite the railroad are the hotels and stores, and steam-boat offices. On the land side of the jetty there stretches a town of low wooden houses standing, when I saw them, in a lake of sluggish water. Anything more dismal than the prospect from the windows of the St. Charles Hotel, out of which I looked over the whole city, can hardly be conceived. The heat was as great as that of the hottest of the dog-days with us; and the air was laden with a sort of sultry vapour we scarcely know of in England. A low mist hung over the vast waters of the Mississippi and the Ohio, and

Edward Dicey, *Six Months in the Federal States* (London and Cambridge, 1863), **2**: 116–19, 132–42.

[1]   The reference is to Dickens' *Martin Chuzzlewit*, published in 1843. Ed.

stole away across the long unbroken line of forest which covered their muddy banks. The sun burnt down fiercely on the shadeless wooden city; and whenever there came a puff of air, it raised clouds of dust from the dry mounds of porous earth of which the jetty is formed. The waters were sinking in the lagoon, and the inhabitants paddled languidly in flat-bottomed boats from house to house, looking to see what damage had been done. A close fetid smell rose from the sluggish pools of water, and fever seemed written everywhere. Along the jetty alone there were signs of life, and even that life was death-like. Long trains of empty luggage vans were drawn upon the rails on which the poorer settlers had taken refuge, when they were driven out of their dwellings by the flood, and in these wretched resting-places whole families of women and children, mostly Irish, were huddled together miserably. The great river steamboats were coming-up constantly from the camp before Corinth, bringing cargo loads of wounded and sick and disabled soldiers, who lay for hours upon the jetty, waiting for means of transport northwards. There were piles, too, of coffins—not empty ones this time—but with the dead men's names inscribed upon them, left standing in front of the railway offices. The smoke of the great steamboat chimneys hung like a pall over the town, and all day and all night long you heard the ringing of their bells and the whistling of their steam as they moved to and fro. The inhabitants were obviously too dispirited to do what little they could have done to remedy the unhealthiness of their town. Masses of putrid offal, decaying bones, and dead dogs, lay within eye-sight (not to allude to their proximity to the nasal organ) of the best dwellings in the city. The people in the street seemed to loaf about listlessly, the very shopmen, most of whom were German Jews, had barely energy enough to sell their goods; and in all Cairo there was not a newspaper printed, a fact which, in an American city, speaks volumes for the moral as well as the physical prostration of the inhabitants. The truth is, that the town is a mere depôt for transhipping goods and passengers at the junction of the Ohio and Mississippi rivers, and the great Illinois Central railroad. There is money to be made there, and therefore people are always found to come and settle at Cairo for a time. But the time, either by choice or stern necessity, is always a very short one. At first, the wounded soldiers from the army at Shiloh were sent up to Cairo, but the mortality amongst them was found to be so great, that the hospitals were closed, and the sick shipped up the river to Louisville and St. Louis, far away as they lay from the scene of action.

It had been my purpose to go on from Cairo to the camp of the western army, and the battle-field of Pittsburgh Landing. Shortly, however, before my arrival, I found that very stringent orders had been issued by General Halleck, then in command, against allowing civilians to visit the army on any pretence, and an attempt to obtain a pass would have necessitated a reference to head-quarters at Washington, and consequently a delay of many days at Cairo. There were ague and fever in the bare idea, and so unwillingly I turned my step northwards to the States of the free West . . . .

In company with the friend at whose house I was stopping in Racine, I went out into the prairie to visit the town of Lanark, situated on the extreme north-western frontier of Illinois. It is no good referring to any map of the United States to ascertain the locality of this city. It had not then completed the first year of its existence, and was inscribed on no chart or map as yet designed. Probably, beyond the circle of twenty miles round Lanark, there were not a score of people who knew that there was such a place in the world, still less that it was a rising locality. In the far West, cities start into existence like Aladdin's Palace. You read of this mushroom growth in books of travel, but it is hard to realize it without seeing it on the spot. You pass through the vast city of Chicago, along its splendid streets and quays and avenues, and are told that thirty years ago no buildings stood there except an old mud fort, raised to keep off the Indians, and that the first child ever born in the city was only married the other day. You are told so, but you hardly believe it, or, at any rate, you form no idea of how the solitary fort grew into the mighty city. To understand the process of development, you must take a baby-town just beginning to stand alone, and not the full-grown giant of a metropolis. It is for this reason, and because, in French phrase, I have "assisted" at the birth of Lanark City, that I have taken it as the specimen of a Western settlement. I was not, indeed, the first representative of the English Press who had been at Lanark. Six months before I was there, Mr. Russell[2] had visited the place with the same friend who brought me thither; but at that time the town was an idea only, and Mr. Russell passed the day shooting over the ground on which the town now stands. I may fairly claim therefore, in a literary point of view, to have discovered Lanark, and, discoverer-like, wish to lay before the world the result of my discoveries.

Between Lake Michigan and the Mississippi River lies the prairie-land of Illinois. From the river to the lakes there run a host of railroads, and amongst them there is one, now in process of construction, called the Racine and Mississippi Railroad. If you take any map of the West, and draw a straight, or what the Americans call an "air-line," from Racine to the nearest point of the Mississippi, you will have before you the exact course of the railroad in question; and twenty miles or so from the river lay the then terminus of the line, Lanark City. It was in company with Mr. George Thomson, the English projector of the railroad and the founder of the city, that Lanark and I made acquaintance with each other. The course of emigration, naturally enough, caused the borders of the great river and lake highways to be first occupied by settlers; and it is only slowly, as population increases, that the inland districts of the Western States become settled. Thus the interior of Northern Illinois is still a great prairie country, dotted here and there with new cities. Railroads are not constructed there to connect existing towns, as much as to open out new ranges of country; and if the Racine and Mississippi had to depend upon the custom of the inhabitants settled along its route before the line was made, its chance of profit would be a small one. For miles and miles our road lay along the silent,

---

[2]   William H. Russell. See above. Ed.

almost deserted, prairie—every now and then a low cutting through a hillock, sometimes a short embankment over a hollow, and then a flat bridge carried on piles across a marshy stream; but as a rule, a long level track, scarcely raised above the ground, and stretching without curve or bend for miles before and miles behind you. Right in the middle of the prairie, the rail came to an end at Lanark.

Alongside the depôt there stood a sort of railway caravan, which had been the first house of Lanark. When the rail was finished, there was not a hut or covered dwelling of any kind on the spot, and so this caravan was sent down there as a shelter for the railroad servants. By this time it had served its purpose, and I heard the order given for its transmission back to Racine, in order to be used elsewhere for a like object. Close to the station there was an hotel built already, not a pot-house or a roadside tavern, but a genuine, well-ordered inn. Of course, being in America, it had a bar-room, a public room with long tables, and public meals at fixed hours. It was clean too, and neatly furnished, as hotels in the Free States mostly are. The only national institution in which it was deficient was a gong. The first landlord—there had been three already—had levanted, taking that inevitable deafening instrument of torture with him on his departure, and happily it had not yet been replaced. There was a piano in the house, belonging to the wife of a gentleman employed on the line, and in his room I found copies of Macaulay's History, and of Gibbon's "Decline and Fall." The hotel was the property of the Company, and had been built by them to induce settlers to come to the place, and it seemed to be doing a good business. Meanwhile, the town was fast growing up around it.

Lanark, like all Western cities, is built on the simplest of plans. The owners or projectors of the settlement buy a certain number of acres, draw out a plan of the town, dividing it into streets and lots, and allow any purchaser to build any sort of dwelling on his lot he likes. The houses may be as irregular and unlike as possible; but, as the spaces allotted for the streets are not allowed to be encroached upon, the general plan of the town must correspond with the chart. The map of the city had been drawn out by a Scotch clerk in the service of the railroad, who had undertaken the task of naming the streets. To display his nationality, he had given Scotch names—Bute, Argyle, Forth, Moray, and Macs innumerable—and had only condescended to American prejudices so far as to permit of there being a Main and a Chestnut Street. Most of these streets, however, were still streets of the future, and the influx of population had as yet only called Main and Bute Streets into existence. The first of these is the commercial thoroughfare of Lanark, and in it there were some twenty shops already established. I noticed two competing ironmongers and tinmen, whose stores seemed plentifully stocked, two or three rival groceries, two saddle and harness makers, and a couple of beer and oyster saloons—a tailor's, a shoemaker's, and a lawyer's office. Besides these, were were two large stores building, one of which was to be a furniture warehouse, and the other, I think, a dry-goods shop. Bute-street consisted of private cottages. A number of shanties, too, were scattered round the place, but not close enough yet to one another to form streets. Every house in the place was of wood, many of them two, or even three, storeys high. The majority of the houses had curtains and green veranda shutters, and even the poorest I looked into were far superior in comfort to an ordinary English labourer's cottage, not to mention their being clean and airy. The streets were mere tracks of prairie-land, hardened by the wheels of teams, of which the town was full; but there were planked footpaths raised along Main-street.

The object, indeed, for which Lanark has been founded is to form a depôt for agricultural produce. The fertile plains of the vast prairie will produce boundless supplies of wheat and corn. There is no clearing to be done before these plains can be cultivated. For some cause or other, which nobody appears to me to have explained as yet satisfactorily, trees do not grow spontaneously upon the prairie, fertile as it is; and for miles on every side of Lanark there was scarcely a tree to be seen. A New England farmer, who had lately removed there, told me he should never feel at home until he had brought some rocks from the Pilgrim

State, and planted trees between their crevices, so as to form a miniature Massachusetts of his own. The richness of the soil is something marvellous. You have but to turn it up some three inches deep, and the land will yield crops year after year without rest or manure. An acre will bear from thirty to forty bushels, and wheat fetches from half-a-crown to three shillings a bushel. Indian corn, or "corn" as it is called there, is so plentiful that in many winters it is burnt for fuel. With such prices the only thing which stops the cultivation of wheat is the difficulty and expense of bringing it to market; and as fast as the railroad removes this difficulty, the cultivation extends rapidly. On one day, within a few weeks of the railroad being opened, three hundred team-loads of wheat were brought to the single station of Lanark. The population therefore of the city consists of farmers, and of dealers who have come to provide for their wants. There is, of course, a great deal of luck about Western towns, as about all other speculations in a new country; and it is impossible as yet to say whether Lanark will succeed in becoming the depôt of its district; but its prospects are flourishing. Its population, as far as I could gather, numbered already about 300 persons. There was no church yet built, but every week there came some minister or other, who preached in a room at the hotel. The people were already making arrangements for establishing schools. One of the chief settlers, with whom I had some conversation, talked of raising 1,000 dollars in the town for this purpose, and said that he hoped to get as much more from the Education Fund of Springfield, the county town of Lanark district.[3] The first public meeting in the town was to be held the week following my visit, to consider the school question, as the railway company had offered to give land for the school buildings at unusually low prices. The site of a church was, I understood, fixed upon, and I had pointed out to me a long square of prairie-land, which is to be hereafter the park of Lanark. If, a dozen years hence, the park were to be surrounded by stone mansions, the growth of Lanark

---

[3]   Here Dicey erred. Springfield, of course, was the state capital. Ed.

would not be more surprising than that of other Western cities.

The railroad was pushing on fast toward the Mississippi. It was strange to any one who, like myself, had seen a good deal of European railroad-making, to watch the rough-and-ready way in which this line was carried forward. The low mound of earth, on which the single line of rails was placed, was heaped up hastily from a trench cut on either side. You would have fancied that the weight of the engine would crush down the embankment, and break through the flat bridges supported on the slender wooden piles. But, somehow or other, American railroads work well and serve their purpose. The cost of construction was low enough to make the mouth of an English shareholder water, being under two thousand pounds a mile. This, however, is unusually cheap even for America; and I believe the cost of the Illinois Central, over as easy a country, was about eight thousand pounds per mile. What makes this cheapness of construction the more remarkable is, that wages were high. The rate of pay for common unskilled labourers varied from four to six shillings a day; and the teams, gangs of which were brought in to the work by farmers settled in the neighbourhood, were paid for at the rate of ten shillings daily. It is probable, moreover, that the farmers worked at a low rate, as the funds for the line were chiefly provided by promissory notes given by them, and secured by the mortgage of their farms. A very large proportion of the workmen were Irish; and the meadows along the line were covered with shanties and gipsy-tents, where Irish women and children huddled together, in as close a proximity to their state of native dirt as the fresh air of the prairie would permit of. The sale of whiskey or intoxicating liquors was prohibited, by a sort of extempore lynch-law; and I was struck by hearing the American overseer go round to the different shanties and tell their inmates, that if he heard of their having liquor on the premises he would pull down the huts over their heads. From what I saw of my friend Mr. Smith, I have not the slightest doubt that, though the most goodnatured man in the world, he would have kept his word to the letter.

In this out-of-the-way spot, as everywhere in the West, the war was the one subject of talk. It was too far North for Secessionism, and the people to a man were staunch Unionists. A report came while I was at Lanark, that Richmond was taken.[4] There was a flag-staff in the main street, and at once the stars and stripes were hoisted in honour of the supposed victory. It was striking, too, to observe how thoroughly all these farmers and settlers were "posted," in American parlance, on the events and politics of the war. To most of them, as Illinois men, Lincoln and McClellan (from his connexion with the Illinois Central)[5] were known personally, and their merits, as well as those of other American statesmen, were discussed freely and often ably. Mr. Stanton[6] seemed the most popular of the public men of the day, chiefly on account of his anti-slavery views. Indeed, in these Northern States of the West, popular feeling appeared to me to be more genuinely Abolitionist than in any part of the Union. There was little sentiment expressed about the negro's wrongs; but there was a strong feeling that slavery is a bad system, and a disgrace to the country; and, still more, there was a bitter hostility—almost a personal antipathy—to the slaveholding aristocracy of the South. Half-measures, or patched-up compromises, found little favour with those plain matter-of-fact Western men: "The slaveowners have made the rebellion, and they ought to pay for it. The North has been half-ruined by the South, and the South is rightly punished if she is ruined altogether. Compensation to rebels is absurd, and loyal men ought not to be called upon to pay for the property of rebels. If the South chooses to burn its cotton, and produce a famine in its own territory, so much the better. The more slaveowners are ruined, the better for the Union." Such was the purport of the sentiments I heard

---

4   This report circulated throughout the North on July 2, 1862.
      It was false. Ed.

5   George B. McClellan, at this time commanding the Army of the
      Potomac, had been chief engineer and vice-president of the Illinois
      Central Railroad from 1857 to 1860. Ed.

6   Edwin M. Stanton, Secretary of War. Ed.

expressed; the form of expression was, in general, a great deal too emphatic to be repeated literally. McClellan, with his supposed pro-slavery views, was looked on with open distrust, and spoken of, even at that period, with undisguised contempt. Lincoln, with his compensation scheme, was thought not to be up to the mark; and the policy which seemed to please this village public best was that of General Hunter, which gave a knock-down blow, for once and for all, to slavery and slaveowners.[7]

Still, in this western world of the North, it was only the rumour of war, not the war itself, that the traveller came across. The great tide of the civil war had not spread so far northwards. Illinois and Wisconsin regiments there were in the fight, and plenty, but the States themselves had been but little affected directly. According to the popular English view, the whole country is in a state of revolution, trade is bankrupt, and the entire progress of the nation stopped for years to come; yet here, in the West, in the very heat of the war, there was a great country growing into existence by rapid strides. The great march of civilization was still, as ever, tending westwards, building railroads, clearing forests, reclaiming wild lands, raising cities, and making the wilderness into a fertile country. This progress westwards across the prairie is the great fact of American history; and those who want to understand the real character of the present civil war, must remember that this progress is still going on without ceasing. The growth of Lanark is one little incident in the history of the West, and it is as such I have dwelt upon it.

---

[7]   Lincoln first proposed compensated emancipation in a special message to Congress, March 6, 1862. On May 9 General David Hunter, commanding the Department of the South, issued an order liberating all the slaves within his jurisdiction. A week later Lincoln annulled the order on the ground that the general had exceeded his authority. Ed.

1871

Sara Clarke Lippincott

Chicago

Millions knew her as Grace Greenwood, author of several volumes of prose and poetry published during the 1850's and 1860's, contributor to many magazines, and a newspaper correspondent who regularly wrote letters from Washington and Europe, which she often visited. Her real name was Sara Jane Clarke Lippincott. Since 1853 she had been the wife of Leander K. Lippincott of Philadelphia, himself an editor. In 1871 she toured the West and two years later published an account of her travels, *New Life in New Lands*. She wrote of Chicago with unabashed admiration, dwelling on aspects of the city's development often ignored by other travelers: the new parks, and heroic efforts to clean up the Chicago River by reversing its flow.

In fast and friendly Chicago, weeks go by like days, and days like hours, and life is almost too rapid to be chronicled. The "glorious Fourth" has already faded into the dim distance. I remember, however, that it was a perfect day, even in a pic-nickian sense. We spent it out of town, some eight miles to the westward, on the prairie, at a gentleman's pretty country seat,—feasting and disporting under noble ancestral trees, some of them as much as four years old! It was fine exercise dodging about under them to catch the flickering shade. But we were quite as jolly as we could have been under the olives of Albano, the cedars of Warwick, or the big pines of California. I have been from Chicago some four years, and in that time its growth and improvement have been absolutely marvellous. It grows on Independence days and Sabbath days and all days. It grows o' nights. Its enterprise, daring, and vigilance storm the land and fetter the sea, defy and override physical laws, and circumvent nature. A great part of the west side of the city seems to me to have been heaved up out of the mud by a benevolent earthquake. I see beautiful and stately marble buildings where four years ago were the humble little domiciles of the Germans, or the comfortless shanties of the Irish emigrants. What were then wastes of sand and rubbish and weeds are now lovely public squares or parks, with hard, smooth drives, ponds, rocks, hillocks, rustic bridges and seats, pretty vine-shaded arbors, and the usual park accompaniments of tame bears and caged eagles.

All this rapid change and progress is as mysterious as it is marvellous, till you know a regular, genuine Chicagoan, and see him go about his business with a drive, a devotion, a matchless economy of time and means, which stop just short of hurry and greed,—of the desperate and the sordid. The very struggle which the men of Chicago have always waged against adverse natural conditions has been to a degree ennobling, and has lifted their

Sara Clarke Lippincott, *New Life in New Lands* (New York, 1873), pp. 7–20.

lives above the commonplace. It is essentially heroic; it is something titanic; it is more creation than development. Foot by foot, inch by inch, they have gained on swampy flats, on oozing clay-banks, on treacherous sand-heaps. Every year has chronicled new enterprises, new triumphs. The sluggish, miasmatic waters, once all abroad, have been driven back, and headed off, and hemmed in, and at last brought to bay in the horrible little river that now creeps in a Stygian flood through the city it does its best to poison and pollute, while sullenly bearing back and forth rich burdens of commerce. But the hour has almost come when that ill-famed stream must take the back track,—double on itself,—actually run up its channel, and through the Illinois Canal into the Illinois River, and so down into the Mississippi. Then Lake Michigan, who does a great deal of mischief for lack of better employment, will have a heavier job to perform in the cleansing line than the rivers Peneus and Alpheus together accomplished for Augeas; and Hercules the canal-digger of Elis will be outdone by one Chesebrough.[1]

I remember the reply of a Washington candidate for the civil service to the question, "Into what do the Northern lakes empty?" It was, "Into the Gulf of Mexico." We smiled at that answer; but the time draws nigh when it shall be vindicated and verified. The young man was a prophet. He spoke for posterity and Chicago. We are all waiting the great experiment with anxiety, as once we hung with wild expectations on the ditching at Yorktown and the opening of the canals at Vicksburg and Dutch Gap. If it succeeds, it will doubtless be a grand thing for Chicago; but what will it do for the unfortunate people who live along the line of the canal? It is said that a ship canal through the Isthmus of Darien may turn the course of the Gulf Stream, and make of England a boreal waste. Is it not possible that this new enterprise of engineering will desolate a smiling country by sending off travelling the fearful smells of this monster sewer, to sicken the sweetest day and hold high carnival at night? Of

[1]   Ellis S. Chesbrough, city engineer, in charge of the project. Ed.

course, it depends on the present character of the Illinois Canal, for cleanliness and wholesomeness, whether the union be a suitable one. If it were our Washington Canal, I certainly should not forbid the banns.

But for a pleasanter theme. Lincoln Park, on the north side, is perhaps the most striking and apparently magical of all the enterprises and improvements of the city.[2] It is already very beautiful, with a variety of surface and ornamentation most wonderful, when we remember that scarcely five years ago the spot was a dreary waste of drifting sand and unsightly weeds. The manner in which these elusive sands, full of the restlessness of the waves from which they have been rescued, are fixed and fettered is very curious. Boards, stones, sticks, leaves, weeds, are laid on them, then clay is added, and so soil enough created to be sown or planted. The modest elevations called "hills," by courtesy, are also, I am told, "fearfully and wonderfully made" out of the most unsightly refuse and rubbish; so that, if future *savans*, taking them for Indian mounds, shall ever excavate one, they may perhaps come upon distinct strata of oyster-shells, tin fruit-cans, old shoes, and broken crockery, with a substratum of hoop-skirts. No means, however humble, for breaking and elevating the surface are despised. I should not be surprised to hear the moles were protected by game-laws. To obtain water for ponds and fountains they have made a requisition on the secret reservoirs of Nature,—on hidden streams that from unknown sources, perhaps as far away as the Rocky Mountains, have been for ages groping their way

> "Through caverns measureless to man,
> Down to a sunless sea."

They come forth into the light and the sweet, vital upper air, leaping and shouting, and make haste to join in the great, busy, restless life around them. Those artesian wells, with the

---

[2]   The city council first moved to establish Lincoln Park in 1860, but little was done to improve it until 1870. Ed.

lake-tunnels, will yet make Chicago more than the rival of Rome in fountains and baths, and in that cleanliness which is next to godliness. The great drive on the lake shore, from Chicago to Evanston, will be another wonder, only surpassed by the system of continuous boulevards and parks, a complete circumvallation of the city, which at no distant day will furnish one of the grandest drives in the world. Citizens of Atlantic cities say they miss their grand rocks and hills, and the sea, "that symbol of the infinite." But Lake Michigan is a respectable bit of water; and the prairie has a beauty and even a grandeur of its own. If a cornfield of several thousand acres is not "a symbol of the infinite," I should like to know what is. The present entrance to Lincoln Park is a little depressing, being through a cemetery, but those old settlers are fast being unsettled and re-established elsewhere.[3] Even the dead must "move on" in Chicago. It were impossible for one to tell where in this vicinity he could take his last sleep. Chicago houses are all liable to be moved, even the "house of worship" and "the house appointed for all living." A moving building has ceased to be a moving sight here. Not only do small frame cottages, that a year or two ago were in quiet rural localities, take fright at the snort and the rush of advancing trade, and prance off to "fresh fields and pastures new," but substantial brick edifices sometimes migrate. A few years ago a Baptist church, on Wabash Avenue, saw fit to change sides, and came over—in several pieces to be sure—to the corner of Monroe and Morgan Streets, where it now stands, looking as decorous and settled and close-communion as ever.

The parks of the west side, patriotically and democratically named "Union" and "Jefferson," though reminding one somewhat, by their modest dimensions, ingenious contrivances, and artifices of rock and water and hillock and bridge (with a "real flag-staff" and "real flag"), of the pious devices of John Wemmick for the amusement of "the aged," are yet sources of

---

[3]   At its south end Lincoln Park displaced the city cemetery. Ed.

incalculable enjoyment and good for all who live in their pleasant vicinity. Wooden pavements, splendid macadamized roads, and the new boulevards are fast bringing the beautiful suburban settlements of Lake View, Kenwood, and Hyde Park into the municipal fold. The city is bearing down upon them at a tremendous rate, and the roar of traffic will soon drown for them through the day the deep sweet monotone of the lake. In the heart of the town Chicago is making worthy preparations to entertain the great floating population of the world setting westward. The work on the new Pacific Hotel goes bravely on. I do not quite like the location, and the court-yard seems to me too small for so immense a caravansery. I am sorry to hear that it is proposed to change its name in order to do honor to one of its most munificent proprietors. No man's name seems to me big enough for such a hotel,—not Montmorency, nor Metamora, nor Hohenzollern, nor Hole-in-the-Day, or Frelinghuysen, nor Lippincott. The old court-house has taken to itself wings to meet the great rush of business in the murder and divorce line; and I hear much of Potter Palmer's new hotel, which is to be a monster affair, capable of accommodating an old-fashioned German principality, to say the least.

In short, all is astir here. There is no such thing as stagnation or rest. Lake-winds and prairie-winds keep the very air in commotion. You catch the contagion of activity and enterprise, and have wild dreams of beginning life again, and settling—no, circulating, *whirling*—in Chicago, the rapids and wild eddies of business have such a powerful fascination for one. Chicago postmen sometimes go their rounds on velocipedes. Chicago newsboys are preternaturally clever and wide-awake. I remember one of the most diminutive of the guild, coming on to the train as I was sorrowfully departing from the city one morning, in war time, and offering to sell me a copy of a leading daily, and that I said, speaking after the manner of a dark-complexioned Republican, "Why, my poor little fellow, where will you go to when you die, if you sell that naughty paper?" He turned his curly red head as he answered, "O, to the good place, I reckon, for I sell *rather* more *Tribunes* than *Timeses*."

I suppose I need hardly say that I like Chicago,—like it in spite of lake-wind sharpness and prairie flatness, damp tunnels, swinging bridges, hard water, and easy divorces. With all the distinctive characteristics of a great city, it has preserved in a wonderful degree the provincial virtues of generous hospitality, cordiality, and neighborly kindness. A lady from the East lately said of it, very charmingly, "It is New York with the heart left in." I do not deny that the genuine Chicagoan has well learned the prayer of the worthy Scotchman, "Lord, gie us a guid conceit o' oursels!" and that the prayer has been abundantly answered; but I do not think that his self-satisfaction often amounts to arrogance, or inclines him to rest on his laurels or his oars. He well knows, I think, that there is small profit in gaining the whole world to lose his own soul, and beautiful churches and beneficent mission schools, quiet deeds of mercy and munificent charities, show that he finds ways of ascent into the higher life, even from the busy dock, the noisy factory, the grim foundry, and the tempestuous Exchange . . . .

July 26.

There was a grand celebration by triumphant Chicagoans in honor of the wedding of the Chicago and Illinois Rivers,— *Othello* and *Desdemona*. There was a canal-boat excursion—which must have seemed like a dream of other days—of the city magnates, and all the power of the press, distinguished strangers, and a stray major-general or two, and many hundreds of the common people,—that is, men not worth over half a million,—all headed by his Honor the Mayor.[4]

They say the going forth of the Doge of Venice to wed the

---

4   The reversal of the current of the Chicago River, diverting the city's sewage from Lake Michigan to the Illinois and Michigan Canal, took place on July 18, 1871. The mayor was R. B. Mason. Ed.

Adriatic could never have been a circumstance to this excursion. There may have been more regal pomp and splendor on those old occasions, but nothing like the bounteous feeding of yesterday. There may have been a richer display of costumes, but nothing like the amount of Bourbon and lager drunk.

I need hardly say that the enterprise of regenerating the Chicago River is a success,—for of course they wouldn't celebrate a failure,—and Chesebrough, the bold engineer, may take up the brave iteration of old Galileo, "It moves!" The great deeps of mud and slime and unimaginable filth, the breeding-beds of miasms and death-fogs, are being slowly broken up, are passing away. One can actually perceive a current in the river at some points, and straws, after some moments of indecision, will show which way it runs. On Monday, washing-day, Lake Michigan really buckled down to her work, and did wonders in the cleansing line. We early drove down to see how far dilution and clarification had proceeded in the thick, black, torpid stream, more interested than though about to witness the annual miracle of Naples,—the liquefaction of the blood of San Gennaro. We noticed first that the color of the water had changed from almost inky blackness to something of the tawny hue of the Tiber after a storm. Then, looking steadily, we perceived it moving sluggishly, sullenly, as though in obedience to an unusual and imperative morning call, —a call from the old Father of Waters himself.

They say there is great rejoicing among the millers and manufacturers along the river down by Joliet at the increase of water which, even at this dry season, sets all their wheels whirling. The change is not only a blessing to factories, but to olfactories. There is an immense modification of the peculiar overpowering odor which was like what a grand combination of the "thirty thousand distinct smells" of the city of Cologne would be,—an odor that only last week sickened the air for half a mile on the leeward side, and for as far heavenward, probably, so that it would seem impossible a bird of delicate constitution could pass through it unharmed.

If I have given a good deal of space to this river-regeneration theme, it is because it does not seem to me a matter of mere local interest. With this city's unprecedented growth and vast increase of commerce, this river nuisance was becoming more and more intolerable and notorious. The fame of it went forth to the ends of the earth. The sailor, arriving from foreign parts, snuffed it afar off; outward bound, he crowded all sail to escape it.

1871

Aurelia R. King

The Chicago Fire

On a quiet Sunday evening, October 8, 1871, disaster struck Chicago. Fire, starting in Patrick O'Leary's cow barn at the corner of Jefferson and De Koven streets, spread east and northeast, and in little more than twenty-four hours consumed the heart of the city. The holocaust destroyed 17,000 buildings valued at $200,000,000, left 100,000 people homeless, and took three hundred lives.

The following account was written by Aurelia R. King, wife of Henry W. King, a wholesale clothing merchant. The King residence stood on Rush Street near Erie.

My Dear Friends All,

Your kind and sympathizing letter reached us last evening, and I should not have waited to receive it before telling you of our fearful experiences, only to tell the truth, I have been and still am so bewildered, I can neither think nor write. It seems a year since the fire, and it will be only two weeks tomorrow evening since it occurred.

We had just moved to the city and had settled ourselves for the winter. I had just laid in all my household supplies of every kind, including every winter garment for my children. We were never so comfortably situated in our lives—our new barn completed, our new house nearly done,—in fact we were on the high tide of prosperity a fortnight ago today. Sunday was an uncommon day with us. We had just finished repairs in our church, had a new organ, a new choir, and two wonderful sermons from our beloved pastor, Mr. Swing,[1] had a delightful communion season, and when we went to our beds, were talking of our joys in rather an exultant manner.

At one o'clock we were wakened by shouts of people in the streets declaring the city was on fire—but then the fire was far away on the south side of the river. Mr. King went quite leisurely over town, but soon hurried back with the news that the courthouse, Sherman House, post office, Tremont House, and all the rest of the business portion of the city was in flames, and thought he would go back and keep an eye on his store. He had scarcely been gone fifteen minutes when I saw him rushing back with his porters, bringing the books and papers from the store, with news that everything was burning, that the bridges were on fire, and the North Side was in danger. From that moment the flames ran

Paul M. Angle, ed., *The Great Chicago Fire* (Chicago, 1946), pp. 37–45.

[1]   David Swing of the Westminster Presbyterian Church. In 1874 he was
        tried for heresy. Acquitted, he withdrew from the Presbyterian
        communion and founded the nondenominational Central Church. Ed.

in our direction, coming faster than a man could run. The rapidity was almost incredible, the wind blew a hurricane, the air was full of burning boards and shingles flying in every direction, and falling everywhere around us. It was all so sudden we did not realize our danger until we saw our Water Works (which were beyond us) were burning, when we gave up all hope, knowing that the water supply must soon be cut off.[2]

We had just time to dress ourselves, tie up a few valuables in sheets, and stuff them into our carriage, when we had to deliberately leave our home and run for our lives. It was two o'clock in the morning when I fled with my little children clinging to me, fled literally in a shower of fire. You could not conceive anything more fearful. The wind was like a tornado, and I held fast to my little ones, fearing they would be lifted from my sight. I could only think of Sodom or Pompeii, and truly I thought the day of judgment had come. It seemed as if the whole world were running like ourselves, fire all around us, and where should we go? The cry was "North! North!" So thitherward we ran, stopping first at Mr. MacGregor Adams,[3] (you perhaps remember Mrs. Adams was formerly Mrs. Charles King) where we found many fugitives like ourselves, tarrying to take breath, every one asking every other friend: "Are you burned out?"—"What did you save?"—"Where are you going?" then running on further north up Dearborn Street to the house of another friend, followed ever by the fire. On, on we ran, not knowing whither we went till we entered Lincoln Park. There among the empty graves of the old cemetery we sat down, and threw down our bundles until we were warned to flee once more. The dry leaves and even the very ground took fire beneath our feet, and again packing our few worldly effects into our closed

---

[2]   The pumping station, on the east side of what is now Michigan Avenue, burned; the water tower, on the west side of the street, survived. Ed.

[3]   On North LaSalle Street near the beginning of the present 900 block. J. McGregor Adams was a member of the firm of Crerar, Adams & Co., dealers in railway supplies and contractors' materials. Ed.

carriage we got into a wagon and travelled with thousands of our poor fellow mortals on and on, at last crossing a bridge on North Avenue and reaching the West Side, where we found a conveyance at noon on Monday which brought us out to Elmhurst—the Adamses and ourselves.

I wish I could give you an adequate idea of that flight, but it is impossible. The streets were full of wagons transporting household furniture, people carrying on their backs the little bundles they had saved. Now and then we would pass a friend seated on a truck or a dray, huddling her children together and her two or three little treasures snatched from the burning. It was only by some look of the eye or some motion [that] we could recognize friends—we were all so blackened with dust and smoke. The ladies, many of them, [were] dressed in a nightgown and slippers with the addition of a sacque or a petticoat. Half of the gentlemen were in nightshirts and pantaloons.

We reached our home at Clover Lawn at six o'clock Monday night, finding Mother and kind neighbors with open arms and sweet sympathy waiting for us. We had had nothing to eat since Sunday at four P.M., and when I said to my little children: "Won't you be glad to get an apple?" they said: "Why, Mamma, haven't we had anything? We didn't know we were hungry." The alarm and strain upon our feelings was so intense that none of us, not even the children, knew what we wanted or what we had been through.

The next day came the anxiety as to the fate of friends, the thrilling accounts of different friends, inquiry into losses, etc., and to this day the excitement increases rather than diminishes. There is so much to see and hear. Our house is full—people coming all the time to talk over respective losses—seamstresses, teachers, workwomen whom we have known, following us out to know what they shall do, what we can do for them. We are much more fortunate than most of our friends in having a roof to cover us, and thankful are we for it, though when we go to Chicago and see the desolation there, see the houseless, homeless creatures there, we feel almost ashamed to be so comfortable.

It is a wonderful change to step from a home where not only every want was satisfied, but luxuries abounded, to a place where we have not the necessaries of life, no pins or needles, not a brush or a comb, a knife or a fork—what a contrast! It would have been hard to bear, only that we are every moment seeing or hearing of some one so much poorer than we, that we are in comparison nabobs. Then too, there is a little touch of the ludicrous now and then which cheers us. Imagine your friend Aurelia, for instance, with a thousand dollar India shawl and a lavender silk with a velvet flounce, and not a chemise to her back![4]—not a pocket handkerchief to wipe the soot from her face. A friend of mine saved nothing but a white tulle dress. Another lady has a pink silk dress but no stockings. I went to town yesterday, and was the envy and admiration of my Chicago friends because I had clean cuffs and a collar. I had to own at last that they were stolen. It was said that when the fire was raging, one citizen left his house and family, and fled on horseback down Michigan Avenue with his portrait under one arm and his lecture, "Across the Continent," under the other.[5] So, you see, we laugh a little, just enough to keep alive.

It seems to me I can never resume the even tenor of my way, my nerves are so unstrung. I do not sleep at night—when I lose myself for a little while I start up, forever running from fires with my children and a bundle. Yet we are so thankful that if we were to be afflicted, it is only by the loss of property. Our dear ones are all alive and well, and we are happy.

[4]   Mrs. King is describing herself. Ed.
[5]   William Bross, one of Chicago's leading citizens. In the Chicago Historical Society's files is a memorandum, written by George M. Higginson in 1881, regarding the Bross incident: "This is probably in part a mere rumor as the citizen mentioned was not one who would leave his family when he considered his house in danger immediately, but he probably thought there was sufficient time to secure some safe deposit for his portrait (which he undoubtedly did) knowing his daughter prized that more than any other household treasure he possessed." Ed.

The hope and cheerfulness which our business men preserve is wonderful. The whole business portion of the South Side is in ashes—there is nothing to be seen from the river to Congress Street, that is, two blocks beyond where Mr. Williams used to live. The North Side is entirely destroyed. There is only one house, Mr. Mahlon Ogden's, between the river and Wright's Grove. The fire stopped at Judge Peck's old house—you will remember Jule going there to a party with me. Such destruction is almost incredible. I suppose such a conflagration was never before known.

The sympathy of sister cities and towns is very sweet. Quantities of provisions, clothing, and money are coming in, but the sufferers are so numerous it is hard to meet their wants. Wooden buildings are going up by hundreds, stoves and bedding etc. are coming by thousands. The work of dispensing is in itself stupendous as I have reason to know, as Mr. King is President of the Relief and Aid Society. He has been obliged to delegate his work in great measure to Mr. Dexter [6] and others now, for his business demands much of his time. His personal losses are large, he thinks not less than $200,000, though he may get more insurance than he expects. He is irrepressible however, full of hope and vim, has taken a store on the West Side, and will open it on Monday next. Mr. Browning, his partner, has been here, and is hopeful and encouraging. I have sent by him to New York for supply of our present needs, and we shall soon have some blankets, pillows, towels, handkerchiefs etc.

Clothing will be easily supplied, but I can't help mourning over my household Gods, the dear things that can never be replaced—my books, the gifts of dear friends, the treasured locks of hair, my Mother's Bible, relics of my little daughter Fanny, my wedding dress, and a thousand things I had saved for my children. My pictures too, and my beautiful statue of the Sleeping

[6]   Wirt Dexter, railroad lawyer and philanthropist, had been president of the Chicago Relief and Aid Society from 1868 to 1870. Ed.

Peri that I did delight in—all gone in a minute, and I can't help a little heart-aching, though they are but the things that perish. Why Jule, I haven't a book in the world, not even a Bible. My children grieve over their little treasures and their books, and I cry with them. I saved my baby's portrait and my Mother's and husband's—my silver, my India and lace shawls, and a few silk dresses, my photograph album, and a little jewelry. The above is my stock in trade, and I feel as if my life were beginning again. I have said too much for myself, only I knew those were the things you wished first to know.

I am going to spend next week in going into the city daily to distribute clothing and food to the suffering, and I want to say to you that if you will have your Blooming Grove contribution sent directly to me, I will distribute to the needy that I know personally. I have already received money and other things from different places which I divide and apportion exactly as I see most pressing need. In so large a work as the present Chicago Relief, there must of course be some donations misapplied. Mr. King feels this, and I thought perhaps it might please your Society to send their supplies where they would reach some of the sufferers directly. I only suggest this, but you may think it wiser to send to the general fund. If you send a letter or anything to me, direct to Elmhurst, Du Page County, Illinois.

I enjoyed the visit of your two brothers amazingly, and grew young in talking of old times. If my house were not already crowded, I would ask you to come out here and look upon the state of things, the like of which was never before known. If either of your brothers has curiosity to come and see, I can give him a lounge to sleep on, and plenty of bread and butter. It is almost impossible to get accommodation in the city, it is so over-crowded. Stores are now re-opening, so we shall, within a week, be able to supply ourselves with shoes and stockings, necessary clothing, and other provisions. We are having delightful weather, which is a great blessing as it gives time for building shanties for the poor, and temporary houses for business. We are all cheerful and hopeful. I have seen only one complainer and that was a millionaire.

Now I have spun you a long yarn without saying much that I wished to, but you must imagine what I had not words to say. With much love to all your family, I am,

Your loving friend,

Aurelia R. King.

1872

John Watson

Chicago, Quincy, River Travel

John Watson, of whom we know nothing except that he was a Scot and described himself as "of Nielsland," visited the United States and Canada in the fall of 1872. Two friends, John and James Hendrie, accompanied him. Watson kept a diary, intended originally for his family, but later published for circulation among friends. He saw Chicago making a startling recovery from the great fire.

Sept. 27. While on the way from Detroit I found the sleeping car very comfortable, bearing a considerable resemblance, as regards dressing conveniences, to a berth on board of a first-class steamboat. Boots are brushed, soap and towels are provided for washing and dressing, as well as other conveniences for making a comfortable toilet; in fact, a man may obtain a good night's rest during a long journey, and be ready to transact business immediately on the arrival of the train at his destination—indeed, I noticed several gentlemen who evidently had such intention. On my arrival at Chicago I drove in an omnibus to the Sherman House, where I found, upon looking at the Strangers' Book, the Messrs Hendrie were staying. Afterwards, whilst driving about, I was much struck by the prominent evidences of the devastation caused by the great fire in October last year, as also by the strenuous and very wonderful efforts which have been made to repair its ravages. New and handsome buildings are being rapidly erected, and I have no doubt that, in a couple of years from this time, all traces of the great conflagration will, so far as covering the old ground with better, larger, and more substantial buildings is concerned, be entirely effaced. All the new houses are being built of stone and brick: such wooden erections as were hastily put up to meet emergencies immediately after the fire will ultimately be replaced by substantial edifices. Any person doubting the energy of the American character should visit Chicago, where he will see how men rise to an occasion. In some places, after such a calamity as was experienced a year ago in this city, the people would have sat down amid the ashes and given way to despair; but in Chicago, so soon as the fire had been got under or had burnt itself out, men began at once to act—to replan, to rebuild—and now the city is rising from its ashes like a phoenix, more wonderful than ever: many of the new buildings being like palaces.

After breakfast, Mr John Hendrie having arrived, we went

John Watson, *Souvenir of a Tour in the United States of America and Canada* (Glasgow, 1872), pp. 42–50.

out, and, obtaining money from the bank, called at the Cunard Office and secured berths in the steamship "Cuba," which sails to Liverpool from New York on Wednesday, 23rd October. Afterwards, accompanied by Mr Hendrie, I called on Widow Russel, and had the pleasure of handing over to her the amount of the subscriptions I had received on her behalf—viz., one hundred and fourteen dollars, a sum equal to £21 sterling. The poor widow, who seems a most respectable and industrious person, and six of her children who were present, seemed very grateful for this unexpected gift, for which they thanked me very warmly indeed. Having a carriage with us, we visited a grain elevator, one of the largest in Chicago, situated between the Chicago River and the railway. We were taken by a person in charge to the top of the building, where we saw a method of elevating, weighing, storing, and loading ships or railway cars with grain which was new to us, and with which we were highly pleased. The elevator or building which we visited belongs to a Mr Buckingham,[1] and is so capacious that it can store one million and a half bushels of Indian corn or wheat, and one and three-quarter million quarters of oats. A vessel of from 500 to 600 tons burthen can be loaded in about three hours, and every bushel of the grain be weighed before being shipped, the weighing being accomplished by large weighing machines placed at every hopper, which can weigh, as a general rule, 350 bushels of oats or Indian corn at a time. Of course the grain is not in bags, but entirely loose, and the elevators are fitted with scoops, on the same plan as dredging boats on the Clyde. The Board of Trade of Chicago has promulgated very stringent regulations as to the weighing and transfer of the grain stored in the elevators, but in spite of these rules I fear there is considerable looseness in the business, and that purchasers do not always obtain their parcel according to sample. I should fancy there are nearly twenty of these "elevators" or granaries in Chicago, and I was told that their storage capacity was equal to 11,000,000 bushels of grain.

[1] See Trollope, "Dixon and Chicago in War Time," footnote 2, above. Ed.

As many as 17,000,000 bushels of wheat reach this busy city in a year. Drove through other parts of the city in order to see still more of the ruins, and observe the activity displayed in the re-erection of the burned portions, and this re-erection is being accomplished in a way so splendid as to excite even the astonishment of former residents of the fine streets and avenues. Dined at half-past four o'clock, having previously had a tepid bath. Met Mr Hendrie's brothers James and William, the latter having been a resident in Chicago during the last twenty-two years. After tea devoted an hour or more to writing up this Diary.

Sept. 28. To-day we were joined after breakfast by Mr Hendrie's eldest brother, Alexander, who had made a run up from Kentucky to see his brothers. The five of us—that is, Alexander, James, William, and John Hendrie (I have placed them in the order of seniority), and your humble servant—then proceeded by street cars to see other places in and around Chicago. We first drove about six miles from the centre of the city to the Union Stock Yards, a large field containing upwards of 200 acres of land, all divided into pens for horses, cattle, sheep, and pigs: the field being intersected by railways at convenient distances, to facilitate the loading and unloading of the various classes of animals.[2] We were much amused by the "stock tenders," or young fellows in charge, not exactly galloping, but gently cantering or pacing at the rate of five or six miles an hour from one part of the field to another, flourishing and cracking their long lasso whips as they drive cattle from the railway cars to be weighed alive previous to being placed in the enclosures. We saw one lot of seventeen cattle driven on to the weighing machine and weighed in a body, the aggregate weight of the lot being 18,904 lbs. I fancy the railway companies charge their carriage rates by weight; and it is advantageous to know the weight either in buying or selling cattle. All the pigs and sheep, after being untrucked, are weighed in a similar way. On enquiry we learned that, during the season,

[2]   The Union Stock Yards opened for business December 26, 1865. Ed.

145,000 pigs and from 20,000 to 30,000 cattle are received at the Union Stock Yards every week, besides large lots of horses and sheep, the numbers of which we did not ascertain. Within the stock yard are three artesian wells, which afford a supply of water to the animals; one of these wells has been bored, at a width of five inches, to a depth of 1050 feet, and the pressure at the outlet, which is about four inches in diameter, is so very strong that, by means of a still smaller pipe, it is raised to tanks 40 or 50 feet high, from which the whole stock yard is supplied. We visited Dexter Racing Park, adjoining the stock yard, where trotting matches are run, and we also visited the pig-killing establishment of Messrs Cuthbert, Bland, & Co., which is near the stock yard. The pig-killing season, however, does not commence till the beginning of November, when the cold weather sets in. The foreman, in conducting us through the establishment, told us that they kill and cure during the season 5000 pigs daily, and that they employ 600 men at this establishment; and at another they have in the city of Chicago they kill and cure half a million pigs every season! The pork-packing business of Chicago employs about fifty firms, who put a fabulous number of swine through their hands annually.[3] In the neighbourhood of the stock yards, towards the south, and as far as the eye can reach, the land has all been originally prairie land, quite flat and without trees; very different, in the latter respect, from those lands we have seen in Canada, and even west from Detroit to Chicago; the stumps of burned trees still remaining in these districts showing that the progress of clearing, subsoiling, and cultivating, has yet to be gone through. Labour is what is wanted in Canada, as well as in the Western States of America, in order to render the land productive. On our way from the pig-killing establishment we observed a gentleman's dwelling-house, two storeys in height, with sunk floor, in process of being placed in position, by means of a multitude of screws, &c., after having been removed from

[3]   The plants of Armour and Morris were still relatively small. Swift and Cudahy had not yet established themselves at Chicago. Ed.

its former site, which might probably be a mile or two distant from where it was now being set down. Many of the largest buildings in Chicago had, both before and since the fire, changed their site by means of the ingenuity and labour of those who contract to do such things. We next visited a cow-killing establishment, where, during the season, the proprietor and his assistants kill, cure partly, but generally send off fresh, from 370 to 400 cattle daily; they had commenced the season to-day, and killed 102 animals in the fore-noon, just before our arrival. We waited for a little time, and saw the men spearing some twelve or fourteen animals, and I must say they got through their work with great rapidity, going about their business in a systematic way; but I will spare you the details of such wholesale killing. Returned to dinner, and, rain having fallen since midday, we kept our hotel in the evening. Posted a few newspapers to friends at home.

Sept. 29. After breakfast I went with Mr John Hendrie and heard a sermon preached in Third Church, Carpenter Street. Afterwards we walked through a portion of the city in order to view some of the recently erected buildings, and to look at those in progress of erection. Three of the best business streets are Madison Street, Randolph Street, and Washington Street, which all run parallel to each other; next there are Clark and State Streets, also running parallel to each other—these are also excellent business streets. Among the new buildings erected or nearly finished since the date of the fire I noticed many that were models of convenience and of fine proportions—indeed, I have not seen better buildings anywhere. The projecting cornices on the top of almost every block or single building are made of zinc or galvanized iron, according to a design furnished by the architect, and look well; of course they are all painted to imitate stone work. One is apt to wonder how the money requisite for the erection of such fine buildings has been obtained; but on making some inquiries on this point I was told that both capital and labour had been abundant ever since the fire. The insurance offices of America and Great Britain were prompt to settle all claims,[4] and money has been freely given on loan or mortgage by capitalists in the United States, Great Britain, France, Germany, and other countries, while at the same time workmen of every trade have flocked in from all parts of the world. In a very few years Chicago will, without doubt, be one of the finest business or commercial cities in the world, as it is the great emporium for the distribution of grain and cattle from various States many hundred miles distant—amongst others Kentucky, Tennessee, Texas, Nebraska, Iowa, and Missouri. All the food stuffs received in Chicago can be redistributed either by water in ship-loads or by railway to New York and other eastern ports, such as Boston, Montreal, and Quebec, with great celerity. It may also be stated, in connection with the American commissariat, that a considerable tonnage of dead meat packed in ice is carried by the railways to New York and other places in the East: we frequently saw cars laden with such produce.

Chicago, which is situated in the State of Illinois, has a population estimated to number over 300,000. Considering that forty years ago the name of the town was not to be found on the best maps of America, the growth of the place has been indeed wonderful. It was so lately as the spring of 1837 that a formal charter was given to the town making it a city, and the population of Chicago in that year numbered 4170 souls; seven years previously (1830) the population consisted of 170 persons; but by the year 1850 Chicago contained no less than 29,963 individuals. The official census of 1870 gives the return of the population as 299,327. The intellectual and moral progress of the people has kept pace with their material enterprise, for Chicago is rich in churches and educational institutions, one of these being a fine university, with a grand library and a most powerful telescope.[5]

---

[4] This was true as far as British companies were concerned, but many American companies were unable to pay claims in full. Ed.

[5] Watson referred to the original University of Chicago, which hardly merited this glowing description. Ed.

There are several excellently-conducted daily newspapers, and one or two luxurious theatres are in course of being built. Altogether, Chicago is a striking place, and may perhaps be classed as the chief artificial wonder of the New World. The city during the hot season is very much infested by mosquitoes, and had not my bed in this hotel been well protected by curtains devised for the purpose, I must have suffered severely. Mr Hendrie's brother James has been very much bitten by these insects during the last two nights, and to-day his hands and face are all covered with spots, as if he had been afflicted with an eruption of smallpox, in consequence of his bed not being protected by curtains. To-morrow we leave at 10-15 for Quincy, via the Chicago, Burlington, and Quincy Railway, intending to sail down the Mississippi River from Quincy to St Louis. To bed about nine o'clock.

Sept. 30. This morning, after the necessary operation of paying our hotel bill had been gone through, we proceeded to the railway station and took tickets for Quincy, for which place we started at 10.15. After passing various places, such as Mendota, Galva, &c., we reached Galesburg, 163 miles from Chicago, about five o'clock, and partook of dinner in the restaurant at the station. Leaving Galesburg, we passed Saint Augustine, Prairie City, Bushnell, Camp Point, and other places, arriving at Quincy about half-past ten o'clock in the evening. After giving up our luggage tokens to a person employed at the hotel, we drove off in the omnibus belonging to the establishment to Quincy House, leaving a part of our train to proceed to Kansas City, which it does by crossing the Mississippi on a bridge at this place. Quincy is 263 miles southwest from Chicago, and contains a population of between 18,000 and 19,000. On our way from Chicago we passed thousands of acres of Indian corn quite ripe but uncut, it being the custom, when the crops are heavy and consequently cheap, to allow the straw to remain on the ground, the ears only of the corn being gathered, and being so left, the straw of course rots, and is ploughed into the ground as manure; again, when the crops are good, and corn only realises the very small price of say from 15 to 20 cents a bushel, the farmers, having moveable fences, drive their cattle and pigs in upon the crops, and so eat them as they grow in the field. The standard weight of cleaned Indian corn is 56 lbs., but a bushel in the husk will weigh about 70 lbs. Each bushel of the corn eaten by a feeding pig will add about 8 or 9 lbs. to its weight, so that farmers easily calculate whether it will pay them better to sell their corn in the open market or feed their pigs with it; when pork is selling, as at the farm gross weight, at three cents—equal to three halfpence of our money—per pound, then Indian corn is worth 25 cents per bushel. A great portion of the land we passed through having originally been prairie land, is very flat and level, producing, however, excellent crops.

Oct. 1. Up this morning about seven o'clock, that I might have a stroll through some of the principal streets before the breakfast hour. Visited the public market, that I might ascertain the prices of butcher meat, which are as follows:—For best boiling beef, 4d. per pound; good beef steaks, 5d.; very best selected pope's-eye steak, 6d. The town, I learn, is *en fête* to-day on account of the successful opening of about 70 miles (Quincy to Kirkville) of the Quincy, Missouri, and Pacific Railway, a line which, when completed, will be about 280 miles in length. There is a street-car railway, as usual, in Quincy. We took breakfast about eight o'clock, and then walked to the river side to procure the steamboat for St Louis due at nine o'clock; but, as usual, the boat was behind time—a too common occurrence both on river and rail in this country—and we had to wait till twelve o'clock ere the vessel put in an appearance, and even after arrival the cargo had to be discharged and coals and a new cargo taken in; therefore it was about one o'clock ere we were able to start. Dined at two o'clock, dinner being included in the fare of three dollars to St Louis. On our passage we touched at Hannibal, a town on the Missouri side of the river; also at Louisiana, Clarksville, and Falmouth, all on the same side. The steamboat was quite crowded with passengers, most of them being on their way to the great State Fair of St Louis, which begins on Thursday first, and continues for nearly a fortnight. About forty of the passengers, of whom we were four, had to sleep in cots put up in the saloon. On our way down the river we grounded two or three times on sandbanks, the river from Quincy as far down as Alton, 140 miles distant, being very difficult to navigate on account of the general shallowness of the water, which is full of shifting sands and bars. We were informed that at present the stream was very low, but that it sometimes overflows its banks, on which occasions the navigation is easier. Got to my cot about half-past nine, previously giving my money and watch in charge to the clerk of the boat, that official having intimated that there were thieves and pickpockets on board, on their way, probably, to the fair at St Louis. During the night our vessel stuck on a sandbar, and was in consequence delayed for three hours. About five o'clock in the morning we were roused by the steward, that the saloon might be cleared and put in order for breakfast; at this time were just passing the mouth of the Illinois River, which is navigable for 250 miles up to a town called La Salle, after which, by means of a canal, the navigation is continued to Lake Michigan at Chicago, a distance from the Mississippi of 300 miles. Having turned out according to order, we were much pleased to find the scenery on either bank of the river grander than that we saw yesterday—more bluffs, rocks, and wooded banks to break the monotony. Breakfasted about seven o'clock, and at nine touched at Alton, a town on the Illinois side, which appears to be the seat of a considerable trade, and from which there is a branch railway to St Louis and other places. This day [Oct. 2], like yesterday, is really delightful—a strong glow of sunshine, but with a fine breeze to temper it. I have been writing the foregoing in the wheelroom, a glass enclosure in which the pilot manages the ship, steers, slows, and stops the engine, the captain not having charge of the sailing department. The wheelroom is on the fifth floor from where the deck cargo is stowed, being about 40 feet above the surface of the water, and, in consequence, commands a fine view of the river, its various islets, and the country round about. Five miles below Alton we passed the mouth of the great River Missouri, another tributary of the Mississippi, and an exceedingly muddy river, so much so that, from its junction with the mighty Mississippi, down to New Orleans and even beyond, the whole waters are quite discoloured and muddy . . . .

About noon we arrived at the city of St Louis . . . .

1876

Henry Sienkiewicz

Chicago and Its Polish Inhabitants

In 1875 Henry Sienkiewicz, the actress Helen Modjeska, her husband Count Charles Chlapowski, and several other Polish intellectuals, depressed by the state of their country and fired by travelers' accounts of the United States, decided to emigrate and found a colony in California. Sienkiewicz and a companion, Julius Sypniewski, were chosen to go ahead of the others and select a suitable location. To pay for the trip Sienkiewicz arranged to send a series of articles to the *Gazeta Polska* and other papers. Some of the letters were collected and published in European languages other than Polish, but they were not published in English until 1959.

Sienkiewicz and Sypniewski selected a site at Anaheim in southern California for their settlement. Sypniewski returned to Poland and brought back eight colonists. The immigrants knew nothing of farming and were physically incapable of hard work. After a few months they admitted failure and returned to Poland. Sienkiewicz resumed writing, and in 1895 published his great novel, *Quo Vadis?*

Twenty-four hours after leaving Detroit we finally reached Chicago. This immense city lies on the southwestern shore of Lake Michigan and serves as a port for all ships sailing between Canada and the United States. Only a few years ago it was almost completely destroyed by fire, but it is being rebuilt with inconceivable speed. Here and there traces of the conflagration can still be seen.

It was already twilight when we arrived; nevertheless, I left the hotel for the street. After my disenchantment with New York and with the dirt and disorder of the famous Empire City, Chicago made a favorable and even majestic impression. The city has an imposing appearance. The streets are unusually wide, the homes are immense, dignified, and magnificently laid out. The sidewalks are elevated above the level of the streets and astonish one by their width and the tremendous stone slabs from which they are constructed. In short, everything is enormous here. One might say the city was built by giants and for giants. It has its own unique characteristics. It is evident that the city is new, built in accordance with the needs of modern living. I had read somewhere a fantastic description of such cities and how they would look in the twentieth century. Chicago reminded me of this description. Everything here is just as that description had said it should be; everything is symmetrically laid out—perpendicular, rectangular. Everywhere are innovations which are not even known elsewhere. Along all the streets stand rows of telegraph poles supporting a vast number of wires. On other wires stretched across the street from one house to another hang signs with all kinds of inscriptions. In the evening twilight which obscures the sight of the wires, the signs appear to be suspended in mid-air without support. As you look down the street, you see entire rows of large and small signs in various colors, almost as if the town were decorated with flags for some celebration.

Henry Sienkiewicz, *Portrait of America*, trans. and ed. Charles Morley (New York, 1959), pp. 47–51, 277–78. Reprinted by permission of Columbia University Press.

On the sidewalks there is tremendous movement. Crowds of people, both white and colored, hurry in all directions with that typical American haste characteristic of business determination. The streets are full of carriages and cabs; the bells of the street-cars clang; cab men shout; everywhere are crowds and tumult, evidence of the great exuberance of life in this young city. Evening has finally fallen, yet it remains as bright as day from the thousands of gas lights. The display windows in the gigantic stores are so brilliantly illuminated by gas flames that they almost have the appearance of real fireplaces. Having selected a street at random, I walked where my eyes led me. In some places the rows of houses broke off suddenly and in their place were empty areas covered with crumbled brick and debris, evidences of the recent fire. In other localities it appeared that a new, gigantic city was being erected. As far as the eye could see I beheld scaffolding after scaffolding, unfinished houses staring out through their empty window frames, storey rising upon storey, heaps of bricks and lime. Then comes a street already built up and completed, filled with the clamor and clatter of people, and the glitter of gas lamps—in short, a city reborn like the phoenix from the ashes.

What strikes one most in these American towns is their vitality and also the almost incredible energy of their inhabitants. A fire of dimensions unheard of in modern times occurred that burned out the city like a cartridge of powder. Its inhabitants were dispersed; commerce and industry ceased; fortunes were ruined; its people were left homeless and without food. Several years elapsed and the city stands again on its former site; four hundred thousand inhabitants find work and livelihood in it; homes, mansions, churches, factories, hotels, stores are being erected. Within a few years no traces of the fire will remain—and if the town should burn again, it will once more be rebuilt. It will be rebuilt twice or even ten times, for the energy of these people surmounts all misfortunes and all disasters.

The extraordinary growth of Chicago must be attributed not only to the energy of its inhabitants but also to its extremely favorable commercial location. Situated on the shores of Lake Michigan, this "Queen of the Lakes" reigns over the entire waterway system connecting Canada with the United States. All of the trade of these inland lakes lies directly in this city's hands. Thus, Chicago might be called a port in the middle of a continent, profiting simultaneously from its inland as well as its port location. Furthermore, as the greatest city on the western route of the transcontinental railroad connecting New York with San Francisco, it unites civilization with the Far West. The East sends out the products of its industry, the West its agricultural products and natural resources, and Chicago is the great market place where the exchange takes place.

Walking aimlessly along the streets, I entered a district which was empty and quiet. Here the town ended abruptly as though cut off, and before me I beheld Lake Michigan. Waves made silvery by the light of the moon broke against the low retaining wall directly at my feet. I could scarcely hear the noise of the city in the distance. Here were no crowds; the air was fresh and all was quiet and peaceful. Only the lapping of the water and an occasional whistle from a far away steamer broke the solemn, poetic silence.

At last I returned to my hotel, the Palmer House, an edifice built of huge slabs of marble in true Babylonian magnificence. Everything within it simply drips with gold, silk, and velvet. My eyes, accustomed but a moment ago to a dim, empty, watery expanse, now blinked under the brilliant lights and the opulence spilling over the brim like the bubbles in a glass of champagne. Indeed, this hotel is the most remarkable sight in town. But in Chicago, too, as in all American cities, there are no stone or marble ruins, no churches or museums to conjure up memories of a historic past. Everything is new and contemporary. Everywhere people look to "tomorrow." "Yesterday" to them means only deserts, primeval forests, and the vast silence of the prairies.

The following day we visited other parts of the city. Since, however, only a few hours are sufficient to become acquainted with most American cities, we saw little that was new. But the day passed quickly and next morning at the break of dawn we resumed our journey westward.

The state of Illinois through whose northern extremity we traveled the entire day is a well-cultivated and densely populated state. Its main difference from the states I have previously described is its general lack of forests and trees, which gives the region a rather melancholy appearance. On both sides of the railroad track, however, can be seen cultivated fields and numerous farms one after the other.

In Illinois, as in Wisconsin to the north, there are many Polish settlements, inhabited primarily by peasants under the leadership of their parish priests. These settlements, although adequately populated, are more or less poor. Their inhabitants lack many necessities of life and long for their homeland in spite of the fact that the settlements are provided with all the conditions necessary to promote prosperity and development with fertile soil and excellent communication facilities. The reason for this is their inability to speak the English language and their unfamiliarity with American customs and local conditions in general . . . .

Since the cities along the shores of the Great Lakes were undergoing industrial expansion and needed workers, it was principally here that Polish laborers settled. Buffalo, Detroit, Chicago, and Milwaukee are full of them. The chief Polish center is Chicago, situated in the state of Illinois on enormous Lake Michigan. In this city of almost a half-million inhabitants there are said to be about 20,000 of our compatriots. The small area occupied by them in the city—a sector sneeringly referred to by the Germans as *Polakei*—leads me to think that this figure is somewhat exaggerated. Most Poles reside along Milwaukee Avenue where they have purchased homes. When I arrived in Chicago at daybreak and visited this part of the city, it seemed at times as though I were in Poland. The morning sun rising from the waters of Lake Michigan illuminated Polish inscriptions and names on the buildings. Only the innumerable telegraph wires and posts—a sight unfamiliar in Europe—and the limitless lake spoiled the illusion. Meanwhile the sun climbed steadily higher. Doors and windows began to open and the illusion was restored for the first words I heard were uttered in Polish. A few minutes later I caught sight of the church of St. Stanislaw Kostka at the corner of Noble and Bradley Streets. About eight o'clock in the morning flocks of children began to swarm here on the way to the school maintained by the priests and situated beside the church. Their childish chirping made a strange impression upon me for despite the fact that these children were studying in a Polish school an English influence was clearly perceptible in their speech.

After the children disappeared behind the school doors, I strolled along further to see the other church between Milwaukee Avenue and Division Street. It was, in a sense, only a branch of the first church, which had proved inadequate for the constantly increasing number of Poles. Unfortunately the new structure was soon seized for nonpayment of its debts.

The Poles of Chicago are united through Polish societies whose aims are to assist new arrivals, to protect their members from foreign influences, and to preserve their national spirit. There are nine such societies, but seven of these are purely religious in character. The two secular organizations are known as the "Polish Village" and the "Kosciuszko Society." Unfortunately, all of these groups do not always work together, following, in this respect, the example of their newspapers, the *Polish Catholic Gazette* and the *Chicago Polish Gazette*. At election time this disunity is harmful to Polish candidates and diminishes the influence that the Poles in Illinois might have in view of their numbers.

VI

The End
of the
Century

1876-1899

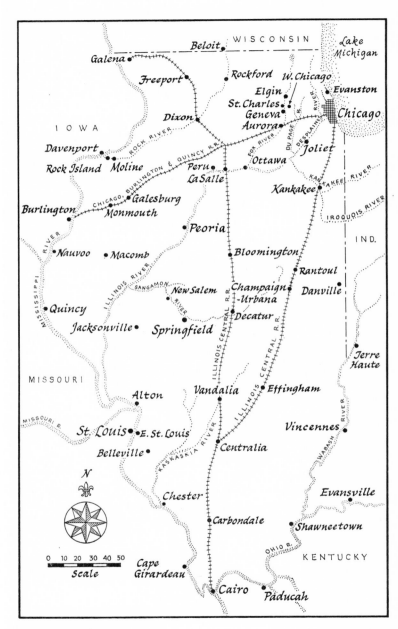

Illinois 1876–1899

In the last thirty years of the nineteenth century the population of Illinois came close to doubling (from 2,539,891 in 1870 to 4,821,550 in 1900). Immigrants came in ever-increasing numbers. While the Germans remained the most numerous element, in the 1880's Austria-Hungary, which then included Bohemia, with Poland and Russia, began to pour their thousands of discontented and ambitious nationals into the New World, and, in particular, into Illinois. Since a large proportion of the newcomers settled in Chicago, the city grew much faster than the state. From 300,000 inhabitants in 1870 it leaped to 1,700,000 in 1900.

As two distinguished Illinois historians[1] have remarked:

> Mere size or growth in numbers is not in itself a desirable thing. The most populous state is not necessarily the best off economically. But in the case of Illinois during the past half century [1870–1920] the growth of population has undoubtedly responded to improving economic conditions, and has in turn stimulated the production of wealth and promoted the economic well-being of the people. . . . The typical son of Illinois—sturdy, independent, restless even, yet conservative and loyal—shows in his composite nature some of the best qualities which have been contributed from so many diverse quarters. In its people Illinois possesses some of the best stock in the nation, whose value cannot be estimated by a mere counting of heads, but whose qualities may be trusted to

[1] Ernest L. Bogart and John M. Mathews, *The Modern Commonwealth, 1893–1918* (Springfield, 1920), p. 29.

maintain the state upon the proud eminence to which they have already elevated it.

Chicago grew phenomenally in more ways than size. Through its location and because of a magnificent transportation system, the city had ready access to raw materials: iron ore, coal, and lumber. To exploit these advantages she had an abundant supply of labor. Many citizens of vision and capacity gave her an additional asset of incalculable value. Their public spirit endowed the city with new cultural institutions: the Art Institute, the Armour Institute of Technology, Lewis Institute, the Newberry Library, and the John Crerar Library. Although the new University of Chicago owed its birth to John D. Rockefeller, Chicagoans supplemented his benefactions generously.

These reasons would have been sufficient to draw visitors to the miracle city, but another event made Chicago a magnet with worldwide power. That was the World's Columbian Exposition of 1893, celebrating a year late the four hundredth anniversary of the discovery of America. Forty-six foreign nations and almost all the states of the Union participated, and in the six months of the exposition it attracted 27,500,000 visitors. The classic lines of its buildings set in a superb man-made landscape awakened millions to the power of sheer beauty. Thousands of exhibits demonstrated the startling advances of the nineteenth century in science and technology. Congresses and conferences drew 700,000 participants and contributed an intellectual stimulus usually missing in world fairs. The Columbian Exposition was undoubtedly the finest achievement of its kind in America, and it made Chicago favorably known throughout the world.

Although Chicago took the center of the stage, the rest of the state moved forward steadily. While holding its rank as first in agriculture, by 1900 it took second place in the value of the products of its mines, and third in the value of manufactures. In slaughtering and meat packing it led by a wide margin; in the production of distilled liquors, flour, iron and steel, men's clothing, agricultural implements, and mill work it stood high. This advance, however, did not come painlessly. Labor troubles, as bitter as any in the country, marked the march toward industrialization. We need only mention the McCormick Reaper strike of 1886, which led to the Haymarket Riot, and the Pullman strike of 1894, which developed into the widespread railroad strike of the same year.

In spite of growing pains, Illinois, between 1875 and 1900, underwent changes that dwarfed those of any comparable period in its history. The historians whom we have already quoted, Bogart and Mathews, sum up its advances in two paragraphs:

> Illinois had emerged from the Civil War a commonwealth lean, forlorn, bedraggled. Mortgages and miasma plagued the lonely, backward farmer. Eight per cent interest and chills and fever harassed his unprofitable days. There was no adequate conception of scientific agriculture. . . . There was no proper understanding of the state's remarkable soil; no sense of the possibilities of its low-grade coals, or of its clays, or of concrete in its manifold forms; no proper employment of drainage, no proper use of fertilizers. . . .

> The advance of Illinois in general prosperity has been in large part the advance of the instructed farmer—an advance which has made Illinois the first agricultural state in the union. Its towns, too, have secured a good share of the general apparatus of amenity: school buildings and libraries, modern waterworks, well-paved and well-shaded streets. Prosperity has followed instruction; and culture—in the sense of a fuller, fairer, richer scheme of living—has followed prosperity.

1876

Sir John Leng

Springfield

When Sir John Leng, editor of the Dundee *Advertiser* and one of Scotland's outstanding journalists, came to the United States in 1876, he did not content himself with Chicago but moved on to Springfield, where he found the presence of Lincoln very much alive.

After three days spent in travelling over the now fertile, wealthy, and populous prairie lands of Illinois, I arranged to spend a quiet Sabbath in Springfield. On the Saturday evening we called on Mr C. M. Smith, a leading citizen in Springfield, and brother-in-law of President Lincoln, who enabled me to write a letter home from the same desk on which the President wrote his inaugural address. My previous Sundays were passed in the great cities of New York, Montreal, and Chicago, where the distances of the churches make even church attendance laborious. Springfield very much resembles an English county town like Doncaster, except that the bells of the tramway cars may generally be heard tingling in the streets. All the principal avenues are planted with trees, that shade the side walks, which are planked, instead of paved or gravelled. The best houses are of brick; but the majority are wooden-framed, neatly porticoed and balconied. One of the simplest of these is the house occupied by Abraham Lincoln at the time he was nominated for the Presidency of the United States, the principal room in which has the same carpet, wall paper, and mirror as on the night when the deputation waited upon him to announce his nomination to the highest office in the country, and the jug is still shown from which he poured out a glass of water to each of the deputies. The best portrait of Lincoln and the most life-like photograph were shown, and some reminiscences of the visit given me by Mrs Harlow, the accomplished wife of Mr Harlow, Secretary of State for Illinois, who now occupies the house, and to whom I was introduced by my travelling companion, who was an old friend of that gentleman. The Secretary, who is an excellent specimen of the best class of Americans—an able, well-informed man, light-hearted, and full of courtesy—drove us to see the State House— the finest building of the kind in the United States. It has been seven years in course of erection, and has cost $3,500,000, or about £700,000, but is not yet completed, another 100 feet having to be added to the dome, which will then be within ten

Sir John Leng, *America in 1876, Letters from the United States and Canada* (Dundee, 1877), pp. 86–92.

feet as high as that of St Paul's. The total cost when the whole building is finished will be about £1,000,000 sterling. The effect of the dome over the central lobby is even now magnificent. The architect has wisely used for the interior pillars and pilasters and the general encasement a Missouri granite very closely resembling that of Aberdeen, which, set off with some enrichments, is very impressive. In the side lobbies and the officers' rooms various coloured Italian and other European marbles have been used, and the decorations are very rich. The Senate and Representative Chambers have sculptured frescoes, in which the artist represents the leading events of American history—one of these, showing the departure of the Indian tribes and the incoming of the immigrants, being quite realistic. In the Supreme Court Room the decorations are all in the Venetian style, and the only fault that can be found with them is that they are rather too gorgeous for a Court of Justice. . . .

From the State House—of which both externally and internally the State may well be proud—we drove to the Lincoln Monument. It is creditable to the Americans that they have so soon done justice to the memory of their martyred Patriot and Statesman by the erection of a lofty obelisk in imperishable granite very like that of Peterhead. This obelisk rises from a broad pedestal containing chambers, in the front of which is a marble sarcophagus holding the embalmed remains of "honest old Abe," inscribed simply with his name, and the motto taken from one of his addresses—"With Malice towards none, with Charity towards all." On one side of the pedestal looking towards Washington is a colossal bronze figure of Lincoln, in which he is represented holding the Proclamation of Emancipation to the Slaves, and with an Eagle bearing an olive branch at his feet. There are also in course of preparation four bronze groups of figures representing the Infantry, Cavalry, Artillery, and Navy of the United States. A very large sum has been spent on this splendid Monument;[1] but I confess, as a pilgrim to the

---

[1]   The Lincoln Monument, in Oak Ridge Cemetery, was designed by Larkin G. Meade and erected at a cost of $180,000, all raised by public subscription. It was dedicated on October 15, 1874. Ed.

home of Abraham Lincoln, I would have preferred that his old house had been secured and upheld, with all its contents precisely as he left it.[2] I can well understand how the feeling of every French soldier that there may be a Marshal's baton in his knapsack develops itself in the breast of every born American citizen, who knows that the humblest American homestead may contain the future President of the United States. In our old countries there is some limit to the career of every one not "born under the purple," but in the great Western Republic it is possible for a river boatman, railsplitter, land surveyor, and country attorney, such as Lincoln was, to become one of the greatest Potentates on earth, to earn a noble and spotless fame, and to die lamented not only by the millions of his own countrymen, but by all enlightened and civilised nations.

[2]   The Lincoln Home was occupied from 1861 to 1871 by Lucian Tilton, and from 1871 to 1880 by George H. Harlow. In 1887 Robert Todd Lincoln, who had become sole owner of the property after his mother's death in 1882, deeded it to the State of Illinois, thus fulfilling Leng's wish. Ed.

1878

J. B. Loudon

The Fox River Towns

Of J. B. Loudon we know only that he was Scottish-born and, at the time of his visit to Canada and the United States, a resident of Coventry, England, famous for its manufactures and Lady Godiva. Like his predecessor Sir John Leng, Loudon wanted to see something of Illinois outside of Chicago.

The first town I visited after leaving Chicago, was Aurora. This place is very pleasantly situated on the banks of the Fox River, 35 miles from Chicago, and as the land on each side of the river rises with a gentle slope, it gives the town a very picturesque appearance. The houses, which were formerly constructed of wood, are gradually giving way to very noble cream-coloured brick buildings. Aurora has a population of over 12,000. It seems to be a very prosperous little town, and has several very important trades in it. All the Pullman cars are built here, and here are many other railway works of great size. After leaving Aurora, I followed the course of the Fox River, and soon found myself in Geneva, Kane County. This certainly is the most charming little town I have ever visited. Here the Fox River is about a quarter of a mile wide, and, as at Aurora, the banks upon each side of the river slope for about a quarter of a mile down to the river's edge, the banks being completely covered with trees of various coloured foliage; while towering above the trees may be seen some very beautiful villas, and as I stand upon the bridge, taking in the whole scene, it looks as perfect a little paradise as it is possible for the eye to gaze upon. I often felt sorry while lingering amongst such scenery, and feeling all the poetic influences such sights called up in my nature, at my utter inability to fully convey to the mind of the reader the beauties of the scene in such language that might, as it were, re-produce a correct picture before the minds of my readers. I hope, however, that they may be able to so draw upon their imagination that they may fully realise the grandeur of the scenery on the banks of the Fox River as seen at Geneva. I was so charmed with the scenery that I made it my home for several days, visiting the various places of interest, and mixing with the villagers in both their joys and their sorrows. One day the village was in deep mourning, owing to the death and funeral of one of their influential and much-respected citizens; and as he was a member of the Masonic Order, the brethren assembled

J. B. Loudon, *A Tour through Canada and the United States of America* (Coventry, 1879), pp. 72–79.

from all round the district, all very nicely dressed, with the various emblems of their lodges. I joined the order of procession to the small village burying ground, where the funeral service was conducted very impressively in the little Church, by a minister from Chicago, and afterwards at the side of the grave by several of the members belonging to deceased's lodge. The whole ceremony in the churchyard, with the surrounding beautiful scenery, was mournfully grand. I think the funeral customs quite an improvement upon those of the old country. Although all friends who attend the funeral are respectably dressed, very few wear mourning; each one dresses just as he pleases. The same applies to those who follow in carriages. Mourning coaches are seldom seen. Their hearses, too, are very pretty; they do not look so dismal as ours. They are painted in white and gold, and ornamented all round with beautifully carved figures. On each side of the hearse there are plate-glass panels, and inside there is a raised dias for the coffin to rest upon, so that all the passers-by may see the coffin if they feel so disposed.

From Geneva I travelled along the Fox River to St. Charles. This, too, is a very sweet little town, similarly situated to Geneva, on either side of the Fox River. It has a population of about 2,000. It is far-famed for its cheese and butter making establishments (they tell me there is a great deal of Cheshire cheese made here). I visited several cheese factories, and was very kindly shown the various processes. One of these places makes on an average 50 cheeses per day, and 420 lbs. of butter. The milk and cream is sent to them fresh from the neighbouring farmers every morning. There are also two or three paper mills for making paper from straw, sent to them from the same persons; so that the farmers round here form a very prosperous community. This is the little town where Dr. Thomas resided, well-known both in England and Scotland as an eminent writer and lecturer on prophetic literature. I heard him deliver a course of lectures to crowded audiences in Edinburgh during the year 1848. I also heard him lecture in Birmingham a few years ago: but he now rests from his labours in the churchyard of this charming little village.

St. Charles is also noted for its mineral springs, which I visited, and drank from the flowing stream; but with this kind of water my thirst is very soon quenched. I then left St. Charles for Elgin, which is ten miles drive, all the way along the banks of the Fox River; and the morning being fine, the drive was one of immense pleasure, the river gradually widening in some places to nearly one mile, and as every bend of the river presents a different view, with little islands here and there covered with trees, the whole scene was one of surpassing beauty. As we neared Elgin the land was very hilly, gradually rising until quite near to the town. Elgin is a very thriving little town, and viewed from the top of the hill, with the Fox River flowing gently through its centre, it looks quite a charming little city. It has several very fine streets, and some very large business establishments. The inhabitants, too, look happy and contented. This place has a very large watch manufactory employing 700 hands, which I also visited. It forms two immense blocks of buildings, one in rear of the other, but connected in the centre, and open at each end. It stands on several acres of land, which is beautifully laid out, and in splendid condition, looking more like the pleasure grounds in front of a nobleman's mansion, than grounds in front of a manufactory. The front entrance to the manufactory is also very spacious, and quite equal to the entrance into a first class American hotel. Being anxious to have a run through an American watch manufactory, I announced myself to the manager, but was doomed to disappointment, as no visitors are now allowed admittance without an order from the President of the Company, who resides in Chicago. I guess, however, that having given my name as belonging to the watch-making city of Coventry, had something to do with my being refused admittance. Not feeling disposed to take all this trouble, I contented myself by having a chat with two or three Coventry workmen I met with at the factory, and very pleased they were to see me. I had many pressing invitations to stay amongst them for a few days. The Coventry men say they are very busy, and are doing very well, but amidst all their prosperity they still retain very warm recollections of their native city, and said how much they would have liked to have returned home with me. It is their opinion, however, that unless Coventry and the other watch-making towns in England bestir themselves by the introduction of machinery, America will very soon run us out of every market in the world. The machine made American watches give general satisfaction, both as to price and quality.

Leaving Elgin, I drove a few miles into the country, and spent a very enjoyable day amongst the farmers, some of whom were friends of my youth in Edinburgh; they are now well-to-do farmers. At one farm they were busy threshing wheat, and getting 50 bushels to the acre. Altogether the farmers all through the State of Illinois present a very pleasing picture of comfort and contentment. They nearly all possess beautiful orchards, and this year there is an abundance of fruit, and being so near to Chicago, they get a ready market for all their produce. I now leave this part of Illinois for Burlington, on the banks of the Mississippi, State of Iowa.

From Elgin I returned to Aurora, and got on board of the Chicago, Burlington, and Quincy Railway for the West. This is a very comfortable line to travel upon, as attached to each train are beautiful dining-room cars, where we got our meals with as much regularity and comfort as can be obtained in any first-class hotel, and at no more cost. The tables are of course rather narrow, and you have to guard against your head coming in contact with the person that may be sitting opposite to you. This, with care, is easily avoided, but, altogether, railway travelling in America is made much more comfortable than in the old country, and long journeys are got through with much less fatigue than short ones are with us. In the construction of their cars, too, all the requirements of human nature are amply provided for; every car has a plentiful supply of ice water, and when passengers get tired of sitting they can have a long stroll from one end of the train to the other, and do a little gossiping here and there as they move about. I found the Yankees as a rule very sociable, and very pleased to talk freely with anyone direct from the mother country. I also observed a good deal of trading being done in the trains, such as in the selling of books and the daily newspapers, also fruits and sweets of every description. I think, however, this trading element is rather overdone, as in a long journey it becomes a bore to be continually asked to buy one thing and another. They have one very good arrangement. While running between stations one of the officials goes through every car and calls out the next station the train will stop at. They are also ahead of us in their arrangement for protecting passengers' luggage. When going by train you give your luggage to the porter; he gives you a brass check with a number, putting at the same time a corresponding number on your luggage. When this is done you have no need to trouble yourself more about it until you get to the end of your journey, when you present your check and your luggage is at once handed to you. My journey from Aurora to Burlington was one of great interest, as the most of this part of Illinois is under splendid cultivation, and looks as green and fertile as our own Warwickshire, until we get to within fifty miles of the Mississippi river; it then becomes very swampy and has a very disagreeable smell, which, I suppose, is caused by the excessive heat of this summer, producing decomposition amongst the vegetable matter in the swamps.

1893

Gustav Kobbé

The World's Columbian Exposition

Of the hundreds, perhaps thousands, who wrote of the World's Columbian Exposition, none had a broader background in the arts than Gustav Kobbé. Born in New York City in 1857, he attended public school until he was ten, when he went to Germany to attend the gymnasium and study piano. Returning to the United States after five years, he was graduated from Columbia College in 1877 and from its law school two years later. In spite of this training, he set out almost at once on a career as a journalist, serving as a music critic for New York newspapers and contributing articles on a variety of subjects to magazines. In this phase of his career he wrote the following account of Chicago's exposition.

Later, Kobbé became an enthusiastic and expert Wagnerian. His writings about the great German composer are still widely read.

It was in the Italian section of the Liberal Arts Building, and I was looking at a fine piece of armor well set up,—helmet with vizor, breastplate, greaves, etc.,—when a woman's voice behind me exclaimed: "It's a diver. I've seen 'em. Ain't he natural looking!"

They were evidently an elderly couple, and she has just caught sight of the armor. I wondered what the smith who had wrought with such patient art would have said could he have heard the exclamation, and have seen the couple walk on perfectly satisfied that they had seen a diver, the husband delighted with his wife's knowledge. The very resemblance which made the mistake not altogether inexcusable made it all the funnier. Doubtless amusing mistakes like this have counted up into the millions at the Fair; yet in spite of these it has not failed in its function as an educator.

It is, however, as an exposition of landscape-gardening and architecture that the Fair will most grandly fulfil this function. If there were not a picture, nor a yard of textiles, nor a ton of machinery, inside the buildings, these themselves, and their disposition about the grounds, would preach most eloquently the gospel of beauty. For this reason the location of the Fair near the geographical center was most fortunate. No unprejudiced visitor to the West can fail to admire many of its characteristics; but cheerfulness in architecture is not one of these. Somberness is rather the prevailing key in the large business blocks of most of the Western cities. In Chicago there is nothing quite so bad as the rows of brown-stone fronts with which post-bellum taste made large portions of New York hideous, but there is generally, a lack of the happy and the engaging. Surely the bright, cheerful buildings of the Fair must have a gladdening effect upon the future of building in the rapidly developing West.

Strolling through this fairy-land of modern enterprise, I often wondered what any one of the intrepid early navigators of this "brother to the sea" would have thought, if, as he

Gustav Kobbé, "Sights at the Fair," *The Century Magazine*, 46, no. 5, September, 1893.

approached this shore, he could have seen the White City rising in all its beauty as if out of the lake itself. Of course he would have laid it to mirage, and, having discovered that it was real, he would have had another and perhaps greater surprise on finding out that it was all in honor of Columbus. The latter, by the way, is not very prominent at the Fair. There is a statue of him on the basin front of the Administration Building, and I presume the central figure in the fine group of statuary on the peristyle was intended for him; but as a whole what started out as the "World's Columbian Exposition" has become simply the "World's Fair."

While the Fair lasts Washington will have to yield to it the title of "City of Magnificent Distances." One does not realize how much physical exertion sight-seeing requires until one has spent a day at the Fair. You are so occupied with looking at things that your fatigue does not find a chance to make itself felt until you turn homeward. Then you begin to wonder if you have any legs left. For this reason the wheel-chairs pushed by intelligent beings clad in sky-blue with white piping are a boon. You can "do" the Fair comfortably and systematically, and if you happen to have the same cicerone several days in succession he is apt to become *en rapport* with you, divining your tastes, and pushing you whither these would lead you. Many of the gracious pushers are theological students, a fact which has gradually fastened upon these chairs the apellation of "gospel chariots." The late Mr. Cook,[1] in the earlier days of his efforts to excite the migratory propensities of the human race, was wont to add to his circulars the announcement that "a number of marriages have been among the results of these tours." From what I have observed, I incline to think that several of the "gospel chariot" excursions will lead to equally felicitous results.

The sum of human happiness being to get about without any effort on your own part, other means of accomplishing this are provided in the electric launches and gondolas. Of these the

---

[1]   Thomas Cook, English tour agent, founder of the worldwide firm of Thomas Cook & Son. Ed.

latter are the more pleasurable, because, as the gondoliers—real ones from Venice—are obliged to work, you are made to feel delightfully lazy, lying back and gliding over the pretty lagoons, and imagining yourself in Venice—providing you have never been there. The illusion continues until your round trip—at an investment of twenty-five cents—brings you near the little wharf from which you started, when one of your gondoliers remarks: "Finis'! Gli gondolieri lika some beer!" Among these gondoliers I found an inveterate fisherman, who, when off duty, could be seen dropping a line in the shadow of one of the arches over the lagoon. Even on illumination nights he would scorn the fairy-like scenes, and seek the shadows of the arch. Possibly the fact that he never caught anything made him feel as if he were at home again in Venice.

If you wish to see the buildings from the lake, there are steam-launches which, passing under the arches of the peristyle, run out to the end of the long steamer-pier, and then, turning north, convey you to the pier from which you can board the brick battle-ship *Illinois*. This is probably the most complete naval exhibit ever made by any country, and it attracts great attention. But I saw one man who did not go aboard. He was not allowed. "Ephraim," exclaimed his wife, "you don't know nothing about ships. It might sink, or it might sail away with you." And Ephraim wisely adopted the advice of his better half, and sailed away with *her*. By the way, I am always struck at expositions of this kind with the fondness of mankind for implements devised for the destruction of mankind. This battle-ship, the models of war-ships in the Transportation Building, the Krupp guns, and the guns shown by our own Ordnance Department, seemed to me the most popular exhibits. The superb guns shown by our Ordnance Department must have created the impression that our forts are as well armed as those of any country. As a matter of fact, each gun exhibited was unique—the only one of its kind at the disposal of our army, except that we have a few more of the fine modern field-pieces, an example of which was shown.

Speaking of the Transportation Building reminds me of the

general subject of transportation to the Fair, and suggests an incident which has a decided Gilbert-and-Sullivan flavor. The Exposition managers were from the start anxious to have the railroads make a low rate to Chicago. Accordingly they appointed a committee on transportation which consisted entirely, I believe, of railroad men whose lines come into Chicago. In their capacity as committeemen these gentlemen passed a resolution requesting their respective railroads to make reduced rates during the World's Fair months. On receiving this resolution by mail the next day at their respective offices, they, in their capacity as railroad managers, wrote letters to the transportation committee denying the request which, as members of that committee, they had made.

The Transportation Building is one of the few instances of color in architecture at the Fair. Its prevailing tone is terra-cotta, and along its frieze, done somewhat after the manner of illumination in old missals, is a line of angels. This frieze is highly artistic, yet the idea of painting angels on the outside of the Transportation Building always had a humorous aspect to me—it was so suggestive of the kind of transportation we are all anxious to avoid, yet (there was a touch of the grim in this) are perhaps most exposed to when we use modern means of transportation. The golden arch which forms the main entrance to this building is probably the architectural detail most admired by the general public.[2]

France figures in a dual rôle at the Fair. She not only makes an exhibit, but shows the other nations of the world how to make an exhibit. After passing along the rows of sarcophagus-like show-cases in which the American textile exhibit is made,—an admirable exhibit so far as the goods are concerned,—it is a positive relief to come within view of the handsome façade with which the French have surrounded the space reserved for them

---

[2]   The Transportation Building, designed by Louis Sullivan, broke with the classical tradition and anticipated the future of American architecture. Ed.

in the Liberal Arts Building. Between the arches of this façade, fronting on the main avenue, are alcoves for the exhibit of furniture, costumes, and other articles requiring an interior for their most effective display. Through the main arch of the façade one enters an apartment hung with rich tapestries, and suitable mural decorations made the *entourage* of the section as artistic as the exhibits themselves. You leave the glare and heat of the rest of the building to find a subdued light and cool shade in the French section; for the French have made ceilings of cloths— some of them with borders or centers cut in lace patterns—to keep out the glare and the heat. Throughout their section they have placed comfortable settees, which are simply a boon to the weary. I have seen exhausted women throw themselves down upon these settees and fall asleep. The French section has become widely known as a place of refuge for those in need of rest. How many of those who admire the setting of this French section, and the humanity which prevails in all its arrangements, realize that it is simply the gracious expression of a national art-sense? Here was a lesson that to be great a nation need not be brutal. When I first arrived in Chicago a feeling of suppressed grief seemed to pervade the ranks of the French employees—even of the marines who stood guard in this section. I wondered what was the matter until I accidentally learned that one of the subordinate American employees in the Art Building had pasted a small label on one of Meissonier's paintings.

The Lyons silk exhibit—which has a "coast-line" of about 1000 feet of show-cases—is in the gallery. For the stairways which lead to the gallery in other parts of the building the French have substituted a broad and easy flight of steps, and the floor of the space occupied by this exhibit has been specially carpeted. The Soieries de Lyon attract a vast amount of attention from women; and, indeed, some of the silks are beautiful enough to be called woven music. This exhibit must equal in money value that of the combined textile exhibits of all the other nations. To show what a Frenchman can do with a loom, I may mention a piece of silk which represents a stretch of sea with sunset colors above it.

It is not a set woven picture, like the woven copy of Gilbert Stuart's portrait of Washington, but a piece of delicate fantasy. Strange to say, the one blot on the artistic arrangement of the French section was in this Lyons exhibit. The cases had been "dressed" about as prosaically as was possible. As an expert drygoods man said to me, they couldn't have been worse if the goods had "just been chucked in for a fire-sale." Yet so beautiful are these silks, that the men who usually rebel at the length of time they are compelled by their wives to remain among the textiles lingered willingly enough here. For myself, I prefer the small but exceedingly refined exhibit of hand-made laces made by the Compagnie des Indes down-stairs, the cheerful human toil which enters into the delicate products giving them an interest which no machine-made fabric can possess.

I happened to witness one rather funny incident in the American silk exhibit. A concern which manufactures spool silk has as a special feature a mammoth artificial silkworm. Under the case is an electrical mechanical contrivance by which raw silk is made to pass into the worm at one end, and spools of silk are caused to drop out at the other. A woman, after watching this for some time, exclaimed, "Well, I can understand it all except how it manages to get the silk colored!"

In the Midway Plaisance is probably the greatest collection of "fakes" the world has ever seen. The proprietors thereof rejoice, however, in the proud title of "Concessionnaires." Whenever I grew tired of formal sight-seeing I would stroll down the Plaisance (which was so popular that everybody soon got the knack of pronouncing it correctly) to the Egyptian temple. Here was the greatest fakir of them all. I am proud to say he was an American. In Egyptian raiment he squatted in front of the temple, and delivered his speech as follows:

"This, ladies and gentlemen, is the temple of Luxor, the tomb of Rameses II. You will find his mummy about the fifth one on the right. On the left the mummy of King Solomon's father-in-law—also his sister-in-law. The sacred dances are about to begin."

To discover, after all this, that the mummies at which people were gazing so reverentially were dummies was an unmitigated joy.

One evening after the Egypto-American above mentioned had delivered his speech about the temple of Luxor and the mummy of Rameses II., a man in the crowd turned to me and asked, "Is this the German Village?"

The personnel of the Plaisance shows reminded me of Thackeray's inventory of passengers in the *White Squall*. There are innumerable Oriental dances—Turkish, Algerian, Persian, and Egyptian, the latter in a theater annexed to the "Street in Cairo." These dances are supposed to be very suggestive, but I think most people must find them simply ugly, and wonder if they really convey the Oriental idea of grace in motion.

Much more interesting is the dancing in the large Javanese village, and in the theater of the South Sea Islanders. The former is really graceful; the latter is the best dancing in the Plaisance. It makes no pretense to grossness, but is simply downright savage. There is a certain indescribable charm about the Plaisance with its varied life; and the crowd which it attracts is an added feature of interest. Not far from the Plaisance was Buffalo Bill's Wild West Show with its Deadwood Coach, "which, ladies and gentlemen, has carried more royalty at one time, than any other coach in the world—Colonel Cody on the box!" It costs about $30 in dimes and quarters to do the Plaisance. But the fakes, including the Beauty Show, are often seen in procession through the grounds.

Very little has been said about the music at the Fair, but it is an important "life" exhibit. I do not refer to the playing of the wind-instrument bands on the out-door stands, but to the concerts in the music and festival halls. At the head of the department of music is Theodore Thomas, who still conducts with his old-time grace and significance, and can get more music out of his orchestra with a simple wave of the hand than many conductors can with hands, arms, head, and body. He is assisted by Mr. Tomlins and Mr. George H. Wilson, the latter being in charge of the arduous duties of administration. Mr. Thomas has a permanent orchestra, which can be brought up to 150 by drawing in some of the players from the bands, who for this purpose become, temporarily, musicians. Choral and instrumental concerts, many of them free, are given nearly every day, and the results cannot fail to be far-reaching.

When I laid emphasis on the importance of the Fair as an exhibit of landscape-gardening and architecture, I had in mind the unusualness of those features as compared with the exhibits as a whole, among which there are necessarily few surprises. The great firms have done about what might reasonably have been expected of them; but those strokes of genius by which individuals hitherto unknown attain on occasions like these immediate and lasting fame are not strikingly apparent. Nor should I say that outside the Art Building and the United States Government Building, residents of our large cities see much that could not be found at home. It must be remembered that our great trade bazaars—which have come up since the Centennial—draw on nearly all industries and all parts of the world, and are really world's fairs. For this reason the location of the Fair in Chicago was fortunate. It has brought things which are familiar to us in the East, where our town and rural population often gets into the large cities, to the cognizance of the great West. Thus exhibits which, perhaps, strike the visitor from a large city as nothing more than rows of show-cases are veritable revelations to the vast majority of visitors.

I have seen many descriptions of the World's Fair, but none has quite expressed what seems to me its most valuable characteristic. That is neither its size nor its magnificence, but its gracious beauty and engaging loveliness, which linger in the memory like the remembrance of a pleasant dream. We Americans are apt to boast of the bigness of various things American; but here we have something as beautiful as it is big—nay, more beautiful. So let us for once overlook its size, and let the world know that we have something that is simply beautiful.

1896

George W. Steevens

Chicago

George W. Steevens, young English journalist, came to the United States in the summer of 1896 to report the presidential campaign of that year for his paper, the London *Daily Mail*. He crossed the country to San Francisco, but went no farther south than Wilmington, North Carolina. No journalist, foreign or American, offered a better description of the candidates, McKinley and Bryan, and the mass meetings and parades of the tumultuous campaign. Steevens wrote with equal vivacity of American cities, especially Chicago.

Chicago! Chicago, queen and guttersnipe of cities, cynosure and cesspool of the world! Not if I had a hundred tongues, every one shouting a different language in a different key, could I do justice to her splendid chaos. The most beautiful and the most squalid, girdled with a twofold zone of parks and slums; where the keen air from lake and prairie is ever in the nostrils, and the stench of foul smoke is never out of the throat; the great port a thousand miles from the sea; the great mart which gathers up with one hand the corn and cattle of the West and deals out with the other the merchandise of the East; widely and generously planned with streets of twenty miles, where it is not safe to walk at night; where women ride straddlewise, and millionaires dine at mid-day on the Sabbath; the chosen seat of public spirit and municipal boodle, of cut-throat commerce and munificent patronage of art; the most American of American cities, and yet the most mongrel; the second American city of the globe, the fifth German city, the third Swedish, the second Polish, the first and only veritable Babel of the age; all of which twenty-five years ago next Friday was a heap of smoking ashes. Where in all the world can words be found for this miracle of paradox and incongruity?

Go first up on to the tower of the Auditorium[1]. In front, near three hundred feet below, lies Lake Michigan. There are lines of breakwater and a lighthouse inshore, where the water is grey and brown, but beyond and on either hand to the rim spreads the brilliant azure of deep water—the bosom of a lake which is also a sea shining in the transparent sunlight. White sails speckle its surface, and far out ocean-going steamers trail lazy streaks of smoke behind them. From the Lake blow winds now soft and life-giving like old wine, now so keen as to set every nerve and sinew on the stretch. Then turn round and look at Chicago. You might be on a central peak of the high Alps. All about you they rise, the

George W. Steevens, *The Land of the Dollar* (Edinburgh and London, 1897), pp. 144–52.
[1]   Louis Sullivan's masterpiece, completed in 1889.   Ed.

mountains of building—not in the broken line of New York, but thick together, side by side, one behind the other. From this height the flat roofs of the ordinary buildings of four or five storeys are not distinguishable from the ground; planting their feet on these rise the serried ranks of the heaven-scaling peaks. You are almost surprised to see no snow on them: the steam that gushes perpetually from their chimneys, and floats and curls away on the lake breeze, might well be clouds with the summits rising above them to the sun. Height on height they stretch away on every side till they are lost in a cloud of murky smoke inland. These buildings are all iron-cored, and the masonry is only the shell that cases the rooms in them. They can even be built downward. You may see one of them with eight storeys of brick wall above, and then four of a vacant skeleton of girders below; the superstructure seems to be hanging in air. Broader and more massive than the tall buildings of New York, older also and dingier, they do not appear, like them, simply boxes of windows. Who would suppose that mere lumps of iron and bricks and mortar could be sublime? Yet these are sublime and almost awful. You have awakened, like Gulliver, in a land of giants —a land where the very houses are instinct with almost ferocious energy and force.

Then go out on the cable car or the electric car or the elevated railroad—Chicago has them all, and is installing new ones with feverish industry every day—to the parks and the boulevards. Along Lake Shore Drive you will find the homes of the great merchants, the makers of Chicago. Many of these are built in a style which is peculiarly Chicago's own, though the best examples of it are to be seen in the business centre of the city. It uses great blocks of rough-hewn granite, red or grey. Their massive weight is relieved by wide round arches for doors and windows, by porches and porticoes, loggias and galleries, over the whole face of the building from top to bottom. The effect is almost prehistoric in its massive simplicity, something like the cyclopean ruins of Mycenæ or Tiryns. The great stones with the open arches and galleries make up a combination of solid strength and breeziness, admirably typical of the spirit of the place. On the other side of the Drive is the blue expanse of lake; in between, broad roads and ribbons of fresh grass. Yet here and there, among the castles of the magnates, you will come on a little one-storeyed wooden shanty, squatting many feet below the level of the road, paint and washed-out playbills peeling off it, and the broken windows hanging in shreds. Then again will come a patch of empty scrubby waste, choked with rank weeds and rubble. It is the same thing with the carriages in which the millionaires and their families drive up and down after church on Sunday. They are gorgeously built and magnificently horsed, only the coachman is humping his back or the footman is crossing his legs. These are trivialities, but not altogether insignificant. The desire to turn out in style is there, and the failure in a little thing betrays a carelessness of detail, an incapacity for order and proportion, which are of the essence of Chicago. Never was a better found vessel spoiled for a ha'porth of tar.

It will be well worth your while again to go South to Washington Park and Jackson Park, where the World's Fair was held. Chicago, straggling over a hundred and eighty-six square miles, was rather a tract of houses than an organic city until somebody conceived the idea of coupling her up with a ring of parks connected by planted boulevards. The southern end of the system rests on the Lake at these two parks. Chicago believes that her parks are unsurpassed in the world, and certainly they will be prodigiously fine—when they are finished. Broad drives and winding alleys, ornamental trees, banks and beds of flowers and flowering shrubs, lakes and ornamental bridges, and turf that cools the eye under the fiercest noon—you bet your life Chicago's got 'em all. Also Chicago has the Art Building, which is the one remaining relic of the World's Fair, and surely as divinely proportioned an edifice as ever filled and satisfied the eye of man. And always beyond it is the Lake. Seeming in places almost to rise above the level of the land, it stretches along the whole western side, so that Chicago is perhaps the only one of the world's greatest cities that is really built along a sea-line. Sparkling under the sun by day, or black beneath a fretwork of stars by night, it is a perpetual reminder that there is that in nature even greater and more immeasurable than the activities of Chicago.

The Art Building aforesaid is now the Field Columbian Museum, having been endowed by a leading citizen of that name with a cool million dollars.[2] Other gifts, with dividends contributed by holders of exhibition stock, brought up the total to half as much again. Chicago has a University hard by, which has come out westward, like Mahomet to the mountain, to spread the light among the twenty-five million souls that live within a morning's journey of Chicago. This University has not been in existence for quite five years; in that time it has received in benefactions from citizens of this place nearly twelve million dollars. Think of it, depressed Oxford and Cambridge—a University endowed at the rate of half a million sterling a-year! Two other prominent Chicago men found themselves in Paris a while ago, when a collection of pictures were being sold; promptly they bought up a hundred and eighty thousand dollars' worth for the gallery of their city. There is hardly a leading name in the business of the place but is to be found beneath a picture given or lent to this gallery. And mark that not only does the untutored millionaire buy pictures, but his untutored operative goes to look at them. It is the same impulse that leads school teachers of sixty to put in a course at the University during their summer vacation. Chicago is conscious that there is something in the world, some sense of form, of elegance, of refinement, that with all her corn and railways, her hogs and by-products and dollars, she lacks. She does not quite know what it is, but she is determined to have it, cost what it may. Mr Phil D. Armour, the hog king, giving a picture to the gallery, and his slaughter-house man painfully spelling out the description of it on Sunday afternoon—there is something rather pathetic in this, and assuredly something very noble.

[2] After the Field Museum removed to its present building in Grant Park in 1921, the Art Building was reconstructed of permanent materials and became the Museum of Science and Industry. Ed.

But there is another side to Chicago. There is the back side to her fifteen hundred million dollars of trade, her seventeen thousand vessels, and her network of ninety thousand miles of rail. Away from the towering offices, lying off from the smiling parks, is a vast wilderness of shabby houses—a larger and more desolate Whitechapel that can hardly have a parallel for sordid dreariness in the whole world. This is the home of labour, and of nothing else. The evening's vacancy brings relief from toil, the morning's toil relief from vacancy. Little shops compete frantically for what poor trade there is with tawdry advertisements. Street stretches beyond street of little houses, mostly wooden, begrimed with soot, rotting, falling to pieces. The pathways are of rickety and worm-eaten planks, such as we should not tolerate a day in London as a temporary gangway where a house is being built. Here the boarding is flush with the street; there it drops to it in a two-foot precipice, over which you might easily break your leg. The streets are quagmires of black mud, and no attempt is made to repair them. They are miserably lighted, and nobody thinks of illuminating them. The police force is so weak that men and women are held up and robbed almost nightly within the city limits; nobody thinks of strengthening it. Here and there is a pit or a dark cellar left wholly unguarded for the unwary foot-passenger to break his neck in. All these miles of unkempt slum and wilderness betray a disregard for human life which is more than half barbarous. If you come to your death by misadventure among these pitfalls, all the consolation your friends will get from Chicago is to be told that you ought to have taken better care of yourself. You were unfit; you did not survive. There is no more to be said about it.

The truth is that nobody in this rushing, struggling tumult has any time to look after what we have long ago come to think the bare decencies of civilisation. This man is in a hurry to work up his tallow, that man to ship his grain. Everybody is fighting to be rich, is then straining to be refined, and nobody can attend to making the city fit to live in. I have remarked several times before that America is everywhere still unfinished, and unless the character of the people modifies itself with time I do not believe it ever will be. They go half-way to build up civilisation in the desert, and then they are satisfied and rush forward to half-civilise some place further on. It is not that they are incapable of thoroughness, but that in certain things they do not feel the need of it. In Chicago there is added to this what looks like a fundamental incapacity for government. A little public interest and a small public rate would put everything right; both are wanting. Wealth every man will struggle for, and even elegance; good government is the business of nobody.

For if Chicago is the lodestone that attracts the enterprise and commercial talent of two hemispheres, it is also the sink into which drain their dregs. The hundred and twenty thousand Irish are not a wholesome element in municipal life. On the bleak west side there are streets of illiterate, turbulent Poles and Czechs, hardly able to speak a word of English. Out of this rude and undigested mass how could good government come? How could citizens combine to work out for themselves a common ideal of rational and ordered civic life? However, Chicago is now setting her house in order. It is thought a great step forward that there are now actually one-third of the members of the municipal body who can be relied upon to refuse a bribe. Some day Chicago will turn her savage energy to order and co-operation. Instead of a casual horde of jostling individuals she will become a city of citizens. She will learn that freedom does not consist solely in contempt for law. On the day she realises this she will become the greatest, as already she is the most amazing, community in the world.

1898

Sidney Webb

The Government
of Chicago

Sidney and Beatrice Webb were well known as leaders of social and economic reform when they visited the United States in 1898, although their reputation would become much greater in the future. Each had produced important works before their marriage in 1892; thereafter they worked and wrote jointly.

Originally a civil servant, Sidney Webb resigned in 1891 to stand for election, on a Fabian socialist program, to the London County Council. He was successful, and served for nineteen years. Naturally, in Chicago he would find out what he could about the city government.

Beatrice Webb kept a diary, only recently published, of the American trip. In it she included the following comments written by her husband.

The government of Chicago, which as far as results are concerned, seems to reach the lowest depths of municipal inefficiency, is, in form, rather of an old type. The charter in force dates from 1870, though it has been much modified by special legislation. There is a single legislative council, of 68 "Aldermen" elected by 34 wards; and in this Council the Mayor[1] presides (the only instance of this English practice that we have come across). But the Mayor seems to exercise no official influence in the Council. He does not, for instance, nominate the Committees, nor is he ex-officio or otherwise a member of them. (By exception, one special committee on the Elevation of Railroad Tracks, is always nominated by the Mayor, and he sits on it.) The Mayor gets $10,000 a year ($7,000 down to 1897), and seems, for all his presiding over the Council, to fill the ordinary place of an American mayor, viz. the chief executive officer. He appoints all the heads of departments who are not directly elected (these latter are the Treasurer, City Clerk, City Attorney); and the principal officers so appointed (viz. the Commissioner of Public Works, the Corporation Counsel, Comptroller and Chief of Police) are said to form the Mayor's Cabinet.

By the way, Washburn [Hempstead Washburne], a recent Mayor, refused to preside over the Council, and confined himself to his Executive duties. Nothing happened except that the Council appointed a President of its own pro-tem.

The Council appoints its Committees by party caucus of the dominant majority, which puts on only such of the minority as it chooses. This, too, is the only instance of this kind that we have found (not counting the U. S. Senate). At present in the Chicago Council the Republicans are 30 to 38 Democrats; and the much more important cross-division of honest men versus corrupt is

David A. Shannon, ed., *Beatrice Webb's American Diary, 1898* (Madison, 1963), pp. 102–7. Reprinted with permission of the copyright owners, The Regents of the University of Wisconsin and The University of Wisconsin Press.

[1]   At the time of Webb's visit Carter H. Harrison the younger was serving the first of his five terms as mayor. Ed.

about the same (30 to 38). As some of the honest Democrats refused to coalesce with the Republicans, honest and dishonest, at the outset of this new Council, the Democratic majority, mostly dishonest, packed the committees to its liking, putting on the committees a very small proportion of Republicans at all, and steadfastly excluding all honest Republicans (and also indeed all Democrats who could not be relied upon to vote without reference to honesty) from all but unimportant committees. Thus, though the reformers this Spring so far gained a partial victory at the polls—for Chicago has not within living memory had so large a minority reputed honest—yet that minority is powerless in the Council, save only that it is large enough to prevent any vote being passed over the Mayor's veto.

When we visited the Council we found the usual disorderly procedure—members smoking freely in spite of a Standing Rule expressly forbidding it; no agenda of any kind; everything read by a reading clerk; voting by call of ayes and nays and members rising to "explain their vote" after the vote had been taken: constant talking among the members, and between them and the visitors "on the floor"; and all the swinging of chairs, opening and shutting of desks, reading of newspapers and writing of letters that marks American public bodies from those at Washington downwards.

As we entered, "Bathhouse John" [John Coughlin], a saloon and private bathkeeper, and leading ward politician, was bawling at the top of his voice in Hyde Park style, reciting a flamboyant resolution denouncing any alliance between the U. S. and England on the ground that England had persistently oppressed all weaker nationalities from Ireland to the natives everywhere; that America had beaten her when America had but three millions of people, and had no need of her now that there were seventy millions; that they were not Anglo Saxons but Americans, and so forth. His claim of urgency for this resolution was lost on the vote, and it was, after another vote, referred to the Committee on the Judiciary! The whole thing was taken as a joke of Bathhouse John's.

It should be stated that the Council had got so far as to have distributed among the Aldermen a type-written list of the improvements they were to vote that evening (pavement, sewers &c. in various streets), and these were all voted en bloc without a word, each Alderman being allowed practically to put in the list whatever he pleased for his own ward.

These "improvements" (which with us would be the ordinary government) are charged, by way of special assessment, upon the owners of the property in the streets in question, and are not, in practice, even undertaken until a majority of the property owners along the street petition for them. Thus whether a Chicago street shall be paved or not, whether its sidewalks shall be of rotting planks or stone, whether its roadway shall be dirt, or wood, or brick or asphalt, is made to depend on a vote of the property owners, largely little property-owners, in the street affected, the vote being in all cases biassed by the feeling of the property-owners, not only that they will be mulcted in an indefinite sum for the "improvement," but also by the well-grounded suspicion that the Aldermen of the Ward and the Contractors will all get their picking out of the job. When a pavement wears out, as is constantly happening, the mere relaying of the pavement is deemed an "improvement" of this kind. Add to this the fact that it is usual to throw all the burden of keeping the pavement in repair on the Contractors for a long term, often 5 years; that the whole administration is so corrupt that no one sees that the contractor lays the pavement decently in the first instance, still less dreams of enforcing his liability to keep in repair—and the reason why the Chicago pavements are bad becomes clear enough.

And the pavements are unspeakably bad! The sidewalks uneven and dilapidated even when of stone in the busy streets, are nothing but rotten planks in the slum streets, with great holes rendering it positively dangerous to walk in the dark. The road-ways in the crowded business streets are, at best, of the roughest cobbles, most unevenly laid, with great holes and prominances. In the slum streets they are usually made of wood—not wood pavement as we know it, squared blocks on concrete—but merely round slices of tree-stems, placed on a dirt surface. This instantly wears uneven, and the unjoined circles of soft wood lie about loose on the mud. Imagine on sidewalks and roadways of this sort, the garbage and litter of some of the most crowded slums in the world, in an atmosphere as moist and as smoky as our Black Country towns, unswept, unwashed, untended from year's end to year's end. On the edge of the sidewalk are "garbage-boxes" large uncovered receptacles, loosely built of unjoined planks, for decaying vegetable matter, which is left to putrefy in the open air until the city's carts come round to empty it.

This utter inefficiency of municipal government so far as the streets are concerned is partly explained by the absurd state of the City's finances. The tax levied by the Council is limited by the Illinois State Constitution to 2 per cent of the assessed capital value of the property. But the assessment is left to the tender mercy of one assessor, elected by the district which he assesses. As there are eight such districts in the city, and no check and no sort of machinery for keeping the districts level, each assessor does his best to keep his own district as low as possible, and usually reduces the total below what it was when he came in. The result of this competition of assessors as to which of them can bring his district down lowest, is that the valuation of Chicago to-day, with $1\frac{3}{4}$ million inhabitants, is less than it was in 1867, when the population was $\frac{1}{4}$ million. In the last six years, it has fallen by more than 10 per cent whilst the population has risen by over 25%. (This system is just being changed; a Board of Assessors to be elected by the whole city; with an appeal to a Board of Review, of three persons also elected by the whole city.)

The result is that the City Council and the Mayor can only levy about eight shillings per head in taxes for all their purposes. If it were not for the fact that they get nearly as much again from other sources,—mostly from saloon licenses—the City would be quite bankrupt. As it is, this City of $1\frac{3}{4}$ million inhabitants spends only £30,000 a year on street pavement repairs for all its 180 square miles, and only £120,000 a year on street cleaning.

The only decent municipal enterprise (beyond the Fire

Department which is good in all American cities and may therefore be good even in Chicago), is the great system of parks and connecting boulevards. There are three Park Commissions, two appointed by the Governor of the State, and one by the Judges—the latter odd way of constructing a municipal body being said to produce the most efficient body. The parks are excellently laid out and kept, those on the South Side in particular, under the Judge-made Commission. This body carries to an extreme the principle of Direct Employment, even running successfully by its own servants, the park restaurants, where municipal ice-cream and other viands are sold. The boulevards between the parks are sometimes broad stretches of green with avenues, sometimes merely an asphalted street through the heart of the city. Thus, Jackson Boulevard is only a street running from West Chicago to the Lake. It was handed over to the Park Commission, and accepted by them, merely as an expedient for getting it paved with asphalt, the necessary outburst of public opinion having been largely supplied by the bicyclists of Chicago. The expenses of the Park Commission are levied as an extra tax on the several districts graduated according to their assumed benefit.

There is a limit of city debt to two per cent of the assessed value, but the Parks, Schools, Drainage, and Water are outside this limit, and have (narrow) limits of their own. The water supply is managed by a separate Commission appointed by the State Governor. The water is simply pumped up from Lake Michigan, and supplied unfiltered. It is thought a wonderful advance that the intakes are now a mile or two away from the shore, instead of close by as was formerly the case.

The drainage of the City is supposed to be diverted from the lake, and sent down a canalised river into the Mississippi (crude).

It should be added that Chicago has, as a city, practically no "Public Charities," these being done by Cook County, of which the city forms the greater part. The schools are under a Board of Education of 21 members, appointed by the Mayor, 7 retiring annually. There is also a separate Board for the Public Library, appointed in like manner.

The citizen of Chicago, in addition to his 2 per cent to the City Council, pays separate taxes to Cook County and Illinois State, and separate taxes also for the Parks, Drainage, Water and Library Commissions—amounting altogether to 8 or 10 per cent of the valuation (capital). But, all told, he pays (as far as I can make out) only about 32s. per head, as against at least twice as much per head in London, where all work costs much less.

1899

William Archer

Chicago

William Archer, Scottish-born and educated at Edinburgh University, was a London journalist by profession. In 1877, when he was twenty-one, he visited the United States; in 1899 he returned for a tour of two months, spending most of his time in Boston, New York, Philadelphia, Washington, Detroit, and Chicago. By his own statement, he came to study the American stage. Fortunately, he did not limit himself to this subject.

Archer's letters first appeared in the *Pall Mall Gazette* and the *Pall Mall Magazine*.

When I was in America twenty-two years ago, Chicago was the city that interested me least. Coming straight from San Francisco —which, in the eyes of a youthful student of Bret Harte, seemed the fitting metropolis of one of the great realms of romance—I saw in Chicago the negation of all that had charmed me on the Pacific slope. It was a flat and grimy abode of mere commerce, a rectilinear Glasgow; and to an Edinburgh man, or rather boy, no comparison could appear more damaging. How different is the impression produced by the Chicago of to-day! In 1877 the city was extensive enough, indeed, and handsome to boot, in a commonplace, cast-iron fashion. It was a chequer-board of Queen-Victoria-streets. To-day its area is appalling, its architecture grandiose. It is the young giant among the cities of the earth, and it stands but on the threshold of its destiny. It embraces in its unimaginable amplitude every extreme of splendour and squalor. Walking in Dearborn-street or Adams-street of a cloudy afternoon, you think yourself in a frowning and fuliginous city of Dis, piled up by superhuman and apparently sinister powers. Cycling round the boulevards of a sunny morning, you rejoice in the airy and spacious greenery of the Garden City. Driving along the Lake Shore to Lincoln Park in the flush of sunset, you wonder that the dwellers in this street of palaces should trouble their heads about Naples or Venice, when they have before their very windows the innumerable laughter, the ever-shifting opalescence, of their fascinating inland sea. Plunging in the electric cars through the river subway, and emerging in the West Side, you realize that the slums of Chicago, if not quite so tightly packed as those of New York or London, are no whit behind them in the other essentials of civilised barbarism. Chicago, more than any other city of my acquaintance, suggests that antique conception of the underworld which placed Elysium and Tartarus not only on the same plane, but, so to speak, round the corner from each other.

William Archer, *America To-Day: Observations and Reflections* (New York, 1899), pp. 102–12.

As the elephant (or rather the megatherium) to the giraffe, so is the colossal business block of Chicago to the sky-scraper of New York. There is a proportion and dignity in the mammoth buildings of Chicago which is lacking in most of those which form the jagged sky-line of Manhattan Island. For one reason or another— no doubt some difference in the system of land tenure is at the root of the matter—the Chicago architect has usually a larger plot of ground to operate on than his New York colleague, and can consequently give his building breadth and depth as well as height. Before the lanky giants of the Eastern metropolis, one has generally to hold one's æsthetic judgment in abeyance. They are not precisely ugly, but still less, as a rule, can they be called beautiful. They are simply astounding manifestations of human energy and heaven-storming audacity. They stand outside the pale of æsthetics, like the Eiffel Tower or the Forth Bridge. But in Chicago proportion goes along with mere height, and many of the business houses are, if not beautiful, at least æsthetically impressive—for instance, the grim fortalice of Marshall Field & Company, the Masonic Temple, the Women's Temperance Temple (a structure with a touch of real beauty), and such vast cities within the city as the Great Northern Building and the Monadnock Block. The last-named edifice alone is said to have a daily population of 6000. A city ordinance now limits the height of building to ten stories; but even that is a respectable allowance. Moreover, it is found that where giant constructions cluster too close together, they (literally) stand in each other's light, and the middle stories do not let. Thus the heaven-storming era is probably over; but there is all the more reason to feel assured that the business centre of Chicago will ere long be not only grandiose but architecturally dignified and satisfactory. A growing thirst for beauty has come upon the city, and architects are earnestly studying how to assuage it. In magnificence of internal decoration, Chicago can already challenge the world: for instance, in the white marble vestibule and corridors of The Rookery, and the noble hall of the Illinois Trust Bank.

At the same time, no account of the city scenery of Chicago is

437

complete without the admission that the gorges and canyons of its central district are exceedingly draughty, smoky, and dusty. Even in these radiant spring days, it fully acts up to its reputation as the Windy City. This peculiarity renders it probably the most convenient place in the world for the establishment of a Suicide Club on the Stevensonian model. With your eyes peppered with dust, with your ears full of the clatter of the Elevated Road, and with the prairie breezes playfully buffeting you and waltzing with you by turns, as they eddy through the ravines of Madison, Monroe, or Adams-street, you take your life in your hand when you attempt the crossing of State-street, with its endless stream of rattling waggons and clanging trolley-cars. New York does not for a moment compare with Chicago in the roar and bustle and bewilderment of its street life. This remark will probably be resented in New York, but it expresses the settled conviction of an impartial pedestrian, who has spent a considerable portion of his life during the past few weeks in "negotiating" the crossings of both cities.

On the other hand, I observe no eagerness on the part of New York to contest the supremacy of Chicago in the matter of smoke. In this respect, the eastern metropolis is to the western as Mount Blanc to Vesuvius. The smoke of Chicago has a peculiar and aggressive individuality, due, I imagine, to the natural clearness of the atmosphere. It does not seem, like London smoke, to permeate and blend with the air. It does not overhang the streets in a uniform canopy, but sweeps across and about them in gusts and swirls, now dropping and now lifting again its grimy curtain. You will often see the vista of a gorge-like street so choked with a seeming thundercloud that you feel sure a storm is just about to burst upon the city, until you look up at the zenith and find it smiling and serene. Again and again a sudden swirl of smoke across the street (like that which swept across Fifth-avenue when the Windsor Hotel burst into flames) has led me to prick up my ears for a cry of "Fire!" But Chicago is not so easily alarmed. It is accustomed to having its airs from heaven blurred by these blasts from hell. I know few spectacles more curious than that which awaits you when you have shot up in the express elevator to the top of the Auditorium tower—on the one hand, the blue and laughing lake, on the other, the city belching volumes of smoke from its thousand throats, as though a vaster Sheffield or Wolverhampton had been transported by magic to the shores of the Mediterranean Sea. What a wonderful city Chicago will be when the commandment is honestly enforced which declares, "Thou shalt consume thine own smoke!"

What a wonderful city Chicago will be! That is the ever-recurring burden of one's cogitations. For Chicago is awake, and intelligently awake, to her destinies; so much one perceives even in the reiterated complaints that she is asleep. Discontent is the condition of progress, and Chicago is not in the slightest danger of relapsing into a condition of inert self-complacency. Her sons love her, but they chasten her. They are never tired of urging her on, sometimes (it must be owned) with most unfilial objurgations; and she, a quite unwearied Titan, is bracing up her sinews for the great task of the coming century. I have given myself a rendezvous in Chicago for 1925, when air-ships will no doubt make the transit easy for my septuagenarian frame. Nowhere in the world, I am sure, does the "to be continued in our next" interest take hold on one with such a compulsive grip.

Culture is pouring into Chicago as rapidly as pork or grain, and Chicago is insatiate in asking for more. In going over the Public Library (a not quite satisfactory building, though with some beautiful details) I was most of all impressed by the army of iron-bound boxes which are perpetually speeding to and fro between the library itself and no fewer than fifty-seven distributing stations scattered throughout the city. "I thought the number was forty-eight," said a friend who accompanied me. "So it was last year," said the librarian. "We have set up nine more stations during the interval." The Chicago Library boasts (no doubt justly) that it circulates more books than any similar institution in the world. Take, again, the University of Chicago: seven years ago (or, say, at the outside ten) it had no existence, and its site was a dismal swamp; to-day it is a handsome and populous centre

439

of literary and scientific culture. Observe, too, that it is by no means an oasis in the desert, but is thoroughly in touch with the civic life around it. For instance, it actively participates in the admirable work done by the Hull House Settlement in South Halsted-street, and in the vigorous and wide-spreading University Extension movement.

At the present moment, Chicago is not a little resentful of the sharp admonitions addressed to her by two of her aforesaid loving but exacting children. One, Professor Charles Zueblin,[1] has been telling her that "in the arrogance of youth she has failed to realize that instead of being one of the progressive cities of the world, she has been one of the reckless, improvident, and shiftless cities." Professor Zueblin is not content (for example) with her magnificent girdle of parks and boulevards, but calls for smaller parks and breathing spaces in the heart of her most crowded districts. He further maintains that her great new sewage canal is a gigantically costly blunder; and indeed one cannot but sympathize with the citizens of St. Louis in inquiring by what right Chicago converts the Mississippi into her main sewer. But if Professor Zueblin chastizes Chicago with whips, Mr. Henry B. Fuller, it would seem, lashes her with scorpions. Mr. Fuller is one of the leading novelists of the city—for Chicago, be it known, had a flourishing and characteristic literature of her own long before Mr. Dooley sprang into fame. The author of *The Cliff-Dwellers* is alleged to have said that the Anglo-Saxon race was incapable of art, and that in this respect Chicago was pre-eminently Anglo-Saxon. "Alleged," I say, for reports of lectures in the American papers are always to be taken with caution, and are very often as fanciful as Dr. Johnson's reports of the debates in Parliament. The reporter is not generally a shorthand writer. He jots down as much as he conveniently can of the lecturer's remarks, and pieces them out from imagination. Thus, I am not at all sure what Mr. Fuller really said; but there is no doubt whatever of the

[1]   A member of the Department of Sociology at the University of Chicago. Ed.

indignation kindled by his diatribe. Deny her artistic capacities and sensibilities, and you touch Chicago in her tenderest point. Moreover, Mr. Fuller's onslaught encouraged several other like-minded critics to back him up, so that the city has been writhing under the scourges of her epigrammatists. I have before me a letter to one of the evening papers, written in a tone of academic sarcasm which proves that even the supercilious and "donnish" element is not lacking in Chicago culture. "I know a number of artists," says the writer, "who came to Chicago, and after staying here for a while, went away and achieved much success in New York, London, and Paris. The appreciation they received here gave them the impetus to go elsewhere, and thus brought them fame and fortune." Whatever foundation there may be for these jibes, they are in themselves a sufficient evidence that Chicago is alive to her opportunities and responsibilities. She is, in her own vernacular, "making culture hum." Mr. Fuller, I understand, reproached her with her stockyards—an injustice which even Mr. Bernard Shaw would scarcely have committed. Is it the fault of Chicago that the world is carnivorous? Was not "Nature red in tooth and claw" several æons before Chicago was thought of ? I do not understand that any unnecessary cruelty is practised in the stockyards; and apart from that, I fail to see that systematic slaughter of animals for food is any more disgusting than sporadic butchery. But of the stockyards I can speak only from hearsay. I shall not go to see them. If I have any spare time, I shall rather spend it in a second visit to St. Gaudens' magnificent and magnificently placed statue of Abraham Lincoln, surely one of the great works of art of the century, and of the few entirely worthy monuments ever erected to a national hero.[2]

[2]   The standing figure of Lincoln in Lincoln Park, east of the Chicago Historical Society. Ed.

VII

A New Era

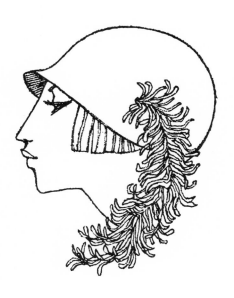

1905-1927

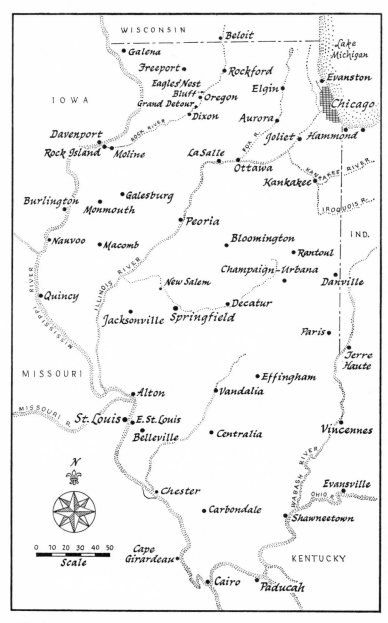

Illinois 1905–1927

Illinois, like the United States as a whole, entered the twentieth century with exuberant confidence. The progress that had characterized the years since the Civil War would continue and at an even faster rate: that few doubted. Both the state at large and Chicago would grow in population; farms and mines would produce in ever-increasing abundance; factory output would mount to unpredictable figures. Few saw the revolutionary implications of the automobile, just beginning to appear on the streets, but all knew that it portended change. What would be the effect of the airplane was less clear.

For the most part the optimists were correct. The state continued to grow—from 4,821,550 in 1900 to 7,630,654 in 1930. Again, Chicago grew even faster, from 1,700,000 to 3,375,000 in those same years. Illinois farms kept the state in first place in agricultural production. In spite of strikes and labor troubles, coal output increased. Factories turned out even larger quantities of goods, and added new products in response to advancing technology.

This, too, in spite of the dislocations of the first World War. Not only did the war divert some 300,000 men from their customary occupations to the army and navy, it also drained available capital into war loans, and taxed factories to their capacities to produce all kinds of war materials. But the war lasted only a year and a half, and Illinois recovered from its effects with surprising rapidity.

In the 1920's Illinois moved to conform to the automobile age. Before 1918 the state had only a few hundred miles of hard-surfaced highways, with most of the mileage built by a few

445

populous counties. Illinois soil becomes almost bottomless mud in wet weather, and the lack of good roads was a serious handicap. With the proceeds of two bond issues totalling $160,000,000, the state embarked on a comprehensive road-building program, with the result that by 1930 it could boast the largest and best system of hard-surfaced roads in the country.

Generally, the twenties brought prosperity, although the farmers were hard hit by the depression of 1920 and suffered declining incomes again in the last two or three years of the decade. In Illinois, as elsewhere, the general public speculated widely and not well. Chicago built recklessly, erecting huge apartment and office buildings with loans that could be serviced and repaid only if the high level of prosperity continued. It did not. In October, 1929, the stock market broke badly. What followed—the Great Depression—is history.

One result of the first third of the century could hardly have been foreseen in 1900. In that year a resident of the state could live a normal life without coming in contact with the federal government except through the post office. In 1913 the federal income tax went into effect, and at least the wealthier citizens met another federal agency. But the penetration of Washington into the lives of the people had only started. World War I meant conscription, regulation of food and fuel prices, operation of the railroads, and federal control in a dozen other ways. Some regulations, of course, were relaxed after the war, but in a few years the measures adopted by the New Deal to combat the depression exceeded anything that even the Illinoisan of 1918 could have imagined. The geography and climate of Illinois remained the same; its society, economy, and political autonomy were permanently altered.

1905

Monsignor Count Peter de Vaya and Luskod

Chicago

Monsignor Count Peter de Vaya and Luskod, a Hungarian nobleman and dignitary of the Roman Catholic church, made several trips to the United States. In 1905 he visited the large eastern cities and Chicago. He was a keen, accurate, and philosophical observer.

The huge railway station of Chicago was in charge of the police. To every passenger—and there were not a few—I counted at least one stalwart guardian of the peace. The large square in front of the station also swarmed with policemen; I even saw some seated on the boxes of the waiting carriages. There was a strike in the town.[1] That great workshop of the United States had once again suspended operations, and all the enormous vitality usually absorbed by the factories and foundries had suddenly broken loose. Like the waters overflowing the banks of a swollen river, so these seething, surging masses of disorganised humanity flooded the town. On my way from the station I saw many sad and evil sights. Workmen and police officers were constantly in conflict, and street fights, regular battles, raged in all directions. The strikers harangued the workmen, urging them to join their ranks, and those who attempted to continue their work were knocked down and mobbed by the infuriated populace. Factories and stores were ransacked by parties of unemployed. Howls and shrieks mingled with the lugubrious sounds of rifle and pistol shots.

Such was Chicago on the day of my arrival. As by chance, it was given me to see this huge mechanism of human labour, unique of its kind, in disorder and confusion. The spectacle was sensational and cruel, such as only the United States are capable of producing. In a few days matters improved, the outbreak was suppressed, the blazing volcano of human passion had spent its force. The daily routine of work was resumed, millions of hands once again seized their tools, and outward peace was restored. . . .

Chicago may be called the city of labour and strikes. Everybody works, great and small, rich and poor, all with the same marvellous intensity. Its favourable situation, in the centre of the country, and within easy access of all the high-roads of communication, makes this town one of the greatest agricultural and

Peter de Vaya and Luskod, *The Inner Life of the United States* (London, 1908), pp. 159–61, 167–70, 172–75.

[1]   A bitter teamsters' strike, called by their union leader, Cornelius P. Shea, in sympathy with the garment workers who were striking. Ed.

448

industrial markets of the world; and Chicago may in truth be regarded as the commercial capital of the United States. The business done from day to day amounts to several million dollars. Factories and foundries of every description abound in the far-extending suburbs. There are establishments where some 10,000 persons find employment, as, for instance, at the Pullman works, where the celebrated railway carriages are made. The Illinois Steel Factory and many other industrial undertakings are towns in themselves, the population being composed of the workmen and their families, recruited from all parts of the world.

I had come to open the first church erected by workmen who had emigrated from my own country. The little wooden structure stands on the Pullman road in South Chicago, about 20 miles distant from the centre of the town. At present it is surrounded by maize- and corn-fields, is, in fact, in the heart of the country, but I was told that in a few years these would all be converted into rows of palatial residences. At Chicago anything is possible, and I have not the slightest doubt that this forecast will come true. . . .

It was on a hot morning in the month of June that my amiable host, the Rev. Father S——,[2] one of the most distinguished orators of the United States and a direct descendant of the great general and popular hero of that name, undertook to pilot me through the labyrinth of the slaughter-houses. To give some idea of the enormous extent of these abattoirs, it will be sufficient to mention that they cover close upon 250 acres of ground. The alleys and passages intersecting this area measure over 75 miles, and the railway net on the premises is approximated at a length of 300 miles of line. It is a town, or rather a world in itself, peopled by the workmen, butchers and pig-killers—a dismal community in truth. We spent the greater part of that long summer day in gaining merely an approximate idea of the organisation and the commercial merits of this vast undertaking, and although, no doubt like every other visitor, I sickened at the sight of so much

2   Thomas Ewing Sherman, son of William Tecumseh Sherman. Ed.

blood, yet at the same time I could not help being struck by the clever management of this wonderful exploitation. It is true that these famous stockyards of Chicago, so often criticised and described, present one of the most sorrowful phases of modern industry but they also show the successful substitution of machinery for manual labour, and a hitherto unrivalled utilisation of the residue. "Nothing is wasted," would be an appropriate motto to place over the packing-houses. Nothing is wasted, neither material nor labour nor time.

The utilisation of these three great factors of successful commercial enterprise, matter, labour and time, is here seen to perfection. Every portion of the animal is put to some profitable purpose. Horns, bones, muscles, skin, hoofs, all are lucratively employed in the manufacture of such secondary products as soap, glycerine, glue, gelatine, ammonias, manures, etc. Labour and time are also scientifically disposed of. Every man's work is limited to one special action. He makes always the same stroke of of the hatchet, the same cut of the knife, until he himself becomes part of the machinery, and moves automatically and with increasing rapidity.

Time—in other words, rapidity and precision—is the third great factor in the administration of these wholesale slaughter-houses, and during our inspection we were forcibly reminded of the familiar saying that the live pig goes in at one door, and comes out as sausages at the other. The quickness of the process is truly dazzling. The animal is fastened to a chain by one of its hind legs and pulled up by means of a revolving wheel. It is then fixed to a steelyard, which moves on rails and brings the body in front of the butcher, who cuts its throat. After a sufficient time has been allowed for the blood to run away, the body is dragged by the same instrumentality to the cauldron of boiling water. Another piece of machinery, no less ingeniously constructed, cuts the body up into the required parts. Head, hams, sides, bones, lard, are no sooner separated, than they are pickled and packed and sent off to the four corners of the earth in the trains ready waiting in front of the buildings.

I have purposely not entered into a more detailed description of the stockyards. No doubt there is much that is objectionable in the manipulation of the abattoirs; they have their evil sides, and voices are raised more and more vehemently against the abuses practised there. Perhaps only the most advantageous side of the business was shown to me, or perhaps the house of Swift, which is the one I visited, is a model establishment. To me it certainly appeared perfect in every detail. The building which contains the offices of the directors and clerks, and where all the business is transacted, might fitly be styled a "Palace of Administration," and is a model of comfort and cleanliness. The offices are tastefully furnished, and have that air of elegance which characterises every American house of business, but is here almost carried to excess. It is a fine iron building, with large windows, and provided with all the latest improvements. The pinewood furniture, the writing machines and telephone boxes, all are arranged on the most approved principles to satisfy the requirements of this growing trade; and to give an idea of the luxury of the establishment it will suffice to mention that by the aid of refrigerators the temperature is always kept at 64° F. The air of the offices is mechanically purified, and by some ingenious contrivance the smells from the slaughter-houses are intercepted so that they cannot penetrate to these precincts.

The directors of this unique establishment entertained me at luncheon in the large dining-room, situated over these palatial offices, which is also kept at a low temperature and artificially aired. This imposing hall is furnished with little tables where the employés can get a good dinner at a very low figure. Adjoining the dining-hall is a smoking-room, provided with books and newspapers, where the business of the day can be discussed over a cup of black coffee. This is the *ne plus ultra* of comfort, and thoroughly in keeping with the American conception of the "Office," where the men spend the greater portion of their life. . . .

Another day I was invited to visit one of the stores. These huge establishments are from twelve to fifteen stories high, and contain every possible article of trade, from matches and bootlaces, to the most exquisite art treasures and priceless gems. Anything, indeed, can be purchased there, even to real estates and country houses. They are "Bon Marchés" and "Whiteleys" on a larger and, if possible, more complete scale, more daring and perhaps more fantastic in their display.

The house I was invited to visit was that of Marshall Field & Co., of almost historical renown, because its growth and success is so intimately connected with that of the city itself. About fifty years ago, when Chicago could scarcely claim to be a town yet, three newcomers, Levy Leiter, P. Palmer and Marshall Field, set up a modest little shop to supply the wants of the early settlers. These three originators were bold and enterprising men, and as the town grew, their establishment increased also, until it has become one of the marvels of Chicago. I viewed all the various departments with interest, and also went into the adjoining ware-house. This has all the appearance of a fortress. It is situated on the banks of the river, and the goods are transported from there by boats to the shop. This is indeed a wonderful establishment. One might wander through it from morning to night without coming to the end of it, without exhausting its hoards, without having seen, in fact, one-thousandth part of all the marvellous confections with which the wealth and fashion of Chicago is pleased to adorn itself. But what impressed me far beyond all the delights of this fairy show, was the person of the originator, the man round whom all this machinery moves—Mr Field, since the liquidation of the firm, sole proprietor of the concern.

The young clerk who was showing me round, and who told me the history of the establishment, came to a sudden stop as we turned a corner, and pointing to a kind of little office, or rather box, with glass partitions, in which a white-haired gentleman was sitting at his desk, he whispered: "The master!" There was a catch in his voice as of fear at the mention of the power upon whom his earthly existence depended. Mr Field was then about seventy years old. His hair was quite white and his face had a tired expression, the result of a life of toil and struggle. My conductor explained that "the master" was always in that place, the first to arrive and the last to leave the premises. Seated in his glass cage, like a spider in his web, he held the threads and concentrated the movements of the whole of this gigantic business. "It is hard work to make millions," the pleasant young merchant remarked, "but it is harder still to keep them." In this land of ever keener growing competition, once relax the hold, and failure is imminent. Respite is synonymous with being swallowed up by legions of competitors. Incessant activity, unflagging zeal, alone can dominate the market, and self-sacrifice is the first condition to insure success.

Suddenly a muffled sound coming from the other end of the building interrupted our conversation. The police were at once on the spot, but the strikers came rushing in from the street and attacked the men who had remained at their work, such as the drivers of the carts and waggons, and the carters carrying out the goods. The noise came nearer. Uproarious vociferations were now distinctly audible, the howls of a delirious crowd mingled with the moans of the wounded and the dull sound of blows. The reason of this tumult was the same as always—a clamour for a small increase of wages. It was but a fresh outburst of that inveterate hatred existing between labourer and capitalist which from day to day is becoming more pronounced. All the sad and bloody scenes which I had witnessed since my arrival in the town were to me so many manifest confirmations of the growing feeling of hostility of the poor towards the rich, and long after I had left that palace of gold and gewgaws, the angry voices of the malcontents sounded in my ears like the refrain of a sordid fanfare. . . .

As my thoughts went back to that glass cage, and the white-haired man toiling at his books from morning till night, I could not help asking myself: Who is more to be pitied, the men who have failed to secure a rise in their wages, or the millionaire who spends his life shut up in a cage?

1913

J. C. Burton

The Rock River Valley and Its Cities

In 1913 J. C. Burton, a journalist, set out to prove that Illinois roads, poor as they were, were passable, and that they led to places of surprising beauty. He chose the valley of the Rock River for his tour.

Emulating the eminent Tom Sawyer, who identified the states over which he passed in a runaway balloon by the color in which they were shown in the grammar school geography, the average motorist thinks of Illinois as an irregular pink spot of the map of the United States, a mental reaction which shows how much we are in debt to Messrs. Rand & McNally.

Maine, with its green pines and silver streams; Massachusetts, famed for the Berkshire hills and its mist of colonial romance; New York, studded with blue lakes and linked to centuries past by trails on which the redskin heroes of the immortal Cooper trod; Florida, with its hard stretches of sandy beach and relics of the Spanish conquistadors' bloody visits to the shores of a new world; Indiana, arrogant in the possession of miles of macadam highways; Colorado, supreme because of its majestic Rockies; California, with its sloping mountains and magnificent missions—all have an irresistible appeal for the motorist, but Illinois is given little if any consideration when a tour is being contemplated.

Is Illinois deserving of such contempt? Is the state of Lincoln, Grant and Logan a veritable slough of despond when compared with other commonwealths, an expanse of prairie where roads are rough, scenery commonplace and touring monotonous? Because the good roads enthusiast has sounded the slogan "Pull Illinois out of the mud," is the supposition correct that there are no highways winding through the fertile fields on which a speed of 20 miles an hour can be maintained without pounding a motor car to pieces and inviting Trouble to jump from Pandora's box to the bonnet of the machine? Are there no historic spots within the boundaries of this neglected state to warm the patriot's heart; no glens, no dells, no rippling streams to invite the admiration of the nature lover?

Crank up your car—if it is an early model and not equipped with a self-starter—and come with me on a journey of vindication. Leave Chicago, Phoenix city of energy consumed, behind

J. C. Burton, "In Defense of Illinois," *Motor/Age*, July 31, 1913. Reprinted by the Illinois Sesquicentennial Commission from *Motor/Age*.

and penetrate a region where the air is unpolluted by smoke, where the restful whir of mowers is heard instead of the wracking rattle of elevated trains, where ancient trails lead by fields of waving corn and bowed wheat.

It is late summer. The prairies are yellow with golden rod. The sky is blue and clear. There seems to be a nectar in the very air you breathe. Life is good on such a day as this.

With two exceptions—Louisiana and Delaware—Illinois is the most level state in the union, the government surveyors tell us, and they are truthful men. This fact is borne out on the 125-mile trip through aristocratic Rockford to peaceful Oregon. There are few hills to obstruct our 20-mile-an-hour progress. The roads are of hard-packed stone and gravel and excellent for touring, especially at this season of the year. For long stretches of the journey the overhanging branches of stately trees shield us from the blistering attack of an ambitious afternoon sun.

Our first stop is at Oregon, a small city of Ogle county and situated on the fertile banks of the Rock river. We have ridden for 6 hours—perhaps a trifle longer—and the air has been especially bracing and conducive to an appetite. We feel a vacuum amidships and are impetuous to enter the screened doors of a neat, quiet, orderly little inn, the Spoor House, where the unpretentious cuisine both appeals and satisfies. The appetite appeased, we are ready to enjoy the scenic beauties which abound in the vicinity of Oregon.

Two miles across the Rock river, in which a fiery sunset is being reflected, but visible for miles around stands an impressive figure of concrete—colossal, brooding and blanketed—on the crest of Eagle's Nest bluff, a mute but formidable sentinel which will keep silent watch for generations to come. This gigantic statue of Chief Blackhawk—it is 75 feet in height and was fashioned by the master hands of Lorado Taft[1]—overlooks the most picturesque spot in the Rock river valley.

[1]   Distinguished Chicago sculptor, 1860–1936. His works include "The Fountain of the Great Lakes," Chicago Art Institute; "The Fountain of Time," University of Chicago; and "Lincoln," Urbana, Illinois. Ed.

The statue of Chief Blackhawk was unveiled July 1, 1911, before an exclusive assembly of 500 sculptors, painters, authors, poets and millionaires. The figure is not a physical likeness of the famous Sac chief, ally of the English in the war of 1812 and enemy of the early settlers, but it is a most noble monument to an unrelentless foe, a redskin forced to don his war paint by unscrupulous whites who beat him, insulted him and encroached upon his fields of maize to ultimately conquer him after a year of slaughter and depredation. It is the statue of a stoic with arms folded across his chest and eyes looking into the great beyond, into the land of the Great Spirit.

At the time of the dedication, the creator of the statue explained how he came to adopt the particular pose that he did. Each evening, he said, he and other members of his family went to the bluff to look across the river and marvel at the color tints on the limitless palette of the Master Painter. Without exception, each unconsciously assumed the characteristic pose of Napoleon, who, with arms folded across his decorated chest, witnessed the defeat of the Old Guard at Waterloo and saw the shores of his beloved France for the last time from the deck of the frigate that bore him a captive to St. Helena. It was the sculptor's belief that he and the other members of his household were doing just what others had done in years past. Gradually he came to think of a great Indian chief standing on the bluff with arms across his breast and admiring the grandeur before him. He was not satisfied until he had modeled such an imperial figure and dedicated it to an inspired posterity.

The colossal figure seems surrounded by a film of mysticism. Steps lead down to the hollow base and echoing interior. Walking early one morning recently near the statue, Lorado Taft heard strange sounds issuing from it. On investigation he found two followers of a strange, if not ancient, religious cult performing their morning orisons with chants and prayers.

A view of the statue also recalls to the mind of the historian an event of historic significance, the meeting of two men, destined to be national figures in years to come, on the Illinois prairies one summer day in 1832. One wore the blue uniform and gold lace of a United States Army officer. He was General Winfield Scott, hero of the Mexican war and Whig candidate for president in 1852. The other was clad in the homespun suit and coonskin cap of the frontiersman. He was Abraham Lincoln, president, emancipator and martyr.[2] Both were in pursuit of Chief Blackhawk, respected enemy of the paleface, and fleeing from the deadly Asiatic cholera which had claimed more victims than the savage redskins.

On the green hillside just below the statue of the belligerent aborigine stands a writhing cedar tree whose gnarled and twisted branches have borne no leaves in the memory of the oldest living inhabitant of Ogle county. Reputed to be over 1,000 years old, it is perhaps the most famous tree in the United States now that Connecticut's historic Charter Oak, which was destroyed by a thunder storm in 1856, is no more. In a pregnant day when its branches were gay with budding leaves in springtime, an eagle built a nest and cradled her young in the venerable cedar. This ornithological tradition prompted Margaret Fuller to name that part of the river bluffs "Eagle's Nest."

The name of Margaret Fuller is linked to Eagle's Nest bluff and vicinity. Three score and 10 years ago, when this distinguished woman of letters visited her uncle, Judge Fuller, an Ogle county jurist of the early days, she became enamoured of the scenic beauties of the Rock river valley and under the branches of the arborial patriarch, she wrote the poem, "Ganymede to His Eagle."

At the foot of Eagle's Nest bluff and only a short distance from the ancient cedar, the waters of Ganymede spring flow from moss-covered rocks. Here a marble tablet, on which are inscribed the particulars of Margaret Fuller's visit in 1843 and the christening of the spring, has been placed by a branch of the Illinois Historical Society. Below lies Margaret Fuller's island, a wooded refuge for the weary motorist, affording an excellent view of the

---

[2]   There is no evidence that the two men met at this time. Ed.

Blackhawk monument and offering opportunities for a delightful drive. . . .[3]

Oregon also is noted for its present celebrities as well as for a genius of another day, it being the nearest station to the Chicago artists' colony, where master and pupil, painter and sculptor, novelist and poet find inspiration, as did Margaret Fuller, in the winding river, green fields, rolling hills and forest of white pine. The colony, which is located on Eagle's Nest bluff, numbers among its members Lorado Taft, Charles Francis Brown, Ralph Clarkson and Hamlin Garland.[4] Perched high on the thickly wooded bluff are the summer cottages where dwell the makers of masterpieces and the writers of best sellers. Pegasus now flaps his wings where the Indian pony once grazed. Easels are set up where the squaws of the Illini, Fox and Sacs pitched tepees for their painted braves.

Only a short distance from Eagle's Nest bluff is Congressman Frank O. Lowden's magnificent country estate of 5,000 acres, Sinnissippi farm.[5] Here "Lowden's lawn mower"—the largest flock of Angora goats to be found in the middle west—moves over the prairie and trims the brush land. An inspiring view of the historic valley is to be obtained looking south from Castle rock, the winding river, dotted with islands and flanked by evergreen-covered bluffs, being visible for miles. Hemingway rocks form another one of the beauty spots in the vicinity of Sinnissippi farm.

Reluctantly leaving Oregon and the scenic beauties in the vicinity of Eagle's Nest bluff and driving down the river road for $11\frac{1}{2}$ miles, we come to the little village of Grand Detour, an isolated hamlet 7 miles from a railroad station and very old as age is computed in Illinois. It was founded by the early French settlers and resembles a colonial town of New England with its towering elm trees, weathered stone houses and antique church

---

[3]   See Fuller, "The Fox River Valley," above. Ed.

[4]   Respectively, sculptor, editor, portrait painter, and novelist. Ed.

[5]   Lowden, in Congress from 1906 to 1911, served as governor from 1917 to 1921. He was largely responsible for the initiation of the statewide hard road system. Ed.

where the great great-grandmothers of the present inhabitants, clad in rustling crinoline and wearing powdered wigs, went to worship.

It was in Grand Detour that the village blacksmith's assistant, John Deere, forged and welded the first steel plowshare ever made and freed the farmer from bondage to the clumsy wooden implement which Adam first fashioned to turn the sod.

The river bank, for a mile on either side of Grand Detour, is studded with cottages which are rented to motorists for week-end parties. Up and down the broad stream play the picturesque boats of the pearl fishers, for hunting for pearls is the leading industry of the quaint old town.

There are no hotels in Grand Detour. Hotels are too modern for a village of this kind. But there are two inns, the Sheffield and the Colonial, where the beaux and beauties of a century ago danced the Money Musk and minuet to the frantic bowing of the village fiddler. . . .

"There are many fine old houses in Dixon of a type built two generations ago when taste was classic and simple," writes a contemporary chronicler. "One is pointed out—a dilapidated, dejected-looking old structure with raw scars of a whilom verandah marring its front walls—as having been the once famous home of 'Governor' Charters, 'Hazelwood.' These decaying walls once sheltered a hospitality so lavish, so all-embracing and ruinous that its owner died utterly poverty stricken, an object of charity.[6] Many gay fetes champetres were given there with champagne flowing ad libitum and the 'governor' (I think the title was purely honorary) danced as lightly as air in spite of his 300 pounds. In his day, the saying was in Dixon, that after you cross the river to the north side, 'all roads lead to Hazelwood.' 'Governor' Charters may rest easy; Dixon is still celebrated for its hospitality as in romantic days of old."

[6] See Fuller, "The Fox River Valley," above. Some years after Burton's account, Mr. and Mrs. Charles J. Walgreen acquired the Charters estate and made it into the showplace it remains today. Ed.

Dixon's 300-acre public playground, Lowell park, is another link that binds the middle west to the east and the learned coterie of which Margaret Fuller was a member. When a brother of James Russell Lowell and his bride came west on a wedding trip they were so enchanted with the beauties of the Rock river valley that they purchased an estate on the shores of the winding stream with the intention of returning and building upon it. The Lowell mansion never was built, however, and at the death of the couple, their daughter gave the land to the city as a public park.

In connection with the popularity of the Rock river valley for touring, it is interesting to note that The Crusaders, a coterie of Chicago society people who have had an opportunity to tour America and Europe, and Friends of Our Native Landscape, a band of ardent nature lovers residing in the Illinois metropolis, have selected Oregon as the objective point in motor migrations this summer. The tourists were so charmed with the scenic beauties of Eagle's Nest bluff and Grand Detour that the services of Eames MacVeagh, the official guide of both organizations, are in constant demand for return visits.

1920

E. Harold Spender

Springfield
and Bloomington

In 1920 E. Harold Spender, English journalist and lecturer, with four of his countrymen, came to the United States at the invitation of the American Mayflower Council. The purpose of the trip was to strengthen friendly relations between Great Britain and the United States. In addition to the larger cities, Spender visited Springfield. The World War, fought ostensibly to make the world safe for democracy, had attracted attention to Abraham Lincoln, the foremost exponent of the democratic ideal, and his home was becoming a place of pilgrimage. On the trip back to Chicago, Spender stopped at Bloomington to fill lecture engagements.

Spender's letters from the United States were first published in the London *Daily Telegraph*.

We started from Chicago early this morning, and travelling in a pleasant Pullman car we have traversed throughout the day the great plains of the Mid-West. We journeyed south-west across the great State of Illinois, one of the most famous States of the earlier American Union. It is the country of Abraham Lincoln, and there seems always a touch of that great man's spirit in the little western towns through which we have passed. From the train we get glimpses of the little two-storied houses with large porches and verandahs, standing in their own grounds, rather shabby and badly painted, a little ramshackle like "Uncle Abe" himself, but always with the same sense of space and freedom that marked his character. Though the houses are small, the roads are wide and bordered with trees. The houses stand well back from the thoroughfares, with no railings or fences, and always with a certain genial openness about the appearance of even the smallest homestead—a hospitable accessibility, like that of Abraham himself.

In the train we found ourselves travelling with that distinguished French soldier, General Nivelle, one of the heroes of Verdun. He has been selected by the French Government as the French representative at the Pilgrim Fathers' celebrations, and it was ordained at New York that he and I should visit Springfield together.

We arrived at Springfield in the dark. The railway station was full of friendly faces and welcoming hands. Committees pounced upon us from the gloom and carried us, bag and baggage, to waiting motor-cars. We rolled smoothly through broad thoroughfares to the Leland Hotel. The lounge of the hotel was full of eager crowds, for many things are happening in this city. A Convention—another Convention!—is sitting here in the capital of Illinois to revise the Constitution of the State, and the town is full of important delegates and lawyers. The revising of the State Constitution

E. Harold Spender, *A Briton in America* (London, 1921), pp. 56–67, 82–89. Reprinted by permission of William Heinemann Ltd.

is a rare and vital event in an American State, and all these men are full of a high exhilaration and excitement. I noticed again in the lobby of this hotel that few of them sat down, but persisted in standing quite as remorselessly as members of the British Stock Exchange.

I have talked to many of the members of this Convention Committee, including several Ministers of the State. I am deeply interested to find that this Convention recognises as the basis of its new Constitution all the great documents of English freedom—Magna Charta, The Petition of Right, The Bill of Rights. Nothing is admitted to their Constitution which is inconsistent with any of these great British standards. The walls of America are built on British foundations, and it is really useless for people to say that British traditions count no more than any other foreign traditions in the making of America.

For in discussing their new Constitution with these men, I realise instantly that they are bound by the laws of British freedom almost as closely as we are ourselves. They inherit the achievement of British ancestors: they build on the deeds of British heroes. All the time they hark back to British origin and think in terms of British faith. Certainly the best Americans can never forget this aspect of their lives.[1]

But while talking to these distinguished men we have been witnesses of a pretty spectacle which presented the lighter and gayer aspect of American life. A fashionable wedding took place in the hotel this evening—for American weddings always take place in the evening. A great party assembled, including all the rank and fashion of the town and all the beauty of Springfield womanhood. Two things have impressed us. One is the grace and charm of the women; and the other is the elegance of their dress. The women in this Mid-West capital are as finely dressed as any women in Europe. Thanks to their great wealth, they can indulge in this taste freely, and certainly there is no sign of excessive thrift

[1] The constitution framed by this convention was rejected by popular vote. Ed.

464

in this matter of dressing. American women are fond of wearing their jewels, and it appears to be a pleasanter habit than that of keeping them in boxes at home. It is surely an amiable thing to share the glitter and delight of your possessions with the world at large!

November 18.

Springfield is indeed the city of Abraham Lincoln. He dominates the place, even in memory. For this is where he lived during that important period of his life between the early Mid-West backwoods experiences and the later grandeur of his Presidency. At Springfield he was something "betwixt and between"—not yet the great man of America, but already emerged from the obscurity of his early days. He had become a lawyer and given up the vague, shiftless life of the Mid-West pioneer store-keeper which he had led for so many years. In 1834 he had been elected a member of the Illinois House of Representatives, and in that house he served until 1842. He was elected to Congress in 1846, chosen by the Republicans for the Presidency in 1860, and elected on November 4 of that year. During all those years—from 1834 to 1860—he lived in Springfield, residing in the little house which has since been bought and furnished by the State, and is now kept sacred to his memory. After his tragic death at Washington his body was brought to Springfield and buried in the cemetery here. A great monument has been erected over his tomb, and a statue of Abraham Lincoln stands in front of the monument. Another statue is placed in front of the State Capitol, the great white-domed building which here in Springfield, as in all other State capitals of America, represents the majesty of State power.

During the morning we have been taken in a motor-car loaned to us, with the usual American hospitality, to visit all these great memorials of Abraham Lincoln's life and death. We have journeyed in this way round this beautiful spacious town, now beflagged in our honour with French and British bunting. We have accompanied General Nivelle to the cemetery and laid wreaths in front of the tomb.

E. HAROLD SPENDER

American cemeteries are certainly a great advance on European. In Europe after we die we are laid to rest in great melancholy, flat, walled spaces, deprived of the companionship of trees and streams, and unpleasantly crowded even in death. England is such a congested country that of late years we have been obliged in the great city areas to keep moving our ancestors' bodies from one melancholy site to another, the living always pushing the dead further away from their company. In England the tomb itself gives no rest. But America, being more spacious, has more room for its dead; and consequently there is not the same movement towards cremation that has gone so fast in England during the last twenty years. At home we are now obliged to burn our dead because they take the space of the living —and after all the living have the first claim. In America there is still room enough both for the living and the dead; and so on the outskirts of their towns you come across these beautiful undulating, wooded spaces, of which Springfield cemetery is only typical. In these fields of sepulture—these " Sleepy Hollows " as they beautifully call them—they do not cut down the trees, they do not dam the streams, they do not crowd the tombs. They put man to rest beneath the shade of the weeping willow or the beech tree, giving him softly back to Nature; they do not attempt to reproduce in the cemetery the crowded conditions of life. The result is soothing and beautiful; death itself is robbed of some of its bitterness.

In the midst of such a cemetery stands the tomb of Abraham Lincoln, a mighty structure with that tall, sombre, melancholy figure of the grim President guarding the portal, and round him at each corner of the tomb four sculptured groups, episodes in the Civil War, made from the cannon captured from the South. Within this colossal tomb is a chamber tended by a custodian—a keen and devoted man, who can remember Abraham Lincoln and can tell you stories from his life. He is a man of the same age as Lincoln's only surviving son.[2] It was pleasant to be taken round by

[2]   Herbert Wells Fay, custodian of the Lincoln Tomb for many years. Robert Todd Lincoln was seventy-seven in 1920. Ed.

466

such a mentor, who could show us with intelligence the collection of interesting relics hoarded in that chamber—memorials of every kind, trivial and important. Pictures, engravings, photographs, letters, and poems—the play bill of the actual drama—"An English Cousin"[3]—which was being performed in the theatre at Washington when he was assassinated. Here are cuttings from contemporary newspapers bringing back to you the immense tragedy of that human eclipse—the blow to the North, the appalling shock to the whole American people, just emerged from the bitterness of war. Perhaps the most vivid memento of this event is a small piece of the brocade dress worn by Laura Keene, the actress, and actually stained by Lincoln's blood, which dropped on to the dress when she knelt down and took Lincoln's head on to her lap after he had been shot. "Now he belongs to the ages."[4] So it is that, looking back past the years that intervene, we see that life and that death fall into their proper perspective, and feel that the martyr's end somehow or other suited the hero's life. Perhaps after all, as Tacitus said of Agricola, he was happy in the opportunity of his death. "Tu vero felix, Agricola, non vitae tantum claritate sed etiam opportunitate mortis."

From the tomb we passed to the house, for our time was short. The Lincoln home is in Eighth Street, four blocks from the Courthouse. It is open to the public at certain times, and we were most graciously received by the charming lady who now owns it.[5] She is the grand-daughter of the sister of Mrs. Lincoln, and she showed us through the rooms with a loving enthusiasm for the man who had lived there. Like the chamber at the tomb, those rooms are full of mementoes. But the simple furniture best bespeaks the life. One gains the impression of a smooth, middle-class existence, intensely domestic: the life of a man who had passed right beyond his pioneering stage, and had settled down to

---

3   *Our American Cousin.* Ed.
4   If this remark was made at all, which is not certain, it was made by Edwin M. Stanton, Secretary of War. Ed.
5   Mrs. Mary Edwards Brown. She was not, of course, the owner of the Lincoln home, which belonged to the state. Ed.

tranquil ways. One wonders how that gawky, long, lank man was contained in those little rooms. I caught a fancy that he was probably more often to be found on the open verandah outside the house, perhaps sitting there in a long chair on the summer evenings with his feet on the railings, pouring out his unending stream of stories to the mixed crowd which probably surrounded him there, as all through his life.

The neighbourhood of the house is full of tales about Abraham Lincoln, many of them bizarre and grotesque. But the one I like best is that which tells how Abraham Lincoln, going down the street outside to an important engagement at the Capitol, passed a little girl who was carrying a very heavy basket. He stopped and insisted on taking the basket from the little girl and carrying it himself all through Springfield. That was characteristic of the man, his indifference to external dignity, his unbounded compassion for the weak, his readiness to bear the burdens of others, his essential and fundamental goodness of heart.

From the house we passed to the Capitol, and there we paused to look at Lincoln's second statue. It is a representation of a younger Abraham, probably during the period of his State political life, and alongside of it stands the statue of his great friend and rival Stephen Douglas—a stout, thick-set little man, rather recalling Charles Fox. The interesting fact about this second statue of Lincoln is that it represents him without the goatee beard conspicuous in the statue presented to London by the United States, and now generally associated with his features. Shorn of that ugly appendage, the face is far more interesting. The close-lipped mouth and the square jaw reveals the secret of his strength and determination, hidden from the world afterwards by the straggling beard.

The story of why he took to growing this beard is interesting and characteristic. In the chamber within the tomb there is a letter from a little girl commenting on his photograph, and telling him that he would look a handsomer man if he grew a beard. It is the solemn fact that Abraham Lincoln brooded over this letter and finally decided to obey this child. It is also the solemn fact that afterwards, having grown the beard, he sought out the child on one of his journeys to Washington and shook her by the hand, thanking her for her advice. It is one of those strange, half-foolish stories about Lincoln which make you wonder whether there is not a touch of folly about all great men. At any rate, there seems always a touch of kinship between them and children.

We now hastened back to the hotel, where we were to be entertained at lunch by the Springfield Luncheon Club. It was a great and enthusiastic gathering, and certainly Springfield did her best to show both England and France what she could do in the way of welcome and hospitality. When I ventured to ask that gathering whether they would, in the end, after they had finished with their politics, come back to the assistance of afflicted Europe, they replied with one unanimous shout—"Yes! We will!" Whether that shout was merely the exhilaration of the moment, or whether it represented the deeper mind of America time alone will show.

We have spent the afternoon motoring round the suburbs, and paying a series of visits to the homes of hospitable Americans, who have overwhelmed us with invitations. I will not trespass upon their privacy except to note the beauty of their houses. We visited ex-Senator Hays, who possesses one of the finest private libraries that I have yet seen in an American home. [6] Then we visited the villa of a rich business man which seemed the last word in artistic luxury. Every bedroom, including also the servants', has a bath room with a shower bath. The guest's room is the best of all, a happy touch in home-making. It has a marble bath worthy of a Roman Emperor. There are sleeping porches and verandahs all round the house for use in the hot weather. The study of the master of the house is in the basement, and is surrounded with pictures of the American Revolution, showing that no luxury abates the patriotism of the true American. [7] We ended by

---

[6]   Logan Hay, lawyer, had served in the state senate from 1907 to 1915.
      Until his death in 1942 he was easily Springfield's leading citizen. Ed.
[7]   Although I lived in Springfield from 1925 to 1945, I cannot identify
      this house. Ed.

glimpsing into a house where the hostess was entertaining a bevy of American girls. For in Springfield, as in most other American towns, the women are quite happy with their own company. A prettier set of girls one could not wish to see: their tea frocks exquisite, with short sleeves, but otherwise covering the body in a way that puts the present nudity of Europe to some shame. One more point—they were really drinking tea, and not smoking cigarettes!

There is no rest for the wicked. This evening General Nivelle and I had to address a great popular audience of 4,000 people in the great Springfield Arsenal. General Nivelle spoke on France, and I tried them with the lantern-lecture on the Pilgrim Fathers. The Arsenal was decorated throughout with French and British flags. The band played and all sang four great patriotic hymns—"The Star Spangled Banner," "America," "God Save the King," and the "Marseillaise."

We spoke with a background of Tricolours and Union Jacks: and there seemed no evidence that America is afraid to display British flags. I would commend that fact to those people in Europe who are hysterically declaring that the British flag cannot be shown in America without a riot.

Looking round that great building, now empty of arms, there came back to mind the mighty poem of peace that Longfellow wrote at the suggestion of his wife—"The Arsenal at Springfield."[8] It is still worth remembering at the present moment in the world's history. Here are two stanzas:—

> Were half the power that fills the world with terror,
>> Were half the wealth bestowed on camps and courts,
> Given to redeem the human mind from error,
>> There were no need of arsenals nor forts.
>
> *   *   *   *   *
>
> Down the dark future, through long generations,
>> The echoing sounds grow fainter, and then cease;

[8] Longfellow was referring to the United States Arsenal at Springfield, Massachusetts. Ed.

And like a bell, with solemn, sweet vibrations,
  I hear once more the voice of Christ say, "Peace!"

                              . . . Bloomington, Nov. 19.
We rose this morning at 5 a.m. in the Leland House Hotel at
Springfield. In the dim dark we finished that precarious process
of packing which "vexes public men" on travel intent.

We had been promised a five o'clock breakfast. But one of the
weak spots in these admirable American hotels is the supply of
early food. The instructions seem to get handed on from one head
of department to another—and it is marvellous how many heads
of departments there are in the smallest of these Mid-West hotels.
The only real "servants" appear to be the negroes. Every white
man or woman becomes a "manager"—of sorts: and managers
don't like early rising. Division of labour leads to efficiency up to
a point, but beyond that point it becomes a form of industrial
stagnation.

This morning at Springfield, Illinois, for instance, it shocked
up against the earliness of the hour and sank in deep water.

Compelled at last to make a bolt for our train we had the
hungry experience of passing our breakfast on our descent to the
hall—we in the lift and the breakfast on the stairs. We climaxed
in a game of hide and seek. The breakfast and the negro dodged
us. At last, despairing of our quest, we took refuge in the hospitable car of our friend and were whisked breakfastless to the
station.

Then came a glorious relief. For lo! there stood to hand in the
station restaurant a gracious breakfast of fresh fruit—apples rosy-
red and grape fruit bulging—steaming coffee and hot rolls—such
as one could not dream of in war-worn Europe. Thus refreshed,
we quickly forgave and forgot.

So we started back eastward to this little town of Bloomington
in mid-Illinois, where I was booked to address the students of the
Wesleyan University at ten o'clock. We travelled in an "Observation Car"—a car attached to the rear of the train, and provided
with "big windows"—which gave us an admirable vision of the
Mid-West prairies and vast corn fields which used to supply

471

Europe with maize at a time when the exchange permitted it. To-day the country is in its winter dress. The golden maize has been plucked and the fields are a dirty yellow, dotted with bare stalks. But it is all new to us, and we loved every little village that we passed—the freedom of the little wooden houses and the pretty thoroughfares.

At the station we expected the usual committee. But instead we were greeted by an old Oxford friend—a contemporary from the eighties—who, seeing our arrival notified in the Press, had walked down to the station to welcome us. My friend is typical of the American human kaleidoscope. He came to America twenty years ago as a railway manager and remained to become an Episcopalian minister. He is now in charge of the principal church in this little town of Bloomington.[9] Although now a fully equipped American, he remains British in heart and memory. How often throughout this tour we have met this type of British American! Prosperous and patriotic, true to "The Star Spangled Banner" but still always, with a touch of the exile, eager to see an English face and to hear an English voice!

"I just thought I'd come and meet someone from the old country," is the way they put it. Or if he is a Yorkshire man then rather wistfully, "And how may they be doing up Bradford way." Or if he be a Lancashire man—"Do you happen to have been down Manchester of late?" Or if he be from Somerset, he grips me with both hands and smiles all over his face when he hears that my native town is Bath.

It is wonderful how long these memories of the old country survive. It is not only the Irish-Americans who love their old country.

We have been lucky to-day. For these good British-Americans —this old Balliol man and his American family—have looked after my travel-weary wife, letting her rest in their house, while I have been lecturing and speaking.

[9]   The Reverend William Baker, pastor of St. Matthews Episcopal Church, 1908–22. Ed.

The sight of the morning was the crowd of eager young faces of the boys and girls at the Wesleyan University—a vast hall packed with young men and women allowed to sit as they liked and with whom they liked—just left to their own sense of discipline and order. When I looked at these glad and happy faces, and received their joyous welcome, I thought of how differently we order these things at Oxford—of the young men and women separated into their flocks and eyeing one another furtively over their books— and I wondered which was the better way, the English or the American!

They are good listeners, these young Americans. But I think we all enjoyed ourselves best when the lecture was over. Then they told me all about their University, and their happy life there, and they brought out their Kodaks and took photographs of me, and made me sign autograph books and do a number of other trivial things, just expressive of their general pleasure at meeting a visitor from England. At the gates we parted, and I suppose I shall never see again any of that great crowd. May they live happy lives!

But America leaves one no pause for regret. My guide and guardian immediately switched me off to eat with the inevitable Town Luncheon Club. What I said at that luncheon does not matter, for most of the time was occupied by a formidable American orator—"spell-binder" is, I believe, the word—who was billed to lecture on Abraham Lincoln. It was a gathering of lawyers, well-dressed, prosperous men, and I think I told them that Europe was not quite so prosperous as they were. But my chief recollection of that luncheon is that our speeches were preceded and followed by a band which played jazz music with amazing violence, and comfortably drowned most of our conversation. Listening to this music I was not surprised to hear from my neighbour that many of the melodies were of African origin. A fearful thought then possessed me—that possibly the musical tradition of America is destined to be submerged by the aboriginal music of the negro!

For it is a curious fact that although America shines in many of the arts—especially in painting and sculpture—she has, as yet, struck no original line in music except along these semi-barbaric paths.

Finding it impossible to talk, I spent most of my time watching the keen, mobile, clean-shaven faces of the men sitting around me, and I became conscious of a certain boredom and weariness reflected on their countenances, as if the endurance of these jazz noises were merely accepted as one of the sacrifices of life offered on the altar of convention.

Luncheon over and its turmoil abated, we enjoyed a few hours of afternoon rest in the British-American home of our hosts. We obtained here a vision of that large American class which has procured no increase of wealth during the war, and feel only the incidence of high prices. It is a class that must never be forgotten if we are estimating the comparative well-being of the English-speaking peoples. For it is through the common experiences of that class on both sides of the water that America and Britain have the best chance of being drawn together.

Here was a household built on an income corresponding to £400 English sterling—with three children ranging from ten to fifteen—a small house but no servants. It is a hard life.

The difference indeed between such a house in America and England is the far ampler supply in America of facilities for cooking, warming and cleaning. Central heating alone saves much work on fires. Shopping is easier and quicker in the wonderful American stores. Holidays are simple and cheap. For such a family in America is freed from the British tribute to the seaside lodging-house keeper. They enjoy an almost free holiday in the vast spaces of this continent. For three months every summer they go camping out on the shores of Lake Michigan, living in tents, fishing, bathing, and renewing their energies in a glorious experience of the simple life. That is one signal advantage to set against the drudgery of the domestic life.

For an hour or so we have wandered about this town, visiting the fine bookshops and other stores, all bespeaking the wonderful wealth and well-being of this Middle-West city. All round you is a sense of national well-being, but perhaps most of all in the multitude of motor-cars which crowd the streets. It is a low estimate to say that one out of three adults in any of these Mid-Western towns possess a motor car. At mid-day you see all the side streets blocked with them. There are practically no chauffeurs: nearly everyone drives their own car.

Our host has been telling us of some glorious examples of the motor-mania which now possesses America. The workmen spend much of their spare cash in purchasing motors, usually on the hire system. A strike crisis recently arose because the workmen engaged on a new building did not consider that sufficient facilities were provided for "parking" their motor cars. Walking around, I expressed a surprise at seeing a number of cars "parked" behind one of the great stores. "You have a rich shopping class here," I ventured to say. My friend laughed.

"It is not the shopping class," he said. "It's the girls in the stores. That's where they put their cars while they are at work."

Perhaps not a bad investment; because, after all, it enables the girls to live out in the fresh air at lower rents instead of being crowded up in expensive lodgings in the centre of the town. But it all speaks of high wages and a great national reserve of wealth and energy.

A lady engaging a charwoman recently in one of these American towns, was faced by the charwoman with the following interesting dilemma.

"Have you room for my car in your garage, or will you fetch me in yours?"

Surely a very perplexing question, and likely to add very much to the problems of the modern mistress.

One last memory of Bloomington. In front of the courthouse there is an Arch of Triumph, on which is recorded all the names of the young Americans from Bloomington who fell in the war. It is a long list, and in thinking of the American war record we must not forget how much these little towns of the Mid-West paid in blood for the saving of the Allies. But what has struck us most is not so much the names, as the little interchange of poetical greeting between the Old World and the New recorded on either side of this triumphal arch.

On one side is written "Message from Flanders Field," composed, I believe, by a young Englishman at a bitter crisis of the war, and addressed to America.[10]

MESSAGE FROM FLANDERS FIELD.

In Flanders Field
The poppies blow
Between the crosses
Row on row
That mark our place.

---

[10]   John McCrae, the author, was Canadian, not English. Spender quoted the poem inaccurately. Ed.

1927

Allen D. Albert

Edgar County

Allen D. Albert spent most of his life as a journalist and free-lance writer. He served as a war correspondent in the Spanish-American War, and as chief editorial writer on the *Washington Times* from 1895 to 1910. In college he had majored in sociology, an interest that led him to deal with city and community problems in many magazine articles. One of these concerned Edgar County in eastern Illinois.

If the pilot of the St. Louis air-mail ever looks down in the moonlight as he crosses from Indiana into Illinois, he sees a prairie landscape fairly representative, probably, of the best of our American midwest.

He is then above Edgar County, an area of some 675 square miles of Illinois black loam and brown silt, fields crisscrossed by thousands of corn rows, clusters of trees breaking the roof lines of farmhouses in gentle rollings of the land, villages every five or six miles centered on church spires, roads converging from all directions upon Paris, the county-seat.

Here approximately 8,000 persons in the one small city and 18,000 outside of it live a life as farmer folk and town neighbors which is the sheer product of a century spent in pioneering and development. There is no great university here, as at Champaign-Urbana, or group of black chimneys as at Terre Haute across the State line. Paris has four small factories which diversify the employment of its people favorably. But Edgar County is primarily an expanse of farms.

If not from the air, then surely from car-windows, have thousands upon thousands of us looked out and wondered what kind of life was lived in the quiet farmsteads we could see as the train sped past. Lately some of us have been given a new light on that subject for this prairie county, and the insight it has afforded us into the tastes and purchases of such representative Americans has proven fascinating.

The thing came about because the president of one of the factories in Paris desired to suit his product more confidently to his consumers. His product was advertising specialties. He concluded he could gain more of what his trade calls "conscious obligation" if he knew more definitely what his consumers liked and what they were able to buy. He gave me the commission of identifying their wants and finding out how those wants were met.

Allen D. Albert, "Where the Prairie Money Goes," *Scribner's Magazine*, October, 1927.

We were not interested in what is called "farm relief." Our concern was with the life these people live as conditions are now, in 1927—whether they get or never get what politicians mean by "farm relief." It is significant of something, let the reader judge what, that a keen manufacturer did not think it dangerous to disregard "farm relief" in a programme to serve the farmer in 1928.

The study spread over the months of December and January. In the entire experience not a single person refused an answer. More striking than that, merchants and officials opened their books freely and called each other by telephone to help. Many of the farm households were within the range of my own friendships; yet it happened sometimes that with all their willingness, these people were unable to furnish the totals and budgets I sought, and we had recourse to the Edgar County Farm Bureau, where, as it proved, we could find out almost anything we needed to know.

Now that the work is done and the report accepted, I suspect that the best beginning to an understanding of the life lived in this county in 1927 lies in the finding that the money income of the county is very great indeed. From major sources alone it passed $11,400,000. This is the equivalent of $2,500 for each household.

Industrial wage-earners in Paris factories earned $845 a year on an average. Storekeepers had an average earning of $2,650 each. Town workers above the grade of helpers were paid $1,100 on the average. All that remain of workers not on farms, that is to say the clerks in the stores, the half-skilled laborers, the waiters in small restaurants, the drivers of delivery-wagons and the like, earned in the towns an average of $830 a year.

Hired help on the farms seemed to be at least equally well paid. There are 2,352 farm units, and four of them out of five took on workers by the year for about $40 a month for each man, somewhat more when the worker brought a family with him. In each case a room was furnished or a house; and for each family the means were provided for the growing of all the green food, all the meat, and all the dairy products the family could use, along with most of its fuel. Perhaps as often as not the workman could add to his money income, if he liked, by raising chickens or selling milk.

In the sense of our cities there is no poverty in all Edgar County. What a remarkable statement that is! Several scores of families live unhealthfully. Hundreds of them, as we shall see, do without things which city-dwellers esteem to be absolute necessities. For all that it signifies, however, here is an American community of some 5,000 families in which not a single household is denied food to keep the body strong or shelter and clothing to prevent exposure.

When it does happen that a family is without food or is deprived of protection against the weather, that follows which our young novelists will find hard to square with their materialistic interpretations of our life: neighbors come from all sides to make up the lack.

A renter moved into a typical small farmhouse a year or so ago, and no sooner were the family belongings in place than everything was lost through a fire. The blaze lighted the sky at four in the morning. At six the homeless little group were in rooms in a finished barn on the adjoining and larger farm.

That afternoon the newspapers of Paris printed a suggestion that old furniture, including blankets and pillows, was needed. Those of us who put off going only a day were informed when we did get there that the needs of the family had all been met.

The next thing to know about these families is that in town and country alike they are spending nowadays all the money they receive. Not a dollar has been added to the savings of Edgar County in two years. On the contrary, the money on deposit for savings has diminished.

This does not mean thriftlessness in most cases. There is plenty of that, here as elsewhere. It means, more significantly, a varying income, an upturned financial structure, a widening range of desires.

More than a hundred young persons go from this county each year to normal schools, colleges, universities, and finishing schools

—to name the institutions of the higher education in progressive order of expense. The total thus outlaid is not far from $102,800. This, of course, is only a beginning of the expense.

The eddy of this process has been in motion for years, growing with the years. As son comes home from the University of Illinois or the University of Chicago, and daughter from the more distant woman's college, phonographs come to be necessities and radios indispensable luxuries. Two-thirds of the homes in Edgar have phonographs now, beyond question; probably half have radios.

In apposition, fifteen farmhouses out of each hundred are believed to have some sort of lighting system better than kerosene-lamps, and ten of each hundred some sort of a water system better than buckets. The aerial is already more familiar than the windmill.

The factor which has most upturned the financial calculations of the Edgar County family is obviously the automobile. On it, twenty-five years ago, these families did not spend anything. In 1926 they spent more on it than the total of their outlays for food to eat and clothes to wear.

Their community income, great as it is, cannot be put much above $12,000,000. The total for food and apparel falls to about $1,990,000. The total for transportation of all kinds is $3,583,306; and of this about two-thirds—the great sum of $2,190,000—is spent for the purchase of automobiles, for garage service and accessories, for gasoline and lubricants.

Edgar County rural sections spend more than one dollar in four of their gross income on automobiling. This is fifteen times what used to be spent on pleasure vehicles for these same farms.

Away from Paris the trade of the county is largely through general stores. Readers who sniff reminiscently at the mention of such emporia and recall the aromatic mixture of scents as it used to be, with a post-office in the front corner and molasses side by side with vinegar in the rear, would hardly recognize these Edgar County general stores.

Somewhat of the old medley remains, but not much. They are package stores now. Candles bearing the names of Eastern manufacturers, crackers sealed against moisture, even beans in little sacks, and rod upon rod of canned goods in orderly battalions on shelves; silk shirts and work shirts; hats of well-advertised and expensive make beside straw hats for ten cents each; brooms and a demonstration vacuum cleaner; binding twine, alarm-clocks, and magazines; lettuce and fruit from a great distance at nearly all seasons—this is the general store with which this representative farm community has come to be familiar. Thereto it sends about a fourth as much trade as to the larger stores of the county-seat.

Less often than one would think—the farmers step on the starter and drive to Paris, Danville, or Terre Haute. Tracing such movement through package delivery by parcel-post, express, and freight, and estimating the goods brought home by automobile, the total is not impressive. It does not make a quarter of the sales of the general store and not much more than a tenth of the buying done from mail-order houses in greater cities farther distant.

Every farmhouse with a permanent tenant in the county receives each year a catalogue from one of the old-line mail-order houses. If you have never seen one, you cannot possibly visualize it from a description.

It is like a telephone directory for a city of the first class. It comes free. It is an invitation to window-shopping. There on the "craftsman" table in the living-room it invites a casual turning of its thousand pages.

You cannot fancy anything not to be found in it, excepting such perishables as fresh food or cut flowers. A speed-lathe for wood-working; a system for measuring men for ready-to-wear clothes; a special farm cyclopædia; sweaters for ladies of large figures; water systems and lace curtains; furniture and family medicines; flour, perfumery, and calf muzzles—all standardized, made by the quantity and all alike, the stream of them into Edgar County is unceasing.

A new method of selling by mail has arisen in late years. All mail-order establishments permit instalment buying. For the oldest of such houses the farmer has only to give the metes and bounds of his land, the town-dweller to give a letter of scant recommendation from his bank, to open an account. The new movement lifts instalment paying into a system.

Suppose that the county papers announce the appointment of a new teacher for a rural school. Her pay may be $90 a month for ten months. Soon a letter comes from one of these companies proposing what is set forth as "budget purchasing."

The teacher is to make up a sizable list of articles she would like to have—a coat with fur trimming, a toilet set for a dressing-table, an outfit of shoes and hosiery, the whole to cost possibly $300. These she can have at once, to use while she pays for them, if she herself will but fix the amount she can pay in monthly instalments and agree so to pay.

The volume of business must be large. More than 500 money-orders are issued for such budget purchases, it is believed, every month from the Paris post-office alone.

All in all, not counting bulk commodities such as coal and building-materials, a full third of all the retail trade of Edgar County is transacted through mail-order firms at a distance.

What kind of a home is the result? I hesitate to say for fear of creating an altogether misleading impression.

These are true homes of true Americans. They have the air of being comfortably lived in. They invite one, as does the shade of a thick maple in summer.

I have thought now and again how the typical city flat-dweller would smile over one of these midwest country homes. In his vocabulary small town and farm people are "hicks" and "rubes." In the county they wash outside the kitchen at a pump. They know when a telephone call is for them by the number of rings. They keep old-fashioned parlors. They have "jay" calendars on the walls and do without refrigerators.

Yet their homes give an impression of stability and permanence that typical flats in typical cities almost never have.

They have this effect of refuge as composites. List their furnishings one by one and you will wonder how it is they have it. The custom is to wash the dishes and let them stand on the kitchen-table; to put writing-materials in the sideboard and not to have a desk; to make a vivid machine-rug and a huge rocking-chair the high points of decoration in the best room; to put vases holding bunches of dyed immortelles on the upright piano.

Why so many do without conveniences they might so readily have is a baffling puzzle. A dollar's worth of hardware, some of the lumber out in the barn, and a rainy afternoon of amateur carpentry would give any tenant farm-wife a cupboard; but not half of them have such treasures. Throughout the Middle West undertakers tell of house after house among tenant-farmers where the children sleep on a mattress made up on the floor.

Stoves must make what heat is to be had in cold weather, and since coal is high and must be hauled in farm-wagons, it is sparingly used. Cream is poured into the jars for butter-making as soon as it is separated. Produce of all kinds goes to market without delay and without fair reservations for family use; so that many a farm in Edgar County and all neighboring communities sells its vegetables only to buy huge quantities of canned goods for the hired help at harvest.

Exterior decoration has made headway in recent years, perhaps because of automobile touring. The spaces set apart for lawns have increased in size and shrubs have been set out. Ramblers are the most frequent of vines. They are the pride of the older women; the girls turn to substituting planting about the house foundation for the old circular flower-bed in the middle of the front lawn like a horticultural pie. The space between the barn and the rear gate has not so far been invaded by change: it is still a muddy mass in wet weather and an expanse of naked, black ugliness in all weather.

A constant cry goes up hereabouts over the taxes, as everywhere in the world. The total paid by the people of the county for all purposes is set at $1,367,000 for 1926. This approximates a tenth of the money income.

Interest on loans of all kinds exacts another tenth, $1,030,423, though the payments to banks and mortgage companies seem not more than $827,000.

It will be observed that these two items together scarcely exceed the outlay for automobiling and that a considerable share of the loans made by the banks must be for the purchase of cars.

One can smile every now and then in the findings of such a study, thus:

All the benevolences reported, including the support of the churches, the Boy Scouts, and the County Homes, do not pass $110,000, which is less than 1 per cent of the chief items of income.

Twelve newspapers were operated in the county last year for $162,000.

Enough of the wealth of the county is productively invested outside to produce an estimated addition to the yearly income of $411,000.

Undertaking costs $100,000 for such a population each year; the upkeep of cemeteries $8,127.

On theaters of all kinds, at home, the county spent $70,000.

One household in four in a representative county-seat uses canned milk instead of fresh.

Well above half the total cost of insurance is repaid to the county each year in claims.

More money was spent on cigars, confectionery, and ice-cream than upon local and long-distance telephoning plus the telegraph.

Each dollar paid into such a community moves in and out the local banks several times, apparently, before it goes away to stay. Wherefore an annual income of less than $15,000,000 becomes more than $66,000,000 in bank clearings.

Of what the people of the area are thinking, and how they are changing their social customs, the study did not treat. It dealt with money income, and the findings which it produces for our more serious thought, it seems to me, are these:

That in a rich countryside all financial operations are now subject to riding in automobiles; that instalment buying by mail is routing direct buying over the counter; that taxes and interest on loans have become lesser items of expense; that at least for the year 1926 money is not being saved; that a relatively small amount of financial planning and reorganization would greatly increase the comfort of these households.

The disclosures are mainly the evidences of a transition out of one age into another, from life at a low gear to life at a very much higher gear. It is reassuring to consider that every social transition produces confusion and lifts up apparently unsolvable problems. We can feel we are on our way to the solution when we see the new problem as it really is.

I look across the winter landscape of Edgar County as I write and reflect how these midwesterners are like unto other Americans in other agricultural areas. In every prosperous American country-side perhaps is the counterpart of the financial overturning we have come upon here. Like you that read, I have confidence these people will work out a sound and wholesome adaptation to their new conditions.

VIII

Mid-Century

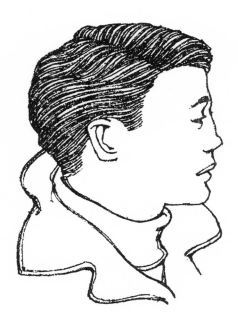

1934-1967

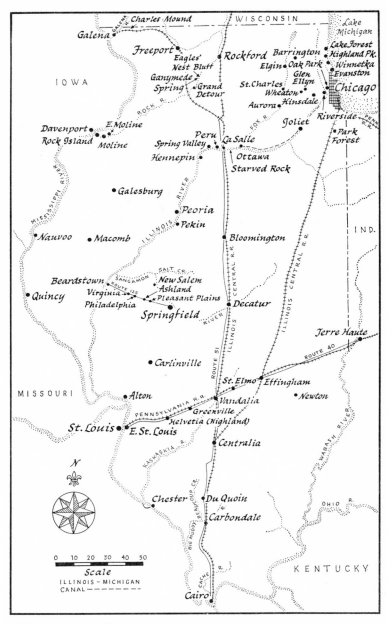

Illinois 1934–1967

Undeterred by the depression, Chicago, in 1933 and 1934, staged the world fair that it had planned in the preceding years of prosperity. The exposition, called "A Century of Progress," was designed to celebrate the one-hundredth anniversary of the corporate existence of Chicago and to demonstrate the amazing progress the world had made in one hundred years. In spite of hard times, the fair drew 39,000,000 in two successive seasons and proved to be an important prop to the faltering economy of Chicago.

In other respects, the course of Illinois was much the same as that of the other industrial states of the East and Middle West. Prohibition was repealed, and with repeal came a decrease in gangsterism; the remedial measures of the New Deal began to have an effect on the economy; and, finally, the production of equipment for a greatly expanded military establishment vanquished the depression. War, from 1941 to 1945, made first claim upon industrial production, and placed restrictions upon civilian activities stronger than those which had ever been imposed before. Meat, sugar, gasoline, and tires were rationed; travel was restricted; ceilings were placed upon salaries and wages. Many thousands of Illinoisans, women as well as men, were drawn into the armed forces and took an honorable part in combat in all theaters of a global war.

In one important respect, Illinois retrogressed during the second third of the century. In population the third state of the Union since 1890, it found itself pushed back to fourth place in 1960. (California was the villain, taking second place after New York, dropping Pennsylvania to third, and Illinois to fourth.)

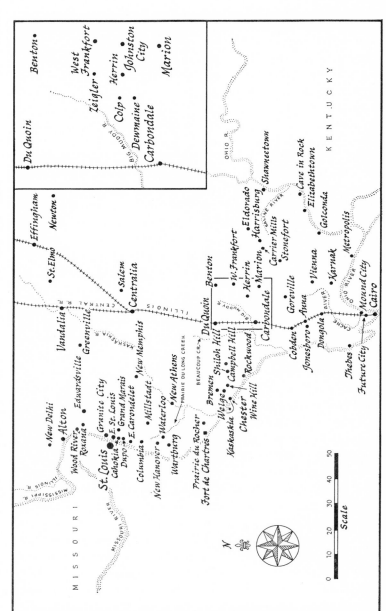

Southern Illinois

For the first time in its history, Chicago lost ground, dropping from 3,621,000 in 1950 to 3,550,000 in 1960.

Chicago's loss was compensated for by the enormous growth of its suburbs. The Chicago metropolitan area, including the city itself, jumped from 5,586,000 in 1950 to 6,794,000 ten years later, a gain of more than twenty per cent. Specific examples are more startling than general figures. The suburban city of Skokie, on the northwestern border of Chicago, had a population of 14,832 in 1950, and 67,865 in 1960. Park Ridge, another suburb, grew from 16,602 to 39,065 in the same decade. Arlington Heights nearly quintupled in population—from 8,768 to 40,622— in these years. And many others could show something approaching the same rate of growth.

Like the rest of the United States, Illinois entered the air age. Chicago had long been the railroad hub of the country; it soon took a similar place in air travel. For years its Midway airport was the world's busiest, and when Midway was abandoned because it could not accommodate big jets, O'Hare succeeded to that distinction. (As this is written, Midway is being readied for service again, and will soon carry a heavy burden of traffic.)

Not even the briefest account of Illinois in the second third of the twentieth century should omit two advances in agriculture: hybrid corn and the soy bean. Credit for the development of hybrid corn cannot be allocated to any one agronomist or to the agronomists of any one state, but the Illinois experimenters were second to none in this spectacular discovery. Moreover, Illinois farmers were not slow to take advantage of the new seed, which quickly doubled and trebled their yield of corn per acre. They were equally quick to plant their fields to soy beans, of which the state is now, and has been since the value of the crop was recognized, the nation's leading producer.

1934

Morgan Philips Price

A Century of Progress

Morgan Philips Price, Gloucestershire agriculturist and Labour Member of Parliament, had been a correspondent of the Manchester *Guardian* in Russia and had represented the London *Daily Herald* in Berlin. In 1934–35 Price covered the United States thoroughly, prying into the farming areas of the Middle West and the slums of the great cities as well as the showplaces. In Chicago, which he visited the fall of 1934, he saw the fair, "A Century of Progress," in the last week of its second season.

My first impressions of Chicago, where we arrived on October 24th, were definitely pleasing. The waterfront along the shores of Lake Michigan offered a striking spectacle. Chicago has more room to be impressive than New York. It is not confined to a narrow tongue of land, but is able to sprawl along the lake shores. The admirably conducted tours round the city give one a good idea of all that a foreign traveller is expected to see of the polished exterior of this great city, whose population exceeds four millions. The flats of the millionaires, with special lifts which hoist their motor-cars to bedrooms behind their masters' apartments, and the exclusive clubs, which none but a few families can enter, show that a section, I think a small section, of the American public is trying to forget its lowly origins and imitate the snobbery of old England. Money indeed has beautified the lake front of Chicago. It has forced back the waters of the lake, and made fine parks arise in their place. The Elks' War Memorial, and a beautiful piece of sculpture in the park, near the University, depicting the Ages of Man in stone,[1] as Shakespeare once depicted them in words, show that Chicago's artistic sense is alive, if not particularly original. We were greatly impressed by the University students who accompany the tourists, in order to earn money during their vacations. They are fine specimens of modern American youth. They avoid the coarse jokes and facetious remarks so usual with the old type of conductor, and really concentrate on giving the tourist a reliable account of the history, social life and art of their city.

One of the first things we did after our arrival was to visit the World Fair. We were lucky enough to get there just a week before it closed down for ever after a run of two years. It had been organized to illustrate a century of development in North America. On the surface, at least, it succeeded in exhibiting a certain kind of development. It was exceedingly imposing. It

Morgan Philips Price, *America after Sixty Years* (London, 1936), pp. 116–19.
Reprinted by permission of George Allen and Unwin Ltd.
[1]   See Burton, "The Rock River Valley and Its Cities," footnote 1, above. Ed.

extended for nearly two miles along the lake shore, and almost all the chief industries on the continent of North America were represented. It certainly showed what its promoters set out to show—a century of progress. But what kind of progress? The great motor firms told the same story that Ford was telling in his private exhibition at Dearborn—progress effected by scientific invention, and by keeping such troublesome things as an interfering Government and a social conscience in the background; in short, Science and Rugged Individualism. And I admit that the scientific side of the show was most impressive. We twice saw *The Wings of a Century*, a pageant acted on the lake shore, demonstrating the progress of transport from the days of the buffaloes and the Indians to the days of the "Twentieth Century Limited," with the actual vehicles employed, from the Erie Canal barge and the old wood-burning steam engine to the super-heated express locomotive and the Transcontinental Streamliner. Without doubt the Chicago Fair showed one that man can produce great instruments of transport and production. But we knew that before, and the crowd from the back-streets of Chicago knew it, for they seemed more interested in the side-shows. After all, these inventions had brought no happiness to them. The Science Building, however, seemed very popular and was patronized by students and people of the middle class from all over the States and Canada, who were really thrilled by the photo-electric cell and the hidden mysteries of the atom. There was also a pleasing exhibit of the more modern types of architecture, buildings characterized by straight lines and broad surfaces. But I think the palm must be awarded to the exhibit of the Federal Government. Perhaps it was possible to see them in other parts of the Fair, and perhaps I missed them there, but it was only in the Federal Government building that I saw the things that really matter in the twentieth century. In the rest of the Fair I saw the things that really mattered in the nineteenth century. I don't know if the advent of the Roosevelt Administration was at all responsible for this, but it was clear that Washington was alive to what the public mind should be focussed on. In the Government building I saw how the Western farmer can grapple with the problem of soil erosion, the legacy of decades of ruthless exploitation of Mother Earth; how the national forests can be preserved and forest belts planted across the prairies; what improvements have been made in the material and moral welfare of the wage-earning class, and what further progress is needed; what a potential market there is for the unsaleable surplus of American agriculture, if only the people have more money to buy. One could go on writing endlessly of the impressions of this great Fair, which, with all its tendency to loiter in the past, showed a definite understanding of the problems of the future. Judging by what I heard, this change of attitude had come about in the last year through pressure exerted by public-spirited people, and, judging by the Federal Government's exhibit, through pressure from Washington.

On our last day at the Fair, three days before it closed for good, I examined an exhibit of a house made of a patent wood preparation and built in sections, so that it could be taken down and transported from place to place whenever the owner wanted to move. I remembered a letter written by my father from Chicago in 1869, in which he spoke of having seen a Chicago family moving its wooden house on rollers to a new site. Since then Chicago had been burnt down and rebuilt. On the Lake front rose the great villas and palaces of the millionaires, many of them empty since the slump. In the back areas, west of the river, had risen the slums. Was this movable modern house a shadow of things to come? Would the twentieth century Chicagoan, stranded in the great city by the depression and change of circumstances, take up his house and move away to new employment in the distant provinces, where industry is being decentralized? In my father's day the population of Chicago was rising by leaps and bounds. Last year, I understand, for the first time it showed a decline. The wings of the nineteenth century carried Chicago to Olympian heights. The wings of the twentieth century may have another destination for it—not perhaps up in the clouds, but on more solid ground, and on a firmer foundation.

1945

Graham Hutton

Chicago

Few Englishmen have written about the United States more perceptively and with more sympathy than Graham Hutton. Although a young man when he came to this country in 1937, he had traveled extensively in Europe and had had experience as a businessman, teacher, and lecturer. For the next eight years he was the director of the Office of British Information, with headquarters in Chicago. He traveled widely in the Middle West, came to know the farms and small towns as well as the cities, and above all, met the people. Likeable and friendly, he was received as readily in the simple homes of small farmers as in the luxurious apartments of the rich and influential.

No more penetrating study of the heart of the United States is to be found than in *Midwest at Noon*, the book Hutton wrote before returning to England at the end of World War II. He not only admired Chicago and its people; he knew the city better than many of its lifelong residents.

Chicago is the metropolis of the West. To describe this great city, now the fourth largest in the world, defies one's powers. Abler pens than mine have done it, and yet Chicago changes so fast that their written descriptions are largely out of date or out of truth in a few years. Here is a city of nearly four million souls, with another two millions in satellite communities round it; composed of almost all Caucasian nationalities, Negroes, and Orientals; and dependent on agriculture, mining, oil, electricity, the seaborne traffic of the Great Lakes or the canals and rivers, and the most intricate texture of railroads and highways on earth.

The most impressive first sight of the New World is when you sail into New York harbor—if it is on a clear day. But the most impressive first sight of the Midwest is when you fly into Chicago at night from the East, descending over the blackness of the prairie to the great, ruddy blast furnaces and steel mills, catching the first winkings of the Lindbergh beacon from the Palmolive Building away on the starboard bow, and watching the brilliant rectangles formed by a thousand square miles of straight streets and buildings. Huge, sprawling city of swamp and prairie; one community of many communities, *communitas communitatum*; it is both a Pittsburgh and a Detroit; a financial and commercial center; a warehouse, department store, mail-order house, granary, slaughter-house, and inland seaport; a repository of great wealth and great poverty; a center of learning; metropolis of that million square miles which is the heart of America. It is something of a national metropolis, too, because of its position. It is the national headquarters of the medical, surgical, and hospital associations; of Rotary and other service clubs; of America's library associations; of the mail-order business; of the musical and juke-box industry, which plays so large a part in American life; of the *Encyclopaedia Britannica*; and of the cinematograph equipment trades. It is a part of all American life.

Graham Hutton, *Midwest at Noon* (Chicago, 1946), pp. 140–50.
© 1946 by The University of Chicago.

Driving into the city from the airport[1] up Archer Avenue, you could be on the outskirts of Warsaw, Budapest, Prague, Bucharest, or almost any other big central or eastern European city except Berlin or Vienna, which have too many apartment blocks. And in a sense you are, for the names above the stores and on the windows of offices speak all European tongues. Little clapboard houses with unfenced patches of garden remind you of a dozen European nations and their cities. Miles and miles of streets go by, with railyards and warehouses, corner stalls and markets, before you see the strange billowing vastness of the inland sea; the great cluster of skyscrapers and the biggest hotels in the world that sprout inside the central "Loop" of the elevated lines, like precocious overgrown plants in a wired-in forcing-bed; and perhaps the noblest front that any city in the world ever deliberately put on: Michigan Avenue.

This great and imposing front was once washed by the waves of Lake Michigan. Then the Illinois Central tracks came along it on piles and wooden bridges. Then the sandy foreshore was drained and reclaimed for the Columbian Exposition in 1892–93. The work was extended, and today Michigan Avenue is mainly built-up on the western side, facing east across the lake, and looking down on reclaimed and man-made Grant Park, the open-air theater, the Greek buildings of the Chicago Museum of Natural History (the old Field Museum), Soldier Field like a Byzantine hippodrome, the elegant Shedd Aquarium and Adler Planetarium, the richly endowed Art Institute, and the imaginative superhighway of the Outer Drive which takes traffic along the lake front from north to south, away from the Loop, for twenty miles. Driving along that highway by day or night and looking across to Michigan Avenue, the Loop behind it, and the big buildings of the Near North Side, you marvel at this noble city of the prairie on a seashore, where the first skyscraper was born.[2]

[1]   Midway Airport. Ed.
[2]   Home Insurance Building, La Salle and Adams streets, completed in 1885. Ed.

Just parallel with the northern boundary of the Loop you cross the Chicago River by the bridge which President Franklin D. Roosevelt opened with his famous "quarantine the aggressors" speech in October of 1937. Just here is an example of Chicago's ingenuity, initiative, and enterprise. The sluggish Chicago River, on the swampy banks of which the first white fur-trader settled a hundred and fifty years ago and Fort Dearborn was put up, used to meander through sand bars and reeds into Lake Michigan. Chicago straightened it, put a lock and harbor at its new mouth, and now the river can either flow into the lake and so into the Atlantic by way of the St. Lawrence, or admit vessels and water from the Lakes, channel them round the Loop and down the canal to the Illinois River, and so to the Gulf by way of the Mississippi. One canal, a few locks, and Chicago became a two-way lake port.

Another side to the story is not so impressive. The cities downstream enjoy the trade and traffic, but they do not like the products of the city's effluents which wash downstream when the locks are opened and the higher level of the lake water puts a "head" on the canal and the streams. This is the cause of a long and acrimonious dispute between Chicago, the adjoining states, the cities on the rivers, their various legislatures or authorities, and the national Congress and Supreme Court. All of these authorities are involved in Chicago's struggle for better sanitation and drinking water (it comes from the lake) and in her neighbors' struggles to avoid inheriting Chicago's dirt while Chicago gets clean.

The fourth city of the world, built by "fools" on piles in a marsh at the southern end of a lake, has other problems, too, which grew with its size, impressiveness, and beauty. Life in all American cities is more varied, mobile, and hectic than in any others in the world; but in none is it more so than in Chicago. Chicago has the best human virtues and the worst vices. It is therefore more truly human than any city, and it tells more about humanity. It tells it frankly, honestly, and openly. Nothing is hidden, nothing hush-hushed. The beauty of Michigan Avenue is offset within five or ten minutes' walk westward by the derelict buildings, dirty alleys, and run-down, overcrowded dwellings that any other city would hide or gloss over. Not so Chicago. Look on this picture and now on that, and see what was done and remains to be done. That seems to be the motto of Chicago. It has more extremes and variety than Istanbul, Singapore, or Shanghai, and ten or a hundred times their vigor. The vigor and vitality of the city amaze the visitor. Like an anthill, it is always moving, day and night. Other cities have their quiet times. Not so Chicago. To find a blasé Chicagoan would almost be a relief, so keen, so hungry and thirsty for new experiences, so curious, so divinely discontented and unsatisfied are Chicagoans of all income brackets and national origins. That is why Chicago holds the quintessence of the Midwest.

In Chicago all the extremes and extremisms of the region reach a grand climax. Within a minute or two's walk of the splendid stores and hotels and offices in the Loop you pass the flophouses of West Madison, Canal, and North Clark streets; the hiring offices for casual railroad laborers ("Good Eats Provided" painted white on the windows); the terrible slums and Negro district near the stockyards; the waste lands near the railyards; the hangouts of the bums and especially of the old, wrinkled, slow-moving, pathetic bums. I think "bums" and "bumming around" are still used more frequently in the Midwest than anywhere else because of the size of the region, the importance of its vast railroad network, the building of that network and its maintenance. It is natural, in the region of the greatest mobility in America, that the Germans' *bummeln* should have thus passed into the general slang.

On railroad maintenance, in thousands of factories, in the stockyards, and down south in the steel mills work the sons of fifty nations, all Americans, all midwesterners, all Chicagoans; and if white and colored, Sicilian and Greek, German and Pole occasionally clash, what of it? It is natural: the naturalness of so many different kinds of human nature. A little bloodletting is a small price to pay for such general tranquillity and order. The police are tolerant and extremely tactful, for they are mainly of Irish but also of German, Polish, Czech, and other national origins. Chicago is a League of Nations, a United Nations in itself. But it has been learning for seventy-five years how to live and let live, when to pay out the line and when to reel it in, when to give ground and when to hit hard. It requires a good deal of management and skill to give such a city order and regularity. As with so much in the Midwest, the wonder is that it has so much order, efficiency, and regularity. You cannot achieve that quickly without some show of toughness and force. You cannot let intolerance abolish order. And yet you must preserve liberty.

Who are the Chicagoans? More than New Yorkers, Jersey Citizens, Philadelphians, Pittsburghers, Clevelanders, Detroiters, St. Louisans, New Orleannais, or San Franciscans, they come from almost every race and people. There are Americans from all regions. Germans form solid districts all over, but chiefly in the north and northwest, like the working-class quarters of Hamburg. Poles with their pseudo-baroque Catholic churches with green cupolas make whole areas look like Cracow or Lodz. Czechs and Slovaks keep their homes and little gardens more neatly and reproduce Brünn or Pilsen, Brno or Plzen, in the Midwest. Lithuanians, Latvians, and Estonians have their homes out in the southwest, looking severe and North European in winter. There are Scandinavians of all kinds; Italians of all kinds, too, who keep their feast days and market days as if in the old country and live in solid blocks of the city; Greeks, Yugoslavs, and Syrians mainly on the West Side; Mexicans, Chinese, and Japanese, in their characteristic quarters; Hungarians down in the South and also on the North Side, mixed in with the Czechs and Germans and Yugoslavs, whom in Europe they dislike; British, Dutch, Belgians, Spaniards, Portuguese, Russians, Ukranians, and Armenians; and, of course, the Negroes.

It was estimated in 1940 that two-fifths—nearly one-half—of adult Chicagoans did not generally speak English (or, as Illinois puts it, American) in their own homes. Nearly all of them can speak it and do, outside, or with their American children. But there are many Chicagoans over the age of fifty who cannot speak it at all; they live in one or other of these compact groupings and do not need to. No wonder there are so many confusing accents in Chicago. New Yorkers and other Americans can make fun at the Brooklyn or Italian accent because in New York these stand out, firm and clear. No one in Chicago makes fun of any particular accent, because there is no single Chicago accent as a standard from which to deviate; there are so many. Chicagoans of German, Italian, Polish, and Czech national origin of the first or second generation, with their children, accounted in 1940 for more than one-third of the people. The others of non-English-speaking origin and the Negroes brought that proportion to more than one-half; a clear majority. Here is a potent source of variety and difference as well as of vigor and restlessness. The same pattern can be traced, with less degree of clarity and intensity, in almost every Midwest city and large town.

Americans from outside the Midwest tend to think of Chicago as Sandburg's "hog-butcher to the world," as being composed of vast stockyards and slaughter houses ("everything used but the squeal"), surrounded by some fairly decent apartment blocks and some necessary hotels and offices in a downtown section called the Loop or the North Side, and peopled by a scared race who go to and from work under a periodic hail of gangsters' lead. Nothing could be more grotesquely inaccurate. The stockyards are vast, surprisingly trim and clean, and localized in a compact area away from the main thoroughfares and traffic (except, of course, the huge railyards which serve them). You can live in Chicago for years and not know that meat-packing goes on there.

Chicago is not the only American city with gangsters; but in Chicago "the Prince of Darkness is a gentleman." They, too, keep to their local haunts, taverns, and night spots. They have a rigid code. The penalty for failure to observe it is quicker and more severe than in normal, so-called "civil" society. The only Chicagoans who see a gangster or hear his shots are those who, out of an inverted sense of snobbery or curiosity, go to the gangsters' haunts to see them or, more rarely, happen to be about in the small hours when the code of gangland is enforced. Even then the gangsters take remarkable care not to shoot up the public. Everything is nicely and neatly arranged so that only the principals—gangsters and police—are directly affected. Crime, racketeering, robbery with violence, other forms of lawlessness—these are more in evidence, as in other big American cities; and on them we shall have more to say later. But the activities and deaths of gangsters are known to Chicagoans in the same way as they are known to all other Americans: namely, in the columns of the newspapers.

The visitor generally sees only the Loop, the Outer Drive, the Near North Side, the offices and hotels, and perhaps one or two institutions on the outskirts: factories, mail-order houses, universities, hospitals. He seldom sees the Chicagoans at home. Their homes are their pride, and rightly so. From over thirty miles north of the Loop to thirty miles west and southwest, or fifteen miles south, and from as near as only three miles, the commuters come into the Loop by steam and electric trains, trolley cars, busses and automobiles. They are very early risers. Chicago starts work at the same hour as New York, where time is an hour later, and often before it. All factories and most Loop offices are working by eight or eight-thirty. From six-thirty in the morning until eight-thirty the commuters go into town; and from four-thirty in the afternoon until six-thirty they go out again. They have little time for lunch; half an hour is quite common. They are a hard-working community.

Their homes are the places where they relax. The variety of suburbs is bewildering. In this respect Chicago is far less standardized than most other American cities. The styles of architecture, layout of the suburb, and density of population per acre vary from the spacious, quiet beauty of Glen Ellyn, Hinsdale, Winnetka, Riverside, Evanston, and Highland Park to the greater uniformity and compactness of Oak Park, Rogers Park, and the South Side, with its more frequent apartment blocks, and then to the still more densely settled communities nearer the Loop. No greater luxury, spaciousness, elegance, and beauty could be found than in the old homes and modern apartments of the wealthy on the near North Side—the "Gold Coast"—or the great homes and estates of Lake Forest, Wheaton, or Barrington. Farther out, too, beyond the thirty-mile limit, are the big estates, summer homes, "farms," or week-end cabins of many of the better-off Chicagoans. But the homes of the great majority of Chicagoans, of the German workers on the nearer Northwest Side and of those of all national origins in separate wood-frame or brick and clapboard houses or in brick, stone, and concrete apartment blocks, are homes indeed. For ten miles around, the terrible grime of the soft coal from the many railyards blackens the windows and the outside, and the drapes or curtains inside; but the interiors are generally kept clean, full of those intimate belongings and that informal atmosphere which make a place a home. Chicago is not mainly an apartment city, like most of New York; nor does it live and eat in public places. It is a city of separate homes to which the visitor or client is immediately made welcome. It is a city of home-proud, city-proud citizens whose fathers and grandfathers came there to "make a home"—and made both a home and a city. And in that it is typically midwestern. It is the product of the South, New England, and central Europe. It is even more of a cosmopolitan city than New York.

This has one interesting by-product. Chicago has little of its own to offer the mere visitor or tourist. It is not a center of entertainment or diversion like New York or Los Angeles, or a national historical center like Boston or Philadelphia, or an old and quaint city of non-American origins like New Orleans or San Francisco. There are beautiful things to see in Chicago; but few tourists want to go to the remarkable Art Institute or the wonderful museums. Children and students flock to them. Few businessmen go, and the life of the Midwest is business. They want relaxation or "fun." The "fun" of the Rush Street or North Clark Street night spots and other such places, many run by questionable persons, is ordinary, vulgar, and raw. For those reasons, these places are well patronized—but not regularly by Chicagoans. The theaters are average; and despite or perhaps because of

Mr. Sam Insull's colossal barn of an opera-house, with its indifferent acoustics, Chicago has no permanent opera and for an adequate performance has to depend on New York. The smaller and more congenial Orchestra Hall, hallowed with memories of Thomas and Stock, provides music and a home for a good symphony orchestra. The movie-houses are vast, numerous, comfortable, and always full—day and night. The big hotels put on the best "entertainment" in Chicago; but because there is so much to see and do on the street and because, as in the early days, taverns and night spots are extraordinarily numerous, the visitor for a few days and nights gets the impression that there is much liquor, "fun," relaxation, and diversion in Chicago and that Chicagoans are always indulging in them. Again that is grotesquely inaccurate.

Chicagoans will put themselves to no end of trouble and expense to take a visitor or client round the night spots, the floor shows, to the theater, or on a round of a few of the many taverns. But that is not how the Chicagoan lives when the visitor has departed. The Chicagoan is like the Parisian in this respect: a very devoted home-lover, judged by visitors who hardly ever see him at or inside his home. He is judged by what he provides for alien palates. For this, the Chicagoans are not responsible, though America may be. Much of the less attractive, noisy, blatant, neon-signed, liquor-smelling aspect of Chicago is there for the millions of visitors, businessmen, and passers-by who have to traverse this vast crossroads city between transcontinental or other trains. (The greatest railroad hub in the world still has no central terminal, no through connection for passengers; you have to change stations, to the perpetual profit of the men who own taxis and hotels.) True, many of the 20 per cent of Chicagoans who live in mean streets and poor housing areas and work very hard at the rougher jobs regularly patronize the taverns; as the small minority of unimaginative and unwise businessmen, condemned by their fellows as unreliable or unstable, regularly patronize the places on Rush Street and elsewhere. That is because both these groups lack imagination, have poorly stocked minds, and have not acquired, or been able to acquire, any other ideas of relaxation. That occurs with the same groups in every big city. Drowning one's sorrows, or giving them bromide, is not unique to Chicago; nor are the sorrows of humanity. But the vast majority of Chicagoans lead quiet, domestic lives in their own homes and with their neighbors, who are friends.

One feature in which Chicago is very like big British cities is in the size of its suburbs. That is scarcely surprising, since the city has grown by absorbing small outlying villages and converting them to suburbs. These are now the home of the middle class, the clerical workers and the professional men. Being the Midwest capital and metropolis, Chicago has a very big middle class—or perhaps, as "classes" are not supposed to exist in America, I had better say, as Americans do, "a great concentration in the middle income brackets." But these Chicago suburbs of the well-to-do and the "middle income brackets," unlike the suburbs of European cities, are very beautiful; they have also far more variety than those of British cities. They have more of a community sense and community life of their own, centered round their community houses, libraries, forums, clubs, societies, or high schools. Places like Oak Park with 70,000 souls—"biggest village in the world"—Winnetka, Riverside, and Hinsdale set a high standard for suburban community life, and though they are not satisfied, they have already outdistanced most suburbs in overcoming the problems of life in a big city. They have community sense and community achievement to their credit, where the suburbs of cities in the Old World have only apathy and bleak failure. Indeed, the suburbs of most of the big cities in the Midwest are way ahead of others, both in and out of America, in this respect; and that is scarcely surprising, because the sense of community is, and always was, so strong in this new region. But, in making these communities, the community sense has been taken away from the city's center. The problems of Chicago, as of the other big cities and towns in the Midwest and everywhere else, are left at or near the center: the "inner ring" of solid and densely settled residential areas where the manual workers live; the areas of slums, dilapidation, or overcrowding; and these are linked with the level of incomes and the grading of jobs. That leaves the problems with the city fathers while the satisfied suburbanites go free. You cannot take the "El" or the Illinois Central out of the Loop and look out of the windows without wondering when and how Chicago is going to clear its slums, its deathtraps, and its breeding-grounds of crime and social problems.

The tempo of life in Chicago has to be experienced to be believed. It is much faster than that of New York. I am sure midwesterners work harder and more furiously than any people. They relax harder, too. One reason for that is the restless curiosity and experience-hunting of the midwesterner, which is greater than that of the more sophisticated easterner, which in turn is greater than that of the European. Another reason is the extra-ordinary gregariousness of all midwesterners, which is part of their sense of community. The Chicagoan is a home-lover, and there he really relaxes. But when he is "on the job," whether it is work or "fun," he (or she) never relaxes. Organized and com-munal relaxation is a business, like American games; "in earnest." The world is the midwesterner's oyster, which has to be opened at sword's point and then quickly swallowed, before he looks round anew for "those of the largest size." In New York, Philadelphia, Boston, there are many different groups in the social or intellectual life of the city. You can join any of them, but not all. Chicago's social and intellectual life is confined to a thinner layer, and whether it is in social affairs, intellectual pursuits, or gay diversions you meet the same people.

In this it is true that Chicago seems still "an overgrown small town"; but that remark is not as unkind as it sounds. The life of the small town rests on more solid social foundations than that of a metropolis. Social and intellectual leaders in such conditions must be prepared to live in the public eye. Thus the great mass of Chicagoans are free to live as anonymously or as publicly as they like, but there is little anonymity for the few hundred social "families" or "big names" of Chicago. They may not want anonymity. Certainly most of them cannot get it; and those who do are thought "snooty." That, in turn, means that life is a very hectic business, somewhat like that of royalty. Like the Red Queen in *Alice through the Looking-Glass*, you have to run as fast as you can to stay in the same relationship to people and events. To a smaller extent this is also true of social life in the other big cities and larger towns of the Midwest. It is not so much a question, as many observers think, of "keeping up with the Joneses"; it is rather a question of just "keeping up"—period. This gives to the surface of things in Chicago an impression of perpetual motion, like the surface of the sea. The analogy is good because in Chicago things happen, and people seem to think, and even move, in waves: waves of thousands or little waves of friends, but always waves. To get an individual alone you have almost to get into an office, bedroom, or bathroom.

Few cities in the world dominate as vast a region as Chicago. London dominates England and, as Cobbett[3] pointed out over a century ago, it has not been altogether for England's good. Moscow dominates a large region of Russia. Paris, Berlin, Vienna, and Madrid do not dominate their countries to that extent. Chicago is still the "big town" to millions of midwesterners; but millions do not like it because of its bigness, vigor, initiative, enterprise, and economic dominance. The other big cities and the larger towns are jealous of it. The farmers distrust it. All of them prefer it to New York; but, for them, that is like preferring the devil you do know to the devil you don't. To many midwesterners Chicago seems, and seemed long ago, like an octopus whose tentacles could not stop growing, extending, reaching out, sucking in. By the same token, Chicagoans have a chip on their shoulder about the entire East, which the East helps to keep there. They also tend to decry the importance, qualities, or achievements of other Midwest cities; somewhat as if they were the New Yorkers, Bostonians, or Philadelphians of the Midwest. Their natural self-assertion and contrariness are thereby heightened.

The oldness of Chicago, the old town, has disappeared with the

---

[3]   English politician and pamphleteer. Ed.

people who made it. The city is always putting on a new dress—but not always changing its underlinen. It is always on the go, going places, seeking "some new thing." If ever anyone tries to build a bridge out of wedding cake in the shape of the letter *S*, I am sure it will be a Chicagoan—and I am sure the experiment will succeed.

The city has surprising beauty. The beauty shines through all of its grime, the dirt of hard work. I have stood many a time, of a fall evening or in the depth of terrible winters, on the Michigan Avenue Bridge and looked west to see the girders of the many bridges over the Chicago River and the skyscrapers and the sunset beyond; and I have wondered why a Midwest school of painting did not spring up here. The rich businessmen of the Midwest buy the old and modern masterpieces of Europe; yet the best European artists would have had a field day if they had lived in the Midwest. Grant Wood and other Midwest artists seem more attracted by farm and rural life. Yet the cities have beauty, too; and it is ignored. You have the most beautifully poised masses and patterns of lines, majestic skies, colors, light and shade, depth and distances. Cross the east-west bridges over the southern branch of the river: look at the fortress-like dimensions of Butler Brothers' warehouses; the Byzantine aspect of the Merchandise Mart. How tiny seem the huge locomotives on the Milwaukee Road's tracks beneath, how their smoke billows over the bridges; how the west winds howl under the Randolph Street underpass below the Northwestern Station and rush eastward into the Loop; how the bridges rise and fall so quickly, one after another, to let ships through—at what cost to the city I cannot imagine, for there is a bridge for almost every street leading north and west from the Loop, and they must all be lifted and lowered again. Stand on the top of a skyscraper and look south, along the curving shore beyond Hyde Park and the University of Chicago, seven miles away, to the steel-gray horizon of the steel mills. Go out west to Halsted Street—the longest straight streetcar ride in the world for eight cents, over thirty miles—and see Greek and Syrian, Sicilian and Armenian, at work and play. Or go to

Maxwell Street on Sunday morning and see London's Caledonian market, Berwick Street, and Petticoat Lane fused into one, with the color and noise and bargaining of all the world's peoples.

See the city under new snow—be sure it is new—and it is a city transformed. "Windy City" lives up to its name, and to see a modern city being snowed in is an experience. I have seen drifts breast-high against the walls and only a few inches deep at the curbstone, right in the Loop. Go to the remarkable observatory on the top of the Board of Trade Building, above the "wheat pit," and walk all round, looking out for miles across railyards, stockyards, great public buildings, hotels, skyscrapers, each commercial building with its water tank atop, and as far as you can see in all directions but one—eastward where the lake runs straight north and south—there are the evidences of hectic activity: producing, transforming, packing, merchandising, printing, transporting, financing, selling, advertising, bustling, jostling, hurrying —all for the needs of six millions in Chicagoland, forty millions in the Midwest, a hundred and forty million Americans, and millions more in other lands. And then think: where Chicago is now there were about a dozen log cabins five generations ago.

1950

A. J. Liebling

Springfield

A. J. Liebling, famed for his mordant yet humorous sketches of
the American scene that were a distinctive feature of *The New
Yorker* until his death in 1963, visited Springfield in order to do a
series of articles on the Lincoln tradition in that city. In the first
article he included a thumbnail sketch of the Illinois capital.

Contemporary Springfield's preoccupation with its pre-Civil War self is not a sign of senescence. The city, which bears much the same relationship to Chicago that Albany does to New York, has a population of almost a hundred thousand, as against only nine thousand when Lincoln left for Washington; it also has more politicians and lobbyists than it had in Lincoln's day, because the population of the state has increased five times as much to lobby for. It has a fairly active industrial life, several good-looking department stores, and a generous quota of pubs. The percentage of visible women who are pretty is higher in Springfield than it is in Chicago; "Springfield's a Southern town," the women you meet there say when you mention this fact to them, as if that were sufficient explanation. Springfield is nearer to St. Louis and southern Indiana than to Chicago, and the eternal whitefish of Chicago restaurant menus loses the place of honor to catfish in Springfield, marking the change from a lacustrine to a river culture. (No great civilization has ever grown up around a lake.) The Springfield countryside is full of fat cattle being made fatter for market, and farmland there sells for more an acre than farm-land almost anyplace else in the United States.

Still, the tall man casts a long shadow. With Lincoln as a competitor, it is hard for any present-day politician to make an impression in Springfield. There hasn't been a major-party Presidential candidate from Illinois since Lincoln was reëlected, in 1864.[1] The current Governor, Adlai Stevenson, is the likeliest prospect in a long time. Democrats close to him act the way the hands around a racing stable do when a horse is working fast. The trick in the Presidential race, however, lies in getting the horse to the post.

I stopped in at the bar of the Leland Hotel, which is older and more frequented by politicians than the Abraham Lincoln, for a

A. J. Liebling, "Our Far-Flung Correspondents, Abe Lincoln in Springfield," *The New Yorker*, June 24, 1950. © 1950 The New Yorker Magazine, Inc.

[1]   Mr. Liebling overlooked Ulysses S. Grant, President of the United States, 1869–77. Ed.

glimpse of contemporary Springfield. While taking a rather harder drink than Lincoln favored, I listened to a couple of large, hearty men commiserating boisterously with a thin, sallow fellow because he had not succeeded in landing a state contract to build an airport in some downstate town. "You had the wrong bull by the horns," one of the large men said to him. "You should have come to me first." It was a congenial barroom. The two bartenders on duty looked as if their fathers might have poured for Lincoln's last law partner, William H. Herndon, who was a whiskey man and survived his senior partner by twenty-six years. I do not mean that it was the whiskey that made Herndon live longer. It was the brandy John Wilkes Booth drank that killed Lincoln.

1950

Simone de Beauvoir

Chicago

Simone de Beauvoir, French author and exponent of the existentialist movement, had published two novels when she visited Chicago in 1950. (Others, to appear later, would add measurably to her already substantial reputation.) She had friends in the city—notably the novelist Nelson Algren—and under their guidance she walked through sections and neighborhoods that a woman alone would not have dared enter.

Between New York and Chicago one flies over a plain that is even more monotonous than a desert; I slept throughout the journey: as the timetable changed, and I became confused with standard time and local time, I do not know how many hours the journey lasted: it seemed to be the same time in the morning when we arrived as when we left. I had the impression of being transported by magic all the way to Chicago: and it was only by magic that I would ever leave. Never had I felt such an impenetrable atmosphere in any city: I felt more lost than on the day of my arrival. I was a prisoner. It was difficult to recognise these streets: they cut across each other at right angles, and yet on the map which I had taken care to procure they gave the impression of complete disorder: they did not alternate with the avenues but ran into canals, vacant sites and railroads: I was lost; they were endless, even on the map.

New York is vast but its layout is quite clear, dictated, of course, by its geography, and it is easy to get the picture. Wide rivers flow into the open sea; to the North the city suddenly confronts the Hudson, faced with high cliffs. In Chicago you feel a claustrophobia, shut in by endless plains; the city lies at the heart of a vast stretch of land; the lake that borders it permits of no escape. From time to time, at the end of a long tram journey, in a train, or again on the overhead railway, the buildings thin themselves out, and one thinks that the city must surely peter out; but it starts again more vigorously than ever. You have only reached a former boundary beyond which new districts have sprung up; beyond them there is another boundary and yet another.

It is not only these extravagant dimensions which make Chicago so vast: Los Angeles is huge, but it is crisp. This city is made of opaque dough without leaven; it reeks of humanity more than any other city in the world, and that is what makes its atmosphere

Simone de Beauvoir, *America Day by Day*, trans. Patrick Dudley (London, 1952), pp. 269–74, 280–84, 288–89. © 1952 Gerald Duckworth and Co. Ltd.

so stifling, so tragic. Neither nature nor the past can enter here, but while lacking in the picturesque it still takes on a sombre poetry. Black is the colour—a proud colour, and brilliant like the facets of a block of anthracite. From north to south, from east to west, the streets are crossed and invaded by the metallic structure of the elevated, commonly known as the El. This low steel ceiling transforms the avenues into dark tunnels; beams that are shaken by the passing trains fill the air with groans that penetrate the houses: it is a great voice like the voice of nature, or that of the winds and the forests. There are viaducts, railroads, bridges, where trucks and engines are moving day and night. Trams jolt about in the middle of the roads. Men's destinies are forged to this clang of metal, in dust and soot. The dirt is so awful that it finally reaches a point when you no longer notice it; soot from coal is not dirty.

When you walk along the Loop on a sunny day, the shadows in the roadway tone so well with the dark colour of the walls that you would think the buildings retain these shadows permanently in their masonry; the blocks are split by narrow alleyways: to right and left the walls are decorated with fire escapes, so tightly packed that one could easily touch hands by leaning over them; from top to bottom of these fissures shadows are thick with dust. Even in the centre of rich districts entanglements of shadow and dark metal proclaim the wretched life in the huge areas that stretch around them. Far from the centre, among the small brick houses and the wooden shacks, the shadows pale; opening out into paved streets are alleys built on earth, blind alleys and yards where dustbins overflow with rubbish: they are emptied once a week; the wind whips up the eddies of grey dust; your eyes are filled with particles of straw and coal grit blown by the wind, while newspaper and fragments of greasepaper curl about your legs. Sometimes there is a smell of burning: as in New York, the children amuse themselves by setting fire to refuse. Yesterday I walked about for two hours in sandals on these pavements: when I got home my stockinged feet were covered with a thick layer of soot. You must walk in stout shoes and clean them four times a day.

And yet on the outer boundaries of Chicago there is a blue smiling zone. On Sunday afternoon I reached a lake surrounded by green lawns; in the sunlight the waters reminded me of silk and flashing diamonds, sailing boats were moving over them: it was the luxury of the Côte d'Azur. To my left, in a heat-haze, the Michigan Avenue skyscrapers stood out; there was nothing to remind one of the squalor with its human wreckage. Crowds of people were sitting on the grass in the bright sunshine; there were well-behaved loving couples who hardly touched hands; young people had got up a game of baseball on the lawns, and children were darting in and out of bushes playing at Indians. I followed the crowd which advanced towards a round building— an aquarium; there were hundreds of fish and thousands of visitors; they looked at each other with mutual astonishment. A spring day made for leisure. Seagulls flew over the lake and Chicago appeared as a city, huge, wealthy and gay.

New York nights had always cast their spell; here I felt stifled. I went out with N.A. and C.L., a young woman who ran a book-shop near my hotel. We strolled for a long time up and down Clark Street and State Street: they are, together with West Madison, the three main streets of pleasure in Chicago: luxury and squalor rub shoulders here in a familiar way. There are movie theatres, restaurants, burlesque shows, *cafés concerts*, dancings and bars without end. The smart ones are bathed in blue and violet light, soft to the eyes; they are quilted, quietly decorated, three-quarters empty—good places to talk in. Close to these quiet, correctly patronised, smart places are pothouses like those I saw during my first visit, full of drunks and tramps, with filthy wooden tables and violent lights in the midst of a steady din. . . .

12th May

. . . The press has a local flavour; of course the *Chicago Tribune* and the *Chicago Sun* are international in content, but there is something of the local press about them; matters of meteorology, highways, crimes and accidents, and civic festivities, occupy whole columns. Pictures are almost entirely given up to views of the Loop or narrow alleys with their rows of dustbins, and parks and monuments. If a citizen of Chicago succeeds in literature or politics, he is proudly acclaimed as a child of the city, a local man or boy. They are not interested in what is happening in New York. The majority of the people just ignore their rival city.

Chicago, however, is not a single town; more than any other American city it is an agglomeration of towns of huge dimensions, grouped round the business centre; the various districts are much more watertight than those of New York: the emigrants have not fused into a single whole. Many of them only speak their native tongue, have their own papers, and develop a kind of chauvinism that leads to brawls and quarrels: the Irish and the Poles hate one another.

N.A. had told me of an episode which shows how deep this segregation really goes: he specialised in the study of the Poles in whose district he lived and, although he described the squalor of his neighbours with sympathy, the Polish newspaper attacked his book in 1941. It accused the author of collaborating with German propaganda directed against Poland, and called him a Nazi agent; nothing extraordinary, the Polish writer added, since the author was of Swedish origin and Sweden was the hereditary foe of Poland. The Scandinavian paper in Chicago extolled the book.

One should not think that Chicago is picturesque on account of its mixed population: nothing is more like the Greek quarter than the Mexican quarter. There is nothing exotic in the Chinese streets: across shop windows names and inscriptions are in Chinese characters instead of Polish or German, that is the only difference. There are also many Japanese in Chicago. On the west coast the Japs were put in concentration camps during the war and regarded as enemies; here they have become so well assimilated with other people that they were looked upon as Americans in the same way as the citizens of German origin, many of whom fought in Europe as G.I.'s.

As soon as one leaves the splendid avenues, one finds, not a quarter of an hour away from the Loop, the peace of villages.

There are little places that seem to be far older than any street in New York; you can still see at the doors of the tobacconists Indians carved in wood, which served as signs in the nineteenth century, and in front of the barbers' shops are posts with blue and red stripes revolving in spirals. The dust that silts up in windows and camouflages walls seems to have been there a hundred years or more. To-day I saw a small forgotten street beside an old station in which the rails were rusting; from time to time an empty tram passed by. And there were wooden houses with verandas where people sat to get a bit of sunshine or taste the evening cool. Each had a tiny garden below street level; they looked like any suburban allotment at home: the lawn had a plaster statue, a coloured ball or a miniature windmill of varnished wood. There were hundreds and hundreds of empty silent streets. They had sprung up anyhow, and their shacks were so rotten that one might easily take them for poor hovels although the interiors were often clean.

I took the overhead and, for mile after mile, we sped over mud-coloured areas covered with dreary shacks built on the hard earth. From time to time one saw some blades of grass, an empty plot, a tree that leant against a wooden paling; trees were never so moving as in this blackened city. They grow so humbly amid all the rubbish, the dustbins, railway tracks, backyards and *culs de sac*, but they are never soiled by the neighbourhood; they look exasperated with their fresh green leaves; the pastures of the Alps or the tropical forests could never express a green as green as this. Older than the houses that they lean against, they are the survivors of a giant clearing, reminding one silently of their prime existence in a kingdom of wild beasts. In an organised world where contingency results from the human will, and where every sign of disorder signifies misfortune, they have the nonchalance of things of nature. Their sight is restful.

Above all it is at evening that this poetry floats in the streets. At the corners of blind alleys children smoke and plot in whispers; women on their porches gaze at city lights that twinkle on the horizon; the groaning El suddenly breaks the silence; the foliage shudders; a cat upsets a dustbin; the slightest sound can be heard for a long time. You feel that you are very far away from human follies, and at the heart of a quietly-ordered life that repeats itself day by day. And yet to-morrow you will read in the papers that they found a corpse cut to pieces in one of these alleys, that two men have slit each other's throats in a nearby tavern, while two yards off the tenant of a bar was shot with a revolver. The silence of the night here in Chicago is only a mask. . . .

14th May

. . . This afternoon C.L. left her bookshop and walked with me through the endless streets of Chicago. On the far outskirts of the coloured district and the Greek and Italian quarters, we came to one of the biggest markets I had seen since the Djelma el Fna square at Marrakesh. It stretches for more than a mile along the road and the sidewalks of a wide street.[1] The heat was stifling, it was a midsummer sun, and dark Chicago had suddenly become an exotic city, hot and colourful, such as I had imagined San Francisco to be. The men wore shirts hanging out over their trousers: they were pale blue, soft green, salmon pink, mauve, sulphur yellow. Many of the women had knotted the flaps of their blouses across their navels, so that a broad strip of flesh showed between skirt and bodice; there were many coloured faces, while others were olive-tinted, bronze or white; and they were often shaded by straw hats.

To left and right in little wooden kiosks they sold silk dressing-gowns, shoes and cotton frocks, jewellery and blankets, tables, lemons, hot dogs, scrap-iron, furs: an amazing mixture of rubbish and solid goods, a junk fair all mixed up with one-price luxury. Small cars were moving up and down the road from which they were selling ices, coca-cola and bags of popcorn. Behind its shield the flame of a little lamp wavered to and fro, its heat made the porous grains pop. A dwarf-like figure in rags, with the face of an Indian and a big straw hat, and with an acoustic gadget fitted to

---

[1]   Maxwell Street, now (1968) succumbing to urban renewal. Ed.

his ear, was telling fortunes with the help of another Indian; his props were complicated, truly magical; he had on a barrow a glass tube filled with liquid in which small dolls were jumping up and down; a customer drew near, a coloured girl. She looked provoking, sceptical and shy as she laid her hand on the glass; the ludions jumped and sank into the depths of the mysterious instrument which ejected a strip of pink paper. The woman's fortune was clearly printed on it.

The machine designed for magic and the acoustic gadget under the exotic hat were a happy combination which gave to the bazaar its unexpected character—an eighteenth-century fair where drugstore products were sold amid the clamour of loudspeakers. Here was a charlatan who had coiled a snake round his neck and sold a dark elixir that cured all ills; but it was only with the aid of a microphone that he described his wondrous panacea. Another specialised in brain diseases and healed them merely by laying-on of hands: he too was talking claptrap through a microphone, and had behind him an anatomical design which looked scientific and purported to represent the human brain.

There were booths upon the widewalks, often in areas as in the Jewish district of New York. Their goods spilled out onto the pavement. Through an open door I saw, standing in a dark room, a gipsy covered with veils, crouched over a basin and washing her dirty linen. The loudspeakers yelled, each emitted its tune. At one street corner coloured folk were holding a religious meeting: the men were in everyday clothes, but the women wore black dresses and dark veils edged with white, just like nuns in certain religious orders; they sang together. Above their heads a coloured family sat on a balcony, lazily listening to them; they were singing spirituals. A little further on a coloured preacher was speaking excitedly; guitarists played dance tunes. A second coloured preacher, with a red cap on his head, gesticulated wildly: he pointed to the other preachers angrily because they preached about the god of white men: as for him, he invoked the coloured man's god, and exhorted his brethren to listen to him and no other.

Sects which are openly against white people have recently

developed, but in strictly limited numbers. Islamic for the most part, they adore the god of Mahomed, not Him of the Christians: it is to the people of Africa and Asia that they look for the salvation of the coloured race. No doubt this preacher belonged to the "Moorish" group, which was not only a religious sect but a small business community with a harem. It comprised altogether some two hundred coloured folk (the majority were women) living in nearby hovels. We listened and we watched. Superstitions, science, food, religion, jewellery, spiritual and corporal remedies, rags, silks, popcorn, guitars and radios—what a mix-up of every civilisation and every race in the course of time and space; in the hands of merchants, preachers and charlatans, the revolving mirrors glittered, like candles attracting moths, and the street was filled with the screeching of bright-plumaged birds. The buildings of Chicago stood out sharply against the bright blue sky; at the end of the avenue that cut across the bazaar, houses, streets and lamp posts were all the colour of dirty water.

15th May

... In the afternoon M.G. took me for a walk in one of the coloured districts. There are several in Chicago. Coloured folk have settled in the city since 1830, but they poured in there at the time of the great strikes in the slaughter yards in 1894 and 1904. They were not numerous then, and were scattered throughout the town and on the outskirts of the well-to-do districts. Towards 1915, and during the war industries boom, immigration was intense; the city was also growing rapidly, but coloured folk were not allowed to penetrate the new districts. The southern section, the biggest in 1910, was much extended. It forms a narrow strip that is called the Coloured Belt; other sections developed, but not a single one in the centre was open to coloured folk.

As in New York, the growth of the coloured population, which multiplied sixfold during the first world war, resulted in strict segregation: even the coloured people of the upper class, whose ancestors lived in Chicago almost on equal footing with their white neighbours, are thrust back into ghettoes and hardly differentiated from "poor darkies," those who arrived more recently from the South. Organisations were set up to prevent property owners from selling or letting to coloured folk; while threats and violence were also used to prevent the negroes from gaining footholds in white districts. At the instance of Roosevelt cheap houses were put up for coloured folk, who in fact inhabit them; but this effort was insufficient. The constant immigration of Southern coloured folk into forbidden zones (which, nevertheless, allow them to percolate) results in a number of families living in one apartment designed for one family, and in their taking lodgers, or converting large apartments into a number of small dwellings, with all the resultant insanitary conditions. This explains the contrast which struck me to-day between the exteriors, wretched for the most part, and their respectable interiors.

We walked down an avenue above which the Elevated sprawled like a blackened ceiling. To right and left were little wooden houses, with narrow stairways leading to tiny hovels. We climbed a stair and went down a balcony where clothes hung out to dry; we saw a yard surrounded by a fence, and other huts with flat roofs; the structure of the Elevated loomed over the district, and the whole house shook whenever a train passed by. Through an open door I saw a tiny room, but it was clean. Further on we explored another building, astonishing on account of its southern picturesqueness; there were terraced stories open to the winds and lined with rooms on both sides; a stairway steep as a ladder climbed up past them, and I noticed a kind of pulley with ropes which could be let down from the roof to the ground floor. In Italy, in Spain, this mouldering house would be full of sordid dwellings. Through the glass doors I saw the interiors but they were clean: there were frigidaires, linoleum, American cloth, and sometimes a radio. Of course, there are many wretched families living in all the shacks which give Chicago its dilapidated air; but there results from the housing crisis, which is just as acute for white people, a situation whereby many people live in houses far inferior to their standard of living. It is not space which is lacking. From the upper terrace, leaning against a balustrade which enclosed the galleries, one had a fine view of skyscrapers on the

Loop and the endless flat grey city; I noticed great spaces there. On foot, in the train, I saw them continually throughout Chicago. But land speculation, the rising cost of building and lack of capital leave them vacant right at the very centre of thickly-populated districts. We went down into the street and turned a corner, to find ourselves in a more populous-looking street, whose atmosphere reminded us of certain parts of New Orleans; the bungalows, of course, were not so romantic, but the rank grass, dwarfed trees, red and blue shirts of the children, and the indolent gait of young people gave one a strong impression of the tropics. And yet, the fact that I could stroll about with a coloured man was the obvious proof that we were now in the North. . . .

16th May

. . . This evening I went for a stroll in the Italian district, Little Italy, with N.A. and C.L. We passed through the Greek quarter, and then the Mexican quarter, whose antique shops reminded me of Santa Fé. At a corner we stopped to look at a carnival, a tiny amusement park such as one often finds in poorer districts in the larger towns: roundabouts, shooting galleries, ice cream, aeroplanes, more or less the same attractions as with us, and there is always a crowd; Americans like these mechanical amusements. A little further on there was a bright shop window; some fifty people were sitting about in chairs and two women in spectacles, one dressed in pink, the other in pale blue, were singing hymns and playing the harmonium: it was a religious meeting and we entered. On the walls we read some edifying texts, and questions such as: "When did you last write to mother?" The majority of the people who took refuge here were tramps over sixty who probably had no mothers. We were given hymn books with a blue bookmarker. Everyone stood and sang, or at least moved their lips. We only stayed a moment, and as we left we handed the precious volume to our neighbour; he shook his head with a wink, and N.A. pointed to an inscription on the wall: "Dinner will be served after the service." Obviously the meeting was a success. A little way further on we came to another; a man was preaching instead of women singing, a zealous person distributed prospectuses before the door. But we preferred to dine elsewhere.

We came to a crossroads which was very famous for the number of murders that took place there in the time of the gangsters, when the Italians worked with specially swift knives. We entered a restaurant which was also a wine and spirit merchant's, with a fine collection of Chianti bottles set out in a row; the tiled floor, wooden tables, and families chattering away in Italian, took me back to Rome; we were given Chianti, *pizzas* and *spumoni*. And then we returned by little streets that were very quiet, and where there were neither cars nor pedestrians, and a single street lamp shone; there was only the murmur of the trees in the wind, and the shadows whispering together under the eaves. There was a smell of the countryside, and under our feet we felt the hard bare earth; only the sky had the suspicious tinge of skies above great cities. There were many people in this huge oppressive city living as peacefully as in a little town in France or Italy.

17th May

This was the last day I would spend in Chicago. This morning I went to see the museum again, and the splendid lake on which white sails sparkled. A young mulatto had fallen fast asleep in the sun-drenched grass with straw hat over his eyes. A grey-blue mist was thinning gradually over the massive buildings of the Loop, so that they no longer seemed to weight the earth. But the blackness was not banished: beside the harbour where the brightly-varnished boats lay still and slumbered, at the edge of satin waters, there were enormous heaps of dust and coal; warehouses streaked with railways and with trucks loaded with black blocks. I crossed an avenue where shining automobiles were moving swiftly, and went towards the canals. I found myself in a subterranean world; it was roofed by a road and very much darker there than underneath the El. It was lit with lamps, and there was a proper street with shops and bars on sidewalks where neon signs shone at midday; I saw in my mind's eye the brilliance of the sun and the blue waters, and this subterranean city strongly reminded me of the film *Metropolis*. The street brought me back to the Loop, in which, alas! I wandered for the last time.

I should miss Chicago. I did not see it at all in the same way as I saw New York, so that I could not compare them. Instead of getting to know a lot of people and many places, I preferred to profit by the friends I had, which gave me a deeper appreciation of at least one of its aspects. My experience was very limited. I did not return to the "smart" districts, of which I had caught a glimpse the first time I passed through; I did not set foot in any of the chic nightclubs, nor did I have any contact with the University, which is most interesting, I was told. But because I had taken up a definite approach I came to be quite intimate with the city, in a way that I had been unable to achieve in New York. At all events it would only be a memory to-morrow. And in three days' time the whole of America would be but a memory. Slowly my phantom had taken on bodily shape; I had seen the blood flow through its veins, and I was happy when its heart began to beat like a human heart. But now it was becoming disembodied with alarming speed.

1955

William H. Whyte, Jr.

Park Forest

Most Chicago suburbs have evolved from small villages planted in the nineteenth century. Oak Park, for example, goes back to 1833. Highland Park grew from a tavern, built in 1834, on the Chicago-Milwaukee post road. Evanston was platted in 1854, at least ten miles north of the Chicago city limits.

In the middle of the twentieth century a new kind of suburb appeared. The prototype was Park Forest, planned in its entirety before a single foundation was laid. William H. Whyte, Jr., editor, sharp observer of the ideology, training, and neuroses of men whose lives are directed by large corporations, described Park Forest and its residents in his book, *The Organization Man.*

WILLIAM H. WHYTE, JR.

This kind of suburbia is a natural phenomenon. They bear a resemblance to such utopian ventures as the Oneida community or the Fourier settlements, but where earlier utopias were an expression of revolt and idealism, the new suburbs are a response to social and economic realities. Park Forest, for example, was set up, quite simply, to make money, lots and lots of it. Looking at the real-estate situation right after the war, a group of Chicago businessmen saw that there was a huge population of young veterans, but little available housing suitable for young people with (1) children, (2) expectations of transfer, (3) a taste for good living, (4) not too much money. Why not, the group figured, build an entire new community from scratch for these people? The group, incorporated as American Community Builders, bought up ·2,400 acres in the cornland thirty miles south of Chicago and brought in a remarkable man, former Federal Public Housing Commissioner Philip Klutznick, as president.

The plan was to build clusters of rental garden apartments (rent for two-bedroom duplex: $92) around a central shopping center, and then, as time went on, build ranch-type houses for sale ($11,995) on the periphery of the area. The housing would be merchandised at bargain rates. The real money would come from the waterworks and the company's cut (ranging up to 10 per cent) of every dollar spent in the shopping center. In effect, the developers were building a city to provide a sort of captive market—a constantly replenished, nonsatiable reservoir of 30,000 people, many of whom would ever be poised at that stage when families just begin to lay up possessions.

When the doors were thrown open in 1948 the rental courts were islands in a sea of mud, but the young people came streaming out of Chicago. The first wave of colonists was heavy with academic and professional people—the place, it appeared, had an extraordinary affinity for Ph.D.s. Since Chicago is one of the

William H. Whyte, Jr., *The Organization Man* (New York, 1956), pp. 282–88. Reprinted by permission of Simon and Schuster, Inc. © 1956, by William H. Whyte, Jr.

great business-training grounds of the U.S., however, another kind of affinity proved even stronger: poised at the nexus of America's junior-executive migration, Park Forest quickly became a haven for the organization man. Out came trainees for the big corporations, research chemists with the AEC, captains and majors with the Fifth Army, airline pilots, FBI men—in total, a cross section of almost every kind of organization man in America.[1]

Why the attraction? Since I am going to emphasize some of the nonmaterial factors let me at once put first things first. The people who went to Park Forest went there because it was the best housing for the money. Some psychiatrically-minded observers have hazarded the thought that they really went there to seek a father image and such, and that Park Forest is not a normal sampling because it tends to select such people. I do not agree. Undoubtedly, it does have some selective appeal, but it should be noted that people in the income and age group of Park Forest have very little luxury of choice in housing. Even though they might dislike the idea of so much propinquity—many Park

---

[1]   The cross section has remained constant. Old settlers at Park Forest like to tell you that they are being replaced by an "element" less worthy, but though the population has been greater each year (about 25,000 in mid-1956), there has been little change in basic characteristics. Median educational level for *all* adults remains about 2.5 years of college—the highest of any Illinois community. As far as occupation is concerned, a check of move-ins to the rental area in 1955 shows no change, save a few less university people. Here is a random sampling of newcomers in 1955: research chemist, Sinclair Oil Co.; salesman, Swift & Co.; major, Fifth Army; investigator, FBI; purchasing agent, Ford Motor Co.; industrial psychologist, Swift & Co.; space salesman, *Business Week* magazine; underwriter, Prudential Life; salesman, Du Pont Co.; buyer, Carson, Pirie, Scott store; trainee, Burroughs Adding Machine Co.; lieutenant colonel, Fifth Army; research engineer, Continental Can Co.; engineer, Western Electric; sales trainee, Atlas Box Co.; engineer, General Electric; pilot, American Airlines; public-relations assistant, Acme Steel Co.; teacher, Rich High School; labor-relations assistant, Ford Motor Co.; writer, Time, Inc.; accountant, Gulf Oil Co.; copywriter, Chicago advertising agency.

Foresters, indeed, say that they almost decided not to go there because of the propinquity—other considerations weigh far more in the balance. The space for the money, the amenities not elsewhere available, and, most important, the fact that it was so well set up for children have been in most cases the dominant factors.

Park Foresters, in short, went there for quite rational, and eminently sensible, reasons. Once there, however, they created something over and above the original bargain. Together, they developed a social atmosphere of striking vigor, and while it might have been as one to ten with the more material attractions, it was to be a significant extra. The developers were quick to recognize it. At first they had advertised Park Forest as housing. Now they began advertising happiness. They retained an advertising agency, Weiss and Geller, famed as the most motivation-minded of all agencies, and after a bout of depth interviews and psychiatric panel discussions, the ads began belting away at the overtones of Park Forest more than the homes themselves.

Here's the way they went:

You *Belong*
in PARK FOREST!

The moment you come to our town you know:
You're welcome
You're part of a big group
You can live in a friendly small town
   instead of a lonely big city.
You can have friends who want you—
   and you can enjoy being with them.
Come out. Find out about the spirit of Park Forest.
(*Ad for Park Forest Homes, Inc., November 8, 1952*)

Here is a magnificent one:

a cup of coffee—symbol of
PARK FOREST!

   Coffeepots bubble all day long
   in Park Forest. This sign of
   friendliness tells you how much

neighbors enjoy each other's company—
feel glad that they can share their daily
joys—yes, and troubles, too.

Come out to Park Forest where small-
town friendships grow—and you still live
so close to a big city. (*November 19, 1952*)[2]

The ads are quite right. Let's take, for example, a couple we shall call Dot and Charlie Adams. Charlie, a corporation trainee, is uprooted from the Newark office, arrives at Apartment 8,

[2] One can only stand in admiration of these ads—and hard selling they were. I have always wondered, however, why the developers and the advertising people neglected another, and quite important, appeal. In exploiting the loneliness of contemporary life they hit a nerve, but they left untouched the more material service of Park Forest as a temporary home for people who know they'll be transferred. Many transients would be better off if they bought a home, and some discover this after a year or so at Park Forest. But often it is when it is too late and the knowledge that buying a home—even for a stay of only two years—as a riskless and economical proposition has not been openly advertised, and as a consequence many transients in the Chicago area never think of this possibility. In time this new concept of home-buying will probably become accepted practice, but it is still an appeal that offends many sensibilities. Those who want to stay put bridle at it. Even the developers themselves hate to say it out loud. They have become Park Forest citizens too, and hard-headed as they are on most things, they are a bit touchy on the matter of Park Forest's turnover. It is quite a normal phenomenon, but they sometimes spend their own good money in ads that imply that nobody's leaving Park Forest any more. The developers have a proper concern, of course, in that it takes some explaining before most nontransient home seekers will recognize that turnover is normal and not a rejection of the community. I still think, however, an opportunity is being overlooked, and since I have great respect for the resourcefulness of the developers I have no doubt that in time they'll be advertising openly how good a way station for transients they have. In a decade or so, indeed, what may worry them is that people aren't *enough* aware of the turnover. Park Forest is not so a home of aging people, of has-beens, they may feel impelled to argue; our junior-executive people get promoted and transferred as fast as people anywhere.

Court M-12. It's a hell of a day—the kids are crying, Dot is half sick with exhaustion, and the movers won't be finished till late.

But soon, because M-12 is a "happy" court, the neighbors will come over to introduce themselves. In an almost inordinate display of decency, some will help them unpack, and around suppertime two of the girls will come over with a hot casserole and another with a percolator full of hot coffee. Within a few days the children will have found playmates. Dot will be *Kaffeeklatsching* and sunbathing with the girls like an old-timer, and Charlie, who finds that Ed Robey in Apartment 5 went through officers' training school with him, will be enrolled in the Court Poker Club. The Adamses are, in a word, *in*—and someday soon, when another new couple, dazed and hungry, moves in, the Adamses will make their thanks by helping them to be likewise.

In the court, they find, their relationships with others transcend mere neighborliness. Except for the monastic orders and the family itself, there is probably no other social institution in the U.S. in which there is such a communal sharing of property. Except for the $200 or $300 put aside for the next baby, few of the transients have as yet been able to accumulate much capital or earthly possessions, and so they share to make the best of it. One lawn mower (with each man doing his allotted stint) may do for the whole court. For the wives there may be a baby-sitting "bank" (i.e., when one wife baby-sits for another she is credited with the time, and when she wishes to draw on it one of the wives who has a debit to repay will sit for her). To hoard possessions is frowned upon; books, silverware, and tea services are constantly rotated, and the children feel free to use one another's bikes and toys without asking. "We laughed at first at how the Marxist society had finally arrived," one executive says, "but I think the real analogy is to the pioneers."

But the court social life, important as it is in rooting the transient, is only part of the acclimation. Before long Charlie Adams may feel the urge to shoot out a few extra roots here and there and, having normal joining instincts, may think a mild involvement in some community-wide organization just the thing. When the matter is bruited to him he may be tentative—nothing strenuous, understand, awfully busy with company work; just want to help out a little. Instantaneously, or no longer than it takes one person to telephone another, the news is abroad. Charlie will never be quite the same again.

He has plunged into a hotbed of Participation. With sixty-six adult organizations and a population turnover that makes each one of them insatiable for new members, Park Forest probably swallows up more civic energy per hundred people than any other community in the country. For the wife who gets fully involved, the blackboard in the kitchen is indispensable, for scheduling oneself to keep from being expected at two different meetings at the same time is not always easy. Every minute from 7:00 A.M. to 10:00 P.M. some organization is meeting somewhere. Looking through the picture windows of one of the community buildings one typical night I saw: on the top floor, the church choir rehearsing; the Explorer Scouts (waiting for a quorum to plan next week's hike); world politics discussion group (to discuss what causes war; a second discussion group was to meet on a different evening to take up American foreign policy). Bottom floor: school board meeting (to talk over interior decoration of the new school); an organizing committee to organize a new organization (the Protestant Men's Club); Husanwif Club (to watch slides on safety rules for children).

As elsewhere, of course, the apathetic greatly outnumber the active—but not by so much as elsewhere, and the active are so active that they generally feel compelled to laugh at themselves for their folly. "Actually, neither Fred nor I are joiners, like some of these silly characters around here," one wife explains, "but it's gotten so now I practically have to make an appointment to see him Saturdays. During the week we alternate; when I have my meetings, he baby-sits for me, and when he has his political meetings, I baby-sit for him." Says another: "What a rat race! Even staying at home I do a lot more than you think. I act as Dick's secretary and handle all the phone calls when he's away, and then there's my League [of Women Voters] work and the

P.T.A. and the Great Books Course. Some of my friends think I'm nuts. They ask me, what do you do it for? Sometimes I wonder myself."

They hate it and they love it. Sometimes it seems as if they are drawn to the participation just for participation's sake—the ease with which signatures for petitions—any petition—are obtained, for example, is nothing short of startling. Nor are meetings necessarily directed to any substantive purpose. Sometimes they appear to be chiefly a medium by which anxious, uncertain people can vent aggressions they must elsewhere repress. Without the disciplining effect of a dominant older group and of custom, they are enticed into precocity, and this, unfortunately, stimulates many to a form of free expression in which name-calling and rancor seems to be an end in itself.

1953

James H. Morris

Lake Forest

Park Forest is one kind of suburb, Lake Forest is another. This
the English journalist, James H. Morris, makes clear in his book,
As I Saw the U.S.A. Morris visited the United States as a Commonwealth Fund Fellow. Of the book he wrote after his return to
England, Sir Denis Brogan, of Cambridge University, whose
knowledge of the United States is unrivaled, commented: "one
of the very best travel books, one of the very best impressions of
contemporary America I ever read."

Chicago has always had, though, a flourishing intellectual and cultivated minority, and it was the center of the great Middle Western literary and artistic movement which had its heyday between the wars. Around its wide perimeters today there are a number of handsome suburbs which, without having pretensions to intellectual distinction, nevertheless represent a comfortably literate way of living, and have not their exact equivalents or equals, perhaps, elsewhere in the world. The word "suburbia" has not acquired those overtones which taint it in England. In the hubbub of American urban life it is only common sense to live in a suburb, though some of the more earnest sociologists profess to be disturbed about the movement away from the centers of tòwns; and the large stores cater to this trend by opening excellent little minor versions of their enormous emporia, scattered about the more expensive outskirts of the cities. The most attractive residential area I saw in America was the suburb built on the top of Lookout Mountain,[1] in the country of the snake-worshippers; but most of the big cities of the Middle West have their counterparts, well-tended, clean, prosperous, complete with their own rich little shopping centers, teeming with clubs, societies, discussion groups and other manifestations of the American social appetite. The Middle West is full of intense local patriotisms, but when a small frontier settlement blossoms into a metropolis Americans demand some more intimate loyalty, and are inclined to scuttle some of their fervor for Detroit or Chicago, let us say, in favor of such desirable suburbs as Grosse Pointe, Michigan, or Lake Forest, Illinois.

Lake Forest is characteristic of these well-fed communities. The best way to reach it from Chicago, if you can endure forty minutes of conviviality, is to persuade some friend to take you on the evening "club car." The American railroad can still be surprisingly personal and flexible in its services—as anyone knows

James H. Morris, *As I Saw the U.S.A.* (New York, 1956), pp. 212–18. © 1956 by Pantheon Books, Inc. Reprinted by permission of Random House, Inc.
[1]   A short distance south of Chattanooga, Tennessee. Ed.

who has discussed a transcontinental ticket at Pennsylvania Station in New York. There is none of the monolithic detachment of British Railways about these lively enterprises. What the customer wants, he gets (providing it pays). Accordingly it is not difficult, on many American lines, for a group of commuting businessmen to arrange for a private coach to be hitched each morning to the 8:15 and each evening to the 6:38; and quite a modest subscription is enough to acquire membership in such a mobile club, and to share the services of the calm and adaptable Negro servant who travels with it every day.

So each evening at Lake Forest, when the club train pulls in, a most cheerful and well-acquainted group of businessmen emerges from its cushioned recesses, and parts with fond expressions of fraternity. How comfortable a process this is, compared with that dreary daily grind from Waterloo to Axshott! There they sit in their swivel chairs, a glass of bourbon in the hand, a selection of friends round about, an attentive lackey padding among the seats, a stack of new magazines, a whole coach to wander in, instead of those dark Satanic cabinets that are all too often provided by the Southern Region, with their gray and aging upholstery, their cramped corridors, and the squeezing anxious crowd that presses into them. Moreover, when these fortunate Illinoians reach the little station at Lake Forest, another pleasant circumstance awaits them; for there parked beside the line are the long polished rows of their limousines and shooting-brakes, a well-dressed wife at each wheel, an expectant child or two skipping about the seat, a couple of poodles or a huge lugubrious mastiff peering through the back window. What a world away from the 'bus queue outside that Surrey station, or the bicycle locked with its padlock in the stationmaster's office, or even the Morris that is beginning to burn oil! There are probably no commuters anywhere in the world who travel home more comfortably than the burghers of Lake Forest.

But there are disadvantages, not always apparent, to so soothing a progression. The wife in her black nylon looked very nice from the station platform, but inside the car there is a dauntingly purposeful air to her ensemble. The Lake Forester will, however, be more depressed than surprised by her air of impending festivity, for dinner with the Rodney Bells, or the Howard J. Spriggses, the Afschleters or the Edmund Browns is something that befalls him frequently. They need only run back and drop the children while he freshens up; it is rarely black tie in America, and he is therefore able to step with scarcely a pause from club car to cocktails.

But the evening is likely to be an agreeable one. The guests will find themselves in one of two kinds of houses: a comfortable and well-preserved little mansion built by some complacent plutocrat in the early years of the century, and having a parklike garden and an atmosphere if not actually horsy, at least distinctly doggy: or a house of uncompromising modernity, with mobiles floating about the drawing room, a hostess who keeps Abyssinian cats, and a host who talks about the G-factor of the roof. Few American households have servants. The wife cooks the meal herself, slipping a crisp and colorful apron over her dress, and inviting her women guests (as the men drink their cocktails) to join her from time to time in the kitchen. If she is unlucky she may be burdened with an epicurean husband, for "knowing about cooking" has become as popular as esoteric exercise among American men as it has among British (though probably no American takes it quite so seriously as the Oxford don who subscribes to *Le Figaro* for its daily recipes). If so, it is the husband who leads the way into the kitchen, placing his Martini on the top of the refrigerator as he demonstrates his techniques. He is sure to have acquired the very best equipment: rows of heatproof dishes, rolls of aluminum foil, and an oven at shoulder height, so that he need not strain his knees bending for the joint. The Americans do not take their eating lightly, and there is no dishing up an old stew or reaching for the sausages when Lake Foresters entertain.

Among many of them, on the other hand, there is a determined rejection of formality, a vestigial relic of frontier times or an inherited reaction (which they would fervently disclaim) against the imperial splendors of Europe. There are many houses in Lake Forest where you can rely upon polished oak tables, monogrammed napkins and candles; but you should be prepared, when you accept an invitation, to eat your dinner literally on the floor. It is the custom to serve the meal in the manner of a buffet, the guests queueing a little self-consciously while the host and hostess, at the head of the serving table, ladle the soup or give encouragement. Having received your portion, you must then dispose yourself about the house to eat it; and for some reason or other—I am never quite sure whether it is intentional or not—there are not enough chairs to go round, so that the more girlish of the ladies, and the more resigned or flirtatious of the men, must sit on the carpet. I know of few less relaxing exercises than that of eating a plate of curried prawns with one hand, clutching the support of a neighboring chair leg with the other, trying to avoid destroying a priceless china dog with one's feet, and discussing the Meaning of Truth with one's companion.

For the conversation is unlikely to be entirely frivolous. You cannot depend upon an evening of utter escapism, as you can in England; you will meet no girls, however anxiously you search, of an utter emptiness of intellect; and few men whom you can trust implicitly not to talk about the next elections. The Middle Westerner has reached his apogee of creature comfort by a commendable gift for labor and application; and he is still, beneath a veneer of sophisticated congeniality, an earnest and a serious person. So is his wife. I remember all too clearly a conversation I had with one Lake Forest woman, sitting on just such a floor, eating just such a curry, in which she displayed some anxiety to arrange in corresponding order the Kings of England and the Presidents of the United States; and in which, while she rattled through the Georges and the Williams, hesitating only over the details of a year or two, I floundered distressingly among the Presidents. Who was the fifth President of the United States? For that matter, who was the fourth? Was Van Buren a President? Who was Millard Fillmore? Luckily she did not notice my inadequacies, for the conversation spread, and soon the entire company was busy discussing the relationship between Catherine de Medici and Bonnie Prince Charlie. There is always an encyclopedia in such a house as this; and the children, poor things, sometimes seemed to me to be weighed down with reference books and inducements to learning. It is an atmosphere healthily demanding accuracy of mind. Though you can survive the wildest opinions, you should try to avoid errors of fact; unless, that is, you are an expert, for expertise is sacrosanct, the specialist is never doubted, and a few technicalities interlarded with authority will make almost any statement acceptable. (A visiting agent for a firm of English sanitary engineers was once introduced to a group of Middle West women reporters, as a somewhat heavy joke, as "Sir Henry Middleton, leader of the 1949 Everest Reconnaissance." "Oh, Sir Henry," they gushed, "tell us, do, what it was like!"—and when with scarcely a pause for reflection he replied that it really wasn't much fun cutting crampons on the West Col, they wrote it down in their notebooks with awed excitement; for though he was portly, sagging and wildly ignorant, he was indubitably an expert.)

The evening is likely to be dominated by women. This is not surprising, for not only are they generally more intelligent, but they form a closely interwoven society of their own. Miss Freya Stark[2] refers in one of her books, describing some very different society, to "the universal sisterhood of women." In the well-to-do suburbs of the Middle West this nebulous mystery is reinforced by the American women's invincible urge to join things. The impression you take away with you from the dinner party is likely to be that while the male guests had not seen each other for a month or two, the women had spent most of that day together, and the day before too, and would be meeting again tomorrow morning if not for breakfast, at least for morning coffee. The highly integrated social activities of these ladies are naturally not quite so straightforward as those of the ladies of Cranbury, New Jersey. There must be Presbyterians in Lake

[2]   English travel writer. Ed.

Forest, but they are a great deal more subdued, and I have heard religious opinions expressed there that would lead to agonizing reappraisals of social standing among the simplicities of Cranbury. The fêtes are smarter and more expensive; the discussion groups more inclined to talk about Kafka and less likely to read *Ivanhoe* aloud in relays; the dance committees much more anxious to secure a foreign title or two for effect. For it cannot be denied that many of the people of Lake Forest, though in theory thorough democrats, have at the back of their minds some slight yearning for a more aristocratic form of society. Many are the obscure English baronets or German princes who are paraded in their drawing rooms or casually introduced to envious neighbors. Subtle indeed are the means by which the arrival of such a worthy is made known to the social columns of the local paper, or even to the gossip pages of the Chicago press. You can meet your thrusting self-made Americans in Lake Forest, proud embodiments of the old legend about office boy to high executive; but you can meet at least as many who will drop a hint about "the old place" in England, or assiduously preserve the faintly European accent they acquired at Harvard, or drive about in an English sports car, or wear clothes of unmistakably Savile Row ancestry. I was once walking down a road in Lake Forest when I heard from over a garden wall the beguiling wail of bagpipes. Could it be, I wondered, that the Stockyards Pipe Band of Chicago, a well-known Middle West institution, had come out to Lake Forest in charabancs for some fashionable carnival? Or was it the band of some ancient regiment of the line, shipped to the Middle West by the ever-active British Information Services, as they once shipped two London buses complete with drivers and direction plates to Hackney Wick? I looked over the garden gate and there, marching solemnly up and down the lawn, were the pipers, two young men in kilts who happened to be identical twins. They were watched by an elderly lady of distinguished appearance, dressed in tweeds, who sat in a chair at the head of the lawn surrounded by admirers, as if she were ordering the sea to retreat, or was expecting the head of John the Baptist. This was a characteristic

Lake Forest occasion. The lady was Dame Flora Macleod, head of the Clan Macleod; the twins were her two grandsons; and they had come to America to meet members of their clan and invite them to visit the ancestral castle in Scotland, a prospect of sublime appeal for those many Lake Foresters to whom the lure of ancient stones and immemorial titles is irresistible.

Lake Forest, indeed, has its own nobility, inhabiting the fine houses that stand along the shore of Lake Michigan. Some of these houses are very grand indeed, beyond the means of all but the most successful Italian marquises, and of a state of preservation and convenience utterly beyond the ambitions of the average English duke. One such house has a splendid staircase leading down to the water, embellished with a series of Grecian figures; and such is the rudeness of the Chicago climate, and such the conscientiousness of the owner, that when these statues are not being used, so to speak, they are enveloped in transparent containers, and stand there modestly and mysteriously muffled, ghosts in shrouds of cellophane. Lake Forest, like a hill station in the evening of an Empire, has its own subtle social tiers, its own barons, landgraves and caciques. It has its sporting club, too, to which in the long summer evenings the commuters are whisked for parties, just as the Major, home from evening stables, would be conveyed to Gezira for dinner with the Lauries of the 9th. This tight little community, living so comfortably among its trees and shady lawns, no longer feels the magnetic pull of the big city, nor the call of the land, but has evolved its own polished and intricate civilization. It has its failings of pretension, perhaps, but it shares a grace and an easy style that is one of the more attractive American contributions to social progress.

1958

Baker Brownell

Egypt

After a distinguished career as a university professor, principally at Northwestern, Baker Brownell became director of Area Services, Southern Illinois University, Carbondale. The experience aroused his interest in the southernmost quarter of Illinois, commonly called "Egypt," and gave him a thorough knowledge of the region. *The Other Illinois* is in sharp contrast to such of Brownell's earlier works as *Art in Action, The Philosopher in Chaos,* and *The Human Community,* but it is an unsurpassed study, informal yet penetrating, of a distinctive part of the United States.

Off to the south of the big-time Illinois and considerably older is another Illinois not well known even to Illinoisans. Though the main show, of course, is a big one that people who live in the long carrot-shaped state take for granted, the other Illinois is something else again. From this Illinois a black report drifts northward now and then, foggy with rumor of a mine disaster, a massacre, or some other desperate instance of life and death, but that is about all that most people hear of it. This southern Illinois sits on the back doorstep as poor as Job's turkey, as beautiful as redbud trees in spring. It may be more passionate, more violent, stubborn, stringy; still it is a sweeter Illinois with soft southern linguals, magnolia blossoms, and a generous heart.

This other Illinois begins at the 39th parallel or thereabouts, in line with Alton and Vandalia, and extends southward into the crotch of the two great rivers down to the 37th parallel. Here at the tip of Illinois Cairo stands with one foot in the Mississippi River and the other in the Ohio and calls itself, not "Kyro" nor "Kayro," but "Kerro." It has about the same latitude geographically as Norfolk, Virginia, with a moral latitude said to be considerably greater.

The thirty-one counties of the south end of Illinois are a hill-top and bottom country wedged down among rivers. On its north line the Missouri and Illinois enter the Mississippi in brown turmoil. On the south the Ohio joins the Mississippi where it enters the Gulf plain and thence moves past the Wickliffe mounds of Kentucky on down more than a thousand miles to the sea. This southern Illinois country was planned by Nature more to delight rivermen, hunters, fishermen, and folks willing to forego good soil for a house on a hill than to facilitate the orderly acquisition of wealth. A central plateau is made of tough, recalcitrant clay pan. The ranges of ancient, sometimes rugged hills in three cases attain the dignity—standardized at 1,000 feet—of mountains.

Baker Brownell, *The Other Illinois* (New York, 1958), pp. 3–22. Reprinted by permission of Duell, Sloan and Pearce, affiliate of Meredith Press. © 1958 by Baker Brownell.

The borderland is a realm of levees and overflowing water, of flood plains along the Mississippi, the Wabash, the Ohio rivers, and the black precious earth.

Southern Illinois is thus somewhat south of prosperity. For the main show and the big incomes begin with the black, generous soils, the glacier-tilled prairie, the corn, hog, and soy culture of the central counties, and include, no doubt, McLean County corn, Kane County butter, the Chicago River, the Tribune Tower, along with lesser items such as the greatest railroad network in the world and the southwest corner of Lake Michigan. To all this our southern Illinois seems indifferent, too much so, perhaps, for it rejects sometimes the accepted codes of prosperity. Says young Dr. Striegel, a veterinarian just new-minted from college and professional school, "I could make more money up north, but I can go fishing here." That remark is typical of southern Illinois.

Egypt is the popular name for the region; no one knows why. A whimsical Egyptophile influence had a part, perhaps, in naming little, new places hereabouts: Cairo, Karnak, Thebes, Dongola, and from them the regional name may have followed. But legend does not have it so. Although the legend probably was invented after the fact, it is persistent. There was drought in the northern counties, says the legend; the wheat fields dried up; the streams died in their beds. But in southern Illinois rain fell and there were good crops, and from the north came people seeking corn and wheat as to Egypt of old. Thus the name, Egypt. Neither the name nor the legend is a good one, but people stick to them. Instead of Egypt it might better be called, if we must be historical, Mesopotamia, or between rivers. Or, still better, the river country.

Who are these people of southern Illinois? Where do they come from? They are not all Abraham Lincolns, to be sure, but many of them look it. The name or something similar, such as Linkon, is not uncommon. And the Lincoln trail, a thousand miles and a hundred years long, from the Atlantic seaboard,

Virginia, the Carolinas, over the Cumberland Gap into Kentucky, and trickling on in slow stages into Indiana and Illinois in the early nineteenth century, was trodden by thousands of southern Illinoisans. These deep-eyed, thin-lipped people were the first to come of those who still remain. Only later by a decade or so, when the Black Hawk War was finished to the satisfaction of the victors, did the white tide, including my own ancestors, begin to flow from New England and New York over the northern prairies. They were the newcomers then. When men from the little swampy town of Chicago came to Shawneetown on the Ohio to borrow $10,000 they were refused because Chicago, they were told, had no future. That, at least, is the story.

The southern Illinoisans were rural and mountain folk who felt at home in this outlier of the Ozarks. They hacked their way into the magnificent hardwood forests, split rails for fences, rolled the great walnut, oak, elm, beech, sycamore, poplar, locust logs together for burning, piled the brush, and grubbed out farms in the uncertain soil. They shied away from the prairie, for in those days prairie soil was suspect. It also was hard to break.

These are called the first settlers but there were men before them. Frenchmen settled in 1699 and 1703 at Cahokia and Kaskaskia on the Mississippi. Under its cliffs of limestone, Prairie du Rocher—usually called Roach-er—was settled a little later. But not much of France remains except names hanging here and there on ancient places, like garments whose owners have gone away and left them. Carondelet, Dupo, Grand Marais, Fort de Chartres, the great stronghold, Prairie du Lang Creek, Beaucoup Creek—usually pronounced Buckup—are some of them.

An old and gentle custom also survives here and there: At Prairie du Rocher ancient singing, "La Gui-Année" from house to house and from drink to drink may be heard in its French patois on New Year's Eve. For two hundred years, with some intermissions no doubt, "La Gui-Année" has been sung in the village, and for twenty of those years Charlie Clerc—pronounced Clare—has led the score of voices and the violins. It is good, say the people of Prairie du Rocher, that the songs of their ancestors should endure. Nor should the drinks be forgotten; they, too, are appropriate. And if one of the singers during this tour of good wishes finds it hard to carry both the tune and the drinks, he can be replaced from a reserve held for the purpose.

It is also good, says Prairie du Rocher, that some of the courtesies of an older day survive. Tom Conner, the big shot of the village and French in all but name, will leave his hardware store and with Gallic grace take a visitor to his home for a little wine and conversation. Thus good things live on, and charming but threadbare little gestures, accents, customs, almost absorbed but not quite, can be found buried under thick strata of modern lingo and habits. They are cultural fossils, delicate skeletons of ancient behavior. Even the slaves of the French retained the intonations and manners of their masters. Their descendants, free men now for generations, have still a hint of the accent and quality of the continental customs to which their people were bred.

But German migrations and the Americans now have covered over the French residues in southern Illinois. The green pastures of the Germans range across the Saint Louis milk shed. The low-pitched little towns gathered around their German-Catholic or German-Protestant churches are thrifty, reticent, secure. They, too, have become old, and in their own way are as American as the hamburger that my teen-age son orders on every possible occasion. German names and Lutheran churches mark a sharp marginal line at the south edge of the industrial slums of East Saint Louis, names such as Millstadt, New Hanover, Waterloo, Wartburg, Columbia, New Athens—pronounced Ayethens—a later stratum covers the old.

Others came. Urged by English capitalists with investments in the Illinois Central Railroad, more than 41,000 English migrants settled in Illinois in the late fifties, most of them south of Centralia. The Irish came by shiploads, and Irish voters as early as 1860 controlled the town of Cairo.

The French, the Colonial Americans, the Germans, the English, the Hungarian, Lithuanian, Polish, and Italian mineworkers, the Negroes, these are the Americans here. The Negroes now number about 67,000 in a total southern Illinois population of 1,009,000 folk. Some of the villages, such as Dewmaine, or Colp, or Future City, are mainly Negro. The Irish had a settlement or so. The Swiss founded a town called Helvetia,[1] and a highly intellectual town it was. The different stocks come and go. Their villages rise and fall. They are new and then old, and new ones come again, for their mobility in time is great. Of the earliest Illinoisans, such as the Kaskaskias, Michigameas, Tamaroas, Peorias, Cahokias, Shawnees, only names, cemeteries, and mounds are left. They, too, have come and gone many times. Their pumpkins and the corn in the fields are older in American lineage than the oldest white men and survive by many years those who first cultivated them. At the Modoc site near Prairie du Rocher, human relics have been found 10,000 years old by preliminary tests. As for Kaskaskia, the Indian village and later the first capital of Illinois, the great river changed its course one day and Kaskaskia now is under water. It was a big town once with 7,000 or more people, or so it was said, and Lafayette visited there. But catfish now are its first citizens. The long, black barges on their way to Memphis slide over it.

The mortality of villages and of men and their institutions in southern Illinois is not alone a matter of floods and natural disaster. It is also economic. There is a high mortality of jobs. The land is beautiful and broken—tragic some would call it—as beautiful in its own idiom as anywhere on earth.

Spring is incandescent here; it glows with strange, soft fire. The autumns are golden and still; each tree in its own way is a transfiguration. There are more kinds of trees in these few counties than in all of Europe. The north and south, the east and west of the continent meet here. But the lovely spring and fall and the mild winter between them are not enough, if there are no jobs. "You can't eat them," says the man looking for work. Even southern Illinoisans, impractical as they are, admit that.

[1]   Since 1843, Helvetia has been called Highland. Ed.

The cost of public relief in the area is higher by more than 50 per cent per capita than in the rest of the state. In some communities the largest source of income is relief payments. Farsighted relief workers are saying that the costs of community rehabilitation and education would be more than covered by the reduction in relief payments.

In Eldorado, a town of 4,000 in the Saline Valley, the last of six coal mines has closed down. Men, like ants in a hill that suddenly has become hostile to their interests, scurry out to find jobs. Scores of them commute daily to jobs in Evansville, Indiana, Paducah, Kentucky, Joppa, or elsewhere, 160 miles or more for the round trip in order to support their families. Their cars wear out and the men wear out, but the worried, harried traveling continues.

"But labor nowadays must be mobile," says the economist, looking up from his desk. "Why don't they live near their work?"

"Hell!" says Jess Chandler, the big miner, now a pipe fitter in Evansville. "That's all those damn economists know about it. Many of us own our homes in Eldorado. We can't sell them; we can't rent them; and we can't pay the high prices in the new place. Our children are in school in Eldorado. Our wives may have jobs there. It's not so easy to move as it looks on paper."

Many men in Eldorado have no jobs at all, and this is repeated in most of the towns of the area. Eldorado, it is true, is now enthusiastically sniffing the air of a local oil boom, but her sister towns drag on as before. It is an old story, decades long. Though magnificent in its resources in coal, in oil, in its spars, marbles, limestones, and clays, its great rivers and railroads, its fruit and forests, its climate and long growing season, its beauty, its hunting and fishing, and above all in its people, southern Illinois seems to feed outside areas such as Chicago and Saint Louis more than the people where those resources lie.

Few Americans and certainly no southern Illinoisans will accept the proposition that one region should exist only as a feeder to some more propitious spot, still the decay of this rich and beautiful land goes on. Cairo, for example, declined more than 15 per cent in population in the last census decade, Centralia 15 per cent, Eldorado 8 per cent, Johnston City 17 per cent, Salem 15 per cent, West Frankfort 8 per cent, Zeigler (pronounced Zigler) 16 per cent. A few towns, including Centralia, Marion, and Carbondale, are picking up again. But the general tendency is down. In the rural areas as well as in the towns the decline is general. The surrounding rural areas have declined, indeed, even more than these towns that serve them. The metropolitan area including East Saint Louis, Alton, Granite City, Wood River, on the other hand, shows gain.

Some of the little towns have responded gallantly to the challenge. Herrin, once the bad boy of America, has accomplished wonders largely through the labor and wisdom of an elder statesman there, O. W. Lyerla. Chester, Du Quoin, Eldorado, and others, with the cooperation of the Area Services of Southern Illinois University, are currently building for better times. They have hopes. A kind of superchamber of commerce of the sixteen southernmost counties, called Southern Illinois Incorporated, led first by Norman Bitterman and now by Goffrey Hughes, has driven head on into the regional problem of underemployment and underindustrialization. Thus the troubles of the area beget resistance and the will to solve them.

In Eldorado, a little north of Harrisburg on U.S. 45, the city hall was physically a mess. It crouched furtively behind a vast flight of concrete stairs that mounted from the street up to the second story. It was a grubby place so unhandy as a building and so passionately ugly as architecture that it became Eldorado's symbol of civic frustration. It acquired ulterior meanings, all of them unpleasant, and because it was a symbol, a kind of vicarious image of the town's defeat, it was selected as the first objective of Eldorado's operation bootstrap.

That was some time ago. Today the city hall has a new look. The gigantic stairway is gone and the building has emerged gracefully from behind it. The whole third floor shines with the gadgets of youth, for it has become the community youth center. The council room and the offices of justice on the second floor have a new glamor. Even the jail on the first floor, painted personally an aspen green by Mayor John David Upchurch, has become attractive—but not too attractive.

All this is more than a paint job or shingles on the roof. This new look is a symbol of an uplifted town. The city hall was restructured, refloored, reroofed at little or no cost to Eldorado. Labor helped, including carpenters, masons, plumbers, along with unskilled laymen filling in where they could. They gave more than 5,000 hours of work free. Businessmen contributed more than $2,500 worth of materials and equipment.

"This will prove to ourselves," said the people of Eldorado, "that we can work together. Never before have we been able to do that."

Thus the symbol of a community's frustration was converted into a memory. The work now has gone far beyond the physical city hall to new parks and a better water supply tinctured with fluorine, to sanitation, better schools and churches, and even an art center, and the documentation of sites attractive to industry. The factories will come, says R. W. Poston, field director of this project. But even if none comes, the work of making Eldorado a better place to live in will be justified. Thus the new look of the city hall becomes a symbol in action, a bright mobile art of red circles and green squares. The artist is the little community itself.

"I never saw anything like it," said Charles Pulley, the University architect. "Fifty men were working on the roof when I went over there one afternoon. Joe Blake, a banker, was sawing rafter angles and Bill Soper, a carpenter, was telling him how. I conferred with Mrs. Draper, the smart little chairman of the beautification committee. She had asked my advice on the color scheme, but in five minites she knew more about it than I did and had a squad composed of a painter, a minister, and a real-estate man mixing the paints."

Meanwhile, over in Chester, high on its bluff above the Mississippi across the state from Eldorado, they are having their art week. With the help of young men from southern Illinois' own university, Chester has gone artistic—and also historical—in a big way. From the highways and byways, from Campbell Hill, Bremen, Shiloh Hill, Welge, Wine Hill, and Rockwood, from across the river in rural Missouri and even from the neighboring penitentiary have come paintings, carvings, weaving, jewelry, craftwork, or, if not work, at least interest and good wishes. Some of the work is good from any point of view, for the fingers of southern Illinoisans still retain old skills and craftsmanship. A traveling exhibit from the Museum of Modern Art occupies one room, a puppet show by fourth-grade children occupies one evening. Hassles on modern art with visiting experts from the University, a flute trio, a school band, each in its own way explores the structures and visions of the arts.

But why all this? For an answer ask Howard Sherman or Alice Beardslee who came over from the University to help. "Well, it's a lot of fun," one of them might say. "Folks get to know one another and find common values and interests. They work together. In the process they become aware of their own community and are proud of it. And they discover the arts of action. How much better that is than those spectator affairs!"

For the historical exhibit ancient rifles, Kentucky style, old documents, dresses, kitchenware, china, a wonderland of quilts and quilting, appeared suddenly along the wall of the high-school assembly room like brilliant fungi from old wood. A modest but telling pageant-drama of the capture of Kaskaskia and the ancient fort upriver from Chester by George Rogers Clark came, like Clark himself, seemingly from nowhere. Scratch the surface of southern Illinois even a little and the mineral glint of the frontier, the middle-border frontier, shows. For a stratum of old-fashioned America underlies southern Illinois.

"There isn't much of this newfangled, twin-bed sort of thing down here," says Bill Lyons, "unless . . . well, it's this way: Smile and the world smiles with you, snore and you sleep alone."

Chester, says Howard Sherman, will make the art and history week an annual affair.

But works of antiquity and art do not tell the whole story of the quality of man in southern Illinois. Below his work and the relics of his crafts his life has layers of reticence and dark dignity. There is no need to romanticize these qualities or make them absolute. The folks here differ among themselves as in any other region, and some of them, as elsewhere, are soiled and shiftless. Usually they are silent, too, with a tough, arrogant silence. Their reticence is like the clay-pan soil of the plateau, stubborn, recalcitrant, unresponsive. Though misfortune may be a man's mistress in this country, though he may beat her or rape her, he rarely will seek refuge from her in noisy drink or begging.

Said the Union County subsistence farmer, too poor to clothe his children, to his more prosperous neighbor, "I won't work for you, if you mean for money; but if you want to trade work— I help you and you help me—that's all right with me."

Pride burns in his vitals, a useless fever, no doubt, that neither nourishes nor kills him. "And," says the visitor from Chicago or Saint Louis looking him over with a kind of urbane malice, "without much of anything to be proud of."

The visitor, of course, is right—outwardly. The so proud man may be slow of speech and limited in grasp. He has sometimes a kind of dismal honesty, to be sure, but this seems to arise less from principle than from lack of facility. Men without jobs do not have the full kit of personal resources and stratagems. The graceful things designed to lubricate a more sophisticated life are not part of their equipment. A miner laid off more often than he works, a subsistence farmer on forty acres, a boy in his middle twenties who never had a job is definitely down on the gravel bottom of life. His rages may seem explosive and irrelevant, his honesty corrosive, his lies without friendly purpose.

But he doesn't whine, not in southern Illinois. He may find symbols for his pride and stubbornness in lonely squirrel hunting, in strange, creative profanity, or sometimes in revival "meetings." These meetings come seasonally in southern Illinois and often mark the top of his moral and emotional cycle.

Southern Illinois is socially residual in its way. But taken as it is, there is a good deal that is preferable to many a place more unctuously prosperous. The people here are not little, leftover men. Far from it. They know hard times, violence, the risks of living. From a quality of man like this, but under other conditions and from different premises, statesmanship of considerable significance, industry, and the arts can be derived. In some ways the quality called greatness is already there. After all, Lincoln, Logan, Robert Ingersoll, William Jennings Bryan, William E. Borah, and many another in law, labor, government, and industry came from this Illinois country.

The great state of Illinois was laid out in the early days of the nineteenth century as a kind of kingpin of the nation. From north to south it is long, with one end in the Great Lakes and the other deep in the south, farther south than most of Virginia, Kentucky, Missouri, almost to the Tennessee line. This midcontinent kingpin helped to hold the North and the South together. It is no accident that the leadership both of the Civil War and of the attempted reconciliation afterward came largely from Illinois. The people there had lived with the problem, debated its pros and cons through years of tension, and were mature in their responses to it. It is said that General John A. Logan, when a brash youth from Jackson County, joined the northern forces instead of the southern only because Senator Stephen A. Douglas, the Democrat who debated Lincoln up and down the state, persuaded him to do so. Logan once drew up a bill for the legislature granting the right to sell into slavery any free Negro who entered the state. It was passed in 1852.

Southern sympathizers were many in the south end of the state, for it is far below Mason and Dixon's line. In what is now Giant City State Park they had a rendezvous. In Alton the abolitionist editor, Lovejoy, was killed.[1] But southern Illinois

[1]   See Thompson, "River Travel, Peoria, Jacksonville, and Prairie Farming," footnote 8, above. Ed

nevertheless became the great salient into the Confederacy from which Grant launched his western campaign. It was the threshold to northern victory.

The road to Elizabethtown drops down through Carrier Mills and Stonefort to Vienna (pronounced Vy-anna), turns east, and keeps on east over the long hills to Golconda and thence to the white clutter of little houses that is Elizabethtown. It is an Ohio river town, like Old Shawneetown, Golconda, Metropolis, or Mound City. From its promontory it overlooks a majestic reach of this great stream. Its hotel, the Rose, sits at the point of that promontory and is the oldest in Illinois. Its catfish, true Ohio River catfish, and its hushpuppies are all that an ancient tradition can demand.

But E-town, as many call it, sits above the river with a serenity that is not entirely congruous with the bloodstained history of the river. Southern Illinois is full of these incongruities, for the gods of these rivers came here with mixed gifts, with cruelty, graciousness, wealth, poverty, pride, beauty, and defeat. Upriver a little way, at Cave in Rock, pirates lived on the plunder of the rafts to New Orleans. Mike Fink was there. He killed pirates according to one story. The Harpe brothers flourished there knee-deep in dark, bloody deeds. These brothers were as sordid an outfit of gratuitous murderers as ever lived in Illinois.

"I'll keep your baby quiet while you go and cook the dinner," said one of them to a woman member of a band that they had waylaid in camp. He rocked the crib a bit, looked down at little Bonnie, and tried to sing a line about going to sleep.

And the baby was quiet, the mother was reassured, and in due time a good dinner was served.

Then the mother went over to her child to care for it. Bonnie was indeed quiet. The baby's throat was cut from ear to ear.

But Elizabethtown is somehow virginal amid the blood and fornication of the ancient, wicked river. It sits demurely on its hill above the vast passion of the stream. The meals at the Rose Hotel are still good after a century and a half of service. If ordered well ahead, a meal there is highly prepossessing. At least it was not long ago. The view from the long, white-columned porch is still magnificent. The rooms are comfortable and in some cases modern. But the prices! They have changed. The rates at the Rose Hotel in 1813, according to John Allen, the well-loved historian of the region were:

Breakfast, dinner, or supper	25 cents
Lodging	$12\frac{1}{2}$ cents
Oats or corn per gallon	$12\frac{1}{2}$ cents
Whisky, a half pint	$12\frac{1}{2}$ cents
Small beer, a quart	$12\frac{1}{2}$ cents

History in Elizabethtown is comfortable. A neighboring town may wear its past—and often its present, too—somewhat grudgingly, but Elizabethtown's past is as friendly as its present is charming. The visitor lingers on. When he leaves, he probably will go by the direct road north to Harrisburg instead of the long circuit by which he came hither.

And yesterday three men were killed in a mine near Johnston City, or if not yesterday, ten days or a month or two months ago. The lift swung sideways, caught on the wall of the shaft, and tipped the men off fifty feet to the bottom. It is a routine item, except to those who die, small disasters and big ones, murder and massacre, explosions, tornadoes, and human deviltry are part of the meat and bone of living in southern Illinois. These unpleasant incidents are probably no more prevalent there than in many other areas with reputations far more serene. But southern Illinois recognizes them as part of the pattern of things and dramatizes them. Here death is not an accident of living, remotely unconsidered like a rumbling stomach never to be mentioned; death may answer problems; it may be intense and culminating.

Southern Illinois is an intemperate land, like Spain, perhaps, or old Greece; and if Greece is sun-bitten, thirsty, shaken by earthquakes, southern Illinois is assaulted by great winds, great floods, and at times by great and bitter passions. There is a window there always open to violence, and people in the northern part of the state who know only the serene good humor of the rich prairie soils do not understand it. Nor did those who lived on the fat lands of the Tigris and Euphrates understand the turmoil-ridden, disaster-beckoned Greeks. The Greeks, too, had their cults of death, such as the Orphic mysteries, along with their bright affirmations of living.

In the oil country around Salem burning gas is flaring angrily from the ground in insolent wastefulness. Around Benton and Zeigler the stink of coal gas lies like low fog across the pastures. But there is April over the hill, a vast basket of peach blossoms. A little later the apple blossoms lift their white banners across the hills near the slag heaps where the Birger gang, the Shelton gang, the Klan gang, and the massacres and murders around Herrin and Marion once tortured the earth. A little white church is under the trees. There will be revival "meetin's" beginning Monday.

Southern Illinois is an angry woman, black and beautiful, a glory and damnation. Still, this Illinois has many quietly lighted moments, ordinary 60-watt moments, that are neither black nor brilliant nor high-powered. The smell of bacon and eggs drifts out of the open doorway on a summer morning as it does from millions of American homes, and if bacon costs too much for many southern Illinoisans, eggs at least are fairly cheap. Boys still play bar-bar-ée and run sheep run on a summer evening although newer games and more sophisticated amusements make inroads. Young men go to work early in life, if they can get jobs; if not, they wait it out. The relative number of college students in the area is only 60 per cent of that for the state as a whole. And the girls are slim, dark, tall, or at least seem that way. Though rarely boisterous, they are as American as a stand of sassafras trees along the Cache River. But their eyes have mystery and darkness such as the Cretan woman had four thousand years ago fixed in eternal profiles on the walls of Minoan palaces.

They are the eyes of woods people, for the forest is never far from the past or even the present of a southern Illinoisan. Long ago the best timber was cut out, burned, or hewed to the uses of the pioneers and farmers, but the memory of big timber, of gunstocks of burled walnut, of dusky walnut furniture of the nineteenth-century Midwest remain. Second-growth timber now surges up from the bottoms and the hills at a rate far greater than consumption. The great hardwoods grow fast here.

This other Illinois has become a symbol of something in America that we cannot afford to lose. The hills and bottom lands, the living forests and the fossil forests below ground, the lakes, the orchards, and the people, always the people, stubborn, bitter, beautiful in their little towns and tattered farms, this is folk America, the germinal society from which our democratic customs, industries, and arts continuously emerge. It is the life of small communities and of fields and farms. We lose it at our peril. But lose it we shall, if we do not bring to its support the advantages of modern education, science, and administration.

It looks as if Thebes, the showboat town, has shot her wad. Once glamorous in her small way, and even more glamorous retrospectively through the lenses of literature and legend, Thebes on her big hill above the Mississippi has lost touch. Her boats do not come in. From Thebes the present has fallen away in tatters. Only the past, like an old-fashioned petticoat, remains to clothe her.

The long barges of oil, or gravel, or automobiles push resolutely by without a signal. The showboat that paused at Thebes and the great packets have gone from the river, and the wharf and tie-up posts, like time, have rotted out both on the near side and on the far side over in Missouri. Back of the hill the orchards now are gone or serve other towns such as Anna and Cobden. The courthouse of 1848 high up the bluff still has the old magnificence of view, but the county seat was moved, and the courthouse, its stone piers out of plumb, its walls out of line, now is a modest library and museum.

Thebes is only a dim light on the river. The streets are empty. Most of the store buildings are vacant. A year or so ago the high school on the hill burned. Then, as a culminating disaster, the proud fire engine was caught in a grass fire and destroyed. After that what more could happen? Once Thebes was gay. Old Man River was a friendly fellow nudging traffic and entertainment her way. But today the largest source of individual income in Thebes, it is said, is the relief check.

These tragedies of little towns take place over much of southern Illinois and for that matter over most of America. Are they necessary? In the case of Thebes it does not seem so. For Thebes as a corporation seems to be comfortably off as to income. The big railroad bridge pays its dues year after year and the treasury is healthy. Thebes is well off corporately; the tall hill still looks west over the river and the view is forever beautiful. The streets are well paved, and the great trees march up the slopes and along the terraced drives. Transportation by road or rail or river is excellent and the view, the view, the view westward over the river, still reveals the destiny of America.

Thebes is well heeled as little towns go, though houses and lots along the bluff can be purchased for very little. There is beauty, a proper quaintness, friendly people. And to ensure its permanent authenticity among the folk groups of America— among honest-to-god Elizabethan folk groups—it has somewhere east of the hill its own variant of "Barbara Allen." This, says David McIntosh, southern Illinois' own authority on folk songs and singing games, may as well belong to Marion or Goreville as to Thebes, but let Thebes have it. The view westward, the river, the good people, the sound treasury, a novel perhaps, an ancient song, Thebes has all of these. But Thebes still lacks one thing: A man can't earn his living.

And Thebes may stand as well as any other for paradoxical, beautiful, impoverished southern Illinois. This river country sits amid wealth, beauty, and vast resources. Its women are lovely and stubborn, its men angry and ingenious. Is there a land anywhere like southern Illinois? I doubt it, except that all lands touched by men and women are alike, and different.

1962

Joseph P. Lyford

Vandalia

In 1958 the Fund for the Republic launched an investigation into the complexities of the American character. Joseph P. Lyford, a staff member, proposed to find out what was going on in a small American town—a town that was not a satellite of a big city, a town not dominated by a single industry, a town with a strong historical heritage. He chose Vandalia, and his choice and project were approved by the Center for the Study of Democratic Institutions, which had been assigned responsibility for the general study.

Lyford, who had spent twenty-five years in journalism and politics, principally in the East, moved into Vandalia with a tape recorder and an armful of notebooks. The people talked to him freely. His report, describing what a small town was really like, what its residents were concerned with, and what they had to say about themselves and their neighbors, attracted attention all over the country.

Judged by the map, the city of Vandalia (population 5,500) has a fine location. It lies across a junction of the Pennsylvania and the Illinois Central Railroads, appears to be the center of a criss-cross of highways, and is on the edge of the Kaskaskia River, which winds its way diagonally downstate to the Mississippi. But the map reader will be deceived. The Kaskaskia, swollen and icy in winter, subsides by summertime into a winding trail of mud and snags; the new superhighways—Routes 40 and 70—pass by to the north, and the only concession by the Pennsylvania's "Spirit of St. Louis" is a raucous bellow as it hurtles through a cut in the center of town an hour before noon. The Illinois Central is more considerate. Occasionally a freight engine shunts back and forth a few blocks outside of town to pick up some crates from one of the small factories along the tracks. "No trains stop here," the stationmaster says. The indifference of the railroads to Vandalia is paid back in full by the town's oldest practicing Democrat, eighty-eight-year-old Judge James G. Burnside. "We don't pay any attention to the railroads any more." he remarks. "They're just passing acquaintances."

A train traveler from the East can alight at Effingham, thirty miles away, trudge through the snow to the Greyhound Post House, and take the 1:30 p.m. bus, which is always overdue. The driver does not smile when along with a St. Louis ticket he gets a request for a stopover in Vandalia, which means that the express bus has to make a ten-minute detour off the main highway. Route 40 runs straight and flat as a tight ribbon through wide umber plains sheeted with winter rain, past farmhouses four or five to the mile. For a few hundred feet at a time the road will stagger and pitch slightly as the land wrinkles into prairie, creek, and brushwood; then it subsides again to a level as monotonous as the roar of the bus. The see-sawing pump of an occasional oil well is the only motion in the fields on a rainy day. There are a

Joseph P. Lyford, *The Talk in Vandalia* (Charlotte and Santa Barbara, 1964), pp. 3–15. Reprinted by permission of McNally and Loftin and by the Center for the Study of Democratic Institutions.

few crossroads villages, then the town of St. Elmo, and, finally, a few miles along Alternate Route 40, the city of Vandalia, once the western terminus of the Cumberland Road, capital of Illinois from 1819 to 1839, seat of Fayette County, and country of Abraham Lincoln of the House of Representatives of the State of Illinois.

The Evans is the taller, hotter, and more impressive of the town's two hotels. A fourth-story room offers a view of the magnificent old state house on the common, a tall-windowed white building, now a museum, where Stephen A. Douglas and Lincoln met with their fellow-legislators more than a century ago. The first-floor windows are not too far from the ground to have prevented a long-legged politician from swinging his leg over the sill when he wanted to make a quick exit. The town's second most noticeable monument is a huge, sand-colored statue of a pioneer woman who gazes down Gallatin Street's rows of two-story buildings, parking meters, vertical signs over a Rexall Drug Store and the Evans Hotel, past a pair of banks standing face to face at the main intersection, and, finally, across the tracks to the Eakin Hotel, the County Courthouse on the hill, and one of Vandalia's many churches.[1]

Robert O. Hasler points out that the town has thirteen churches and ten lawyers. It is his business to know odd statistics because he is president of the Chamber of Commerce. He is handy to the main source of such information because his office is in the Town Hall just above the city clerk. Some time ago Hasler prepared a typewritten economic profile which begins, "Vandalia, centrally located in the heart of the Midwest, is seventy miles from St. Louis, ninety-five miles west of Terre Haute, 245 miles southwest of Chicago . . . total labor force of county 7,778, unemployed 276, self-employed 738, oil production 536. . . ." Under the heading of "Resources of Transportation"

---

[1] First Baptist, Second Baptist, First Methodist, Mother of Dolors (Catholic), Church of God, First Christian, Holy Cross Lutheran, St. James Lutheran, Assembly of God, Free Methodist, Pentecostal, First Presbyterian, Bethel Tabernacle.

appears the information that on the Pennsylvania and IC railroads goods are "in transition" from Chicago, St. Louis, and Indianapolis—a politic way of saying that Vandalia is a way station. The figures on the sheets are from 1959, but Hasler says this is not a serious matter. "Things around here don't change very much from one year to another."

The township of Vandalia is grouped in three economic units. On its outer ring are the farms, the town's main support, ranging from sixty or eighty acres to several hundred, the average being somewhere in the middle. The chief crops are corn, soybeans, and livestock—mainly hogs and cattle. The land is worked with modern machinery by farmers who combine their own land with leased acreage—as much as they can get.

On the western edge of town are four factories, which employ altogether about 850 people. They are the Princess Peggy dress factory; United Wood Heel, manufacturers of heels for women's shoes; the Johnson, Stephens and Shinkle shoe factory (the largest single employer with a work force of 475), and the Crane Packing Company, which turns out mechanical seals for automobiles, machines, appliances, etc.

At the core is the town itself—the stores, the banks, professional offices, churches, schools, filling stations, garages, plus the Elk, Mason, Moose, Odd-Fellow and Legion Halls, the Town Hall and County Courthouse, one movie theatre, restaurants, and nine of the only taverns in a county noted for its religion and its aridity. Vandalia's supermarkets are big and modern; its dry-goods stores range from the antique-looking Fidelity Clothiers to the Hub Department Store which has quality merchandise at New York prices. Only one commercial establishment—Radliff's Pool Parlor—remains open for business seven days a week. The local newspaper plant is built of yellow brick and houses the editorial staff of two weekly papers, the *Union* and the *Leader*. Most of the business district lies south of the Pennsylvania tracks except some hardware and feed stores, the Farm Bureau offices, and a cleaning establishment. On the north side of town the streets are lined with small frame houses, and a few large and attractive

Victorian homes. Some blocks further out are the new County Hospital, the million-dollar Vandalia High School which is the community's pride, and a new development of luxurious, ranch-type homes. Beyond the high school is the intersection of Route 51 out of town and Route 40, which has given rise to a cluster of motels, restaurants, and filling stations. To the west lie the factories and on the far side of Shoe Factory Hill, along the Pennsylvania Railroad, are patches of dilapidated wooden dwellings which make up the hopeless part of the town. To the east is the Kaskaskia River. The southern part of town peters out rather quickly a few blocks below the Post Office and the white frame house which is the home of Charlie Evans.

When he is not in the front parlor of his home, which he uses as his office, Mr. Evans is in the lobby of the Evans Hotel. He built the hotel in 1924 and, along with a hardware business and various real estate dealings, it made him probably the richest man in Vandalia. Last year, his eighty-first, the $106,000 library he gave to the town opened its doors. "We were a money-saving family, all of us," he says. "We're Welsh by descent. I was never a man to sell, I always bought and added to it. When I sold the hotel I'd been saving all the time. I guess I'd saved too much. I didn't have any use for the money, so I built the library. When I built it, I didn't try to cut corners. I didn't try to save as if I was building for myself."

Mr. Evans leans back, and crosses his arms when he talks about his town. "This is a historic city. When they moved the capital from here to Springfield in 1839, our population was only 400. We've gained a little bit all the time. Population-wise we've never had a setback. We've never had a boom. We held our ground. A big percentage of people own their own homes, including a lot who work at the factory. This makes us a good town for a factory. The companies know our workers are not fly-by-nighters. Their employees are here to stay. They have money invested in our town. Homes today build from $12,000 to $18,000, and we have a good building and loan program. Banks will lend money to anybody here who wants to build a building. We have good, sound, sincere bankers. Back in the late 20's, when people were trying to buy more and more land for their farms, the bankers warned them against it. When the crash came, we weren't so badly off as some. We had hard times in 1932, oh mercy.

"I think the town is going to develop pretty well. Rental housing is pretty scarce. The homes here are good ones, and people have made substantial payments on them. I don't know what we're going to have to do to keep our young people here, though. When they go to the city, they don't come back. They want new people to get acquainted with. Industry might be the answer. We should have more opportunities for skilled workers. The Crane Packing Company has been very good. They have a training program for employees and they are expanding. The shoe factory is a shoe factory. Their idea is how much work you can get out of your help. It's as good a shoe factory as there is. It's a good town, but we have one bad problem. It's the farmers. The farmers are in trouble."

Evans is not the only person who worries about the Fayette County farmers. The towns-people think and talk a great deal about them these days. They have always depended on them in the past, and they are no longer sure of them. The uncertainty may explain why the business of farming, traditionally honored in the State of Illinois as an independent way of life, is undergoing rapid sanctification. Probably more speeches are delivered at Kiwanis and Rotary clubs on the virtues and contributions of the tillers of the soil than on any other single subject; it is also the favorite topic of the county's political circuit-riders during campaign season. The community's businessmen prepare banquets in honor of local agriculture; the Junior Chamber of Commerce's first big dinner of 1962 was held to proclaim Siebert Hoover the "Outstanding Young Farmer of the Year" and present him with tickets to a Miami or New York vacation.[2] Agricultural experts from the University of Illinois and the Department of Agriculture,

[2]   Mrs. Hoover said she'd rather have a new refrigerator.

armed with pamphlets on fowl disease and hog pest, criss-cross the territory with advice on all phases of scientific farming. Secretary of Agriculture Freeman's emissaries from Washington are available to discuss the farm program at the smallest gatherings. The Farm Bureau offices have special classrooms where experts lecture local farmers and their wives on the economics of farm management. And, in contrast to the days of the Great Depression in other parts of the nation, the banker and the farmer maintain friendly, interdependent relations throughout Southern Illinois. The two bank presidents in Vandalia talk about farmers as if they were business partners and mutual allies under attack by the rest of the nation's economic interests.

The popularity of the farmer in the abstract has not always thawed out farmers in particular, some of whom still harbor ancient resentments against the town. (One farmer says he wants his children to stay in the rural schools because Vandalians think that "farm kids still piss on stumps and never heard of inside plumbing.") But many of the farmers seem to feel closer to the town than before the war, partly because of the knowledge that a lot of other people besides farmers are involved in their economic troubles, and partly because the farmers' own social life has become more and more interlaced with the life of the town. As the one-room rural schoolhouses have dwindled, over the farmers' opposition, from three dozen in the school district to a half dozen, farm mothers have become members of the PTA's of the Washington, Lincoln, and Central elementary schools. There is more talk in the homes of educational problems jointly shared with the townspeople.

Those farmers who work in the factories—"Saturday farmers," J. B. Turner, the county farm agent, calls them—have a growing association with non-farmers, and some even join labor union locals in the shoe and heel factories. Also, the growing cost of running a farm because of the new machinery required and the rising prices of land have increased the extent of the farmer's dependence on local financial institutions. The farmers buy more and more of their food locally—most of them have disposed of

566

their dairy cows and buy their milk at the Tri-City Supermarket and the A & P. The farmer's machinery is repaired by local mechanics. Feed-dealer Norman Michel, who has carried a few thousand people on his credit rolls, is a farmer's banker in his own way. Vandalia shapes its commercial activities to suit the farmers' tastes, and the farmer, his wife and children, and his trucks are a regular part of the scenery on Gallatin Street. This is not to say that the town has been taken over by the farmers: in one sense it is the farmers who have changed their habits and tastes—even in dress—to fit the town.

The farmer has responded in other ways to the town. He participates more in local events. He comes more to the city's churches. One outstanding farmer is chairman of the school district's Board of Education. Many of the more prosperous farm families contribute their women's time to fund drives. The high school's football and basketball teams are getting a little more help from the farm youngsters who used to shy away from extra-curricular activities after the last school bell. One still hears complaints from the townspeople that the farmer is hard to reach, 'but he is less and less remote.

Partly as a result of his accumulating difficulties, the political attitudes of the farmer seem to have become less distinct from those of his fellow-citizens in town. If anything, his views on such matters as health insurance, social security, the United Nations, even labor unions, have often become more tentative than those of some of his city brethren. The realization that government may be the only power capable of restraining the technological and political forces gnawing at his economic position has affected the farmer's outlook considerably, and more than he will admit.

In matters of local politics, the farmer rarely finds himself at odds with the town, probably because politics in Vandalia is not a serious matter. The last great political controversy in the memory of the dean of Vandalia's lawyers, ninety-year-old Will Welker, was over temperance. Only on the school issue, not one that divides on party lines, does the farmer sometimes dig in his heels and refuse to budge. His stubborn desire to hold on to the one-room country schools defeated two attempts to float bond issues for elementary school construction in Vandalia. Even in this case, he was finally won over to support of the bond-issue program once he had the assurance that the rural schools would be allowed to continue. On those rare instances when a farmer talks world politics, his views are unexceptionably moderate on one side or other of the center: the voice of the John Birch Society is hardly audible in Southern Illinois. President Kennedy, feared by many tight-jawed Lutherans and Baptists during the campaign as a possible threat to ancient Protestant values, is now spoken of mildly enough, and more often with praise than not.

The growth of the farmer's ties to his community, and the pleasant folklore of which he is the center, are not especially helpful to him in his present extremities, and this is true of farmers all over Southern Illinois. Businessmen's eulogies of the farmer's "way of life" seem to have become louder and more frequent in direct proportion to the approach of his economic doom. No amount of talk about how the farmer is the backbone of the nation alters the fact, as farmer Phil Gehle points out, that a tractor that cost him $1,600 in 1946 has a price tag now of $2,400, and that a bushel of corn in 1946 brought $2.25 as compared to $1.00 or less in 1962. The praise that rings in the farmer's ears has a little too much nostalgia in it to be entirely reassuring. It is almost as if he were hearing distant relatives discussing his virtues while he was being lowered into his grave. The farmers, least of all, have any illusion about the future. Those who remain on the soil around Vandalia live among ruins of abandoned farmhouses which are visible in almost any direction. The sturdy, independent way of life that makes Senator Dirksen's heart beat faster is rapidly becoming an anachronism in Fayette County.

The farmer's decline casts a cold shadow. Vandalia would suffer without its factories—their loss would be a fearful blow to the town's hopes for the future—but it could not survive without its farmers. As Dr. Josh Weiner puts it, "the job of people in town is to supply the farmer all the services he needs." Even the factories, with the possible exception of the Crane Company, depend heavily on the farmers and their families for their labor supply. Saddled with a heavy investment in farm machinery, the farmer must cultivate at least 250 acres or seek extra employment. Any less will usually not be enough to bring him the income he must have to pay his debts, maintain a household, and handle his interest payments to the farm-equipment dealer or the bank. So the small farmer turns to the heel and shoe factories for additional income, and often his wife and daughter work in the shoe factory or the dress factory. Without the "Saturday farmers" and their families, it is doubtful whether the plants could get their employees from any other large source at the $1.15 per hour that is the starting pay at all but Crane.

J. B. Turner, the county farm agent, a heavy man in his sixties who looks like an unfrocked Southern Senator,[3] says that while Fayette County has 1,467 commercial farms, averaging 231 acres and bringing in a total income of over $13,000,000, nearly 500 people who live on these farms have other jobs as well. Almost half of them work 100 days or more a year in the factories, in the oil fields as servicing and maintenance personnel, and at the Norge plant in Effingham and the Caterpillar Tractor Company in Decatur, thirty miles away. The farmer is able to handle both a farm and a job because he is mechanized. Most of the farms have electrical equipment and modern conveniences; out of 2,100 county farmers who answered a poll by the University of Illinois, 1,400 had telephones and a slightly smaller number had freezers or refrigerators. Farmers own an average of two tractors apiece.

With all this capital equipment, the farmers are not getting any richer. It is estimated that the average net income of a Fayette County farmer is somewhere around $3,400 as compared to a state average of $4,500. But the fact that he has had to become more and more of a capitalist has certainly made his life more complicated. To stay afloat, he has to become a mechanic,

---

[3]   A misleading impression. Turner is a Republican with a tough carapace that enables him to hold his post even under a Democratic national administration.

an expert on governmental policies, a soil scientist, and a book-keeper. For some, the economics and the competition have been too much. For others, farming has become distasteful because it has turned in a very few years into a totally different way of life.

In this new era a Vandalian who has become more and more important to the farmers is Harry Rogier, president of the First National Bank. His institution, and its competitor across the street, the Farmers and Merchants Bank, have never inherited the traditional rural dislike of the money-lender. This is partly because there happen to be some farmers in Rogier's own family tree—Rogier himself grew up on a farm and still puts in many hours a week of hard physical labor on his acreage before and after banking hours—and also because the financial decisions of his bank have provided the underpinnings of a great many of the surrounding farms. Rogier's bank, which has a "friendship room" in the basement, complete with piano, for community use, is not cast in the cold, impersonal mold of lending institutions which earned so much bitterness in other parts of the country during the depression. The same applies to the bank's officers. One vice-president, Dale Tedrick, is a leading county Democrat. He says that President Kennedy's feed-grain bill is "the best thing that ever happened to the American farmer," and he often wears a Franklin D. Roosevelt campaign button to banking conventions.

As a matter of fact, most of Vandalia's bankers and those in other rural Southern Illinois communities speak about the economic policies of both Republican and Democratic administrations in the past fifteen years with an impartial bitterness and vehemence that has much of the flavor of the old Populists. The recognized spokesman for bankers like Rogier is the *Independent Banker*, which holds that the farmer has been the victim of a conspiracy by every organized economic pressure group in the society, and that the farmer has "suffered the worst economic depression in the history of the United States since the turn of the century." The alliance of rural banks like Rogier's with the farmers, who in Fayette County are largely a debtor class, gives them a character quite unlike most banking enterprises in the East.

"If we have a bad year, the bank will carry us along for a while until we have a chance to get back on our feet," says Fred Mattes, one of the community's most Republican—and most solvent—farmers. During the disastrous burn-out of 1954 the local banks outdid the FHA in its efforts to relieve the farmers' distress when their crops were pretty well ruined by a combination of scorching heat and a tornado that cut corn production to twelve bushels an acre. "There was a meeting of farmers in Greenville to talk the thing over. The bankers came and said that they would wait until next year for their loan payments if the farmers would just pay their interest charges." The "moratorium" was successful, and in a year transactions between banker and farmer were nearly back to normal.

1967

Anthony Monahan

Beardstown

Anthony Monahan, young newspaperman, came from the Pacific Northwest in 1965 to become assistant editor of the *Chicago Tribune Sunday Magazine*. "I'm often asked," he writes, "why I ever left Seattle and the mountains, forests, and ocean. Well, I had never seen an Iowa corn field. I anticipated seeing the Midwest (the non-urban Midwest) much like that Iowa farm boy anticipates his first grittycold step into the Pacific Ocean. We've spent our vacations roaming through the heartland in an increasingly dusty Rambler—from Galena to Clinton to Hannibal to Louisville, etc. Beautiful."

Affection permeates Monahan's sketch of Beardstown—static, a little somnolent, and nostalgic over its past.

On the winter road to Beardstown: Pleasant Plains . . . Ashland
. . . Philadelphia . . . Virginia. Towns of Illinois. Downstate
country, frosted miles of crop-stubbled Illinois farmland as the bus
carrying its taciturn cargo along State Highway 125 downshifts
through the sporadic clusters of buildings, lurching to half-minute
stops beside rusting gas pumps and weathered depot-diner-
grocery centers. (Inside the steamy windows, brittle cakes and
doughnuts under torn strips of cellophane; dusty racks of postcard
scenes—illustrated farm humor, Lincoln's boyhood home, a
floodlighted Marina City; scrawled 30-cent checks impaled on
overflowing spikes; winter-weather musings drifting from dim
rear booths.) Quickly the bus is grinding gears again, accelerating
along the highway. Generations of buses have carried generations
of restless youths of this downstate land in the *other* direction, away
from the soil, as Illinois 125 became a road to the magnetic cities;
for many, the familiar throb of the bus is the last link with a home
place where the struggle with the land has priority over the
struggle with the self.

The sky is a granite ceiling across the horizon as the bus fights
the distance, the highway a strip of transience laid abruptly
across the millennial layers of loamy brown, sandy soil. Artifacts
of roadside American culture have been planted poorly, anonymously: Mary's CAFE-HOME Cooking; Stop HERE LINCOLN did;
RESTRESTREST HERETOURIST REST; Beardstown FUN Capital
of Illinois.

For many Chicagoans, their pictures of downstate are collages
of earnest, starch-collared Rotary clubbers urging us on from
those full-page, Our-Land-Is-Grand, telephone company ads;
plump, toothy 4-H girls patting record-weight cows—or were they
sheep?—in back-page wire-service pictures, meshed with vague
remembrances of town names from one of Sandburg's Lincoln volumes. To downstaters, *their* town is the one that was once (1850
or so) larger than Chicago, and would *still* be larger, if only . . .

Anthony Monahan, "A River Town, A Lincoln Place: Beardstown,"
The Chicago Tribune Sunday Magazine, January 15, 1967. Reprinted courtesy
of *The Chicago Tribune.*

Beardstown—quiet, sturdy, and neat as it nestles close against the Illinois river—was founded in 1829 and today has a population of 6,256 (6,080 in 1950; 6,344 in 1930; 7,111 in 1920; 6,107 in 1910, etc.). The town exports, thru tourist promotion, its most durable noncitizen, Abraham Lincoln. The town's most renowned noncitizen today is Oscar Mayer & Co., whose new hog-processing plant has a "kill line" that accommodates 750 hogs an hour. Beardstown's century-old struggle against the flooding Illinois river is now aided by an imposing concrete seawall which keeps the brackish water out of the downtown store aisles, but which also puts the town on less intimate terms with the river. The river today is exploited ("central Illinois' gateway to the St. Lawrence seaway"), but it is no longer feared and cursed. Once the town's mistress—lanquid, angry, threatening—the river today is Beardstown's serene, little-talked-about maiden aunt.

Still, Beardstown's history and geography begin at water's edge: "You should have heard the sound of the calliope drifting up the river as the showboat moved toward the town," says Miss Annabelle Colvin. "Then soon the boat itself would come into view, the lights over the water and the horns blowing and the music playing . . ." Miss Annabelle, 70ish, unofficial town greeter from her perch behind the desk of the Park hotel, watches the buses stop and start twice a day alongside the hotel lobby, directs tourists, and reminisces with hotel regulars—most of them between-trains railroad men or retired river boat men. ("When I ran for mayor in 1958," says Beardstown business man, John Glenn, "I had two men just working to get out the vote among the river people—barge captains, deck hands, etc.") Miss Annabelle, daughter of generations of river men, was born in a houseboat moored beside the town—and lives today in the same dwelling, now converted and perched on dry land, like a weathered family ark, on a quiet Beardstown street. During the town's memorable flood of 1926, she operated a do-it-yourself taxi service, rowing up and down the streets in a small boat, ferrying supplies and residents to and from buildings awash under the river waters.

"This was a *river* town, a port town, a *young* town," Miss Annabelle says of her Beardstown—before the highway-railroad networks pushed the big barges from the mainstream of the economy; before radio, then the movies, dimmed, then shut off forever, the glitter of the showboats. Today, the last showboat to moor at Beardstown (the Goldenrod, in the 1930s) is a museum in St. Louis; today, on a week-end night in Beardstown, two blocks away from the darkened riverfront where the musical Goldenrod swayed, Elizabeth Taylor cavorts in garish-flesh, wide-screen color at the Princess theater, directly across State street from the City hall.

The courtroom on the second floor of City hall was the scene of Beardstown's Main Event—Lincoln's "almanac trial" of 1858. Rural lawyer Lincoln, just three months away from his campaign for the United States Senate against Stephen A. Douglas, defended one Duff Armstrong, accused of murder in the death of James Metzker the night of Aug. 29, 1857. Armstrong was said to have struck Metzker with a "slung shot" outside a bar set up at a religious camp meeting. (Although state law banned the sale of "ardent spirits" within a mile of the large, emotional meetings, rings of crude taverns often sprung up at the mile-fringes of the evangelical campouts.) The lone prosecution witness testified that he saw Armstrong strike Metzker; although standing a good distance away, the witness "could see by the light of the moon" who slung the fatal shot, because "the moon was shining bright, about where the sun would be at 1 o'clock on the afternoon."

Lincoln, rumpled in his shirtsleeves, knitted suspenders dangling at his sides, had the witness repeat this account several times. Then with a flourish Lincoln produced the Old Farmer's Almanac, which showed that on the night of Metzker's death, the moon was in its dim first quarter, and not even visible at the time of the alleged violence. The jury balloted once and unanimously for acquittal. Lincoln gained some new election support, his legend gained a pivotal anecdote, and Beardstown gained an everlasting tourist lure.

At the restored trial scene today, sharp odors of floor wax and disinfectant enhance the museum aura of the almanac court-room ("church pew from first church in Beardstown, built in 1841, German Evangelical church—donated by Miss Minnie Pauk," proclaims a placard taped to a courtroom bench), al-though it is used today for Cass County Circuit court proceedings. It was one of the last courtrooms in which Lincoln practiced law before moving from his downstate land to the center stage of history.

Earlier, it was in a Beardstown park that Lincoln, newly elected captain of a company of farmers' sons who volunteered for the Black Hawk Indian war of 1832, was drilling his troops when suddenly the company, marching in several files, swiftly approached a narrow, single-file gate. Novice commander Lin-coln, unsure of military procedure but sure of his men, com-manded: "Company dismissed for two minutes. Fall in again on the other side of the gate."

"Of *course* you've heard something like that attributed to most generals and leaders sometime during their career," muses Mrs. Vivian Rogers, Beardstown historian and former editor and publisher of the *Beardstown Illinoian-Star*. "But it sounds so typi-cally Lincoln."

The almanac trial was re-enacted some years ago, with local lawyers and judges sitting in, and Beardstown citizens acting as jurors. "The re-enactment was well-attended," Mrs. Rogers says. "Everybody had a good time, although the Historical society thought our jurors were too *young*—Lincoln picked a very young jury, all men of Duff's age and temperament. Of course, our jury at the re-enactment was a little noisy. One man fell off his chair, and someone said that a jug had been snuck in, but I don't think *that's* true. . . ."

Downtown Beardstown's appearance is dominated by the town square—a tree-studded, memorial-dotted green island in the traditional village square manner. Facing the square is a large old house, an ornate, imposing classic in a town of classic old structures. Now owned by a local real estate firm, the Mount

Vernon-like house of curving iron grillwork and gracious lines lies unused and crumbling. Old-line Beardstown residents know the old house would be a prime attraction if restored, but the costs of rehabilitation are prohibitive.

"Only one thing could save that house," says Mrs. Rogers. "If only Lincoln had *slept* there. . . ."

1967

Robert Paul Jordan

Illinois

Early in 1967 the *National Geographic*, to commemorate the Illinois Sesquicentennial, commissioned Robert Paul Jordan, one of its senior editors, to cover the state and describe its cities, towns, farms, and mines for readers who think of the commonwealth primarily in terms of Chicago. Mr. Jordan's careful portrait is full of meaning both for the state's own residents and for the people of the entire nation.

Illinois contains some of the Nation's most valuable farmland.

You begin driving into it less than an hour's ride from downtown Chicago. From the superhighway the panorama of dairy farms—white-fenced, white-barned, green-pastured—fills the eye. When you turn onto a country road, it becomes an aisle cutting through a tall forest of corn.

Not far beyond Chicago the somber spoils of strip mines also begin to rise above the plain: desolate ridges tossed up by huge shovels as they gouged the earth to bare the coal beneath.

Then, continuing south a few hours, you reach the oil fields. When the oil boom was at its height back in the 1930's, you could read a newspaper at midnight by the light of hundreds of gas flares miles away.

Coal underlies two-thirds of Illinois. Fourth among the states last year with 63 million tons mined, it has enough coal in reserve to supply the world for a century. Illinois still pumps oil, too. Seventy million barrels flow in a normal year from nearly 30,000 wells.

Nature brought other boons. When the glaciers smoothed the land into its gentle southerly slope, they made it easier for the Nation to expand. Wagons moved over it without obstacle, and then railroads. And the ice sheets scraped out the lake basins and created the rivers for men to use as highways of trade.

On the east bank of the Illinois River, about 100 miles southwest of Chicago, lies Hennepin, Putnam County seat. Originally it was a trading post named for Father Louis Hennepin, a Franciscan missionary, who with La Salle explored the area in 1679–80. At its zenith more than a century ago it was a busy steamboat port of 2,000 inhabitants. In those days, passage to Peoria, about 50 miles downstream, took four hours; the round trip cost a dollar.

I drove into Hennepin one sunny day and found that it had dwindled to a few blocks of frame houses bordering a fine old

Robert Paul Jordan, "Illinois: The City and the Plain," *National Geographic*, June, 1967. Reprinted by permission of the National Geographic Society.

courthouse, population 400. But great change was coming. Industrial development—or, rather, explosion—soon would galvanize this sleepy village on the Illinois Waterway. Jones & Laughlin Steel Corporation has acquired 6,000 acres adjoining it and plans to spend $150,000,000 in the first phase of building a steel mill that will employ thousands.

Main Street hadn't yet changed. It was deserted. I parked in front of the Putnam County Bank, walked inside, and introduced myself to Ernest Bassi, the cashier.

"Where's all the activity?" I asked him.

"It's only starting," he said, showing me a $16,000 check he'd just received in the mail.

I looked at it, puzzled.

"We had a small mutual telephone company," the crew-cut banker related, "with 200 subscribers. Each became a stockholder when he paid his $2 membership fee. I was the president. We charged $5.50 a month for a business phone, $3.20 for a four-party line, and we were making money.

"When Jones & Laughlin announced their plans," he continued, "we realized that our little common battery company couldn't serve this huge operation, so we decided to sell. We hoped to get $25,000 or $30,000."

I handed the $16,000 check back to him. "You didn't do too badly," I said.

Mr. Bassi laughed. "That piece of paper represents 10 percent down. We will get $160,000. Each stockholder will receive about $750 for his $2 investment."

I asked Mr. Bassi, who also sits on the Town Council, about reactions to the forthcoming steel mill.

"We have mixed emotions," he replied. "We were a quiet bedroom community. People commuted to work in Spring Valley, Peru, and La Salle, all close by. Now everything is taking on new proportions."

When I called on Mayor Frank Biagi, a bridge operator for the New York Central System, I found him up to his elbows in paper work at the kitchen table.

"We've formed a school district and a fire district," he said. "We've worked out a water district that includes a sanitation system. A bigger police force will be needed. Someday Hennepin will have its own shopping center. . . ."

Mayor Biagi's voice trailed off. "It's going to be a complete change for all of us."

Today the men who explored this land for France would marvel at the expanding industrial network that is filling in the open spaces along the Illinois River Valley from the Chicago area to St. Louis.

The Illinois Waterway stretches about 330 toll-free miles from Lake Michigan to the Mississippi. Barges glide up- and downstream carrying coal, petroleum products, grain, sand and gravel, chemicals, and iron ore. Cities along the Waterway naturally become manufacturers and shippers.

Joliet is famous for wallpaper and produces a lot of steel. Ottawa, La Salle, and Peru manufacture marbles, window and safety glass, and other glassware; clockmaking is another big industry.

The activity around Peoria and Pekin, I can testify, is enough to make a visitor blink. All told, more than 350 industries hum day and night, turning out close to a thousand products. I went to sleep lulled by the champing of distant freight trains, and awoke to the insistent moans of towboats.

The Prairie State's biggest private employer, Caterpillar Tractor Co., makes its headquarters in one of Peoria's many striking new buildings. Of Caterpillar's more than 57,000 employees, nearly 40,000 work in Illinois, and most live in this vicinity.

Peoria also is a major distiller and brewer. Hiram Walker & Sons, Inc., the world's largest bourbon distiller, stands on the riverbank here. Food processing and chemical and paper manufacturing bolster the area's economy.

Rivers have always been the state's lifeblood. Pioneers built mill dams on them, and settlements grew up. Aurora, diversified manufacturing center, and Elgin, maker of plastics and electronics, started as mill sites on the Fox River.

When I reached Rockford, in north-central Illinois, I learned that it dates back to a sawmill built in 1834 on the Rock River. Rockford has grown into the state's second largest city—and it saws more wood than ever as a furniture manufacturer. But machine tools are its leading product.

West of Rockford I began cutting through rolling terrain; the leveling glacial sweep missed this region. Charles Mound, at 1,235 feet the highest point in Illinois, rises in the north-west corner. From it I looked into Wisconsin and Iowa; the Mississippi River shimmered in the distance, a silvery line dividing them.

Close by I came upon Galena, "The Town That Time Forgot," wearing its lavender yesterdays bravely and a little sadly in the hills above the Galena River.

Laid out in 1826 as men thronged to rich lead mines there, Galena (Latin for sulphide of lead) grew into a clamorous city while Chicago was still a swamp village. For years it was the most important port north of St. Louis; as many as a dozen steamboats tied up to the levee at once.

Prosperous citizens built splendid homes on terraces above the river, and the population swelled to around 15,000. In 1855 the five-story, 240-room De Soto House opened on Main Street, "largest and most luxurious hotel in the West." Abraham Lincoln spoke from its balcony in 1856.

In April, 1860, Ulysses S. Grant, erstwhile Army captain, poor-luck Missouri farmer, and unsuccessful St. Louis business-man, sailed up to Galena with his wife and four children aboard the side-wheeler *Itasca*. He clerked for a year in his father's leather store at $600 per annum, and then marched off to the Civil War.

The city went wild when General Grant came home in August, 1865, commander of all the Union Armies. Proud citizens presented him with a stately brick home. As Republican candidate for President in 1868, Grant maintained headquarters at the nearby De Soto House and enjoyed the comfort of his handsome residence while his opponent, Horatio Seymour, stumped vigorously, to no avail.

Today, some melancholy sense of all this lingers on—the mute reproof, perhaps, of a town long jilted by fortune. I know that I searched in vain for the glory that was Galena. The lead deposits near the surface were depleted many years ago, and the railroads stole Galena's waterborne commerce. Population has shrunk to 4,400. One last indignity remains: The broad river, once 300 feet across, has silted over to a sullen trickle 30 feet wide.

I wandered into the De Soto House; it continues to welcome guests, although the upper two stories and balcony were removed in 1880 as the city declined. I strolled past the gracious old mansions, architectural heirlooms all, cameos carved into the hills. I paused in the venerable Methodist Church; the Grant family pew was marked by a small United States flag with 48 stars.

And I savored the Grant home, a state memorial since 1932. Its long-time curator, Mrs. Sadie Allen, showed me around. The dining room, she said, was her favorite; we admired its oak table softly agleam with china and silver used by the Grants in the White House.

"By thy rivers gently flowing . . ." begins the official state song, written in 1892. The lyrics still pertain. A short, pleasant drive down-Mississippi from Galena took me to the industrious Quad Cities—Rock Island, Moline, and East Moline in Illinois, and Davenport across the way in Iowa.

No place in the world builds more farm machinery, thanks in part to John Deere, a former Vermont blacksmith who in 1837 at Grand Detour on the Rock River hand-shaped a self-scouring steel plow that knifed through the sticky soil. Establishing a factory at Moline, Deere advertised that "The Prairie Queen" gave "unequalled satisfaction." It certainly did. Together with Cyrus Hall McCormick's reaper, manufactured at the same time in Chicago, it revolutionized agriculture.

Touring the Quad Cities area today, you pass plant after plant making farm implements and earthmoving equipment— Deere & Company, International Harvester, J. I. Case, and others. Their storage yards are jammed with brigades of brightly painted planters, corn pickers, loaders, dozers.

And plows. An automated production line can turn out a plowshare every six seconds.

Rock Island offered further proof that the more I saw of Illinois, the less I could dissociate past from present. Rock Island Arsenal spreads over 946 acres of limestone in the river, much as it has since its establishment in 1862. Indians lived there before then; to Black Hawk, a leader of the Sauk and Fox, this was "the best island on the Mississippi."

The white man practically annihilated the Indians in the Black Hawk War of 1832. Abraham Lincoln served in the debacle; his only combat, he recalled in later years, consisted of "a good many bloody struggles with the musquetoes."

Illinois was beginning to grow up. Pioneers from the South had used the Ohio River as their highway into the state, and settled in the lower part. With completion of the Erie Canal in 1825, New Englanders, Scandinavians, and others began swarming in via the Great Lakes, filling in the upper two-thirds of Illinois. Population swelled from 157,445 in 1830 to 476,183 a decade later.

In 1839 Joseph Smith, founder of The Church of Jesus Christ of Latter-day Saints, led his persecuted band of Mormons from Missouri to a marshland beside the Mississippi by the Des Moines rapids. They drained the land, laid out streets, built homes—often firing brick on the site—and planted orchards.

Nauvoo, Joseph Smith named it, saying it meant "beautiful place" in Hebrew. Mormon converts flocked there by the thousands. Within a year after its founding, between 250 and 300 brick houses had been constructed. In a short time, with more than 15,000 inhabitants, it turned into Illinois' largest city.

Just as rapidly did Nauvoo decline. The Mormons' growing strength alarmed their neighbors, who displayed increasing animosity. Prophet Smith and his brother Hyrum were shot to death on June 27, 1844, by a mob in nearby Carthage. Soon most of the Latter-day Saints set out on their historic hegira to the Valley of the Great Salt Lake.

I have seen Nauvoo in both spring and autumn, and I too find it beautiful. Today's town, population 1,000, sits on the bluff; old

Nauvoo reposes on the grassy flat. In May I caught the fragrance of apple blossoms and lilacs riding the river breeze, and watched aged vineyards renewing their annual promise. In September orchards drooped with the weight of firm-fleshed Jonathans and succulent golden pears, and blue-black Concords clustered thick on the vine.

At first glance, Nauvoo seemed to me just another quiet agricultural community, its economy enhanced by wine and cheese making. Not so, I found, for down on the lowland the old Mormon settlement is coming alive. Many of its homes and other buildings are being restored by Nauvoo Restoration, Inc., a nonprofit corporation of the church, which has acquired more than 1,000 acres. Already streams of visitors are appearing.

Over the next 10 or 15 years, Elder J. Byron Ravesten told me, 40 to 45 buildings will be restored or rebuilt.

Elder Ravesten kindly left off harrowing a field to show me about. A big, soft-spoken man, he began with a direct question: "You are a Christian?"

"Yes."

"It would be wonderful to be able to visit the homes of Christ's disciples, the Twelve Apostles, and see how they lived, wouldn't it?"

I nodded in agreement.

"We look at Nauvoo in that light."

My host pulled up in front of a handsome colonial brick house, a gem of New England ancestry with a widow's walk and a white picket fence.

"This is the home of Heber C. Kimball, completed in 1845," he said. "He was one of our church's original apostles."

As I departed, it struck me that Nauvoo is becoming a new Jerusalem to Latter-day Saints, and a kind of Colonial Williamsburg to others.

I pointed my car south and turned east at Quincy, a thriving industrial and shipping center on the Mississippi.

It was September. Dogwood had changed to russet dress. The land lay full with autumn's bounty. Roadside stands offered the yield of orchard and field: apples, peaches, pears, plums, pumpkins, gourds, peppers, cider. Always cider.

Presently I reached the village of Pleasant Plains. I hoped to see an up-to-the-minute farm in operation, and Illinois' Department of Agriculture had suggested that John W. Lehmann's land nearby would serve as a showcase.

"I don't think many people realize what modern agriculture involves," John Lehmann said as we began our tour. "It's more than just a seven-days-a-week job."

He soon convinced me. Mechanized farming requires not only a large capital investment but a working knowledge of several professions. A little luck with the weather always helps.

John is a University of Illinois graduate in animal science and agronomy. He works his 333-acre general farm with the aid of one full-time employee. Farmstead and pasture for a small herd of registered polled Herefords occupy about 100 acres; corn takes up the remaining land. His attractive blond wife Betty keeps the books—in addition to caring for their four children.

We halted beside a field of ripe corn and the farmer squinted at the rustling crop. "Because of the drought, I'll be glad to get 100 bushels to the acre here. In a good year this corn runs around 125 bushels," he said.

A little later we entered a large white barn, its pens full of fat sows surrounded by squealing piglets. "Ever hear of confinement hog raising?"

I confessed ignorance.

"We raise and sell as many as a thousand head of purebred Duroc hogs a year," John said. "We confine them here from birth to market. They never touch the ground—they're always on concrete. We control their diet and give them vitamins and antibiotics. Air conditioning ensures the proper temperature, and keeps pneumonia away."

A high-quality product results, lean and tasty. Lehmann hogs and cattle have won enough ribbons at fairs throughout the Midwest to paper a couple of rooms, I'd guess.

"What," I asked, "does it take to be a farmer today?"

586

John grinned. "Unceasing work." He reflected a moment.

"I have to be a veterinarian, agronomist, chemist, and nutritionist," he said. "I have to be a lawyer, practically: Farmers are liable for just about everything, like the pesticides we use.

"Most of all, I have to be a businessman. I've *got* to keep my thumb on the market."

Farm families used to go to market every Saturday with the keen anticipation of nomads approaching an oasis, making a social occasion of the visit. Nowadays they pop in and out on weekdays, and the town square is virtually deserted after nightfall.

I learned the reason in Carlinville, a calm and prosperous agricultural center about midway between Springfield and East St. Louis. "Everybody's home watching television," said policeman Melvin Churovich. "I still work until 9 p.m., but there's nothing to do. I haven't written a ticket on Saturday night in two years."

The truth is that Melvin Churovich goes out of his way *not* to write tickets. Most people leave a nickel on their car's hood when they shop. If the parking meter runs out, he cheerfully feeds the coin into it. "Creates good will," he observed.

Carlinville brimmed with good will, and conversation was easy. Strangers nodded on the street, greeting me with a "How-do." In the Elks Lodge, a wisp of a retired miner named Pat Cunningham spoke of his 54 years digging coal nearby: "In 1922 I scooped 260 tons in 12 days, loading it into carts pulled by mules. Eight-hour days they were; 92 cents a ton. I'd do it again."

Half a century fell away when I entered Ralph Surman's drugstore, still very much in business with its old white-tiled floor and apothecary jars standing on oak shelves. The labels intrigued me: calumba, cambogia, gum acacia, ipecac and opium, precipitate of calamine. Beneath were drawers filled with other wonderful things: boneset, malena salve, soapbark, Indian turnip, indigo madras, chestnut leaves, bloodroot.

I was delighted to find a pack of Cubebs for sale in Mr. Surman's fine establishment, and to renew an acquaintance with these formidable cigarettes—tobaccoless, medicated, acrid, and unforgettable—that dates back to a misspent boyhood. Then I strolled about Carlinville.

The United States flag presided over City Square Park and its marble bandstand (concerts on summer Thursday evenings). I circled the square—like many town squares, it is round—and wandered a block to stare at the majestic Macoupin County Courthouse, its 100-year-old painted dome looming 191 feet over the gentle countryside.

Beyond the courthouse, sunlight pierced canopies of elms and maples and oaks, and dappled peaceful residential streets. Here and there Victorian houses charmed me with their large towers on one corner, big bays, wide porches, and overhanging pediments.

On the edge of town I walked across Blackburn College's attractive campus with President Glenn L. McConagha. He spoke proudly of the college's "Self-Help Plan," under which students work 15 hours a week, building classrooms and offices, preparing and serving food, operating the laundry, snack bar and library, and performing numerous other chores. "Students are glad to participate," he said. "The plan lowers their expenses considerably."

Before leaving Carlinville, I dropped in on Mayor Howard C. Heinz, a frank and friendly man who operates a furniture store and funeral home established by his grandfather in 1854.

"English, Germans, and Scots settled this part of Illinois," he told me, resonant voice filling the living room of his commodious old house. "My grandfather was a 'forty-eighter' from Bavaria."

I asked how he would describe Carlinville.

"It's a very stable community," Mayor Heinz replied. "The population 100 years ago was 5,800; today it's 5,400. As a marketing and shopping center and the county seat, we serve around 18,000 people. We haven't much industry—a creamery, a glove factory, and a pipe fabricating firm."

He glanced out the front window. "It's just comfortable small-town living," he said. "We resist change. People are fiercely independent here. They want to be left alone, and they want no government interference.

"We're only an hour and 15 minutes out of St. Louis, so the big city is readily available. A lot of us work over that way, in the Alton-Granite City-East St. Louis area."

"Work" indeed characterizes the East St. Louis region, where giants of industry hold sway along the Mississippi for 30 miles.

I headed south through bustling Alton. Abraham Lincoln and Stephen A. Douglas held the last of their Great Debates here on October 15, 1858—and a Nation heard the distant sound of Civil War bugles. The city was an important shipping point and trading center then; today it is a busy manufacturer as well, fabricating steel and brass, making munitions, chemicals, boxes and box board, and much more. Owens-Illinois, the world's largest glassmaker, began here in a single building.

Beyond Alton I passed the oil refineries of Wood River and Roxana, crossing buried pipelines that run all the way to the Atlantic, the Gulf of Mexico, and Canada. Coming into Granite City, I saw steel mills daubing brilliant orange smoke against an azure sky.

In East St. Louis, warehouses and railroad yards dominated the waterfront, and mills and factories hummed on the south side. For me, one thing only relieved this stark industrial panoply: Across the river in Missouri rose the 630-foot Gateway Arch. Tallest monument in the Nation, it loomed over the old St. Louis levee in stainless-steel splendor.

Just south of East St. Louis I paused in Cahokia, the state's oldest town in continuous existence, now engulfed by suburbia.

Founded in 1699 by French missionaries, Cahokia soon grew into a center of French culture. Here and at Kaskaskia, 60 miles south, *habitants* tilled fields, *bourgeois* conducted business, and *gentilshommes* directed civic affairs. . . .

I drove to Kaskaskia and saw that the original village has vanished, devoured long ago by the Mississippi; a state park overlooks the scene. Then I plunged on into the land popularly known as Egypt, the wedge of southern Illinois between the Wabash and Ohio Rivers and the Mississippi.

I peeked at the village of Thebes; it perched somnolently on a bluff, and I did not want to disturb it. In late afternoon I reached the old steamboat port of Cairo. It was napping in the Sunday sun.

The Ohio and Mississippi marry here. The delta marks Illinois' lowest point: 279 feet. Cairo, some say, got its name from the lowland's fancied resemblance to the Nile's mouth, and the region became Egypt.

Whatever its origin, the name has taken hold. In one locality, for example, I changed a bill at the Bank of Egypt, watched a movie at the Egyptian Drive-In, and dined amply at the Little Egypt Smorgasbord and Restaurant.

Now I must tell you that I think it all adds up to an engaging misnomer. True, there is the delta. But this Egypt also encompasses the smiling valleys and wooded hills of the Illinois Ozarks, and the billowing plains farther north. Coal and fluorspar mines and oil wells are part of it. So are peach and apple orchards and silvery lakes with Canada geese rafting on them.

Much of Egypt has strong ties with the South. I saw magnolias and bald cypresses, canebrakes and cotton mills. I heard the soft speech of Dixie blend with the twang of the rolling mountains.

Still, the people of this land remain sturdily independent. When they run out of Egyptian names like Karnak and New Memphis, they call their towns Eldorado and New Delhi and Vienna—and pronounce them Eldor-ay-do, New Del-high, and Vie-enna. Cairo becomes Care-o, shading sometimes to Keer-o or Cay-ro.

I hold a warm affection for this Egypt, with its friendly people and lovely face. In all of Illinois I came upon no place more beautiful. Yet I felt an air of sadness hanging over it. People spoke of a decline in farm work, and of coal miners out of jobs for years.

Coal has been southern Illinois' major industry since the 1890's. Many mines are producing. But unemployment ranges up to 12 percent in some counties, and averages 6 per cent. When I called on David Richmond, an official of the State's Department of Business and Economic Development, he summed it up this way:

"Before a mine was mechanized, 2,400 men were needed to dig 15,000 tons of coal a day. Now, 400 miners produce the same amount."

I met Dave at his department's office in Herrin, and he took me on an extensive tour of southern Illinois. Herrin itself provided an insight. In the summer of 1922, near here, 23 men were killed in a clash between miners and strikebreakers. Then came years of severe economic depression. Today the city has brought in several industries and enjoys full employment.

A few miles north, Dave and I drove up to Freeman Coal Mining Corporation's Orient No. 3 Mine—one of the deepest in the United States.

We donned coveralls, hard-toe shoes, and hard hats with lamps attached, and rode an elevator 800 feet to the shaft's bottom. There I saw tunnels stretching out like fingers in several directions. Assistant Maintenance Foreman Paul Kirk led us to a battery-powered personnel carrier, and we clattered interminably along uneven rails.

After about a mile, Paul halted the car and we got out. Coal dust hung in the air thick as fog. Our lamps cut three narrow paths through the murk; pinpoints of light danced in the distance, and I heard something like the rumble of far-off thunder.

Then we walked to the source of the noise—a roaring monster called a continuous mining machine. Torrents of water spewed from its snout, keeping dust down; its huge steel teeth ripped boulders of coal from the seam and scooped them onto a conveyor which then dropped them into a shuttle car.

"A machine like this can tear out a dozen tons of coal a minute," said our escort, "and it only takes seven men to run it."

Back on top, I thanked Paul Kirk and asked what he thought of a coal miner's life. He smiled. "Well," he said, "I'm just about to retire. I guess half a century of it is enough."

I wondered what steps were being taken to improve the region's economic outlook. In Carbondale, I sought an answer from President Delyte W. Morris of Southern Illinois University. He received me in his pleasant office on the campus.

591

"Not many years ago," he said, "there was a feeling of despair here. People were convinced that nothing could be done. Well, things have changed."

Some of that change resulted because S.I.U. reached out to the people, I learned. "We began by helping the public schools to help themselves," Dr. Morris told me. "Our motive was selfish—we were greatly interested in the students they would be sending us."

Today, the university's popular Vocational-Technical Institute offers 18 to 20 areas of study, ranging from blueprint reading to the training of medical and dental technicians. In addition, ten thousand men and women are enrolled in adult education courses. And experts of S.I.U.'s Community Development Service counsel town officials on how to attract industries.

The university has pulled itself up also, noted its slim, energetic president. "Only a couple of decades ago the student body numbered fewer than 3,000," he said. "This fall we're expecting around 18,000 students here in Carbondale and 8,000 more at our new Edwardsville campus near East St. Louis."

I left Dr. Morris, hopeful that a better day had finally come to southern Illinois. Then I headed northeast for the oil fields a few hours' drive away.

Illinois ranks eighth in the Nation as an oil producer, reason enough for me to look in on its petroleum industry. Besides, black gold had been rediscovered a little earlier in Jasper County, a nearly depleted area.

Near Newton, I found, Union Oil Company of California had routinely redrilled a dry, concrete-plugged well—and struck oil in a previously bypassed formation.

"The rush was on," said J. J. (Jerry) Wasicek, the company's District Operations Superintendent. "Leasing activity took place for miles in all directions. In a month's time about 20 rigs were drilling. Now, four months later, about 50 wells have been completed.

"It was exciting for a while," he went on. "We saw quite an influx of cowboy hats, boots, and white Cadillacs. But the wild-catters are gone now."

I asked what had happened.

Jerry rolled up the map we had been studying. "It's a fact of nature and the oil industry that these wells can't keep flowing at their initial rates," he replied. "They decline rapidly. Our discovery well now produces less than 100 barrels a day."

And by this time my own discovery of today's Prairie State was nearing its end. One last quest remained. Up and down Illinois I had crossed the trail of Abraham Lincoln—a trail marked by memorials and plaques. Every license plate proclaimed "Land of Lincoln." Portraits of the Great Emancipator looked out on eternity from countless walls.

Now I sought to find the spirit of the man. Perhaps I succeeded —in a small and very personal way—at New Salem, in Springfield, and on a windswept knoll not far from Decatur.

Abe Lincoln arrived in the little mill town of New Salem in 1831 and spent his early manhood there. He studied by the light of a fire made from cooper's shavings.

Today's New Salem is a superb reproduction, as painstakingly reconstructed as is humanly possible. I spent hours in the village, and from the outset it seemed to me that the young Lincoln still lived there—that he might come along any minute.

He left New Salem in 1837, riding a borrowed horse into Springfield to hang out his law shingle. Here, seven years later, he moved with his family into the only home he ever owned. Three of his four sons were born in it and one of the "dear codgers," little Edward, died in it. The house still stands and welcomes all of us. Inside, I felt the gentle strength of Lincoln, husband and father.

From Springfield he went to Washington in 1861 as President-elect of the United States, and returned in death just a little more than four years later. In the Lincoln Tomb, in the hush of evening, I sensed the majesty and meaning of Lincoln in his full greatness.

And the windswept knoll? It rises about ten miles southwest of Decatur, a green and peaceful tract above the sycamore-lined Sangamon River. Here, in 1830, began the saga of Abe Lincoln of Illinois. Arriving from Indiana, he and his family settled on this plot, putting up a log cabin and sowing a crop of corn.

A simple marker states as much. But beyond it I could see—as Lincoln must have seen—this good land spreading to the horizon. I think I came closest then to knowing him, and Illinois.

1959

Donald Culross Peattie

The Best State of the Fifty

Donald Culross Peattie, botanist and author, was born in Chicago
and educated there and at Harvard. His mother was the literary
critic of the *Chicago Tribune*, and perhaps it was her example that
led the young man to publish three books before he was thirty.
Many others followed. In them he combined the scientific knowledge of a naturalist with rare felicity of style and expression.
Although he left Illinois to take up permanent residence in California, his love for his native state never diminished. His tribute
to Illinois, though slightly out of chronological order, makes a
fitting conclusion to this book.

I'll call Illinois the best.

I don't expect anyone to agree with me except several million suckers (natives of this state, so called for the ugly-faced fish that feed at the bottom of its sluggish streams), and in Washington, D.C., my friend Senator Paul Douglas, and—wherever he is— Adlai E. Stevenson.

I hear cries of protest and ridicule: "What's good about Illinois?" "Chicago has the worst crime rate in the world." (It hasn't, not any more. Several cities excel it, including Los Angeles.) And then there's always the trite one: "It is a good state to come *from*." That last could be a blade turned against me, for at 20 I left the state. I did come back to it and stayed for years, but now I live in California because my work as a naturalist takes me to that so-various state with its forests and deserts, mountains and long seacoast.

Why, then, do I say Illinois is best? It has no gorgeous scenery, no stately ante-bellum mansions, no hallowed customs and no true cosmopolitanism like New York City's. In fact, just the opposite. Illinois is the best state precisely because it is so American.

More, it is heartland. As Castile is of Spain, as the plain of Beauce is the granary of France, or Tuscany of Italy, so Illinois is core America. Yes, even in the large number of the foreign-born in Chicago. It is American in its unappreciated beauty of plainness—something that Thoreau would have understood perhaps, something that the three poets of the state who really sound to me like Illinois give voice to—Sandburg all the time, Vachel Lindsay sometimes, and Edgar Lee Masters in the one truly great book of poetry that he produced, "Spoon River Anthology."

Illinois is beautiful, it seems to me, as only a great fertile plain can be beautiful. If I cannot have a range of snowy mountains, then give me a great teeming plain, and not mere hilliness which

Donald Culross Peattie, "The Best State of the Fifty," *New York Times Magazine*, April 26, 1959. Reprinted by permission of The Estate of the Author and his Agent James Brown Associates, Inc.

shuts off rather than provides a view. In Illinois you can see right down to the horizon. You have 180 degrees of an arc of sky, be it the aching blue of spring, when meadow larks and bobolinks throw the twinkling gold of their songs into your ear, or a sky with vast moving clouds, castle-in-Spain clouds, in the days of summer thunderheads.

A tree, too, on the prairies, has meaning for me as mere woodsiness never has. When in Illinois you need a tree, for shade or the vertical breaking of the horizontal lines, there is a tree. In the Atlantic coast states, for example, such a tree as a cottonwood is just another tree, shortlived and too tall for you to back away and look at it because of the woodsiness around you. But in one of the first accounts of the Prairie State, "Waubun, or the Early Day,"[1] by the wife of a captain at old Fort Dearborn, the single beauty of a far-off poplar is described, now near and clear, now mistily distant on the prairies. So with me, a cottonwood is a short-lived queen whose last golden raiment falls from her smooth body in the hour before the little death that is winter.

"Yes," I hear some saying, "I have been to Illinois several times. I motored across it as fast as I could." Or, "I took a train, pulled down the curtains against the sheer monotony of the state, and went sound asleep until I was well out of the place."

Good-by, stranger; next time take a faster train; step on that accelerator; my state is not for you. I'm sorry you didn't have the time to drink from Ganymede Spring, the best, the coldest water I ever tasted, as it comes rushing, crystalline, from the base of a famous bluff. Eagle's Nest Spring and bluff were both named by that fearsome bluestocking, Margaret Fuller, who said of the view from the top of the bluff: "Florence and Rome are suburbs compared with this capital of Nature's art."

And I am sorry for you if you had no time to go to Starved Rock with its wild primroses, the true subarctic mistassini primrose with pale lavender petals and yellow throat. Francis Parkman found it worth his while to go there in the days when travel was

---

[1]   See Unonius, "Chicago," footnote 2, above. Ed.

difficult, to see the spot where, on a high natural castle of rock, La Salle established a French fort in 1682 and, according to legend, a band of besieged Illinois Indians later met starvation. They would not be dislodged and stayed, in their pride, till death overtook them.

Yes, and I'm sorry that you could not see the lofty and murmurous virgin white pine groves. You didn't know we had such places? No, how could you? These spots don't advertise on billboards, they don't charge admission. Illinois is the least touristical of states. Nobody comes to Illinois for the climate, heaven knows; nobody comes to see the sights unless in Chicago. Illinois is just itself, soliciting nobody. Yet the French soldier-explorer La Salle and the Jesuit priest Marquette said of it, over and over: Beautiful beautiful!

Typically Illinoisan, it seems to me, was the canteen set up in a station on the Santa Fe Railroad during World War II. Where other canteens had long, official-sounding titles, or were members of some alphabet-soup organization of that period, this kitchen was called simply "The Parents' Canteen." You saw it at all hours staffed with middle-aged women belonging to no organization but their own, waiting to serve the uniformed sons of other parents.

Corny? If you like. You could call Florence Nightingale corny, or Clara Barton, or Walt Whitman in his letters and poems as a male nurse in the Civil War. Illinois is corny. It produces the best corn grown in this country, or anywhere in the world.

I never heard a place where birdsong and the spring song of the frogs sounded so sweet. If you camp out on some hillock where swamp and orchard and prairie grass meet, you will hear full more than half of the species of land birds of eastern North America—the wild telegraphy of crows, the "flick-up wick-up" of flickers (called high-holers in Illinois), the golden rolling call of orioles, the jingling doorbell cry of redwings. And there is always the raucous call of herons (farm boys call them cranes) and the warning cries of king rails to their tiny coal-black chicks.

And the frogs! What I still hear in my dreams is the rising, bubbling sound of the swamp tree frogs, a thin "pee-yee-yeep." And the trilling tree toads who, like the stuttering black-billed cuckoos, prophesy rain.

The state flower is the modest violet, and it is a good choice, for there are scores of species—the butterfly, the sister, the hooded, the larkspur, the longspur. What some call dogtooth violet is a member of the lily family. And that flower called shooting star, with its upward-and-backwardly flaring petals, like some pointed comet-head rushing to earth, is really a close relative of cyclamen.

In early spring, when the plum thickets fume with snowy blossoms on the dark, gnarled old finger-twigs, comes the moment when millions of spring beauties spread a carpet under the thicket. In autumn, the prairies change like the colors of the sea, with the rough purple of ironweed, the royal purple of Liatris, the purple and mauve of joe-pye weed, the smoky drift of asters through the woods.

For there are woods, of course—the prairie groves and, in every county, a strip called "the river woods." But there are three completely characteristic trees besides the cottonwoods: the bur oaks and the red haws (we called them thorn apples) that lean old elbows on the ground, making a perfect playhouse for every Illinois country child and, towering above, the shagbark hickories that, like Homer's soldiers who fought naked in their leathern armor, stand soldier-straight in their long strips of bark that is forever being sloughed off and replaced.

I love, too, the old-timiness of Illinois towns, with their streets deep-shaded in vaulted elms and their yards never fenced against neighbors so that the children run in and out of each other's frame houses or play those favorite dusk games all over the block, while the June bugs bang against the screens.

I like the typical county courthouse of an Illinois town, be it Boomtown Byzantine, Catfish Corinthian, or bearing some faint mansard-roof resemblance to the Paris Opera. I even like the bad statuary—the blackened greenish copper of a Civil War soldier standing on a granite pedestal, with his kepi and cape and the pyramids of cannonballs which do not look as if they would ever fit the long-nosed cannons beside them.

Some of the towns are true gems. I'd pick St. Charles on the Fox River, for simple and mellowed beauty. I'd call Galena a positive museum piece, redolent of times when hopes were high in the now-abandoned lead mines.

I sometimes wish I lived in one of the old towns on the Mississippi, where the gulls make it seem like a seaport and the houses rest low on the ground, the long grass almost on a level with the old porches, to which only lilacs or clematis give a partial privacy. And fondly I remember Grand Detour, with its unpaved streets, its two famous rival hotels where the Negro cooks tried to outdo each other with luscious chicken and custard pie.

Most antique of all Illinois' settlements is the carefully restored hamlet of New Salem. Photographs show that the last of it was tumbling downhill into the Sangamon River when it was saved from final disaster by the state parks system. Here Lincoln clerked in that famous store, read law, and here, fond tradition holds, he loved the girl Ann Rutledge, the real love of his life.

I never saw a better job of restoration than that of New Salem. Every last bit of pewter, every account book is there, every house. They even have the right weed growing around the privy! It's pokeweed, with its inky berries, edible "greens" and poisonous roots.

You can go, too, to the Lincoln House in Springfield, where he lived most unhappily with his wife, Mary Todd Lincoln, who, for reasons no one knows, recognized the future President of the United States when she saw him as a small-time lawyer.

Then follow up the towns that lie on the path of the Lincoln-Douglas debates. They fought in Ottawa, in Quincy on the Mississippi, at Alton, at Galesburg and in Freeport, where 15,000 came from all about to hear these two, and stood in a light drizzle or sheltered in their wagons.

These towns are still there, not totally changed from the days of the great debates. Only in Chicago are Lincoln's quiet traces obliterated. Elsewhere his greatness marches invisibly across the wide, plain land. For there are mighty footsteps in the prairie grasses, as they bow before the wind—footsteps of a brave and simple past; leading to a confident tomorrow.

Index